Possessing Albany, 1630–1710

Possessing Albany, 1630–1710

The Dutch and English Experiences

DONNA MERWICK
University of Melbourne

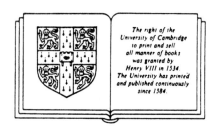

The right of the
University of Cambridge
to print and sell
all manner of books
was granted by
Henry VIII in 1534.
The University has printed
and published continuously
since 1584.

CAMBRIDGE UNIVERSITY PRESS
Cambridge
New York Port Chester Melbourne Sydney

PUBLISHED BY THE PRESS SYNDICATE OF THE UNIVERSITY OF CAMBRIDGE
The Pitt Building, Trumpington Street, Cambridge, United Kingdom

CAMBRIDGE UNIVERSITY PRESS
The Edinburgh Building, Cambridge CB2 2RU, UK
40 West 20th Street, New York NY 10011–4211, USA
477 Williamstown Road, Port Melbourne, VIC 3207, Australia
Ruiz de Alarcón 13, 28014 Madrid, Spain
Dock House, The Waterfront, Cape Town 8001, South Africa

http://www.cambridge.org

First published 1990
First paperback edition 2002

A catalogue record for this book is available from the British Library

Library of Congress Cataloguing-in-Publication Data
Merwick, Donna.
Possessing Albany, 1630–1710 : the Dutch and English experiences /
Donna Merwick.
p. cm.
ISBN 0 521 37386 7 hardback
1. Albany (N.Y.) – History. 2. Anthropo-geography – New York
(State) – Albany. 3. New York (State) – History – Colonial period, ca.
1600–1775. 4. Dutch – New York (State) – Albany – History – 17th
century. 5. British – New York (State) – Albany – History – 17th
century. I. Title.
F129.A357M47 1990
974.7'4302 – dc20   89–33210
CIP

ISBN 0 521 37386 7 hardback
ISBN 0 521 53324 4 paperback

Transferred to digital printing 2002

I dedicate this book to my husband,
Greg Dening, in gratitude for the life we have
possessed together.

Contents

Acknowledgments

In this book on Albany's Dutch people, there are many things I have tried to say. I could not have said them without listening to and reading the work of scholars like Greg Dening, Marshall Sahlins, Clifford Geertz, and Svetlana Alpers. I owe them an extraordinary debt. I needed the support of archivists in Albany, New York City, The Hague, Amsterdam, and Arnhem as well. It was generously given. I am indebted to librarians of the Gemeentearchief Amsterdam, the Koninglijke Bibliotheek in The Hague, the Rijksarchief in Gelderland (Arnhem), the New York Public Library, the Albany County Court Building, and the Albany Institute of History and Art.

Peter Christoph, Charles Gehring, and James Corsaro offered me every assistance at the Special Collections Room of the New York State Library in Albany. Together with Paul Huey, Charlotte Wilcoxsen, and Stefan Bielinski, they were more than expert archivists: They were the historians, colleagues, critics, and friends who helped me understand what I was trying to do. I thank them sincerely and fondly. Colleagues in the Netherlands and the United States gave shape to this book as well: Jan Willem Schulte-Nordholt of Leiden University, Stanley N. Katz and John Murrin of Princeton University, Patricia Bonomi of New York University, Sung Bok Kim of the State University of New York at Albany. Kenneth Lockridge believed in the worth of this book from the start, and my gratitude to him is inestimable.

To colleagues in Melbourne who either listened to parts of this book as conference papers or offered critical comments, I have a debt that can only continue to grow, as I expect to remain dependent on their vigorous concern for fine historical writing. In many ways, I came to possess Albany because of conversations with Inga Clendinnen, Greg Dening, and Rhys Isaac. They encouraged me to think that the processes of cultural transformation in colonial New York could be translated into narrative form, and they helped me shape such a narrative by wisely and affectionately reading early versions of the manuscript. Frank Smith, as editor for Cambridge University Press, shared my interest in trying to write about culture. If the lines of New York's early culture emerge strongly in this book, it is because of his superb editorial skills and his ability to understand what a writer is trying to say, even at a stage when it is very awkwardly said. Sharon Ayre Fell, who typed the manuscript, extended a generosity in editing the text that went beyond my deserving. To her I am deeply grateful as well.

I completed this book while doing research as a Fellow at the Shelby Cullom Davis Center for Historical Studies, Princeton University. There the pleasure of seminars and conversations with colleagues, especially Lawrence Stone, Susan Amussen, Rudrangshu Mukherjee, and Angelo Torre, kept me from turning my possession of Albany into an obsession. They showed me other sites that had been or could be excavated in the wide and rich lands where historians set down their tools and begin to work. This book was initially funded by the Australian Research Grants Commission and has also been supported by grants from the University of Melbourne.

Abbreviations

Archives

AIHA	Albany Institute of History and Art
BL	British Library (British Museum)
GA	Gemeentearchief Amsterdam
HL	Huntington Library, California
NYPL	Manuscripts Room, New York Public Library
NYSA	Special Collections, New York State Library, Albany
OCCA	Office of the County Clerk, Albany, New York
RG	Rijksarchief Gelderland, Arnhem

Major Collections

AA	Joel Munsell, ed., *The Annals of Albany*, 1–9 (1849–59)
CHA	Joel Munsell, ed., *Collections on the History of Albany from Its Discovery to the Present Time*, 1–4 (1865–70)
CNYHS	Collections of the New-York Historical Society
Corr JvR	Van Laer, A[rnold] J. F., ed., *Correspondence of Jeremias Van Rensselaer, 1651–1674* (1932)
CRB; CRA	A[rnold] J. F. Van Laer, ed. and tr., *Minutes of the Court of Rensselaerswyck, 1648–1652; Minutes of the Court of Fort Orange and Beverwyck, 1652–1656*, and *Minutes of the Court of Fort Orange and Beverwyck, 1657–1660; Minutes of the Court of Albany, Rensselaerswyck and Schenectady*, 3 vols. 1668–85 (1922–28)
DHNY	O'Callaghan, Edmund B., ed., *Documentary History of the State of New York*, 1–4 (1849–51)

xi

DRCH	Brodhead, John Romeyn, Fernow, Berthold and O'Callaghan, Edmund B., eds., *Documents Relative to the Colonial History of the State of New York, Procured in Holland, England and France, 1–14* (1851–81)
ER 1–4	Pearson, Jonathan and Van Laer, A[rnold] J. F., eds., *Early Records of the City and County of Albany and Colony of Rensselaerswyck*, four volumes (1861; 1916–19)
L-RP	Livingston–Redmond Papers
RNA	Fernow, Berthold, ed., *The Records of New Amsterdam from 1653 to 1674, 1–7* (1897)
VRBM	Van Laer, A[rnold] J. F., ed., *Van Rensselaer–Bowier Manuscripts, Being the Letters of Kiliaen Van Rensselaer, 1630–1643, and Other Documents Relating to the Colony of Rensselaerswyck* (1908)
VRMP	Von Rensselaer Manor Papers, SC7079, NYSA

Introduction

This book is a narrative history of a colonial North American town between the time of its early settlement and the time when it can be perceived as a community in 1710. I do not take its history, however, to have been an evolution. I take its past to have been layers of time when a single site, Albany, was made and remade as a result of successive, socially constructed interpretations. The generator of change in Albany was interpretation. There was no "Albany" making its way toward to-day's version. Rather, there was continual reinterpretation, rediscovery, and reaffirmation (or disaffirmation) of cultural meanings. In the process, the site, or object of interpretations, underwent change. It altered as successive groups of individuals interpreted, say, its topography from 1630 to 1710 and, out of those understandings, operated upon it. It became the location of a cultured order of things.

In the same process, however, individuals underwent change. The land-scape, to enlarge this example, was appropriated into meaning: it allowed individuals to influence themselves, to change, much as a novel or any text permits readers to change, however slightly. The residents' values and self-identity as well as their ambitions, images, and anxieties changed. Yet neither we nor contemporaries can ever be privy to changes that are not expressed, that are not represented. So the tale bearers of meanings, choices, and fears are the landscape, the rituals of political behavior, the religious liturgies, and the details of vernacular architecture of which we have a record. They are a people's values or self-identity set out for them in structures that must be called symbolic because they were those values re-presented. They are set out for us in the remaining artifacts.

Each of the chapters of this book takes possession of Albany at a different cross section of time – always by attending to the individuals who figured and imaged it. Facing the New World, they were people always inserting new possibilities into available combinations made up of memories, imaginings, and feelings. Their figuring cannot be caught in the word, rational. Yet it followed a set of cultural rules for the proper ordering of part-to-part and part-to-whole. In each of the chapters, I try to discover how Dutch men and women understood Albany at different layers of time, how they made it a particular kind of Dutch spectacle to which they felt a belonging. In Chapter 1, "Possessing the Land, 1630–1652," I have reconstructed Kiliaen van Rensselaer's changing interpretations of Albany over fourteen years. The artifacts are so dense that one may take each year as a layer of time valuable for analysis. In Chapter 3, to offer another example, I have largely used the artifacts from a single year, 1664, to reconstruct how three sets of Dutch men and women understood the surrender of New Netherland to the English. In Chapter 5, I have reconstructed how Dutch men and women – now New Yorkers – made sense of what we call Leisler's Rebellion in 1689–91.

The book presents the "possession" of Albany in chronological order. This is important for the reader. Although time is constructed by all historians as their sequencing of constructed events and is not something natural, a chronological progression that is familiar allows the story to be more pleasurably digested. However, at the same time, each chapter asks the reader to reflect upon the complexities of dealing with interpretation – for example, that written histories are not necessarily narratives of influences, that histories can be narratives of successive forms as *disjunctures* on a single geographical site. And it is in order to join readers to my own sense of both the uses and frustrations of discovering and re-presenting the interpretive acts of colonial Americans that each chapter is intended as a variation on the theme of interpreting as much as it is meant to say something about Dutch people in early upstate New York.

For this reason, the book is structured as an archeology of interpretations and experiences. If Albany's past is viewed according to a spatial mode of depth rather than a linear one of chronological progression, then it is exposed as layers of time when configurations of meanings were enacted. Albany is in fact a place better understood by its differences over time than its continuities. As it happens, it discloses its disjointed character far more than most colonial towns. From about 1614 to 1652, it was Fort Orange and the surrounding patroonship that Kiliaen van Rensselaer called Rensselaerswyck. In 1652, it became Beverwijck when Petrus Stuyvesant, acting as resident director of New Netherland for the West India Company, excised space for a town north of the fort and within Rensselaerswyck. In 1664, the conquering English changed its name to Albany. But even if the site had always been known as Albany, it would still have been, as all sites are, successive and unstable combinations of meanings hidden in the apparent stability of a proper noun. Albany, then, was a site upon which a series of individuals took different perspectives over time. Ours – mine as I complete this book, yours as you read it – are only the latest.

We cannot, of course, understand seventeenth-century Albany the way its Dutch townspeople did. We cannot grasp the cultural rules as they did. We can, however, use the surviving artifacts to reconstruct some of the performances that illustrated their culture. They displayed their values and self-identity in a range of behaviors, none of which is trivial to us because, in the world-in-a-grain-of-sand way, each performance was a cultural text. The trick is – even as in reading a novel or medical report – not merely to understand a phrase here or character portrayal there, a narrative sequence here or a figure of speech there, but to discover the structure.

The structure is most plainly seen in the actions that shaped and gave meaning to the landscape. As the Dutch inhabitants pushed and pulled it into proper order, they could read it as a set of symbols. It was a set of representations that assured them of their Dutchness and of "first and last things" set in proper order.

Houses, palisades, dikes, bridges, forts, and landings were all parts of the built landscape of seventeenth-century Albany. But they were parts-to-a-whole. What was the whole? What was the configuration that gave the parts proper meaning? Into what elemental order were the townspeople repeatedly fitting houses and roads, farmlands and town spaces, house lots and public buildings? I think it was caught up in *burgerlijk* (for the moment, "civic," "mercantile") and its relational opposite, *onburgerlijk*. *Burgerlijk–onburgerlijk* was the fundamental categorizing principle of the physical environment. It was also their organizing principle of "personal space, of social class, of events and actions, of cultural time." It was their central cultural metaphor.[1]

I have tried to catch that metaphor in one of my own or, rather, brought the processual element in *burgerlijk* into prominence by using the term "navigating the land." The Dutch privileged purposeful movement. Lands and seas, continents and oceans, river lands and rivers, all were merely background to movement. They put the physical environment in order by setting *burgerlijk* over *onburgerlijk*, that is, city over countryside, dynamism over stasis, change over permanence, the mercantile use of land over its mere occupancy. In ways that are set out more fully in the

1. Greg Dening, *Islands and Beaches, Discourse on a Silent Land: Marquesas, 1774–1880* (Honolulu, 1980), 87.

final reflective chapter, it was an image that gave a unique shape to the land in the Low Countries and New Netherland, where cities and arteries of trade were valued for allowing purposeful movement, encounter and exchange, while the countryside was less valued because it did not provide a space for those activities. It was an image in which cities and inland trade routes were prized for allowing one to navigate over the land, just as ports of call and sea-lanes allowed one to navigate over the seas.

At home, the intricately constructed canals were not like the irrigation passageways of early modern Indonesia. They were not waterways established to ensure the success of a rural economy. They amplified municipal rule, magnifying a city's well-being while enforcing the dependence of the countryside.[2] They served to enlarge a city's prosperity by multiplying its residents' opportunities to trade in commodities, in business partnerships, in the buying and selling of European cities and overseas trading stations. Yet the acts by which the Dutch people organized space were not, of course, merely economic. They were acts with a wider force of propriety. They gave moral and aesthetic satisfaction. The cities and the inland waterways that made them ports of call to one another were symbols of a physical environment set in proper order.

They were to the Dutch people's taste. By the time Albany was settled, the people of the Netherlands had vested sovereign power in great trading cities and, in the same process, had given them supremacy over the landscape. Two million Netherlanders had entrusted political rule to two thousand town councillors in the United Provinces, effectively handing them rule over the physical environment.[3] Properly sorted out, the land let the Dutch viewer celebrate a *burgerlijk* society and its political variant, republicanism.

In New Netherland, these elemental features and relationships were comparatively primitive but structurally the same. The Albany settlers were positioned at the farthest point of a trade route that began in Amsterdam and pushed its way deep in the heart of northeastern North America. But that did not diminish the force of that image. Rather, it enhanced it. New Amsterdam, Esopus (Kingston), Fort Orange (Albany), Fort Good Hope (on the Connecticut River) and Fort Amstel (on the

2. See Jan de Vries, *Barges and Capitalism: Passenger Transportation in the Dutch Economy, 1632–1839*, in *Afdeling Agrarische Geschiedenis Bijdragen* 21 (Wageningen, 1978).
3. Herbert Rowen, *John de Witt: Grand Pensionary of Holland, 1625–1672* (Princeton, 1978), 133, uses the figure of 2,000 for 1660. Using the figures of B. H. Slicher van Bath, G. De Bruin records the Dutch population growing from about 1.5 million in 1600 to 1.9 million in 1750. About 50 percent lived in Holland in the seventeenth century; see "De soevereintiet in de republiek: een machtsprobleem," *Bijdragen en Mededelingen Betreffende de Geschiedenis der Nederlauden (BMBGN)* (1979), 94:29.

Delaware River) were compact ports of call along promising trade routes and were, therefore, homologous with Rotterdam, Leyden, and Zutphen in the Low Countries. And as in Europe so in New Netherland: The landscape celebrated a burghers' society and a republican one. In seventeenth-century North America, it was the only one to do so.

Comprehension of these people who created and sustained a version of the Dutch Republic in the New World will be very difficult for us English-speaking outsiders. We have inherited and now perform Anglo-American cultural ways. In encountering the Dutch in Albany, we do a common thing: We quickly rush to analogy or resemblance, making the strange familiar. We bring strangers like the Dutch into our present-day culture; we assume they made our improvisations in life. Or we make seventeenth-century Dutch colonials into seventeenth-century Anglo-Americans.

The seventeenth- and early-eighteenth-century Dutch and English were essentially different. They were men and women of different cultures. They knew it then. We, upon reflection, know it now. I insist upon the force of that difference and its manifold repercussions by calling on navigating the land again and again.

The extent of the difference will be shown in looking at the English conquest of 1664 and subsequent events. The English had a different central metaphor for organizing the physical environment. It was expressed in something like "landownership" or what I would call "occupying the land."

There was, then, a Dutch way of looking at land, a Dutch way of seeing a landscape and its iconographical representations. There was a Dutch way of describing and surveying it, of inscribing it on maps – of buying and bequeathing, owning and talking about it. And there was an English way. The Dutch and the English each "possessed" Albany according to their own central metaphors.

1

Possessing the Land, 1630–1652

In 1884, Arthur James Weise described the settlement of Albany in the early seventeenth century. He told a story that differed little from those we associate with colonization elsewhere in northeastern North America. On the bank of a river, "where a narrow, verdurous plain lay pleasantly sheltered by the westward hill," he wrote, "the little band of Walloons with a few Dutch freemen disembarked." The May day of 1624 was one of quiet serenity, he thought, and in the warm sunlight, the colonists began to explore places where "the hearth-stones of their new homes were to be laid."

The colonists wandered "speculatively" over corn fields abandoned by the natives. They soon occupied land "to cultivate" and "began the humble house building." They constructed bark cabins and "with resolute hearts and active hands began to till the land." As they did so, "the men in the service of the West India Company were constructing, near the river, a small log-fort."

Meanwhile the colonists sowed wheat and rye. "Active housewives" began caring for small vegetable gardens. "The warm summer's sun quickly germinated the seed in the fertile fields" and soon too "upon the tables of the settlers appeared the productions of their gardens – the first returns for their laborious cultivation of the virgin soil of New Netherland."[1]

The images that hold our attention here are those of the discovery of land and then the bonding of men and women to it as agriculturalists. They capture the New Netherlanders in activities that seem natural or universal in character or, if not that, then predictably European. As men who brought the land under a farmer's scrutiny, who (some of them) went about selecting house sites out of a sense of being freemen, and whose interest was to await the germination of seed in "fertile fields," they seem to recapitulate the acts by which English settlers first made

---

1. Arthur James Weise, *The History of the City of Albany, New York, from the Discovery of the Great River in 1524, by Verrazzano, to the Present Time* (Albany, 1884), 21–4.

sense of Plymouth, Shawmut, and Jamestown. That was, of course, not the case. The men and women who came to the lands of the upper Hudson River did not act out of universal rules, but out of seventeenth-century Dutch culture. This story of their settlement's earliest years will be constructed by discovering Dutch meanings of origins, beginnings, and possession.

Within Weise's description of the landing – though underdeveloped because he thought it had negligible evocative force – there is a picture of "the men in the service of the West India Company ... constructing, near the river, a small log-fort." As Weise presents it, the task they were undertaking there was an adjunct to the larger, more richly symbolic, project of settling agricultural land. Yet Weise had the significance of the activities backward. The men who were tillers of the soil (the *boers*, the farmers) were adjuncts to the Company and its objective at the fort: trading. They were to victual whatever number of soldiers and traders might live within the fort. Little more.

If the proper context for the colonists was the fort, the fort itself was set within the context of Dutch exploration along 't Noordt Rivier since 1609. Its forerunners were the ships of Henry Hudson, Cornelis Jacobsz Mey, and David Pietersz de Vries, vessels that were sailed to the site of the small fort (Fort Orange) and moored along the shore. They were, afloat, what the fort was meant to be in a beached version. Both were *handelsschepen*. The first were platforms of decking with gunnels over which men traded with natives, and the second, the fort or trading station, was an enclosed space with palisades over which trading was carried on as well.

We know that efforts to maintain the small fort met with difficulties and were sporadic in any case. The settlement of 1624 was, in fact, abandoned, and it was only in the late 1620s that the Company and men like the Amsterdam merchant Kiliaen van Rensselaer began to give the area their continual attention. Even then, the settlement was not a solidly founded community, certainly not like one of those that would characterize, for example, seventeenth-century New England. Being Dutch, it would not, under any circumstances, have been a place of binding written covenants, town fathers, and prescriptive political formulas. This settlement, however, lacked the basic elements of continuity in a notable way. It had no founding moment. Until 1652, it had no political, juridical, economic, or geographical center. Until that time – when it was given the name, Beverwijck – it had no single name, but was Fort Orange and Rensselaerswyck.

The settlers of 1624 and those who began to arrive in small numbers in the early 1630s either as soldiers and traders at the fort or as van

Rensselaer's colonists were part of a process we now call the expansion of the Dutch overseas empire. They would have understood the proprieties of that extended but interconnected order. And they would have known their proper roles within it. One of those roles was to fulfill tasks worked out in the Low Countries, especially in Amsterdam. The land would be made into a Dutch landscape, not only out of their own decisions, but out of those made in Amsterdam as well.

It is tempting to argue that possession of Fort Orange and the surrounding land occurred out of the dialectic between Kiliaen van Rensselaer's interpretations of it and those of his colonists. But this would be to use a misleading model. Discovering what happened in the Hudson River valley between 1630 and 1650 is a matter of recognizing that van Rensselaer and the soldiers, traders, and colonists around Fort Orange shared cultural rules at one end of a space, as it were, and values at the other end. It was in the area of choices about how the two were best related and how they might be properly enacted that differences occurred. One promising way of approaching this task is, first, to recover the interpretations out of which van Rensselaer made decisions for Rensselaerswyck and, second, to measure the degree to which those decisions were in fact actualized.

Van Rensselaer never came to North America. Verbal reports and, more significantly, correspondence gave him possession of the *colonie* to which he first sent settlers in 1632. Words – in speech, and in inscribed accounts, letters, inventories, reports, and logs – were all his experience of New Netherland. They turned his ownership of Rensselaerswyck into its possession. They gave him the power to make decisions for the *colonie*, to possess it in images and plans, some of which were valuable and others useless. The meanings he put on Rensselaerswyck were often wrongheaded. Many were incongruent with a range of actualities in the valley after 1629. Nor were they the only meanings that gave shape to the *colonie*.

Nevertheless, van Rensselaer's meanings were decisive. Over fourteen years, he bent every effort to get adequate and precise knowledge of his patroonship. In the end, the effort frustrated, embittered, and defeated him. Yet he made and enforced decisions. In the process, the land became an artifact distinctively Dutch – and distinctively his.

Rensselaerswyck: Images and "Realities," 1630–1634

In 1643, Kiliaen van Rensselaer died. His direct influence upon the Hudson Valley had come to an end. Certainly by that time, Rensse-

aerswyck was firmly possessed. Yet it was not the patroonship customarily described in history books as one that ran for twenty-three miles
along the Hudson River and inland for about twenty-four miles on both
sides. It was not the possession of a landed estate of about a million
acres, as described in 1685. Rather, it was a place with the topography
that the men and women of the 1630s and early 1640s chose to experience. It was the land that they – out of their own choices and those
made by van Rensselaer and the Company – brought under interpretation. Some sense of the choices and resultant interpretations can
be taken from reconstructing the geography they had made theirs by
1643.

Prologue

Every man and woman who came to Rensselaerswyck possessed it differently. Although the land itself limited interpretive possibilities and
Dutch behavior on it was conventional, each settler took possession in
a unique way. We cannot retrieve all of those experiences. However, by
1643, there were about two hundred men, women, and children in the
colony, that is, about 20 percent of the settlers in New Netherland itself.[2]
By that date, they had their bearings on the land.

Men explored in all directions. They may not have known Lake Champlain (Het Meer van Irocoisen) with any greater accuracy than contemporary European mapmakers – who generally placed it too far to the
south and east or gave it outrageously large proportions, making it the
source of all the great rivers that emptied into the Atlantic – but, by
1643, they knew it accurately enough for their purposes.[3] They were
already using it like a rope that, taken hand over hand, led to Canada
and trade. Dutch traders from Rensselaerswyck and Fort Orange also
knew the Catskill area and the Connecticut River valley. They probably
knew the Versch Rivier (Connecticut River) more fully than they cared
to reveal, certainly in cartographic detail. They did not exploit the "old
Boston road," that later linked Albany and Boston. Perhaps they had an
exaggerated image of the distance. Joan Blaeu's 1635 map of northeastern
North America and a copy of one executed in Pieter Minuit's time had,
we know, doubled the distance from Albany to the Shawmut Peninsula.

2. John O. Evjen, *Scandinavian Immigrants in New York, 1630–1674* (Baltimore, 1972
   reprint), 9. Oliver A. Rink, *Holland on the Hudson: An Economic and Social History
   of Dutch New York* (Ithaca, 1986), 146, placed the colonists from 1630 to 1644 at
   174.
3. Isaac Newton Phelps Stokes, *The Iconography of Manhattan Island, 1498–1909* (New
   York, 1915), 2:84; 72.

Whatever the case, the colonists chose to reach Boston by navigating down the Hudson and along the coast.[4]

Most of all, the colonists had mastered the Hudson River, which linked the settlement to Manhattan Island and New Amsterdam. By 1633, skippers had given the Company's director in New Netherland a chart that provided accurate soundings up to Fort Orange. Later maps exaggerated the length of the river from New York City to Albany – and one that the British military were using in 1756 also skewed it absurdly to the east.[5] But the first generation of colonists had calibrated the river into fourteen reaches, named navigational sites, settled on islands, established landings, and estimated travel times. They had also demarcated the strands and water gates (*waterpoortjes*) in New Amsterdam that received cargo destined for Rensselaerswyck and Fort Orange.

The settlers had also come to know the land northwest of the settlement. Individuals remembered how they came to that knowledge. Symon Groot testified in 1688 that, exactly fifty years earlier "being a boy and ...in ye Service of ye west India Company," he lived at the fort with Bastiaen Janse Krol. Krol then "had a great trade with ye Sinnekes & oy^r Indians to ye westward" and ten years later, as Groot recalled it, he himself was "in ye Maquase Countrey."[6] The Mohawk River valley was the gateway to the fur trade. For a man like Groot, it was ownership enough to have access to native customers, to voyage into their country, and return. It was the trade route every settler soon knew and strove to master.

The immediate environment had also become Dutch by 1643. To catch this process we might think of the colonists as a troupe of medieval players deftly and inadvertently transforming the roof of a cart into the proper setting for action. Isaac Jogues, a French Jesuit who was in the settlement in 1644, saw the stage arranged in that year but was unimpressed. Farmers were scattered "2 or 3 leagues" along the river lands. Each was an "outliver" to his neighbor because he com-

4. See Stokes, *Iconography* 2, Plate 32, following 90, and Plate 39 following 120. In each, mensuration is the *Duitsche Mylen* rather than the English mile. I am calculating the geographical mile like Van Laer, that is, as 4.611 statute miles (see *VRBM*, 847); sending letters "by New England" was accepted procedure by 1635 (see KvR to Jacob Albertsz Planck, May 24, 1635, *VRBM*, 315. Kiliaen van Rensselaer (hereafter KvR).

5. Philip J. Schwarz, *The Jarring Interests: New York's Boundary Makers, 1664–1776* (Albany, 1979), 11; Lois Mulkearn, ed., *A Topographical Description of the Dominions of the United States of America: T[homas] Pownall* (New York, 1976) 8; See William A. Foote, "The American Independent Companies of the British Army, 1664–1764" (Ph.D. diss., University of Michigan, 1966), 142, 143.

6. Deposition of Symon Groot, July 2, 1688, Lawrence H. Leder, ed., *The Livingston Indian Records, 1666–1723* (Gettysburg, 1956), 144.

peted in the fur trade and was "satisfied provided he can gain some little profit."[7]

Jogues blamed the dispersal of settlement on the desire to trade. He was correct. In 1643, the northernmost settlements on the west bank of the Hudson, for example, were the farms of Cornelis Teunisse and van Rensselaer. The patroon's farm was about five miles north of Fort Orange. It was arable land watered by a creek. Undoubtedly those were advantages that counted in its selection. But van Rensselaer wanted his farms west on the bank and north of Fort Orange for the same reason that he wanted the majority of his settlers on the east bank and south, at Greenbos, now Rensselaer. He wanted his farm established where his overseer could forestall furs being carried to the Company's traders at the fort, while he wanted those of his artisans and farmers erected at a distance from the same trade routes.[8] Poest's farm was the northernmost area under cultivation on the east bank of the river. It was also arable land on both sides of a kill, but its occupancy also had to do with the fur trade.

From those northernmost farms, intermittent settlement reached south along the river in the narrow bands noted by Jogues. The southernmost area along the west bank was one that drew van Rensselaer's attention again and again. To curtail traders coming into the area, he was intent on placing a subordinate there and, by 1643, had managed to place two men on an island in the vicinity. On the east bank, opposite the island, the land was still uncultivated.

Midway on the land were the only two areas of what might be called concentrated settlement. The fort of the West India Company stood on the west bank of the river, about 180 feet from the shore. It was a building thirty-three rods square and in continual disrepair until its demolition in the 1670s. Possibly nine dwellings backed onto the inner lining of its walls.[9] Here the "free traders" lived, perhaps as many as twenty-five men licensed to traffic in furs.[10] Twenty-five soldiers were thought to live in the fort during these years as well, but they were more likely half that number.[11] On the east bank of the Hudson, opposite but slightly south

---

7. A description of New Netherland in 1644 by Father Isaac Jogues, Jesuit Missionary, *DHNY*, (Albany, 1851), 4:26.
8. S[amuel] G[eorge] Nissenson, *The Patroon's Domain* (New York, 1937), 50, n. 51; KvR to Arent van Curler, March 16, 1643, *VRBM*, 666.
9. Deposition concerning the buildings erected in different places in New Netherland during Director van Twiller's administration, *Dutch, I (Register of the Provincial Secretary, 1638–1642*, ed. Arnold J. F. Van Laer, added indexes by Kenneth Scott and Kenn Stryker-Rodda (Baltimore, 1974), 110.
10. See "Description and First Settlement of New Netherland" [from Wassenaers, *Historie Van Europa* (Amsterdam; 1621–1632)], *DHNY*, 3:47.
11. KvR to de Laet, June 27, 1632, *VRBM*, 200.

of Fort Orange, the second concentration of Dutch men and women, possibly a dozen artisans, was at Greenbos.

A man's proximity to the fort or, less so, to Greenbos meant convenience to points where furs, merchandise, or seawan (wampum) were exchanged. But as one Dutch visitor remarked at the same time, "every boor . . . [was] a trader," and those who held outlying farms could more easily forestall trade without surveillance.[12] In every sense, the settlement was not one of farmers as opposed to artisans or traders: The residents were not related as yeomen to townsmen, with each drawing an identity from the contrast. Clearly the farmers were not traders – their participation in the fur trade was illegal before 1639 and curtailed after that date – but they were decidedly mercantile.

Van Rensselaer thought that he had sent three distinct occupational groups to the *colonie*: traders, artisans, and farmers. In fact, the colonists blurred the distinction from the start. When a Dutch historian described the roles of the New Netherland population to Amsterdammers in 1626 as "men work[ing] there as in Holland: one trades upwards, southwards and northwards, another builds houses, the third farms," he used a model that was in van Rensselaer's mind. It placed the Dutch men and women overseas in proper occupational and geographical categories.[13]

However, the model was irregular around Fort Orange. Moreover, the settlement had not one, but two, generative centers. Each was in a muted but meaningful rivalry with the other. At Fort Orange, on the west bank of the river, the Company had dominance but no domain, since the directors had inadvertently ceded the land where the fort stood to van Rensselaer when authorizing the patroonship. He, however, had domain without dominion. Greenbos was a center in name only. The logical center was the fort. Only the removal of its power would give van Rensselaer uncircumscribed authority. Yet much as he contemplated it, he dared not interfere with an outpost that the Company had operated since 1624.

Charting the Land

Van Rensselaer was patroon of Rensselaerswyck for fourteen years. During that time, he possessed it in a series of images and plans. At one point in the 1640s, for example, he and an associate imagined their vast property on 't Noordt Rivier as a polder. It was useless land that they had reclaimed, populated, and made valuable. They could now expect

12. De Vries, quoted in Allen W. Trelease, *Indian Affairs in Colonial New York in the Seventeenth Century* (New York, 1960), 112.
13. Stokes, *Iconography*, 2:107; Description from Wassenaers, *Historie DHNY*, 3:42.

from it the same profits that other Amsterdam businessmen were winning from polderization projects in the Low Countries. "Everything," his associate wrote, "belongs to us in common just as if it were a newly diked-in polder that has not yet been sold in lots."[4]

Van Rensselaer's images were varied, but not boundless, flights of fancy. They were cultured – that is, they were constructed by the conventions that entailed Dutch thinking about land and settlement. Most of the schemes were thought out at his canal house in Amsterdam. There upper-story windows gave him a view of ships riding in the harbor as well as lighters plying the Amstel River and moving along the canal before his door. He could see his cargo loaded on lighters and, at a distance, reloaded on the *handelsschepen* that would carry it from Amsterdam to Texel and then New Netherland. In the house, he also wrote the impassioned, petulant, and prolix letters that bore his schemes to America where they were enacted, distorted, or secretly rejected.

Before 1643, the year of van Rensselaer's death, the Dutch public would have seen New Netherland only on three printed maps, two *paskaarten* and one globe. The first map appeared in Johannes de Laet's second edition of *Nieuwe Weraldt ofte Beschryuinghe van West Indien* (1630). It was reprinted by Johannes Janssonius in 1636, a year after Blaeu's printing of the "Figurative Map" of Adriaen Block. Blaeu also produced sea charts (1617, 1621) and a globe in 1622. On de Laet's and Janssonius's maps, Dutch men and women would have seen Fort Oranje (Fort Oranjen on Jansonnius's map) but drawn on the east side of the Hudson. Only after 1650 – seven years after van Rensselaer's death – would they have seen Colonye Renselaerswijck printed in the way familiar to us, that is, as lettering on both sides of the upper reaches of the Hudson (Figure 1.1). But had that map escaped attention, the Dutch public would have concluded, erroneously, that van Rensselaer's possessions were at the southern tip of Manhattan Island, where the letters Rensselaers Hoek rode proprietarily over the harbor on one map of 1660 and another inserted in Adriaen van der Donck's *A Description of the New Netherlands* (Figure 1.2).[5]

Van Rensselaer did not live to see the family name on a printed map of New Netherland. And generally he got little cartographic information from the *colonie*. For example, after 1635, as far as we can judge, he had only verbal descriptions of the Mohawk and Connecticut river

14. De Laet to KvR, February 8, 1641, *VRBM*, 542.
15. Stokes, *Iconography*, 2:70, 71. It is possible that the first printed map of Beverwijck came before the Netherlands people in "Beverwyck nu Albany. Ruwe schets van kort voor 1664" (Hague, n.d.) [from Geschiedkundige atlas van Nederland, Kaart 17, De Kolonien, Blad 18] (747), 1664–1914 (f), NYSA.

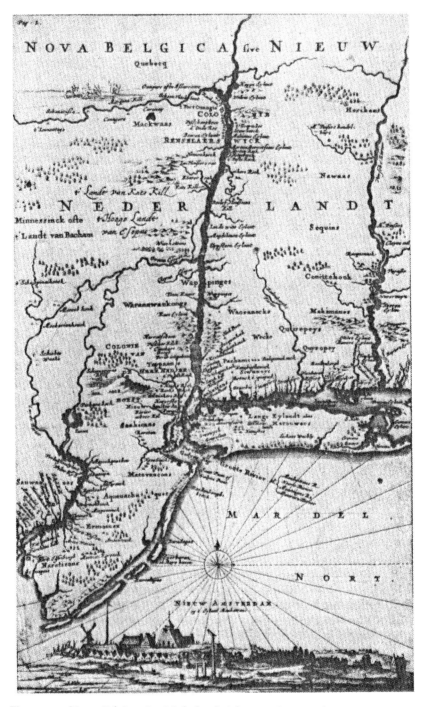

Figure 1.1. Nova Belgica sive Nederlandt (the van der Donck map and view).
Courtesy of the New-York Historical Society.

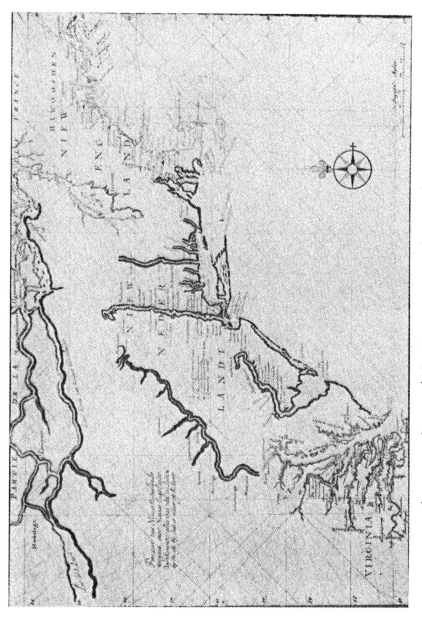

Figure 1.2. Copy made ca. 1660 of a map of Minuit's time, ca. 1630. Courtesy of the New-York Historical Society.

areas.[16] Efforts to get information before 1635 were more successful, possibly because he was especially persistent and specific about his needs at that time. It was information he could add to data available from Block's and Cornelis Hendricksz's early maps of New Netherland.[17] Though the maps were still held by the States General and unpublished, van Rensselaer should have had reason to see them. He was a prominent shareholder in the West India Company, a consortium that replaced the merchants licensed by the States to explore and trade in North America after 1621.[18] Even if he were denied access, he was a close associate of Johannes de Laet who had certainly seen Hendricksz's map of New Netherland by 1630.

Cornelis Hendricksz's map of 1616 accompanied a report on the feasibility of trade in the New World. He had reconnoitered the land in the proper way, that is, charting from the *Onrust* and undoubtedly taking bearings from prominent points along the shores. To map the interior and local settlements of potential trading partners, he used natives or other informants.[19] The finished map was three feet in length, drawn in color, and laid on paper (Figure 1.3).

Hendricksz's map would have given van Rensselaer the Hudson River area as territory served by a substantial river system. It pictured a splendid harbor giving access to a "great... River" already marked with *rakken* and forcefully penetrating a succession of tribal lands. It particularly highlighted islands within van Rensselaer's lands. Two were greatly exaggerated in size, and others south of these were inaccurately multiplied to suggest a chain of islands small in size but capable of impeding access north if required.

However, by 1632, van Rensselaer was in a position to interpret this data alongside more advanced hydrographic charting of 't Noordt Rivier and to see the contours of his lands more precisely. Pieter Minuit, the director at New Netherland, had given him a map of his land purchases but had also commissioned surveys in 1630 that resulted in three others:

16. See KvR to Toussaint Muyssart, February 5, 1641, *VRBM*, 536.
17. The engineer Crijn Fredricksz returned to Amsterdam some time in the early 1630s. Specifications sent to him for building the fort were signed by van Rensselaer, so it is likely he got a verbal report of Manhattan Island from him. See, *Particuliere instructie voor den Ingenier ende lantmeter Cryn Fredericysz... (Special Instructions for the Engineer and Surveyor Cryn Fredericksz... (April 22, 1625), Van Laer, tr. and ed., Documents Relating to New Netherland, 1624–1626 in the Henry E. Huntington Library*, (San Marino, 1924), 164; KvR to van Twiller, July 27, 1632, *VRBM*, 231.
18. Van der Donck was denied access to Company documents because of his fifty-page criticism, *Vertogh van Nieuw Nederlandt (1650)*. See *Description of New Netherlands*, CNYHS 2nd ser. (New York, 1841), 1:128.
19. KvR to Muyssart, February 5, 1641, *VRBM*, 536; Stokes, *Iconography*, 2:73, n. 49. reads "that he [Hendricksz] also traded with the inhabitants of Minquuas."

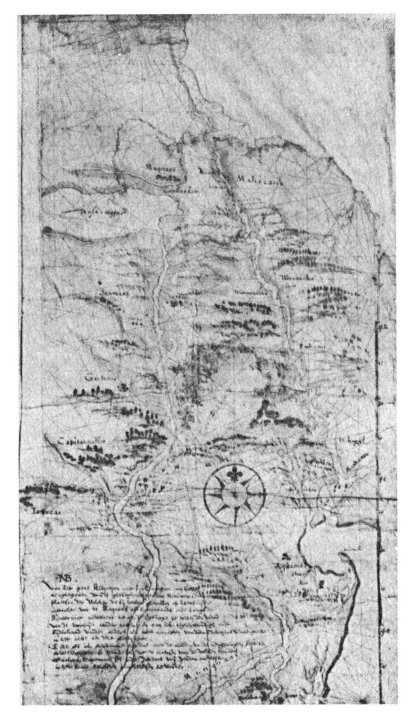

Figure 1.3. Map of a part of Nieuw-Nederland by Cornelis Hendricksz, 1616.
Collection Leupe. VEL 519. Courtesy of Algemeen Rijksarchief, 's-gravenhage.

a detailed map of the bay of New Netherland, a hydrographic chart of 't Noordt Rivier, and a territorial map, "Pascaart van de Nieuw Nederlandt, Virginia ende Nieuw-Engelandt."[20] Each of the maps corrected a good deal of Hendricksz's misinformation. The "Manhattes" was now clearly an island, 't Noordt Rivier was a waterway deep enough for successful navigation, and Nieuw Nederlandt showed itself as territories already characterized by a permanence and solidity. The mapmaker was pleased to dramatize this firm degree of possession by drawing heavy lines to accentuate Dutch lands and using fine lines to mark those of the English (See Figure 1.2).

By summer of 1633, van Rensselaer had in his hands a richly detailed bird's-eye view of his patroonship.[21] It was a map commissioned by him and drafted in Amsterdam. The map was on parchment and measured 22.5 by 70 inches (Figure 1.4). Its delicate geographical detail and skillful cartouche work show that van Rensselaer was willing to spend a substantial sum for a proper visualization. In many ways, it was the culmination of four years' effort to see the patroonship. In January 1630, he had set in motion the first purchases of land from the aboriginal inhabitants of Rensselaerswyck. He commissioned Bastiaen Jansz Krol to make the transactions but could not be specific about the land he hoped to acquire. Basically (and, again, wrongly) he imagined Krol would be looking at expanses of "flat and arable land" but would "meet... [some] woods and mountains." Krol was to make his appraisal of the land by charting from the river. As well as piloting he was to "measure by pacing" the land verging on the riverbanks. At that time, van Rensselaer also expected Krol to substantiate an image lodged in his own mind from seeing Hendricksz's map: There were islands in the river and these were to be carefully charted. Krol was to detail "how many islands there are from the uppermost to the lowest part in the said river, how wide and long they are and what kind of soil they have, to wit, each island separately, also how far apart the same are from each other and from the mainland." He was to buy "*the islands* ... [pay] the respective chiefs ... [and] confirm the purchase before the director and council."[22]

20. KvR to de Laet, June 27, 1632, *VRBM*, 197; Stokes, *Iconography*, 2:111 the "Minuit Maps," following 111.
21. The map, in my judgment, has to be dated at 1633, not 1632. Van Rensselaer had some sort of map from Minuit (*VRBM*, 197), but it is highly unlikely that it is the extant map. It could not have been executed in 1632 as he was still seeking cartographic detail from two men, Krol and Dieterinck, he knew would be in Amsterdam in 1633 and who could not have arrived before that year. They brought sketches of their own (but commissioned in late July of 1632), and Philip Janse van Haarlem also arrived in late July. For Van Laer's reasons for accepting 1632, see "Introduction," *VRBM*, 33.
22. Instructions to Krol, January 12, 1630, *VRBM*, 159; 159; 159; 160; 159 (my italics); 159; Instructions to Krol, January 12, 1630, *VRBM*, 159, 160.

Figure 1.4. Map of the colony of Rensselaerswyck, ca. 1632. Courtesy of the State University of New York Library, Albany.

From other evidence, we can be fairly sure that Krol performed his tasks and sent van Rensselaer some cartographic information. Soon he had a map that would allow him and de Laet to see "the situation and condition" of their "private colony." He knew now that its extent on the west bank was "6 hours walk" (4.8 miles). It began at a southern point (Beeren Island) – known from Minuit's 1630 map – and extended north to a point he could now specify as "Memnenis Castle." He also now knew a good deal about the land purchased on the east side of the river and urged these details on de Laet, even specifying a creek running "far inland and in which rock crystal is found." Less than a month later, he apparently discovered that Krol and the Company's agent at Fort Orange, Albert Dieterinck, were about to be recalled to the Netherlands and could bring him further sketches. He commissioned one of them to make surveys and was now able to be more specific. Three distinct areas for farmlands were to be measured, and a skilled pilot, Philips Jansz van Haarlem, paid to "make a map thereof."[23] The map that resulted from this flurry of reconnaissance was the bird's-eye view of 1633.

Van Rensselaer's map located many notable features with a care for detail. The conventional motif for a town, for example, is repeated in four exquisite miniatures. Each has towers and streets in the finest pen work.[24] Yet this map, like all others, was not an inch-to-the-mile actual world. First, it was what van Rensselaer wanted to see, modified by what he wanted others, especially his partner, Johannes de Laet, to see. Second, it was what the overseas surveyors and draftsmen wanted van Rensselaer to see. An early-twentieth-century scholar discovered some of this. He noted "especially puzzling" errors in the representation of the Mohawk River but left the problem unanswered.[25] In my judgment, van Rensselaer commissioned a map that would deceive de Laet in some details, but his own surveyors had already used their opportunity to deceive him. Although his attempt to distort de Laet's visualization of Rensselaerswyck failed, that of the employees succeeded. It prevented the van Rensselaer family's consolidation in an area to which

23. KvR to Krol, July 20, 1632, *VRBM*, 217, and KvR to de Laet, June 27, 1632, *VRBM*, 197. Stokes, *Iconography*, 2:116, accepts Gillis van Schendel as compositor and printer; KvR to de Laet, June 27, 1632, *VRBM*, 198; KvR to Dirck Duyster, July 20, 1632, *VRBM*, 215–18. Dieterinck was apparently *commis* at Fort Orange; Janse was a pilot at one time for de Vries. (See *Short Historical and Journal Notes*, CNYHS, 2nd ser., [New York, 1856], 3(Part 1):142); Stokes, *Iconography*, 2:116 and "Introduction," *VRBM*, 33, 34.
24. The map is held at the state archives, Albany. The fine workmanship is not apparent in the 1908 reproduction. For a description of towers as symbols of towns, see Johannes Keuning, "XVIth Century Cartography in the Netherlands (Mainly in the Northern Provinces)," *Imago Mundi* (1952), 9:46.
25. A. J. F. Van Laer, "Introduction," *VRBM*, 34.

all colonists wanted uncontested access – the basin and the reaches of the Mohawk River.

Van Rensselaer expected his map to be read as verification that the real estate investment underwritten by himself and four partners was progressing properly. So he placed the names of himself and his partners – Godijn, Blommaert, Burgh, De Laet, and Rensselaer – on the map as "commemorations."[26] The names made the landscape look properly mercantile and properly Dutch. Their placement also signified land correctly distributed. Each partner's name overlay a prominent island in the Groote Noord Rivier. At a distance and in keeping with the practice of distributing profitable lands evenhandedly, the merchants' names appeared again where lands lay alongside creeks. These afforded flats for farming and waterpower for milling, transport, and trade. So the seemingly unwise dispersal of possible places for settlement – Blomaert's Kil 1.7 miles from Blomaert's Eyland and Godijn's Kil across the river and north of Godijn's Eyland – would have struck van Rensselaer as a successful display of fairness.[27]

The map made multiples of the van Rensselaer family name. This was not a denial of the partners' claims but simply an acknowledgment of the efforts of the most active among them. Rensselaerswyck and Renselaer's Eyland appeared alongside Renselaer's Burgh, Renselaer's Kil, Renselaer's Kil [and] vatervall. Further van Rensselaer family names were added, with Bijlaer's Dael, Weely's Dael, Twiller's Dael and Pafraet's Dael. These meanings ordered an unfamiliar wilderness into appropriable parts.

Most of the names never took.[28] Nevertheless, the map gave van Rensselaer his patroonship. The sets of lettering, claiming portions of the land and contributing to the visual conquest of the whole, gave him a patroonship that he could see properly unified.

The map was part of van Rensselaer's promotional scheme to market the east side of the Hudson River. The draftsman had created a map that exaggerated the commercial benefits of the islands, flats, creeks, and waterfalls there. At the same time, he had taken care to cut back on the features of the river's west bank. Drawing the west shore midway from Renselaersburgh to the northernmost landmark, Memnenis Castle, he sketched no details, and he drew only one icon, Fort Orange. Drawing in the area south of Renselaersburgh, he recreated a topography familiar

26. KvR to de Laet, June 27, 1632, *VRBM*, 197.
27. For van Rensselaer's one-fifth shares in three other patroonships, see Colonies and shares in New Netherland, February 1, 1630, *VRBM*, 164, 165.
28. Even he abandoned Rensselaer's Eyland for West Island by midsummer of 1632 (KvR to de Laet, June 27, 1632, *VRBM*, 198, 489).

to the Netherlander, showing *vlakland* (flatland) and *verdronken land* (land subject to flooding) just north of Smack's Eyland, and from Smack's Eyland south to van Renselaer's Eyland he depicted extensive farmlands in considerable detail. Otherwise he drew only the entrances of creeks and left the configuration of the piedmont undramatized.[29]

The draftsman gave copious, and misleading, attention to the east side of the river. In exaggerating the advantages of land on the east bank, the map was a deceit. The *colonie*, as we know, was already emerging as two parts: settlements on the eastern side, which did not have natural access to the fur trade, and those on the western side that did. East on the Hudson lay the lands of the Mahican, a tribe with whom the Mohawk would not trade and who had little access to large stocks of fur-bearing animals after 1626.[30] Only on the west bank could one take advantage of the pattern of Mohawk–Dutch trade operating intermittently since 1612. The Mohawk were able hunters and willing to act as brokers between the Dutch and tribes farther inland. This trade was the reason for the patroonship's existence. Yet the mapmaker reversed these economic realities, shading promise and embellishing loss.

By 1632, Van Rensselaer knew these realities and had already instructed his officer in Rensselaerswyck to convene the colonists – "no one excepted" – and read his prohibition against their attempts to "barter any peltries with the savages" on "forfeiture of their earnings and all their other effects."[31] De Laet may have known the facts as well and smarted at a letter that reinforced van Rensselaer's control over him. "I have commemorated your honor's name," he wrote, "on the east side."[32] But he was powerless to get a foothold on the west bank. Van Rensselaer's growing determination to monopolize the fur trade was already imprinting on the land the binary character of the river community – one in *mirror image* to the commissioned map. It was a feature about Albany that would need different descriptions as the years passed. The split between settlements on the east and west banks of the river was often shaped by new influences as strong as or stronger than those operating at the time of origin. Before van Rensselaer's death, however, the community was already one settlement in two places.

Van Rensselaer realized that it was his responsibility to determine a

29. "Introduction," *VRBM*, 35.
30. Memorial to assembly of nineteen, November 25, 1633, *VRBM*, 245, and see Van Cleaf Backman, *Peltries or Plantations: The Economic Policies of the Dutch West Indian Company in New Netherland, 1623–1639* (Baltimore, 1969), 91.
31. Memorandum of KvR to van Twiller, July 20, 1632, *VRBM*, 209. See also Memorial of van Rensselaer to assembly of nineteen, November 25, 1633, *VRBM*, 235.
32. KvR to de Laet, June 27, 1632, *VRBM*, 198.

center for the settlement. His choices lay between gathering his artisans, minister, baker, skipper, surgeon, ferryman, and teacher in a "settlement" (*"byeenwooninge"*) on the east side of the river, where they would be suitably hampered from participating in the fur trade but would do nothing as a presence to dislodge the Company at Fort Orange, or taking the gamble of settling them on the west bank, where they might usefully challenge the Company's operations but would somehow have to be restrained from competing in the fur trade. He decided on the former, placing the core of settlement on the east side, at Greenbos. Nevertheless he was indecisive about the nature of the settlement, calling it simply *het byeenwooninge*, then *kerkbuurt* (church neighborhood). As late as 1642, he was still trying to fix the location of the church neighborhood. Meanwhile, the community bore the marks of indecision and lack of focus. Van Rensselaer's own properties were on the west shore: Greyenbos (a farm near Watervliet), Rensselaersburgh (an island with arable land just south of the fort), and Beeren Island farther south. When he referred to Greenbos in 1641, he called it *het overquartier van de Colonie* (an outlying section of the colony), acknowledging its distance from the center.[33]

Van Rensselaer's motives were a source of the emerging landscape of Rensselaerswyck. Those of his overseas informants were also significant. As the map shows (Figure 1.4), he had been denied complete data on Rensselaerswyck, particularly the area where the Mohawk River entered the Hudson. Instead, he was given a river basin fed by two substantial looking creeks and, well below, a wider river labeled Renselaer's Kil en 't waterval, apparently meant to represent the Mohawk, but occupying the wrong position. As a result, van Rensselaer, who was able to be specific about other kinds of information he wanted over the years, never knew enough to ask useful questions about the valuable trade route leading into the Mohawk River valley.

Van Rensselaer visualized a geography of rivers and seas. "Land and coast, sea and river," he wrote, made New Netherland more a maritime world "than all the seventeen provinces of the Netherlands." Trading would be a matter of navigating between trading posts like Fort Orange and New Amsterdam. Just as a sailor had been one of the two men doing preliminary surveying for him so, now, a skipper would distribute spirits from his distillery, piloting all the way to the English colonies. He imagined his supply of brandy stowed on a sloop under the care of "a skipper

33. KvR to van der Donck, May 4, 1641, *VRBM*, 547, n. 18 and 547. Today's spelling would be *overkwatier*; for use of the term in Gelderland, the province of van Rensselaer's birth, see K. A. Kalkwijk, *De Hertog en Zijn Burchten, Kastelen in de Gelderse Geschiedenis tot 1543* (Leiden, 1976), 108, and Robert Fruin, *Geschiedenis der Staatsinstellingen in Nederland tot den val der Republiek* ('s-Gravenhage, 1901), 223.

... [who would] cruise along the coasts of New Netherland and the adjacent settlements and sell it."[34] The upper reaches of the Hudson, now possessed in maps, seemed eminently suited to support such maritime enterprises.

Coming to Know the Land

Over the fourteen years of his patroonship, van Rensselaer intensified his possession of Rensselaerswyck by calling on a host of informants. He corresponded with at least sixteen men about the colony. As a result he could find representations of the patroonship structured in the numerous pages of his own letterbooks. Looking at these he could build his reflections and narratives about it. At different times, at least three or four clerks were employed in inscribing his letters, submitting them for revision, and then composing them into proper correspondence.[35] They then made duplicates, usually on paper 34 by 23 cm, and on these van Rensselaer penned his careful marginalia. As with the East India Company, letters were generally dispatched overseas in batches. They were carefully numbered or alphabetized. On one Sunday in April 1634, van Rensselaer alerted the Company's director at New Netherland to a packet of letters en route. "This letter I send separately ... and the documents herein mentioned, from No. 1 to No. 20, in another packet ... also No. 22, being a letter written by Domini Badius ... No. 23, a letter from your honor's father; No. 24. one from Thomas van Wely" (van Rensselaer's brother-in-law).[36] In tone, the letters could be petulant or pious, often shamelessly prying.

But all were a *cri de coeur* for information. Van Rensselaer was never satisfied with the correspondence he received from New Netherland and was increasingly distrustful of it toward the end of his life. But he never relented in pressing for a greater volume of information. To follow the aggregation and reaggregation of his knowledge to 1643 would be to drown in detail, but we might look carefully at one three-year period, 1630–3. The years seem to require an uncomplicated sort of analysis because colonists were few, the patroonship was taking its earliest bearings, and we have already considered his acquisition of geographic information. Actually there are complexities, but these allow generalizations that, in my judgment, hold for the subsequent ten years.

In 1630, van Rensselaer's knowledge of the patroonship was minimal.

34. Memorial to assembly of nineteen, November 25, 1633, *VRBM*, 235; KvR to van Twiller, April 23, 1634, *VRBM*, 283.
35. "Introduction," *VRBM*, 21.
36. KvR to van Twiller, April 23, 1634, *VRBM*, 287.

It was a year of more demanding enterprises, with the partners taking measure of their own and competitors' various projects. He, for instance, took note that one burgomaster and his partners were investing in Tobago. Meanwhile, his old associate Samuel Blommaert was investigating an island in the Barbados, and Michael Pauw was interested in the lower reaches of the Hudson River. It was also a time when van Rensselaer had no one in New Netherland who could act authoritatively for him. Wolfert Gerritsz of Amersfoort was there by September of 1630 and was a reliable farmer. He was expected to send "all the particulars" of van Rensselaer's New Netherland investments to him, but his instructions suggest the patroon's realization that, for the present, he would have to play a larger role on Manhattan Island than upriver at Fort Orange. He expected Gerritsz to plant grain and get in winter seed at Rensselaerswyck between April and November, but most of his tasks would be carried out on a farm on Manhattan Island where he would collect animals, seed, wagons, plows "and all other things" preparatory to the arrival of colonists and removal of all "near Fort Orange."[37] He was only an occasional source of information on the colony's affairs.

By January of 1631, van Rensselaer was dealing with his colonists in two ways. Both were disorderly, but he seemed to recognize this only in 1632. First, he was intent on making an individual contract with each artisan or farmer. With Gerritsz, for example, he agreed to a contract for four summers with 20 guilders for each month of service and the option to "end the contract after one or two summers." In 1631, he drew up a complex contract with Marinus Adriaensz van der Veere binding him to cultivate tobacco for three years. He would pay half the cost of "four good firelocks" and an unspecified number of "axes, adzes, shovels, and spades." He also agreed that, "If it is at all convenient," he would build Adriaensz a house. Some colonists were obliged to make a yearly trip to Manhattan Island "without having any right to claim compensation." Some settlers got the same wages "over three years," while others contracted for incremental wages, that is, "the first year gl 60, the second year gl 70, the third year gl 80 and in hand paid gl 12 as an advance." For some, contracts expired "whenever it pleases him." For others, terms were quite specific. He hired Hendrick Fredericksz van Bunnick at gl 120 yearly plus a pair of boots every four years, and Cornelis Thonissen van Meerkerck for an annual wage of "80 guilders and two pairs of boots."[38]

---

37. Registration of colonies with Chamber of Middelburg [before December 21, 1630], *VRBM*, 176; Registration of Blommaert at Barbados, April 17, 1630, *VRBM*, 166; Registration of Pauw on North River, January 10, 1630, *VRBM*, 158; Instructions to Gerritsz, January 16, 1630, *VRBM*, 161; 162.
38. Instructions to Gerritsz, January 16, 1630, *VRBM*, 161; Agreement between KvR and

Van Rensselaer sought to bring all this intricacy into order. He often obliged tenants or artisans to send "by every ship and yacht . . . proper reports and accurate accounts of everything in all sincerity without concealment." But his calls for reports invariably fell on deaf ears, and he was not satisfied with his accounting. The solution was an agent, a *commis* to serve the *colonie*'s owners, as a supercargo did the principals of a *handelsschip*.[39] Without such a man, the chaos of affairs, which can be seen forming by midsummer 1632, could only worsen.

At this time, van Rensselaer also allowed land to be taken up on a first come first served basis. As a result, he soon had difficulty locating properties and tenants. Quite forthrightly, he advised Marinus Adriaensz to begin cultivating tobacco "on the north side of the fort (*if* the same has not been occupied before his arrival) as the first comer has the preference." Otherwise, Adriaensz was free to locate where he wished. In fact, no one was farming north of the fort at the time. In any case, Adriaensz was working land south of the fort, at Godijnsburgh, in 1632. In 1631, van Rensselaer employed three Scandinavians for the colony. (In fact, two set sail.) They were to erect a sawmill and then a gristmill nearby. The choice of location was their own, though van Rensselaer offered two sites. If they wished to establish farms, they were free to do so anywhere. At this time, van Rensselaer had it in his mind that "ship planking" and "gunwale timber" might be marketable. But his agreement with the Scandinavians that they could fell trees "standing in the *entire* colony . . . and for seven leagues next adjoining" the projected sawmill argues that he had only a vague image of the landscape.[40]

By early winter of 1632, van Rensselaer had taken the opportunity of conferring with at least four men from New Netherland. Dirck Joosten would have arrived in late 1630 or early 1631 introducing himself for whatever favors van Rensselaer might confer and perhaps traveling to van Rensselaer's home with Jan Brouwer, another company employee. Brouwer was one of five men who had signed the deed certifying van Rensselaer's ownership of lands west of the Hudson and was an associate of Wouter van Twiller, the patroon's nephew who was director of New

Adriaensz, January 12, 1631, *VRBM*, 178; 178; Agreement of KvR and Adriaensz, February 17, 1631, *VRBM*, 180; 181; Inventory, January 1, 1632, *VRBM*, 193; Agreement of KvR and Andries Chrisiensz and others, July 2, 1631, *VRBM*, 186; Memorandum of engagement of farm laborers [June 15, 1632], *VRBM*, 196; 196.
39. Agreement of KvR and Adriaensz, January 12, 1631, *VRBM*, 179, and see 163; Agreement of KvR and Christensz, July 2, 1631, *VRBM*, 188.
40. Agreement of KvR and Christensz, January 12, 1631, *VRBM*, 176; 176; List of men on the farms, July 20, 1632, *VRBM*, 222; Agreement of KvR and Christensz, July 2, 1631, *VRBM*, 187 (my italics).

Netherland. It is likely that he would have encountered van Rensselaer's close questioning. Pieter Bylevelt was at van Rensselaer's home in July 1632. He was one of the Company's councilors and an astute man who knew its methods of operation and the means by which its ships and laborers could be brought to serve a private investor like van Rensselaer. He especially knew the ins and outs of agriculture – how to get seed, when to manure, where to get strong animals. Now he had been recalled to Holland and was selling out to van Rensselaer. So the patroon purchased his animals and farm and also got a wealth of information, enough to provide a structure on which to build some order.[41]

More reliable than Joosten, Brouwer, or Bylevelt was Minuit, who returned in the summer of 1632. He came with maps, shining assurances about the economic viability of van Rensselaer's venture, and properties to sell. Van Rensselaer was offered land, stock, and shares in New Netherland, all investments that promised as favorable a future as he would ever encounter. Van Twiller was about to replace Minuit as director in midsummer and would be opportunely positioned to serve van Rensselaer's interests as well. As it proved, he was less effective than van Rensselaer would have wished, never provided enough information, and was eventually removed from office because of the *bewindhebbers'* (directors') distrust. But in the summer of 1632, it boded well. And Minuit's deal was not one to be dismissed lightly.

Nor was his information firsthand. Enough has been said of the geographical reconnaissance shared. It gave van Rensselaer decision-making powers. It enabled him to tell colonists where he wanted them to settle. Although this was not done with exactitude, it did allow him to put the names of colonists alongside place-names decided upon by 1632 and lettered onto the 1633 map. Gerrit Teunisse de Reux was the first man meant to actualize one such name. Under a contract of June 15, 1632, he was to begin a farm "near the fourth creek now called Blommaert's kil." Brandt Peelen was the first man conceived of as farming "next" to another tenant. Now, too, van Rensselaer could give Albert Dieterinck a surveying project with reasonable specifications – "to wit... [survey] opposite Fort Orange; also near the mill creek [Normanskil]; further above the pine wood to the falls [above Watervliet]; from there to Moenemins Castle" – because it was possible to know "how many farms there could be... giving every farmer 20

41. Symon Pos to KvR, September 16, 1630, *VRBM*, 170; Certificate of purchase, August 13, 1630, *VRBM*, 168, Pos to KvR, September 16, 1630, *VRBM*, 170, 172; KvR to van Twiller, July 27, 1632, *VRBM*, 230; "Introduction," *VRBM*, 60; KvR to van Twiller, July 27, 1632, *VRBM*, 231; 231; 231.

or 30 morgens [of] arable land besides pasture and meadowland."[42]

Minuit also came with assurances in this important summer. Van Rensselaer learned that there were whales in the South River (Delaware River) and that rock crystal was to be found in de Laet's Creek. He discovered that Minuit had accidentally found a profitable way of cultivating tobacco. This led him to think it "a new invention which . . . would surpass all others," and by 1636, van Twiller was cultivating it opposite Breuckelen on Manhattan Island. Minuit also gave assurances that the Company would have to keep "some 25 men" at Fort Orange, and van Rensselaer began to foresee a promising future for the *colonie* in victualing them and drawing a profit of "some 2500 guilders a year." Similarly, someone was telling him that with a brewery he could "provide all New Netherland with beer," and by distilling brandy, he could capture the market of the English colonies. Van Rensselaer purchased Minuit's assets, convinced he had made "offhand over 100 pounds Flemish" on the transaction.[43] As it eventuated, the *colonie* gave van Rensselaer fewer diversified enterprises than he anticipated. Yet as late as 1642, he was matching the advice of Minuit against later (more realistic) reports of Rensselaerswyck and complaining that farmers were disloyal in demanding larger farms than Minuit had judged necessary.

During June and July, van Rensselaer used Minuit's and Bylevelt's information to put his colony in order on paper. By August 1, he had a lengthy contract signed by a prospective farmer and glossed by his own marginal note, "29 years old." He had a shorter one inscribed with the marks of three laborers, the signature of a fourth worker, and an apostil reminding himself that one could "write a little." They would all sail immediately. He made copies of thirteen documents and entrusted them to van Twiller who sailed to New Netherland on July 27. The first was a simple cover letter and the second was a memorandum that indexed the abundant data in the documents, listed van Twiller's tasks, and provided a way of recalling him to his responsibilities – provided he was disciplined enough to consult his records. (Unfortunately he was not.) With these documents went lists of five Rensselaerswyck farms and thirteen farmers and a classification of the stock with detailed "specification."[44] Four additional documents were copies of papers concerning the assets purchased from Bylevelt and Minuit. All were the orderly classi-

42. Contract of KvR and de Reux, June 15, 1632, *VRBM*, 193; KvR to Krol, July 20, 1632, *VRBM*, 218; 219.
43. KvR to de Laet, June 27, 1632, *VRBM*, 197; 198; KvR to van Twiller, July 27, 1632, *VRBM*, 233; 233; KvR to de Laet, June 27, 1632, *VRBM*, 200.
44. Contract of KvR and de Reux, June 15, 1632, *VRBM*, 193–5; 196; Memorandum from KvR to van Twiller, July 20, 1632, *VRBM*, 204–8; list of men on farms, July 20, 1632, *VRBM*, 222; Inventory of goods and animals, July 20, 1632, *VRBM*, 223; List of animals, July 20, 1632, *VRBM*, 220.

fications that he tried in vain to teach each *commis* appointed at Rensselaerswyck. Finally, he sent five letters to farmers and officers, expecting van Twiller's secretary in New Amsterdam to duplicate them and retain copies of each among his papers.[45]

Van Rensselaer could see in his letter book a consolidation of the *colonie*. An *ondercommis* of the Company at Fort Orange was likely to "stay there" and see to his interests. Wolfert Gerritsz was there to send frequent "advice." Finally, van Rensselaer now had in his letter book documents enacting his first considerations of Rensselaerswyck as a political landscape. They were the notarized papers empowering him to appoint a *schout* (law enforcing agent) and five *schepenen* (a council of lesser aldermen), together with copies of their instructions and a memorandum to van Twiller setting out the proper "solemnities" of installation. Van Rensselaer shared with a company official in New Amsterdam his sense of satisfaction with these undertakings and with the future generally. "I have already brought some order in my colony called Rensselaerswyck."[46]

The *Soutberg* sailed with van Twiller and nine colonists. There also went a silver-plated rapier and a black hat with plume for the *schout*-designate and four black hats with silver bands for the *schepenen*. The packet of correspondence also crossed to New Netherland. The question arises again, however, whether van Rensselaer's order on paper became the real world. Did his decisions take any better than Weely's Dael and Bijlaer's Dael? Or was it that, in the jostling of his meanings of Rensselaerswyck against those of his colonists, they had equally little substance?

The Patroon, the Company, and the Settlers: 1632–1638

A consideration of the years from 1632 to 1638, when van Twiller was recalled to Hólland in disgrace and Arent van Curler took up his duties as *commis*, offers some answer, for van Rensselaer's copybooks covering the years of van Twiller's stewardship, 1632–8, give copious indications

45. List of animals, July 20, 1632, *VRBM*, 220, 221; Bill of sale, July 20, 1632, Promissory note, July 20, 1632, Receipts for payment on same, February 24, 1634, Bill of sale of animals, July 20, 1632, Promissory note, July 27, 1632, Receipts for payment of same, November 11, 1632 and February 24, 1634, *VRBM*, 225–9; KvR to van Twiller, July 27, 1643, *VRBM*, 230; Inventory, July 20, 1632, *VRBM*, 223, 224.
46. KvR to Notelman, July 20, 1632, *VRBM*, 213, 214; KvR to Duyster, July 20, 1632, *VRBM*, 216–17; 217; KvR to Gerritsz, July 20, 1632, *VRBM*, 219; Power of attorney to van Soest, July 1, 1632, *VRBM*, 203; Power of attorney to van Twiller, July 1, 1632, *VRBM*, 201–3; KvR to Duyster, July 20, 1632, *VRBM*, 215.

of both how and why his decisions had limited effect. First, the order projected by his image in 1632 was not duplicated on the land because his knowledge about Rensselaerswyck continued to be inadequate and skewed. Second, the West India Company was making its decisions, and the colonists were enacting theirs. Finally, his communications with the colony paradoxically undermined the authority they were meant to realize.

Van Rensselaer clearly considered 1632 a turning point in the colony's fortunes. He argued this vigorously before the Company directors the next year, particularly citing its promise as a reason for opening the fur trade more fully to the struggling patroons. His own colony, he argued, had been limping along "year to year *until in July 1632* ... [when] he was provided with people and animals enough to start five farms." Such success should be matched by a more generous policy toward trade. But even in his tidy records of 1632, van Rensselaer had been deceiving himself. There were not, for example, five farms as set out so neatly in the list copied for van Twiller, but only three. In fact, he was unable to get a resident farmer to take the third farm as late as April 1634. There was still no fourth or fifth farm. Three-quarters of the colonists who had arrived before 1633 were gone by 1634. Two years later he knew of six farms but probably had no specific detail about them.[47]

Other projects, like the distillery, brewery, and fisheries that had shape in the paper world of his and Minuit's inventions, were also either much delayed or never tried. The information needed in order to make proper decisions was either not forthcoming or tardy. Facts about his Manhattan farm did not arrive until he was well into litigation over it; specifications for the supplies needed by colonists did not arrive with regularity. Van Rensselaer wrote of having no way of "knowing what I should send," on one occasion, "as I have no advice at all." By 1637, he had abandoned the hope of knowing the locations of all his farmers and artisans. When he sent over two blacksmiths in that year, he told *commis* Jacob Planck to "find ... [them] room *somewhere*." He knew they required a place for "a shop" but could not suggest a location.[48]

Both Planck and van Twiller were irresponsible in keeping records and sending accounts. Van Twiller's general negligence was the talk of the Strand in Amsterdam in 1637 and 1638. Yet van Rensselaer bullied him

47. Memorial, November 25, 1633, VRBM, 242 (my italics); in 1632, there may have been fourteen tenants. This number included the two Scandinavians and a man helping Andriesz with tobacco cultivation. Neither of the two operations is on van Rensselaer's list, VRBM, 222; KvR to Coenraet Notelman, January 10, 1636, VRBM, 317.
48. KvR to van Twiller, April 23, 1634, VRBM, 275; KvR to Planck, September 21, 1637, VRBM, 354 (my italics); 354.

for information in every letter and did the same with Planck. "If I am to keep the administration" of the colony in order, he begged him in 1636, "I must have . . . better information." He was shown all too little, and Arent van Curler's appointment as Planck's successor merely began a second and, for van Rensselaer, final round of equally unheeded imprecations.[49]

The Patroon and the Trading Company

Rensselaerswyck continued to be a landscape constructed on van Rensselaer's faulty and inadequate information. That, in turn, meant a flawed understanding of his whole investment in New Netherland. To be sure, land was only one component given consideration in most Dutch overseas enterprises, and it was valued well below other ways of gaining profits. In this, van Rensselaer and the Company were alike. The Company's persistence at Fort Orange depended squarely on a continual assessment of the fur trade made in Amsterdam. About the trade, the *bewindhebbers* generally had better information than van Rensselaer.[50] But their anger at the inadequacy of van Twiller's official correspondence with them suggests that they too felt an insecurity about their venture. As a result, the directors tacked again and again with respect to the whole New Netherland enterprise.

Historians have generally agreed that the Company was a "structural monstrosity." The Groningen chamber felt rancor at "everything the Company did" and a thoroughly chaotic administration presided until 1671.[51] But the directors' intentions for the upper reaches of the Hudson remained the same: to make the fort the only trading center north of Manhattan Island, that is, to maintain it as the place to which all furs – those of the natives, the Company's licensed traders, soldiers, and before 1639, van Rensselaer's colonists and *commis* – were brought. The *commis* purchased skins and saw to their shipment downriver to Manhattan Island. Profits were enticing. If successful, a *commis* could hope to send 13,000 skins downriver. At gl 8 the pelt, this amounted to gl 104,000.[52]

An incident in 1633 exemplifies how van Rensselaer's visions were thwarted by the Company. The directors had employed Hans Hunthum

49. KvR to Planck, October 3, 1636, *VRBM*, 323.
50. P. J. Van Winter, *De Westindische Compagnie ter Kamer Stad en Lande* (Hague, 1978), 13, n. 43.
51. Oliver Albert Rink, Merchants and Magnates: Dutch New York, 1609–1664 (Ph.D. diss., University of Southern California, 1976), 88; Van Winter, *Westindische Compagnie*, 10, 17–18.
52. KvR to van Twiller, April 23, 1634, *VRBM*, 273.

as *commis*, a man whom van Rensselaer considered "a rogue."⁵³ The decision had disastrous consequences for his farmers. Hunthum *was* a rogue and within a short time had so cheated the Mohawk that they retaliated by burning the Company's yacht and slaughtering cattle. As a result, the farmers were in a state of destitution that the patroon's well-laid plans for shipping animals upriver could not have anticipated. Another effect of Hunthum's actions was his recall to Amsterdam in 1634 where he underwent a lengthy interrogation. In evidence given by a former *commis*, Krol, the exceptional value of the land immediately around the fort began to emerge. Hunthum, it appeared, had allowed an English trader, "Jacob Eelkens," to trade from his sloop "directly in front of the wall" and "in a tent he had erected behind Castle Island [Rensselaersburgh] on the mill creek [Godijn's Kil]."⁵⁴ Further testimony revealed that Eelkens had traded there for "four or five weeks" and in that short time had obtained "about 400 skins."⁵⁵

Van Rensselaer was not privy to this interrogation. But van Twiller had supplied him with sufficient data on Hunthum to make him see that trading near the fort meant increased profits.⁵⁶ Six days after responding to van Twiller's description of Hunthum's activities and eight weeks before the inquiry, van Rensselaer informed the directors that he "intend[ed] to establish . . . [farms] around the aforesaid fort."⁵⁷ This did not mean moving down on the fort from the north since there was only a small area of flat land (some of it swampy) above the installation and then thick forests covering steeply elevated land.⁵⁸ Moving up from the south must have seemed more feasible. With farms at Rensselaersburgh and Welysburgh (on Castle Island), a few colonists were already in possession of land less than a mile south of the fort. The *colonie*, however, was now short of both colonists and farm animals. Van Rensselaer was in no position to encircle the fort nor could he prevent interlopers like Eelkens tenting near Godijnsburgh and having meals there with a corrupt agent of the Company.⁵⁹

---

53. Ibid.
54. Examination of Krol, June 30, 1634, *VRBM*, 304, 303; for de Vries's firsthand observations on the affair, see "Extracts from the Voyages of David Pietersz de Vries," G. Troost, tr., CNYHS 2nd ser. (New York, 1841), 1:256.
55. Examination of Krol, *VRBM*, 303.
56. Ms. is not in his papers, *VRBM*, 302, n. 59; KvR to van Twiller, April 23, 1634, *VRBM*, 273.
57. KvR to Director and Council, April 29, 1634, *VRBM*, 298.
58. William Smith, *The History of the Province of New-York, from the First Discovery, to which is annexed A Description of the Country, an Account of the Inhabitants, their Trade, Religious and Political State, and the Constitution of the Courts of Justice in the Colony* (London, 1776 [Preface dated 1756]), 15.
59. Examination of Krol, June 30, 1634, *VRBM*, 303.

Van Rensselaer liked his relationship with the West India Company to be "one hand washing the other," but it was seldom that way. Generally he desperately needed the Company – its wharves and rivercraft at New Amsterdam, its *boweries* on Manhattan Island, and its fort for "protection and defense." In return he occasionally required colonists to keep night watch at the fort and perform other duties.[60] But there can be no doubt that he was biding his time, awaiting his chance to eject the Company from the upper Hudson altogether.

Meanwhile, the Company continued a policy of carefully limiting its physical presence in the valley. It was satisfied with a minimum of land. "A ruling presence," as in the East Indies, "was more important than the number of people involved."[61] Van Rensselaer's veiled threat of establishing "farms around the fort" in the mid-1630s had little effect. But its actualization after 1646 altered the policy of the Company. It gave the director, Petrus Stuyvesant, no option but to enforce the Company's restricted but absolute tenure. In 1652, he claimed all land "within a cannon shot of the fort." This measurement was a conventional one. In fact, it was in keeping with countrymen who still measured land according to methods that one Dutch authority has teasingly described as exceeding "even the imprecision of medieval land measurement."[62] But in such a way was the land possessed by a Company with no desire to tame the wilderness – but every intention of controlling the trade (Figure 1.5).

The Patroon and the Colonists

To the rivalry of van Rensselaer and the Company was added the opportunism of the colonists in shaping the landscape in the upper Hudson Valley. In the first place, men of all kinds – farmers, smiths, sawyers,

60. KvR to Director and Council, April 29, 1634, *VRBM*, 298; 298; for example, see that van Rensselaer would let his people do "double work watching the fort by night and working by day," in KvR to van Twiller, April 23, 1634, *VRBM*, 287.
61. I. Schoffer, "Dutch 'Expansion' and Indonesian Reactions: Some Dilemmas of Modern Colonial Rule (1900–1942)," in H. L. Wesseling, ed., *Expansion and Reaction: Essays on European Reaction and Reactions in Asia and Africa* (Leiden, 1978), 85.
62. KvR to Director and Council, April 29, 1634, *VRBM*, 298; these properties were his artisans' dwellings, not farms. See Cornelis van Dyck's continuing struggle with van Rensselaer's director, A[rnold] J. F. Van Laer, ed. and tr., *Minutes of the Court of Rensselaerswyck, 1648–1652* (Albany, 1922). Van Laer edited five volumes of the court records: *Minutes of the Court of Fort Orange and Beverwyck, 1652–1656*, 1; *Minutes of the Court of Fort Orange and Beverwyck, 1657–1660*, 2; *Minutes of the Court of Albany, Rensselaerswyck and Schenectady, 1668–1673*, 1; *Minutes of the Court of Albany, Rensselaerswyck and Schenectady, 1675–1680*, 2; *Minutes of the Court of Albany, Rensselaerswyck and Schenectady, 1680–1685*, 3 (hereafter CRB for those before 1664 and CRA for those after 1664); Cornelius Willem de Keweit, *History of South Africa: Social and Economic* (London, 1942), 16.

Figure 1.5. Silver coin of 1683 cast on the order of the directors of the West India Company, Groningen Chamber. Courtesy of the Groninger Museum.

and artisans – soon found their callings obstructed and unrewarding. They were therefore increasingly tempted to position themselves so as to engage in the fur trade. Furthermore, they soon realized that the soil would reward industry and resourcefulness only slowly and ungenerously. True, by 1642, they had learned to sow beans and peas in soil that was "foul and needy," but they also came to know that the patroon was not in a position to turn Rensselaerswyck into the bountiful fields and pastures that his ambitions promised.[63] Their determination to compensate themselves by engagement in the trade was heightened proportionately.

Throughout the 1630s, van Rensselaer continued to convince himself that the lands of Rensselaerswyck were fertile. They would yield sufficient crops so that "each farmer according to his thrift may prosper a little."[64] In 1634, when he had the patroonship on the market, he unintentionally exaggerated the promising composition of the soil. Admittedly it was clay, but it was splendidly improved by the annual "overflow" of the Hudson. There were already 1,200 morgen of arable land on the east shore (about 2,400 acres), and 210 morgen of cleared land on the west side were "now ready" for grazing, "raising hay, and cultivating with the plow."[65] So convinced was he of these easily won livings that, after 1635, he increasingly lost patience with the farmers' lack of success. Some of his myopia about his "fertile lands" upriver arose from contrasting them with his farms on Manhattan Island. There, he thought,

63. Van der Donck, *Description of New Netherland*, CNYHS, 2nd ser. (New York, 1841), 1:157.
64. KvR to Planck, October 3, 1636, VRBM, 327.
65. Account of Rensselaerswyck, July 20, 1634, VRBM, 307; 306.

his land had become so "overworked and poor" that it would have to be sold and the animals moved upriver as quickly as they could be profitably distributed to colonists. In 1636, he was still writing, "The Manhattans are mostly exhausted and my land [upriver] is still luxurious and fresh."[66]

The contrast continued to feed van Rensselaer's vision, but the colonists knew better. Delaetsburgh on the east bank of the river, for example, was land that van Rensselaer described in 1634 as having beautiful groves, a watermill and farm. Yet Roelof Jansz had been unable to make a living there and in the same year either "wanted to leave" or was in the process of being dismissed from it. At the time he was "drawing provisions" from van Rensselaer's agent but "grossly running up . . . [his unpaid] account."[67] Whatever sort of farmhouse he had, it was one of only two in the area. Laurens Laurensz lived in the attic. He was the Scandinavian meant to build the sawmill on de Laet's Kill and roam the seven surrounding leagues for trees. Laurensz lacked both equipment to fell trees and the animals to drag them. He had managed to erect a farmhouse and, at some distance, a gristmill. Neither a sawmill nor a workable farm was to be seen. Laurensz's situation was desperate but not unusual. His companions had deserted him, he lacked the wit to bargain for good conditions in his initial contract, and no provision for board had been made.

By 1637, Laurensz and his wife were gone, and Pieter Cornelisz van Munnickendam, a carpenter, was trying "to get the mill ready for operation." He and a number of associates whom van Rensselaer was pleased to call "the mill company," were promised handsome profits. Trees could be steadily felled and the mill brought to producing boards to be "sold readily to my people, at the Manhatans, and also to the English both to the south and to the north, who will no doubt come to fetch it at your place." Houses would be needed, even by the natives. The land could be built up with "houses and huts," which "the chiefs and others of the savages . . . can shut with doors and windows."[68] Yet as late as 1638 (and until 1646) farmers were using the inconvenient and often unworkable mill across the river on the fifth kill.

In 1638 other farmers on the east bank of the Hudson were desperately clinging to their contracts with van Rensselaer. Michael Janse and his

66. For van Rensselaer's comparisons with the Betuwe and Beemster region, see ibid., 311; KvR to van Twiller, April 23, 1634, *VRBM*, 278; List of papers and memoranda sent by KvR to Planck, October 4, 1636, *VRBM*, 331.
67. KvR to van Twiller, April 23, 1634, *VRBM*, 282; 281.
68. KvR to Piéter Cornelisz van Munnickendam, September 21, 1637, *VRBM*, 350; 351; 351.

wife were the first to farm the land along de Laet's Kill in 1638. Janse, who was an inexperienced farmhand when he left Holland in 1638, left the *colonie* in 1646. Meanwhile, Guert Teunisse de Reux had succeeded Roelof Janse at Delaetsburgh. It was no doubt due to his efforts that seventy-six acres were cultivated and wheat harvested worth gl 2,535 in 1640. Mauritz Janse van Broeckhuysen was less successful with another "new farm" on the east bank and immediately south of a swamp. He retained it only one year, probably not managing to cultivate the land then or soon thereafter.[69] Similarly uncultivated was the nearby farmland assigned in 1638 to Teunis Dircksz van Vechten. To the south, Symon Walichsz and Cornelis Maesen had chosen land at Papscanee Island and were just beginning to bring it under cultivation.[70] In short, there were four or five farms, but only Delaetsburgh was an established one.

On the west side of the Hudson and to the north was the farm worked by Broer Cornelis (Cornelis Anthonisz van Breuckelen) since 1634. Inaccurately, van Rensselaer reckoned that this was exceedingly promising land, set on gently sloping hills, unforested, and suitable for cultivating fruit trees as well as vines. Whatever the case, Anthonisz was far more interested in participating in the fur trade than farming. The position of his land was its value: the closest possible farm to the major trade route into the Mohawk Valley. It was what van Rensselaer himself wanted, that is, "a farm, on the fifth kil far from the fort and where nobody lived." Anthonisz's land remained underdeveloped. He did not give the patroon a tenant's fertile stretches of farmland but, quite the contrary, competition in the trade.[71]

Below Anthonisz's farm in 1638 lay the land that would one day be a most contested piece of land around Fort Orange, *de vlackte* (the flats). Yet it remained undeveloped until 1642 when van Curler alleged he planted "10 to 12 morgens of oats." In 1643, he had perhaps twenty horses there. But as he openly admitted, his subordinate was residing there "to trade."[72] Untilled land reached farther south as well, to Castle

69. Account of Rensselaerswyck, July 20, 1634, *VRBM*, 307; Settlers of Rensselaerswyck, *VRBM*, 818; KvR to M. J. Scrabbekercke, June 25, 1640, *VRBM*, 499 (de Reux died in 1639); Memorandum of KvR for Megapolensis, June 3, 1642, *VRBM*, 619. Van Broeckhuysen left the colony in 1631 or 1632, and in 1639, when de Reux died, van Rensselaer leased Delaetsburgh to M. J. van Broeckhuysen, but the arrangements were mutually unsatisfactory.
70. KvR to Planck, May 10, 1638, *VRBM*, 412; KvR to Planck, October 3, 1636, *VRBM*, 326.
71. KvR to Planck, May 10, 1638, *VRBM*, 414; 414; KvR to M. J. van Broeckhuysen, June 25, 1640, *VRBM*, 503; Leases and agreements, August 25, 1650 to September 11, 1658, *VRBM*, 749; KvR to van Breuckelen, June 25, 1640, *VRBM*, 496; see Memorandum of farms in colony, 1651, *VRBM*, 742, 743; 740; Settlers, *VRBM*, 809.
72. KvR to Planck, May 10, 1638, *VRBM*, 414; A[rnold] J. F. Van Laer, "Arent van

Island almost a mile below Fort Orange, where Brandt Peelen had the
sole farm. In 1634, van Rensselaer had envisioned 272 arable acres here.
It was a grossly exaggerated estimate of an island measured as seventy
acres in 1869.[73] But for van Rensselaer there had to be "not 2 but 3
farms... each of which would have 40 morgens" and, on rethinking,
"there could easily be six." Visualizing the family property near his
birthplace at Nykerck, he wrote van Twiller that it "has not even 20
morgens of cultivated farm land... and what a fine farm that is." The
farmers could have their pastures of hay on "another island" (he did not
know exactly where that might be) and meanwhile "take care not to let
the arable lie fallow." In 1634 he was both wrong and disingenuous
about these farms just below the fort. He was mistaken in thinking that
the soil could be worked yearly without proper manuring, yet the natives
had recently slaughtered the available cattle as he well knew. He was
also wrong in thinking the farmers could easily travel with animals across
what he called "the creek" dividing the island from the mainland. Later
evidence shows the waters could be dangerous and valuable animals lost.
So the demand of the two occupants for what he called "a great deal of
land" was reasonable enough.[74] Yet it all fitted his purpose of moving
as many colonists as possible near the fort.

By 1638, and contrary to van Rensselaer's projections, only Brandt
Peelen was farming on the island. It was a farm in its sixth year, and he
had four farm helpers. It is unlikely that he had extended his holdings
over the whole island; after 1643 the island was leased to two farmers.
On the mainland near the island, Albert Andriesz cultivated tobacco.
With the assistance of his brothers, two farm laborers, and a young lad,
his yield was considerable. In 1640, there were three houses on this
Normanskil property.[75] At a farther distance south, van Rensselaer had
a farmer at Bethlehem. Altogether, an aerial view of the whole colony
in the early 1640s would have shown only twenty-five or thirty houses

Curler and His Historic Letter to the Patroon," *The Dutch Settlers Society of Albany,*
III (Yearbook 1927–1928) 20; 21; 21.
73. Instructions to van Soest, July 20, 1632, VRBM, 208; Arthur B. Gregg, *Old Hellebergh:*
Historical Sketches of the West Manor of Rensselaerswyck, including an Account of
the Anti-rent Wars, the Glass House and Henry R. Schoolcraft (New York, 1975
reprint), 76, quotes a figure substantiated by Joel Munsell's investigations of 1869.
74. KvR to van Twiller, April 23, 1634, VRBM, 286, 287; 286; 286; KvR to Director
and Council, April 29, 1634, VRBM, 297–9, see testimony of C. Davidsz, Ord. sess.,
September 2, 1649, CRB, 91; 286.
75. KvR to Planck, April 23, 1634, VRBM, 214; in 1634, Marijn Andriessen had erected
a "dwelling house... outside of Fort Orange in which... [he was] living with his family
... [and held] an enclosed plot of two morgens in which to sow tobacco, "Account of
the jurisdictions, management and condition of the Territies [*sic*] named Rensselswyck
... July 20, 1634," VRBM, 309. Perhaps the remains of his house were still to be seen,
but he, his family, and farm helper had left the colony in 1634 (List of settlers, VRBM,
806); KvR to Andriesz, July 2, 1640, VRBM, 506.

– probably including the shops of the two free colonists, two carpenters (and an assistant), one blacksmith, and a shoemaker. A brewer, Goose Gerritsz, had just arrived but had neither house nor lot; one carpenter was still hoping to erect a gristmill and brewery. In 1642, even van Rensselaer had no evidence for a "clustering" at Greenbos.[76]

From van Rensselaer's viewpoint, the lands of Rensselaerswyck were extensive. They were always capable of division into smaller, yet still profitable, units. Yet Cornelis Teunisz, the only colonist whose sense of measurement we have, "always stated" to him that the cultivated lands were smaller than he judged. Although the gap between the calculations of the colonists and the patroon was real, it was not the cause of the complaints that crossed the Atlantic. The colonists did not correlate riches with expansive farmlands. Rather, like van Rensselaer himself, they wanted and needed "many strings to their bows."[77]

That meant, above all, trading for furs and therefore knowing and using more land than one's farm. It meant making one's farm, whatever the size, merely a *pied à terre*. So Broer Cornelis spent what van Rensselaer considered undue periods of time at Manhattan – where merchandise could be purchased at prices lower than those set by van Rensselaer who was asking 50 percent above costs in 1635 and 100 percent over costs in 1643. Jan Labatie came as a carpenter but within twelve months knew the lands of the Seneca well enough to explore them for the Company and exploit the trade for himself. Lubbert Gysbertsz came as a wheelwright in 1634 with van Rensselaer's promise of a farm. He also negotiated a contract to construct twelve wagons over the next three years at gl 30 each. Two years later, van Rensselaer thought "it may well be that Lubbert gysbertsen has a farm" but was not certain. The next year Gysbertsz was illegally trading beaver. If the purchase price per pelt was the standard gl 8, his transaction of 43½ beaver that year would have earned him gl 348, a sum slightly double the yearly wages then being paid to a laborer on Peelen's farm. It would have almost matched the total income from making the patroon's wagons – an order, one suspects, never filled.

76. Jogues, quoted in Van Laer, "Arent van Curler's Letter," 17; List of settlers, *VRBM*, 811; Memorandum of KvR for Megapolensis, June 3, 1642, *VRBM*, 619.
77. KvR to Muyssart, February 5, 1641, *VRBM*, 536; van Rensselaer's divisions of land were not particularly mean (for example, Director Kieft granted fifty acres to each of four men in 1646 on the Delaware River; see C. A. Weslager [in collaboration with A. R. Dunlap], *Dutch Explorers, Traders and Settlers in the Delaware Valley, 1609–1664* [Philadelphia, 1961], 144; and at Table Bay in 1657, 13.5 morgen [27 acres] were considered a useful, if not generous, landholding; see Leonard Guelke and Robert Shell, "An Early Colonial Landed Gentry: Land and Wealth in the Cape Colony, 1682–1731," *Journal of Historical Geography* 9 [1983], 266); KvR to de Laet, June 27, 1632, *VRBM*, 200.

The examples could be multiplied. As in so many other things, van Rensselaer was wise to be uneasy in 1642 that his *commis* and chief carpenter were "not personally interested in farms."[78] The colonists' sense of an orderly *colonie* was, unsettlingly, not his.

Images from the Fatherland:
The Veluwe and Manorial Structures

As early as May 1638, van Rensselaer feared the Company would open the fur trade to independent entrepreneurs. Consequently, the next four years were a struggle to bar strangers by enforcing legal jurisdiction over the area. His image of Rensselaerswyck shifted. Formerly he had envisaged his domain as enclosing and beseiging Fort Orange: Now his own borders were at risk. He came to make sense of the land as a fief. It was not so much that he wished to be a feudal lord. In 1641, he thought Rensselaerswyck might be "five lordships," and in the end, he remained too much the Dutch bourgeois landowner, valuing land for its "financial ... rather than social role."[79]

But a manor gave the right of exclusion. The notion collided directly with the views of his partners and was always entertained with some tentativeness. By 1641, however, van Rensselaer was claiming to hold "high jurisdiction" over the colony. Under pressure, he tried to clarify his rights with Adriaen van der Donck, a young man who had taken out a law degree and who had clearly impressed him. The outcome was disappointing. For after getting "into an argument about feudal rights," van der Donck finished by saying that "the professors at Leyden" considered them exceptional in Holland and that "it was useless to waste one's time on them." Van Rensselaer was later dismayed to learn that his proposals for the colony had been discussed publicly, in Latin and "at length" by "certain advocates or lawyers in going by boat from Utrecht to Amsterdam." But he persisted. So while de Laet reminded him correctly that "no example will be found where the entire administration [of a company] is entrusted to a single individual" and again called him back to the image of Rensselaerswyck as a "polder ... belonging to us in common," van Rensselaer awkwardly ex-

78. KvR to Planck, October 3, 1636, *VRBM*, 326, "Redres van de Abuysen," September 5, 1643, *VRBM*, 689; KvR to Planck, May 10, 1638, *VRBM*, 414; for Labatie's deposition, see Leder, ed., *Livingston Indian Records*, 98; Contract of KvR and L. G. van Blaricum, April 15, 1634, *VRBM*, 259; KvR to Planck, October 3, 1636, *VRBM*, 326; KvR to Planck, May 10, 1638, *VRBM*, 417; see 410, 411; Memorandum of KvR for Megapolelsis, June 3, 1642, *VRBM*, 617 (but see 446 for van Rensselaer's promise of promotion and "merchandise for the Indian trade" to faithful tenants).
79. KvR to de Laet, February 4, 1641, *VRBM*, 533; Jan De Vries, *The Dutch Rural Economy in the Golden Age, 1500–1700* (New Haven, 1974), 44.

plored ways to make himself a manor lord and entertained images suitable for what he now called "the patroon and the participants [the partners] of the colony."[80]

In the spring of 1640, van Rensselaer put the idea to director Willem Kieft. He compared Rensselaerswyck to the feudal holding, Amstelland, whose bailiff's jurisdiction encircled Amsterdam just as his jurisdiction held Fort Orange captive.[81] The comparison was based in fact and law, but there is no record of him returning to it. Instead, Rensselaerswyck's problems provoked comparison with another district, that of the Veluwe in his home province, Gelderland.

The Veluwe's appeal is not difficult to understand. Van Rensselaer was not a man to write of geographies. But it is plain that his knowledge and feeling for the Low Countries lay on an east–west axis from Amsterdam to Deventer. Amsterdam had been his home for forty years, and just east of it lay *het Gooi* (goylant), and the farm used to hold cattle destined for New Netherland. Some twenty-five miles farther east lay Nykerk and, four miles southeast, the family estate, Rensselaersberg.

Here the Veluwe began, with Rensselaersberg situated on one of the stretches of high heath country that alternated with dense forest over the next twenty-seven miles before descending to the IJssel River. Like the upper Hudson, the Veluwe was a north–south valley. Cut by the IJssel, it was bordered on the west by the Veluwe heights and on the east by less substantial hills. Sand and clay soils profited from the river's annual overflow, much as they did in Rensselaerswyck (Figure 1.6).[82] Variations in the terrain were those that van Rensselaer now thought characterized the *colonie*. Both were lands of contrast: high terraces and drowned land, hills and crumpled gullies, and dense forest thinning out to heathland.[83]

More important, the Veluwe was an image that served van Rensselaer's understanding of the problems he faced with the colony. The English were increasing numerically in the Connecticut Valley and threatening to invade the colony from the south and southeast, exactly the direction from which the Veluwe was then under threat from German and Spanish armies.[84] The rebelliousness of his farmers also stirred explicit comparisons. They had complained bitterly throughout 1641 and 1642 at his

80. KvR to de Laet, February 4, 1641, *VRBM*, 534; 534; KvR to Muyssart, March 25, 1641 *VRBM*, 544; De Laet to KvR, February 8, 1641, *VRBM*, 542; 542; KvR to Muyssart, January 25, 1641, *VRBM*, 524–5; Instructions to van Breuckelen, August 4, 1639, *VRBM*, 459.
81. KvR to Kieft, May 29, 1640, *VRBM*, 475.
82. See S. J. Fockema-Andreae, *Studien over Waterschapsgeschiedenis, I: Polderdistrict Veluwe* (Leiden, 1950), 4, 5, for a fine map of the Veluwe in 1550.
83. Wim K. Steffen and A. B. Wigman, *Schoonheid van de Veluwe* (Amsterdam, 1953), 53, 55, 53.
84. For van Rensselaer's anxieties, see KvR to van Twiller, May 6, 1638, *VRBM*, 401; Kieft to KvR, August 14, 1638, *VRBM*, 422; KvR to Gerrit van Arnhem, January 29,

Figure 1.6. The Veluwe District, ca. 1550. Courtesy of Bibliotheque Royale, Brussels.

Note 84, *cont.*
    1641, *VRBM*, 526. For the situation in the Veluwe, see M. K. E. Gottschalk, *Stormvloeden en Rivieroverstromingen in Nederland, III (1600–1700)* (Amsterdam, 1977), 71, map 72, 108, 109, 144; see also A. Th. van Deursen, *Holland's Experience of War During the Revolt of the Netherlands*, in A. C. Duke and C. A. Tamse, eds., *Britain and the Netherlands, IV: War and Society, Papers Delivered to the Sixth Anglo-Dutch Historical Conference* (The Hague, 1977), 34.

determination to act as manor lord and collect tithes. He answered them with charges of their profiteering in the fur trade and enjoying "too much luxury"; while "those who are located here on the [Veluwe] frontier where war is would thank God to have such conditions." Two years later, he compared "the work of the farmers in the Veluwe" with that of the complainants and found them doing "but half as much work."[85] Hardworking Veluwe farmers were actually a depressed peasantry, but the comparison was a reasonable one, at least geographically. When van der Donck was in the *colonie*, he described a resemblance between the Mohawk and Issel rivers, and David Pietersz de Vries, a skipper who visited Rensselaerswyck in 1640, later wrote of the *colonie*'s mountains as covered with bilberries and blueberries "such as in Holland come from Veeluwes."[86]

The Veluwe district also offered a useful political model to a man who wanted to claim manorial rights without thinking himself a political anachronism and who wanted to institutionalize economic control without contesting a modern mercantile corporation like the West India Company. The area was a distinctive assemblage of different but basically harmonious juridical units. Individual nobles and independent municipalities like Deventer and Zutphen held lands side by side in a customary Dutch pattern. The necessity of diking and constructing watercourses along the IJssel had produced a structure in which economic and political control was notably dispersed. Deventer, for example, had considerable economic power beyond its walls but was itself subject to small, independent communities like Welsen and Marlo in vital matters of flood control. Since control of the river meant the continual creation of polders and then decisions about their political status – as a parish (*kerspel*), a neighborhood (*buurschap*), a town (*dorp*), a municipal dependency (*ommeland*) or a part of a manor – a variety of coexisting political units operated.[87]

The Veluwe, then, allowed van Rensselaer to think that, in the Hudson Valley, Fort Orange could retain its primacy as a trading center but, like Deventer, expect that its security would require the exercise of seemingly contradictory systems of landholding and jurisdiction in close proximity. In the Veluwe, the requirements of mutual security diminished potentially conflicting political and economic roles. It could be the same in the Hudson River valley.

85. KvR to van Curler, July 18, 1641, VRBM, 561; KvR to van der Donck, March 9, 1643, VRBM, 640.
86. Thomas F. O'Donnell, ed., *A Description of the New Netherlands: Adriaen van der Donck* (Syracuse, 1968), 12. David Pietersz De Vries, *Voyages from Holland to America, A.D. 1632 to 1644*, Henry C. Murphy, tr., CNYHS 2nd ser. Part I (New York, 1857), 3:90.
87. Fockema-Andreae, *Studien*, 6, 19, 30–4.

The feudal model, however, did not resolve van Rensselaer's need to ensure political control over his colonists. He held back from calling Greenbos a town (*dorp*) because that meant conferring political office. So he called it simply a *byeenwooninge* or a *kerkbuurt*, that is, something like a parish, that called for no political appointees who might challenge authority.[88] Greenbos became such a place. Yet it never became the core of a community in any sentimental or legal sense. It was not even the place of manorial authority. Van Rensselaer's officials chose to live on the west side of the river. Van der Donck, for example, served as *schout* after 1642 but, with a surer eye for the fur trade than the patroon's interests, settled north of Fort Orange, at the flats. Van Rensselaer insisted that he wanted him living at the south entrance to the colony – exactly where is still unclear – but he did not comply.[89]

By this time van Rensselaer had added military imagery to his feudal model. He now referred to himself as the "hereditary commander of the colonies on the North River" and appointed two men as *wachtmeesters*, that is, sergeants of the gunnery with the obligation of residing on Beeren Island and regulating river traffic by collecting tolls and enforcing the right of "bulk-breaking of all merchandise" on the river except that of the Company. Van Rensselaer made the power of the new officials real to himself by renaming the place of their authority. "The island commonly called Beeren Island," he directed, " . . . [is] now named Rensselaers Steijn."[90]

Van Rensselaer's determination in 1643 was unswerving. Envisaging a tollhouse where warnings could be posted, he arranged that two such placards and a fourteen-page pamphlet be printed by Teunis Jacobsz at his shop in nearby Wolvenstraat and sent from Amsterdam. In due time, the notices did arrive, and were among the first printed materials specifically used in the upper Hudson Valley (Figure 1.7). The notices warned traders against illegal entry into the patroonship, whereas the pamphlet reprimanded the "malevolent" colonists and outlined redressive measures. But van Rensselaer was still ignorant of where his settlers were,

88. Memorandum of KvR for Megapolensis, June 3, 1642, *VRBM*, 619, 662; see Robert DuPlessis, Urban Stability in the Netherlands Revolution: A Comparative Study of Lille and Douai (Ph.D. diss., Columbia University, 1974), 489.

89. Memorandum for Megapolensis, June 3, 1642, *VRBM*, 617. For van Rensselaer's placement of "the church neighborhood" at Greenbos, that is, "opposite" the southern end of West Island, see KvR to van Curler, March 16, 1643, *VRBM*, 660. Yet there is some suggestion in the memorandum to domini Megapolensis (*VRBM*, 617) that it was a "district" he had in mind south of Fort Orange and on the west bank.

90. See Notice against private traders, September 8, 1643, *VRBM*, 697, and a self-reference as "Patroon en Commandeur" in *Insinuatie, Protestatie ende Presentatie van weghen den Patroon van de Colonie van Rensselaers-wijck* (September 8, 1643), *VRBM*, opp. 697; Commission to Croon and van Bremen, August 26, 1643, *VRBM*, 681; ibid.,

REDRES
Van de
Abuyſen ende ffaulten in de
Colonie van Renſſelaers-wijck.

rAMSTERDAM.

Gedruckt by Thunis Iacobſz, Woonende in de Wolve-
ſtraet/in de Hiſtorie van Joſephus/ Anno 1643.

Title-page of *Redres Van de Abuysen ende Faulten in de Colonie van
Rensselaers-wijck*
From *V. R. B. Mss* 6t. Original size

Figure 1.7. Title page of Redres Van de Abuysen ende Faulten in de Colonie van
Rensselaers-wijck (1643). Courtesy of the Nederlands Scheepvaart Museum,
Amsterdam.

of whether they had clustered in Greenbos, and, if so, where they might
be relocated to achieve greater control. In 1642, he was again looking
for a place where his authority and their dwelling places might coincide.
This time, he envisaged a "refuge" on Beeren Island.[91]

680. For evidence that copies of the *Insinuatie* circulated in the colony, see Printed
Broadsides, Insinuatie, Protestatie, en de Presentatie, September 8, 1643, SC7079, Box
34 (Folder 4), VRMP, NYSA.
91. See *Waerschoveinge, Verboth ende Toe-latinghe, weghens de Colonie van Renselaers-
wyck t' Amsterdam Gedrukt by Thunis Jacobsz Woonde in de Wolvestraet ... Anno*

In all of this, he imagined regular enactments of lordship. He set up a court and provided his law enforcement officer with a handbook on criminal procedure, Damhouder's *Practycke in Criminele Saecken.*[92] Yet he used his representatives more as commercial agents than as manorial officials. Ultimately he opted for mercantile over feudal ways of possessing the New World.

Appropriations of the Land: The van Rensselaer–van Curler Correspondence, 1638–1643

Seventeenth-century Dutch men and women were remarkably self-conscious about letter writing. They took great pleasure in paintings of fellow countrymen composing, reading, gazing at, and musing over letters. They also enjoyed seeing calligraphy. Van Rensselaer shared this selfconsciousness about letters. He composed them as pictures for the eye's enjoyment but was also concerned for discourse (Figures 1.8 and 1.9. So letters to his nephew, Wouter van Twiller, instructed him on the proprieties of the worldly wise. They gave lessons on the role playing and social masques that turned grace into power. In short, they imparted a cosmology to a youth from the best of all sources, the man of experience.[93]

Letters to his grandnephew, Arent van Curler, were uniformly more self-serving. He had commissioned the young man as his Rensselaerswyck secretary and accountant in 1637 and wrote him regularly from 1638 to 1643. The young man's adventures in the colony, however, were meant to be secondary to the older man's need for profits; his self-advancement was to be tied to the patroon's gain. The young man's most absorbing adventures were expected to be those experienced in regularly and conscientiously corresponding with van Rensselaer. So, when the older man saw signs that this isolated work with accounts and letters was not filling van Curler's time, his letters became unrelentingly more censorious than

1643; *Insinuatie, Protestatie ende Presentatie van weghen den Patroon van de Colonie van Renselaers-wijck,* VRBM, 682–9; Memorandum for Megapolensis, June 3, 1642, VRBM, 619; *Redres van de Abuysen,* September 5, 1643, VRBM, 688.

92. KvR to van Twiller, April 23, 1634, VRBM, 281. The manual went through several editions, making it impossible to know which one van Rensselaer sent. See Damhouder, *Practijcke in Criminele Saecken ghemaecht door Joost De Damhouder van Brugge . . . 1642.* (Rotterdam, n.d.) For the later use of Damhouder's *Practijcke* (chapter 50) in the Beverwijck court, see Ex. sess., August 23, 1676, CRA, 147.

93. See KvR to van Twiller, July 27, 1632, VRBM, 229, 266–88, KvR to van Twiller, September 25, 1636, 319, and KvR to van Twiller, May 6, 1638, 400. For the Dutch fascination with letters, see Svetlana Alpers, *The Art of Describing: Dutch Art in the Seventeenth Century* (Chicago, 1983), 194, 196, 206.

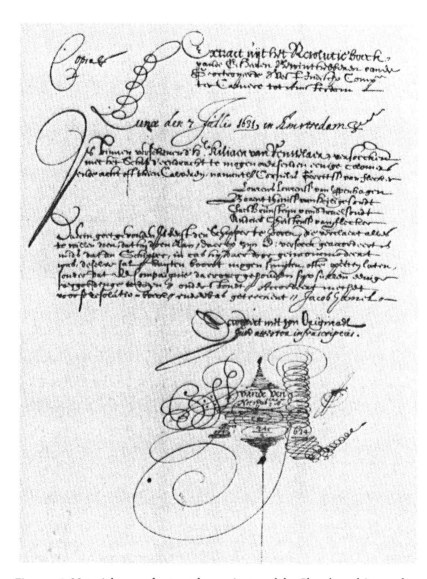

Figure 1.8. Notarial copy of extract from minutes of the Chamber of Amsterdam of the West India Company, July 7, 1631. Courtesy of the Nederlands Scheepvaart Museum, Amsterdam.

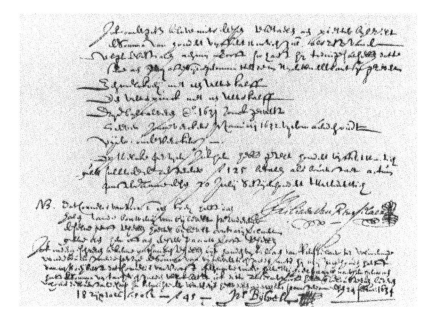

Figure 1.9. Promissory note of Kiliaen van Rensselaer to Pieter Bijlvelt, July 20, 1632, with receipt of February 24, 1634. In handwriting of Kiliaen van Rensselaer. Courtesy of the Nederlands Scheepvaart Museum, Amsterdam.

those sent to van Twiller. To those familiar with later sets of the family's correspondence, there is nevertheless a certain poignancy in watching the old man giving a grandnephew the instructions and advice that his own youngest son, Jeremias, received largely from his brothers, and then often on the run.

The Koopmanshuis

As far as we can judge, all the letters that van Rensselaer wrote to van Curler between 1638 and 1643 were written from his home, 277 Keisersgracht. The house was the place of his business and the information center that constituted his life. There he stored overseas merchandise, displayed the signboard '*t gekruiste Hart* (The Crossed Heart) and, above all, kept his record books.[94] There were paydays at the house, times when he had large sums of money out of the bank for business transactions.

94. H. Voorheem, Jr., "Kiliaen Van Rensselaer," *Amstelodamum, Maandblad voor de Kennis van Amsterdam: Orgaan van Het Genootschap Amstelodamum* 39 (1949), 113.

Figure 1.10. Verzaameling van alle de Huizen en Prachtige Gebouwen langs de Keizers ed Heere-Grachten der Stadt Amsteldam ... Caspar Philips (1767). Courtesy of Gemeentearchief Amsterdam.

He dictated letters daily, many on Sundays and Mondays. He sent 108 letters to New Netherland from 1638 until his death in 1643. Three-quarters of them were written between May and October, months when the *handelsschepen* crossed to the colony.[95]

Van Rensselaer boasted that residence in Amsterdam greatly excelled living in The Hague or Utrecht. His business and the city expanded together. In fact, the same overseas expansion that dictated the spatial arrangements of countless non-Europeans' lives structured those of Amsterdammers as well. So van Rensselaer's *koopmanshuis* fitted into the burgomasters' farsighted design for Amsterdam's areal expansion in 1612. It was one of the "large business houses and town houses for merchants" planned to front onto one of three semicircular canals entering the Ij through the Amstel River and canal. Near the harbor, Warmoesstraat continued to attract many distinguished burghers, offering immediacy to the harbor – where as many as 3,000 ships might await unloading – and access to a canal that carried goods directly to merchants' houses.[96] But the city now provided that service to *koopmanshuizen* along the three new waterways: the Keisersgracht, the Princengracht, and the Herengracht.

Van Rensselaer owned four adjoining houses on the Keisersgracht. They were on the uneven side – as it is now designated – facing away

95. Calculations are based on *VRBM* in which letters dealing with New Netherland – and not other projects – are printed. I am excluding letters written about the colony to the Company.
96. T. K. Looijen, *Herbergen en koffiehuizen van Amsterdam, Een bloemlezing uit de geschiedenis* (Amsterdam, 1977), 65; Jacob van Lennep and Johannes ter Gouw, *Het Boek der Opschriften* (Amsterdam, 1869), 69.

from the harbor. House No. 275 had only a 3.35 meter frontage and was built in 1620. No. 277 was a double *koopmanshuis* built at the same time but 8.78 meters broad, that is, 2.5 feet wider than the average. Here the patroon resided. He owned another double *koopmanshuis* at No. 279 and No. 281. Each lot was 180 meters deep and abutted on the gardens of canal houses facing the Herengracht. Van Rensselaer's houses were between Hartenstraat and Wolvenstraat, where he owned additional properties (Figure 1.10).[97]

Merchants with *koopmanshuizen* along the Keisersgracht near van Rensselaer used the canal as he did. They oversaw the transport of their goods on lighters moving from the harbor, along the Amstel, and into the Keisersgracht. At No. 38, No. 40, and No. 44 the Greenland Company rendered blubber at three warehouses built shortly after 1620.[98] Seven lots from van Rensselaer's houses, two buildings were used to sort wool. Samuel Blommaert, one of his partners in Rensselaerswyck, resided nearby, at No. 158. In 1628, the merchant David van Baerle bought No. 222, and in 1639 he purchased a double *koopmanshuis*, No. 198. Van Baerle's son was a business associate of van Rensselaer's son Jeremias in the 1650s. Jeremias also engaged in business with Isaac Sweers. His was a prominent family that owned three houses nearby and on the uneven side: Nos. 437, 439, and 441. Directly across the canal from van Rensselaer's dwelling, Hans Auxbrebis lived in De Eenhoorn (and so named

97. E. van Houten, *Grachtenboek, naar de Oorspronkelijke Tekeningen van Caspar Philips Jacobszoon te Amsterdam* ±1767 (Amsterdam, 1962), 45; ibid., 13; JvR to Johan van Wely and Jan Baptist van Rensselaer, September 27, 1671, *Corr JvR*, 444.
98. H. F. Wijnman, *Historische Gids Van Amsterdam* (Amsterdam, 1971), 401.

to this day). His was a merchant family to which van Rensselaer's youngest son, Nicolaes, was apprenticed.[99]

Within a short distance, the Becker family owned property on the Herengracht near Leidesstraat. Their interests indicate that a good deal of the power and leadership of the West India Company lay in this small area where the reflecting surface of the water doubled a prosperity already amplified by overseas trade. Marriages consolidated this concentration. Samuel Becker lived on the Keisersgracht and traded to New Netherland with Jeremias van Rensselaer. He had married into the van Baerle family. David van Baerle was a director of the West India Company during Kiliaen van Rensselaer's lifetime and had, in turn, married into the Godijn family and was therefore related to Samual Godijn, van Rensselaer's partner in Rensselaerswyck. The merchant Johannes LeThor occasionally lived on the Keisersgracht and served as a director of the West India Company.[100]

Merchants stored large volumes of merchandise in their *koopmans-huisen*. The functional nature of the houses and the constant traffic of goods on the canal made sense of the area. Van Rensselaer, for example, had access to the Company's warehouse for storage but clearly enjoyed storing and examining merchandise at his house (or houses) along the canal. On one occasion, he had duffels for Rensselaerswyck counted and packed by his man and then oversaw their dispatch by canal to a waiting ship. At the same time he expected other duffels to arrive from Leyden. Toussaint Muyssart, who frequently furnished merchandise for the colony, sent it directly to his house.[101]

Van Rensselaer was also a jeweller. His role in this trade suggests the demands on his time that Arent van Curler would have to endure were he to become the successful businessman the older man expected. As I have said, van Rensselaer was not a retailer nor was the narrow path along the canal a street for a guild of jewellers. But several decades after

---

99. Van Houten, *Grachtenboek*, 45; Wijnman, *Historische Gids*, 403; ibid., 405; Johan E. Elias, *De Vroedschap van Amsterdam, 1578–1795, met een inleiding woord van den archivaris der stad Amsterdam, Mr. W. R. Veder* (Haarlem, 1903–5), 2:561, 563; Van Houten, *Grachtenboek*, 52; Jan Baptiste van Rensselaer (hereafter JBvR) to JvR, August 9, 1657, *Corr JvR*, 53: JBvR to Jeremias van Rensselaer (hereafter JvR), [?] September, 1651, *Corr JvR*, 9, Nicolaes van Rensselaer to JvR (beginning of December, 1657), *Corr JvR*, 66; Wijnman, *Historische Gids*, 413; van Houten, *Grachtenboek*, 45; Anna van Rensselaer to JvR, December 5, 1656, *Corr JvR*, 35.

100. For Cornelis Becker's substantial investments in the Company ca. 1638, see John B. Murray, *Amsterdam in the Age of Rembrandt* (Norman, Okla., 1967), 34; Elias, *Vroedschap*, 2:562, and JBvR to JvR, April 8, 1662, *Corr JvR*, 286; Elias, *Vroedschap*, 2:563; 560.

101. KvR to Muyssart, July 18, 1643, *VRBM*, 671; KvR to Muyssart, June 18, 1641, *VRBM*, 554; KvR to Muyssart, May 3, 1640, *VRBM*, 467, 468.

his death, Wouter Valkenier, a diamond merchant, bought No. 401 Keisersgracht. Like van Rensselaer, he was a leading figure in the merchant oligarchy, a man who dealt in precious gems on the import–export market. The two men's interest in gems put obligations on their time in several ways. First, it meant taking an active part in a large overseas trading company, one of whose purposes was to locate mineral deposits. Van Rensselaer, of course, looked for profits in North America, where the discovery of "crystal" on his own land aroused his intense concern. By 1636, he had a fragment of it but wanted "better samples...of the purest rock." He feared that the deposits might go to others and on one occasion directed Planck to "take a trip at once into the country" above de Laet's Kill and send him two barrels. In 1640, he was still the jeweller. "As to the crystal," he wrote overseas, "keep that matter as secret as you can.... Have some barrels of it dug, good and bad, large and small, and send it to me: I shall know then what price it will bring.... Make an estimate as to the labor it takes for each barrel and look out carefully that the people do not keep back the whitest and largest and clearest pieces, for they are the best."[102]

Jewellers like van Rensselaer also conducted business at the Exchange of Amsterdam (Beurs van Amsterdam) and the Exchange Bank (Wisselbank). They also attended auctions. Wholesale merchants attended then as vendors or buyers. In Amsterdam, such public sales were held at all hours of the day. In 1710, Valkenier, for example, auctioned "loose diamonds...beautiful pearls and unique coloured gems" in midmorning, at "*10 huur precis in de Doelenstraat.*" Another jeweller, Hendrick Dubbels, set his auction for 8 o'clock on a Wednesday morning. The auctions were surrounded by the same small rituals that were enacted in the Hudson Valley. In both places, for example, vendors arranged that a broadsheet describing the auction be printed (or inscribed) and copies circulated. They anticipated customers who could read but also made allowance for nonliterate townspeople. The last line of the announcement was the conventional device: *Segget voort* (Spread the news).[103]

Van Rensselaer's many enterprises had made him a wealthy man. When three appraisers valued his Keisersgracht and Wolvenstraat properties in 1653, they put the total value at gl 63,000.[104] If his investment portfolio

102. Wijnman, *Historische Gids*, 413 and Elias, *Vroedschap*, 2:563; KvR to Planck, October 3, 1636, *VRBM*, 330; KvR to van Scrabbekercke, June 25, 1640, *VRBM*, 500.
103. Juweelen te Koop, in Amsterdam, Op Donderdagh 15, October [1654], File N58.01.001, GA; "Factuurboekje van een Partije Extraordinarij Schoone Gemaakte Jeweelen en Loose Diamanten...Als mede Schoone Paarlen en eenige Couleurde Steenen...[of] Heer Mr. Wouter Valkenier," in zijn leven Bewindhebber van de VOC. [April 10, 1710], File N58.01.002, GA; *CRB*, 106.
104. Petition of Anna van Wely for appraisal, November 6 and 8, 1653, *VRBM*, 745.

resembled those of other members of the Amsterdam elite, that is, if he invested 12 percent of his wealth in houses, then his assets would have totaled close to gl 525,000.[105] This estimate, which may be high, nonetheless excludes properties possibly owned elsewhere in the city – for example, at one time he was part owner of a tobacco warehouse.

Van Rensselaer belonged to a world of wealth that presented itself above all on paper. Frequent auctions and meetings with Company directors demanded attention, and there were dramatic scenes, such as the episode in which he waited for hours in the anteroom of the chamber of the West India Company, was then called in to receive a decision of the presiding officer, shared a bumper of wine, and finally departed, as he described it, gaily.[106] But for van Rensselaer there was also a continuing format of dramatic action, silent and withdrawn. Most of his time was spent with his accounts. Good account books were a conspicuous display of wealth, much like the volumes in a medieval monastic library. Bindings, quality of paper, specially designed tables, all of these, quite as much as content, suggested a merchant's status.

But the cost was high. Accounts pertaining to jewelry, for instance, had to be kept separate from those relating to Rensselaerswyck or other enterprises. They demanded close attention and some ingenuity. Valkenier kept a *factuurboekje* (small book of invoices) simply for the sale of one parcel (*partje*) of gems.[107] Another jeweller meant to entice a customer by sending his prospective buyer a single sheet to which he had meticulously stitched eighty-eight sized garnets (presumably representing diamonds) and listed appropriate prices. This was a variation of a practice notable in Albany account books. There, merchants took bits of the thread that otherwise served to join sheets of account book paper and stitched odd memoranda, receipts, and invoices to the pertinent pages.[108] This was the sort of attention to detail that van Curler would have to master and that van Rensselaer knew meant the difference between success and financial ruin.

Rensselaerswyck was a possession of which Kiliaen van Rensselaer had only the signs. He handled barrels of tobacco and clover seed; he saw colonists depart and heard tales: They were the tangible signs of the

Van Rensselaer left no record of the total value of his assets, exercising a secrecy widely practiced by individuals and corporations.
105. Peter Burke, *Venice and Amsterdam: A Study of Seventeenth-Century Elites* (London, 1974), 588, "Appendix," using portfolios of eighteen men in 1700 calculated that 82% of their wealth was in stocks and bonds, 12% in houses, and 6% in land.
106. KvR to Amsterdam Chamber, October 25, 1640, *VRBM*, 519.
107. See n103 this chapter.
108. Unsigned and undated folio, N58.10.002, GA.

distant enterprise, the particles that he had to know – all that he could know – to estimate the whole. As he was acutely aware, however, greater numbers of them were in his account books and copybook. "The pen," he wrote to one colonist, "must convey to me what personal speech cannot."[109] In such books, detail was recorded and respected but also controlled and pared down. Good copybooks did this in the way of good bibles. Narrative matter in van Rensselaer's books was given in the large blocks of script, and small blocks of writing in the margin offered comment on its message. In this way, calligraphic miniatures decorated the page – sometimes the patroon's glosses on his own letters, often those of a secretary or associate. They afforded a quick summary, an immediate refamiliarization.

Reading to diminish detail was the proper way of encountering the surface of the page. It was the proper way of knowing the Word of God – and knowing an enterprise like Rensselaerswyck. The pages seen by van Rensselaer would have been more like those of a medieval manuscript than we might initially realize. In the place of marginal illuminations were his blocks of script, usually no more than twenty-five words. In a detailed contract with Gerrit Theusz de Reux, he jogged his own memory with the marginal note "29 years old." Elsewhere he returned to the text of an agreement with Claes Brunsteyn van Straelsundt to summarize in the margin: "N. B.: ran away."[110] Order lay in such paring down of detail. Disorder was sprawl in writing and prolixity in speech. At times, van Rensselaer found it a fault in himself. He accused himself of sometimes talking too long and too much, and he was deeply resentful when he learned that a partner had revealed his "prolixity" to others.[111]

Prolixity also directly contradicted his concept of the proper functioning of government. In 1639, he compared a "loose mass of people" to a large block of unannotated text but construed their representatives as a useful apostil that tightened and made sense of the mass. "One must sufficiently understand," he wrote in admiration of the government of the United Provinces "what difference there is between commanding a loose mass of people and ruling through representatives from different orders of society, according to the custom of this country, a republic composed of different members each of which in the first instance prevents as far as possible all acts of insolence in its own sphere, *so that*

109. KvR to P. C. van Munnickendam, May 8, 1638, *VRBM*, 407.
110. Contract of KvR and de Reux, June 15, 1632, *VRBM*, 193; Memorandum, May 27, 1631, *VRBM*, 180; for further examples, see *VRBM*, 251, 252.
111. KvR to Muyssart, January 25, 1641, *VRBM*, 523; KvR to Muyssart, March 25, 1641, *VRBM*, 544.

*only great and important matters resulting from the lessed ones are re-
ferred to the ... presiding officer.*"[112]

It was a statement that only a Dutch man or woman in mid-
seventeenth-century Europe could have made. It described the Low Countries as ascending, and constricting, planes of political consent, with the
town councils, then the provincial Estates, and finally the States General
somehow taming the Republic into order. At the same time, it was a
latent comment on the artifacts that tamed the daily realities of life. Good
copybooks and accounts were among those artifacts. They recuperated
republican ideology, and in the same sense, those that van Rensselaer so
carefully archived and so desperately sought from his New World agents
were cosmological statements as well.

The Agent Who Would Not Write

Arent van Curler was expected to describe Rensselaerswyck for van Rensselaer in regular reports. He was meant to help transform the wilderness
into a profitable colony and inscribe that economic transformation on
paper. Hours should be spent with ledgers and letter books. He knew
something of Amsterdam's financial world before departing for New
Netherland. As a young man he had completed a merchant's appren-
ticeship with the Sweers family who had close connections with the East
India Company.[113] He had also studied Latin and Greek. He used the
languages in an account book kept in Rensselaerswyck but with a light-
heartedness that would have seriously discomposed the patroon. Uncon-
ventionally, he printed his name vertically and in large letters down the
cover of the book, writing, "Arent Van Curler 1640." Parallel to it he
inscribed *"Est nomen meum Cato & inquit Rem Tuam"* (My name is
Cato and I inquire into your affairs). In the index – which was even more
frivolous, certainly unorthodox – he displayed his scholarly accomplish-
ments to himself, listing his patroon's tenants and artisans – indeed Mijn
Heer Rensselaer himself – under the letters of the Greek alphabet. Robbert Hermensz fitted logically under "Ro." Colonists named Jan went
under "Gamma." To us, the result is a delightful hodgepodge. To him,
twenty-one years of age and just assuming his authority, it made formal
a moment of inauguration. The Greek and Latin must have pleased the
eye. The book must have looked to be scholarly and a cut above the
average. It must have been a pleasure to handle.[114]

112. KvR to Kieft, May 12, 1639, *VRBM*, 428, 429. I have substituted "presiding officer"
      for Van Laer's "general chief," 429; italics added.
113. Elias, *Vroedschap*, 2:919.
114. Ledger, debit–credit account, 1634–8 for colonists at Rensselaerswyck, SC7079, Box

Over the years van Curler kept other accounts. A journal from 1644 to 1644, for example, gives some indication of his activities, though it should not be taken as accurate for these or subsequent years.[115] In it he recorded the names of tenants who presumably arrived at his house to exchange produce or goods for a range of van Rensselaer's supplies. In 1642, he conducted only 285 transactions or an average of 32 for each of the nine months he kept the accounts. His encounters with customers were spread unevenly across this period. He was available the last week of April, all of May and June, the first week of July (as well as the seventeenth and twenty-eighth), the first three weeks of August, early and late September, all of October, November, and December. In May, June, and October he was busiest, with 57, 77 and, 42 transactions respectively. In May, he had eight customers in one day. On June 13, he saw fifteen people. From June 10 to June 18 he dealt with 37 customers.

But that was a peak. Even in June (77 entries), the average demand upon him was less than three persons a day. On 99 of the 125 days when he was available, he dealt with three persons or less. The years 1643 and 1644 were more desultory. He had 82 transactions in 1643 or slightly under seven a month. In all he was engaged 69 days of the year. On three occasions he catered to three colonists; otherwise he saw only one or two. Yet this was a year when, according to van Rensselaer's books, he had received gl 36,000 in goods.[116] He answered even fewer demands in 1644, making 23 entries in the ledger or less than those for a single week of June in 1642. He transacted business on 18 days. He could have been on extended trading journeys or attending to his own affairs at almost any time.

Understandably, van Rensselaer did not receive this account book for examination. Instead he got a letter from van Curler laboriously excusing himself about the books and admitting "the matter has been neglected."[117] It seems he had not come to the New World to acquire skills with figures or retailing. His principal pleasure was in being mobile – in coming to know and appropriate the land as an official and farmer, and, above all, as a trader. He established a farm, but he had also come to know how to treat the Indians and how to become a trader independent of his granduncle. The structure of his life is caught fleetingly but solidly

14, Ledger No. 1, VRMP. A notation near an entry for March 23, 1644, reads, "Carried over to folio 103," suggesting he undoubtedly kept other accounts that have not survived. I am grateful to Peter Christoph for the suggestion that van Curler's handwriting points to his recopying earlier entries in the account book at one sitting.

115. Ledger, 1642–1644, VRMP, SC7079, Box 21 (3) (A), NYSA.
116. Van Laer, "Arent van Curler's Letter," 13.
117. Ibid., 18.

in the chance remark of David Pietersz de Vries. Indians had guided him along the Mohawk to the falls. But back at Fort Orange he accumulated information from van Curler, "who had [also] been at the Indians' fort" up the river. This was one year after Symon Groot had helped the fort's *commis* "trade and Pack up 37 thousand Bever... [for] ye West India Company" because he "had a great Trade with ye Sinnekes & ye oyr Indians to ye westward."[118]

Although the old man fretted that van Curler would be unoccupied and urged Jacob Planck to "let him occupy himself in shooting game and catching fish... [and] send him all over the colony to arrange things," the young man was gathering such knowledge without prompting. He had sailed to the colony with seven young men between the ages of fifteen and twenty-five. They were the sort with whom he continued to associate: young, likely to be accused of living with native women, and looking for quick profits in the fur trade. A skipper, paid to command van Rensselaer's sloop, was piloting for him and doubtless transporting his furs and merchandise.

Within eighteen months, van Rensselaer came to suspect all of this. He warned van Curler "not to mix with the heathens or savage women" and accused him of being "into private transactions you do not wish me to know about." He acknowledged that he meant "to do right by [him] ... [so] *write* of such things to me and I shall not refuse you anything to your advantage which is fair." He schooled him, with some patience, in letter writing. Avoid dating letters at top and bottom, he instructed, "once is enough." Avoid also "the general style followed in the schools, for example, 'If it were otherwise I should be heartily sorry.' " Economize, simply give a gloss. Shun "words... [that] fill the paper but give no advice." He had also asked Minuit to instruct van Curler in "the processes of ships' bookkeeping as well as in the keeping of land accounts." And in 1643, he tried to show him and Anthony de Hooges (*onderboekhouder*) how to put together an inventory. Take the paper "lengthwise," he wrote, "and in that way many more columns [can be] made. The cows of the same age must be put on the same line, and after them the horses." He enclosed an example. Now in 1639, though he needed to point out that he had never seen any of van Curler's work, he promised promotion and confirmed him provisionally as secretary and bookkeeper.[119] In fact, he had little alternative.

118. Deposition of Groot, Leder, ed., *Livingston Indian Records*, 113.
119. KvR to Planck, May 10, 1638, *VRBM*, 414; KvR to van Twiller, December 29, 1637, *VRBM*, 395–8; Koet Burnham, "Arent Van Curler, Alias Corlear," *de halve maen* (Spring 1978), 53:16; van der Donck, *Description of New Netherland*, CNYHS 2nd ser. (New York, 1841), 1:191, KvR to Arent van Curler (hereaftrer AvC), May

With hindsight one can begin to see van Rensselaer's loss of control over the colony at this point. He neither recognized that the land was making his colonists independent nor that van Curler was emblematic of it. The young man sent no account books, inventories, or yearly accounts.[120] To van Rensselaer he was both inefficient and disloyal – interchangeable vices. The young man and the colonists were participating in the fur trade and exchanging pelts for supplies from the Company against his directives. In a letter of 1640, he insinuated as much. "I hear that you spend too much time in the woods; that ought not to be." In 1643, he found himself unable to write calmly to van Curler and, instead, sent him a desperate and enraged letter.[121] The rhetoric was more than the customary cry against imposed ignorance. It was now that of the powerless competitor, and his further direction of the colony would arise more out of suspicion and pique than policy. A community built on mutual esteem was almost out of the question.

Van Rensselaer had some success in collecting information from colonists other than van Curler. But it came by encouraging them to inform on one another. He encouraged domine Johannes Megapolensis to report on van Curler, learning, for example, that the young man had built himself too expensive a house and was drinking not just occasionally but like one "completely addicted." Megapolensis also reported on van der Donck, Kieft, and de Hooges, while de Hooges was encouraged to report on Megapolensis. Abram Staats and Mauritz Janse reported on van Curler. Van der Donck as *schout* informed on colonists and in 1643 was meant to report the names of some twenty-five inhabitants whom van Rensselaer suspected of defrauding him. Oloff Stevensz van Cortlandt of New Amsterdam was asked to "write . . . [his] opinion of the colony . . . and how the people conduct themselves, especially the officers." His advice would be kept secret. It is little wonder that, by the spring of 1643, colonists were accusing the patroon of "sending informers into the country."[122]

13, 1639, *VRBM*, 443; 443; 439; 438; KvR to van Twiller, December 20, 1637, *VRBM*, 398; KvR to Minuit, December 29, 1637, *VRBM*, 395; KvR to AvC, March 16, 1643, *VRBM*, 663; KvR to AvC May 13, 1639, *VRBM*, 441.

120. Instructions to van Bruekelen, August 4, 1639, *VRBM*, 460; van Curler "would have him [van Rensselaer] pass his life without ever knowing how his property had been administered" (quoted in Nissenson, *Patroon's Domain*, 75).

121. KvR to AvC, May 30, 1640, *VRBM*, 486; KvR to van Curler, March 16, 1643, 658.

122. KvR to Megapolensis, March 13, 1643, *VRBM*, 646; 649; KvR to van der Donck, March 9, 1643, *VRBM*, 632; KvR to Megapolensis, March 13, 1643, *VRBM*, 647; 649; KvR to de Hooges, March 18, 1643, *VRBM*, 670; KvR to Megapolensis, March 13, 1643, *VRBM*, 652; KvR to van der Donck, March 9, 1643, *VRBM*, 643; 643; KvR to Oloff Stevensz, March 16, 1643, *VRBM*, 656; KvR to van der Donck, March 9, 1643, *VRBM*, 642.

Van Rensselaer had laid a circuitry of distrust. He prided himself on good administration but could not see the flaw in his policy. Although he made metaphor of his practice at one point – "A prudent and vigilant captain divides his officers over several guardposts... [and] in addition has someone make the rounds" – he was unable to allow for inventiveness and independence. He wanted each officer and colonist to correspond with him directly. To his credit, he tried to write each of them, until the number of colonists became too great in the 1640s. But the correspondence was one of mutual criticism, evasiveness, and often against his own good judgment, malicious gossip. A letter from van Rensselaer compromised integrity.[123] It was a mode of fiercely seeking loyalty by means bound to produce treachery.

In his handling of disquiet over tithes in 1640, van Rensselaer's approach must have been evident to all. He sent each of those he took to be rebels a letter in a packet addressed to van Curler. He ordered him to "read them through carefully and copy what is of use to you and then give them to each one individually. Give Maurs his letter first before he has spoken to anyone and see how he takes it. Then give Cornelis Teunisse his letter without anybody being present and see whether he takes it well or not, thereafter give Pieter Cornelisse his letter, also alone." He continued, "The other letters you must give one by one but in such a way that one does not know about the others and as soon after each other as you can." In this way, he hoped, "the bond... [of the threateners] will be broken... which will prevent them from inciting each other as they have done."[124]

The New World had become an epistemological problem for van Rensselaer. In one respect, it changed his understanding of European life. He interpreted the Low Countries in meaningful analogies with North America. As we have seen regarding war in the Veluwe, his problems in North America brought him to understand life in Holland better. But the otherness of the New World was not a dominating puzzle.[125] Perhaps this was because his grasp was upon the trade. Beyond that his curiosities did not go. In another respect, his epistemological problem was an in-

123. KvR to van der Donck, March 9, 1643, *VRBM*, 642; KvR to Planck, May 12, 1638, *VRBM*, 417, Settlers, *VRBM*, 816. KvR to Megapolensis, March 13, 1643, *VRBM*, 647.

124. See KvR to AvC, July 2, 1640, *VRBM*, 509, 510; see *VRBM*, 343, for his chastisement of three colonists who cooperated in writing him one letter rather than each composing a short letter, and see *VRBM*, 418, for another example of urging another to "quietly investigate one after the other; for threateners," see KvR to van der Donck, March 9, 1643, *VRBM*, 632.

125. For the New World as an epistemological problem for Europeans, see Wayne Franklin, *Discoverers, Explorers, Settlers: The Diligent Writers of Early America* (Chicago, 1979).

formational one. If his anger is any indication, Rensselaerswyck eluded him as no other project did. It was not that the profusion of things American invalidated ordinary categories of meaning. Rather, they were too few and unavailable in a systematic way.

Interests in trade limited van Rensselaer's concern for the social formation of the colony. Local officials weakened it even further by denying him information. As a result, the little cohesiveness that the community had was out of its own resources. Like everything else, the community's record of its formation was underdramatized. The record in the following passage was written by the colony's secretary in January 1648 on page 73 of his book. It recounted an occasion when the settlers determined to construct a bit of Dutch landscape. The court found it necessary, the clerk wrote, "that some bridges be built, to wit, one across the first kill, in the settlement (*byeenwooninge*) with railings and benches to sit on; one across the third kill; one across the beaver kill, with railings."[126] The imagination affecting the landscape here had elements supplied by both van Rensselaer (*het byeenwooninge*) and the colonists (the first kill and the third kill being terms they had created). It was an image of the Old World – a Dutch townscape with bridges, railings, and benches over waterways – that affected the colonists' knowledge of the New World. Their epistemological problem was to set the geographical structures of the homeland into the new topography of the upper Hudson Valley. Chapter 2 demonstrates how highly successful they were in the 1650s and 1660s.

Men and Myths: The Land Possessing

Kiliaen van Rensselaer and Arent van Curler possessed the land for their own needs. Those were more than can be recorded. They arose from the structure of Dutch society and quirks of personality. They were at once pragmatic and aesthetic, greedy and honorable.

The land also, then and later, took possession of the two Dutchmen out of its needs. And those needs were also beyond counting. Of the two men, van Rensselaer alone had long-range plans and hopes for the colony. Neither consistent nor generous, his plans were often simply tied to his own financial gain. Yet there were moments, many of them, when he envisioned a corporate future for all.[127] Van Curler had no sense of that.

126. Ord. sess. January 12, 1650, *CRB*, 141.
127. At times, it was linked to "populating" the country in order to "propagate ... the Holy Gospel" (KvR to Planck, May 24, 1635, *VRBM*, 314), or expressed by sending homelitic literature to the colonists (KvR to Planck, May 12, 1638, 418). For the

Incontestably, he was liked in the colony. One colonist bestowed his name on a cow, perhaps out of affection or good humor. He shared good times, his office and background gave him credentials all could lean upon, and he was apparently a fine and trustworthy interpreter. Yet the man of forty-one who wrote, "There is little entertainment here [in New Amsterdam] ... [as] you can judge from the [extended] length of this letter," was one who used time for himself. He let the ambitions of the beachcomber underpin the many enterprises that brought him contact with natives. In this role, he crossed into their lives and he became the legendary "Corlear" well before his death.[128]

So it is ironic that van Curler, and not van Rensselaer, is remembered as the man of vision. Myth has it that he was a man driven to found Schenectady in 1662, either by the feudalism of the Company and the patroon or by the vision "to migrate westward and there form a new settlement based upon freedom and equal rights." Single-handedly he rescued the French forces outside Schenectady in the winter of 1666. He was "a man who was great in goodness, as well as renowned in statecraft," the philosopher "who dared the wild beast and the wild man, to assert the supremacy of thought."[129]

Inventions of the imagination always dominate social life, and Arent van Curler was one of New York's. For mid-to late-nineteenth-century New Yorkers, he served a number of needs. Historical knowledge was not yet the preserve of academics but was the serious interest of amateurs

opinion that the patroonship's success was more a measure of the abilities of the "proprietors" than the qualities of the area, see John H. Thompson ed., *Geography of New York State* (Syracuse, 1966), 125.

128. AvC to JvR [April 1661] *Corr JvR*, 252; see, "Answers to Proposal Made to the Chiefs of the Maquas, July 9/19, 1666," Leder, ed., *Livingston Indian Records*, 30.

129. Address of Charles Alexander Richmond, in *Arent Van Curler, Founder of Schenectady. Addresses Delivered at the Erection of a Commemorative Tablet by the Netherlands Society and the Schenectady Historical Society, September 29, 1909* (The Tablet Committee, n.p., 1909), 5; see William Elliot Griffis, "Arendt Van Curler, First Superintendent of Rensselaerswyck, Founder of Schenectady, and of the Dutch Policy of Peace with the Iroquois," *Transactions of the Albany Institute* (1887), 11:170; 172; James R. Truax, *Life and Character of Arent van Curler*, in *Arent van Curler ... 1909*, 7 and for van Curler as philosopher, see Francis Whiting Halsey, *The Old New York Frontier: Its Wars with Indians and Tories, Its Missionary Schools, Pioneers and Land Titles, 1614–1800* (New York, 1963 reprint), 45; Truax, *Life and Character of Arent Van Curler*, in *Arent Van Curler ... 1909*, 7; for other versions of the myth, see Margharita Hamm, *Famous Families of New York* (New York, 1901) 2:118, and John W. Barber and Henry Howe, *Historical Collections of the State of New York, containing a General Collection of the Most Interesting Facts, Traditions, Biographical Sketches, Anecdotes, etc. Relating to Its History and Antiquities, with Geographical Descriptions of Every Township in the State* (New York, 1842), 46 who write that the "military despotism [of Dutch authorities] drove some of the [Beverwijck] traders to the Schenectady flats."; Griffis, "Arendt Van Curler," 172.

who liked to cross their history with archeology, and their genealogy with ethnography. They strove to preserve historic sites and historic personages for their visible and uncomplicated access to the past. They did all this at institutes, lyceums, and local historical societies.

Upstate New York was no exception. Van Curler fitted in well. In 1883, a speaker at the Albany Institute urged the marking of historical local sites with white marble posts. For the memory of Corlear he asked lasting recognition: The greatness of American frontier settlement, where nature had married civilization, shone in men like van Curler who had joined savages and kings.[130] Others put the theology differently. On the American continent the "white race" was now exhibiting a "supremacy of Anglo-Saxon rule" that rested on entrepreneurs like van Curler and not monopolists like van Rensselaer.[131] In short, van Curler was a person around whose mythic construction the elements of progressivism could be collected.

At the same time, New York was also affirming a Dutch heritage earlier scorned. Late-nineteenth-century patterns of wealth and travel affected this as much as self-confidence. Even ordinary citizens of a small town like Schenectady could be heard offering firsthand travelers' accounts of the townhall of Leyden and "Het Loo in the grand old Batavian wood" the Veluwe.[132] They could now travel to New York City to see its first purchase of Dutch masterpieces, "two by Rembrandt, one by Frans Hals, and one by Vermeer."[133] Alongside paintings of the Dutch masters, moments and figures of the Dutch past also served to glamorize the present United States. George Washington's character, for example, compared well with that of William the Silent.[134]

The world of upstate New Yorkers had grown larger. After 1897, citizens of Albany never saw their city pictured alone on a map. Now there was always Rensselaer or, after 1944, Troy and Schenectady.[135] In 1909, Schenectady also grew, enlarging itself by becoming a daughter

130. "Proposed Erection of Historical Monuments; Report of Special Committee on Archeology," *Transactions of the Albany Institute* (1883), 10:140; 143; 144; 143.
131. Truax, *Life and Character of Corlear*, 7; 11.
132. "Proposed Erection," 138; Truax, "Life and Character of Corlear," 8.
133. "Address of Richmond," 6.
134. Truax, "Life and Character of Corlear," 8.
135. Before 1897, official maps pictured Albany alone, with the exception of an 1857 map, "City of Albany with villages of Greenbush, East Albany and Bath, N.Y." [Maps: 74743 Poster Case, Dr 1] NYSA, and a county map (1876–1885) [74742], NYSA, being "insurance surveys of factories in Albany, Cohoes and West Troy." From 1897 to 1944, maps combining Albany and Rensselaer (Greenbush) dominated. After 1944, maps of Albany, Troy, and Schenectady replaced those of Albany and Rensselaer.

city of Nijkerck, Gelderland. Van Curler, they felt, made it possible.[136]
His deeds became citable. Like a Rembrandt, he became a cultural
treasure. Much of the myth of Arent van Curler constructed by the
nineteenth and early twentieth centuries, then, was a pastiche made
out of their needs. But his image was also the result of mythmaking
from the 1660s to the end of the colonial period. It was during this
time that his role in Rensselaerswyck became a distortion. The needs
of the Mohawk and the English led each to look for leadership in a
single individual. They located this in van Curler. The Dutch in Albany did not. He was never delegated sole authority.[137] He was never
commisary-general or superintendent of the colony, as some later
thought. Much less was he its director.

In a Dutch world that divided authority, he shared it, on occasion. In
the rescue of the Jesuit priest, Isaac Jogues, from Mohawk captors, he
played a leading role but was accompanied by Jacob Janse van Amsterdam and Jan Labatie.[138] Jogues's later reference to him as "governor" is
a mistake arising, no doubt, from the priest's unfamiliarity with the.
complex structure of authority at Fort Orange and the *colonie*.[139] The
records also show that groups of Dutch men aided the French ambushed
in 1666. The memory of Jan Labatie about these events is significant.
Questioned in 1688, he made no mention of van Curler.[140] Finally, in
1662, Stuyvesant patented the flats south along the Mohawk River to
fourteen men, of whom van Curler was one. The patents gave no jurisdictional authority and certainly did not set one man above the others.
Van Curler was in Schenectady not as founder but as trader, interpreter,
and – together with the obvious advantages it brought – in-marrier with
the natives.[141]

Those advantages were crucial to van Curler. Whether he was as trusted
by the natives as later myth would have it, we cannot know. When made
to speak of him after his death, they certainly said he was. They called
him "ruler" and "wise man" and expected "that another 'good ruler'
would be appointed over them."[142] For them, the place of his sudden

136. Truax, "Life and Character of Corlear," 15.
137. For a meeting with the Mohawk in which he was, I believe typically, one represen-
    tative, see List of settlers, *VRBM*, 809.
138. Van Laer, "Arent van Curler's Letter," 27.
139. The Jogues Papers, tr. John Gilmary Shea, CNYHS 2nd ser. (New York, 1856), 3(Part
    I): 211, 212, 213.
140. Deposition of Labatie, Leder, ed., *Livingston Indian Records*, 145.
141. Ruth L. Higgins, *Expansion in New York, with Especial Reference to the Eighteenth
    Century* (Columbus, Ohio, 1931), 19. For van Curler's two illegitimate children, see
    Charlotte Wilcoxen, "Arent van Curler's Children," *New York Genealogical and
    Biographical Record* 1979, 110:82; for van Slyck, see Deposition of Labatie, Leder,
    ed., *Livingston Indian Records*, 146.
142. JvR to van Cortlandt, August 27, 1663, *Corr JvR*, 327.

death by drowning cast magical spells. John Schuyler reported an instance of this in 1690. He himself seemed confused about van Curler's Christian name, writing that of his wife, Antonia, in his report. But the natives knew Corlear. A "savage" knew where Corlear was drowned, Schuyler reported, and "fell into convulsions, charmed and conjured by the devil."[143]

Richard Nicolls, the governor of New York after the English conquest of 1664, immediately realized that van Curler was the most useful man in Albany. He quickly promoted him to the local court and consistently addressed him with the respect due a gentleman. He appointed him emissary to Canada and used both the man and the myth for the continuity they gave in trading relationships with the natives and French. Van Curler's death in the summer of 1667 left him extremely troubled and even prepared to blame the trader's companions for allowing the drowning.[144]

In the environment of culture contact where exchange was continually made, Nicolls took an image of van Curler for his own uses. It was distorted in the taking – van Curler was nobody's gentleman – but that is the way of it. The English appropriated "Corlear" for use in manipulating the natives. The Iroquois had used it to make sense of their complex relationship with the Dutch. Now it was the name for English governors.

Whether it all matched reality was of little consequence. "Ghostly it must have seemed to royal governors to have the personality of the dead founder of Schenectady thrust upon them to the effacement of their own," wrote one nineteenth-century commentator.[145] Not at all. The English took van Curler's name even before death took him. In the summer of 1666, English Indian commissioners in Albany wrung concessions from the Mohawk in the name of Corlear.[146] By the end of the 1670s, Albany – where van Curler had never been nominated for political office and where burghers who had fought his patent to Schenectady for eleven years still resided – was allowed to be "this house of Corlear."[147] For the Mohawk, the name made the site politically neutral and was therefore advantageous for both sides.[148]

Van Rensselaer's story is its contrast. In 1649, Rensselaerswyck's res-

143. Journal of John Schuyler, August, 1690, *DHNY*, 2:286.
144. Nicolls to Commissioners at Albany, August 17, 1667, Livingston Papers, BW 10272, Group B (2), NYSA.
145. Truax, "Life and Character of Corlear," 13.
146. Leder, ed., *Livingston Indian Records*, 30.
147. Griffis, "Arendt Van Curler," 179.
148. See, Answers to Pynchon's Propositions, May 17, 1681 in Nathaniel B. Shurtleff, ed., *Records of the Governor and the Company of the Massachusetts Bay in New England, 1674–1686* (Boston, 1854), 5:320.

ident director declared before the local court that the (second) patroon received "less recognition than a total stranger."[149] It is an apt statement for New York's memory of Kiliaen van Rensselaer. The family name, of course, survived in "Rensselaerswyck." But colonists immediately found names for creeks, meadows, and islands other than those he had intended. His son Jeremias never used such terms as Wely's Dael or Rensselaersburgh. He called Rensselaer's Eyland, Kasteel Eyland, and when an old settler wrote the history of Helleberg he remembered its earliest name as Castle Island. Another son, Jan Baptiste, used Beeren Island for a place near Rensselaers Steijn rather than identical to it.[150] Patroon's Creek may later have referred to the first patroon but was, in any case, a change from the name he gave it, Blomaert's Kil.

The institutes and historical societies that brought Arent van Curler to attention also discovered van Rensselaer, but only just. One amateur historian in 1883 drew incidental attention to the "good old Patroon";[151] another wrote fondly but, again, dismissively of "old Kiliaen Van Rensselaer, the pearl merchant of Amsterdam."[152] In 1924, a revisionist descendant wrote that the patroons were "princes in everthing except name." But they were feudal barons to the eighteenth-century revolutionaries whom the antiquarians were now discovering as their forebears. To them, van Rensselaer was a "thinly disguised feudal chieftain" and his "progeny" were tormentors of the "farmers of the Hudson valley" for two hundred years.[153] In the rediscovered accounts of the rent riots of the eighteenth and nineteenth centuries, the patroons were on the side of monopoly as against men like "Arent van Curler ... whose plea was always for unshackled commerce, free trade and farmers' rights." At the Hudson–Fulton celebrations in Schenectady in 1909, the principal speaker praised van Rensselaer for his management of the *colonie*: He was an "organising brain in a business that had wide relations and re-

149. Court Proceedings, February 4, 1649, *CRB*, 63.
150. JvR to Johan Van Wely and JBvR, September 27, 1671, *Corr JvR*, 444, 445; Gregg, *Old Hellebergh*, 76; JBvR to JvR, October 8, 1659, *Corr JvR*, 182.
151. David Murray, "Industrial and Material Progress, Illustrated in the History of Albany," *Transactions of the Albany Institute* (1883), 10:89. He considers Patroon's Creek to have been named after Kiliaen van Rensselaer.
152. Truax, "Life and Character of Corlear," 8; Gregg, *Old Hellebergh*, 1.
153. Mrs. John King van Rensselaer [in collaboration with Frederic Van de Water], *The Social Ladder* (New York, 1924), 10; Edward A. Collier, *A History of Old Kinderhook from Aboriginal Days to the Present Time: Including the Story of Early Settlers, Their Homesteads, Their Traditions, and Their Descendents: with an Account of Their Civic, Social, Political, Educational, and Religious Life* (New York, 1914), 41, and see 42; Henry Christman, *Tin Horns and Calico: A Decisive Episode in the Emergence of Democracy* (New York, 1945), 3; Hendrik Van Loon, *Life and Times of Pieter Stuyvesant* (New York, 1928), 159; Carl Carmer, *The Hudson* (New York, 1939), 31.

quired able management." But he was, of course, of secondary significance to van Curler and only "take[n] account of" in respect to him.[154]

In the same year, New Yorkers across the state were celebrating the tercentenary of Henry Hudson's discovery of 't Noordt Rivier. The Hudson–Fulton Celebration Commission invented a range of suitable festivities. The river was central. Accordingly, it set up a statewide Committee on Naval Parades and Details. In Albany, members of the Naval Parade Committee agreed upon appropriate celebrations. They included yachts illuminated at night and decorated in the daytime and prizes for the best illuminated and decorated residences along the river. The public could view the arrival of a fleet of ships (including the *Half Moon* and *Clermont*) and celebratory river sports such as Captain Jack Apple's bold leap from the Maiden Lane Bridge.[155]

Historical consciousness had its day. In New York City, the Aquarium Building displayed species of fish present in the Hudson River in 1609. Gardeners in the Bronx Park Botanical Garden marked with an "H" all trees "growing on Manhattan Island and in the Hudson River valley at the time of Hudson's arrival." Members of the Historical and Carnival Parade Committee were embarrassed that floats of Governor Dongan, Philipse Manor Hall, and Governor Leisler and the Huguenots came along out of chronological order, but onlookers seemed nonetheless pleased.[156]

Among the state's scholars, projects went ahead as well. One was the publication of the *Van Rensselaer–Bowier Manuscripts, Being the Letters of Kiliaen van Rensselaer, 1630–1643, and Other Documents Relating to the Colony of Rensselaerswyck.* These were van Rensselaer's letter books, certificates of land purchases near Albany, petitions of sailors in New Netherland, ledgers and logs of ships crossing the Atlantic, ordinances of Rensselaerswyck, inventories, contracts, in all, 909 pages of previously unpublished material. But just as the popular celebration of Hudson's voyage was contexted in the wider matrix of early-twentieth-century folk culture, so the commemorative volume had the markings of

154. [Ballad] "At Two Dollars Per Day," *Freeholder* [Albany] n.p., n.d., in "Anti-Rent Riot Songs," in Christman, *Tin Horns and Calico*, 338. Munsell, *CHA*, 3:321, who cites Albany newspaper editors of 1866 as being sympathetic to van Rensselaer's position in the riots; Griffis, "Arendt Van Curler," 179; Truax, *Life and Character of Corlear*, 8; for van Rensselaer as "enterprising" and "fortunate" in his choice of officers, see Christman, *Tin Horns and Calico*, 3.

155. Henry F. Snyder [Chairman of the Hudson–Fulton Celebration Commission] to John E. Scopes, May 21, 1909, File 14847, NYSA; Minutes of the Naval Parade Committee held in the Supreme Court Room of the City Hall, June 21, [1909], File 14847, NYSA; Edward Hageman Hall, *The Hudson–Fulton Celebration, 1909. The Fourth Annual Report of the Hudson–Fulton Celebration Commission to the Legislature of the State of New York* (Albany, 1910), 2:1020.

156. Hall, *Hudson–Fulton Celebration*, 1:190; 191; 288.

New York's high society. And like the festivities of the masses, the *Manuscripts* was self-defining and self-congratulatory. It showed that proper cultural leadership was in place and more than ready to be activated by such moments as the tercentenary.

Three institutions collaborated in the publication of the *Manuscripts*. The frontispiece froze them into cooperation: the New York State Library, the New York State Education Department, and the University of the State of New York. New York's best families were also represented, sufficient of them to say that guardianship of the past was a privilege of the social, as much as of the academic, elite. The names Vander Veer, Pruyn, and Delancey M. Ellis gave the appropriate impression.

Elite New York was saying something about itself. If the limited copies of the edition were seldom consulted and the 909 pages of evidence never used, it would not have been a grave disappointment. For example, Mrs. Alan Strong (at page 39, Susan DeLancy van Rensselaer Strong) wrote one of the introductory essays. Van Rensselaer's name was never mentioned. He was cited simply as "the famous first patroon" from whose loins the thirty-three subsequently listed van Rensselaers had surged forward to present eminence. He and the importance of the documents for knowing his life went without mention.[157]

For the most part New York cared little about van Rensselaer. He would not have expected a white marble post erected to his memory – nor was it suggested – but, irascible as he was at untidiness, he would have been dismayed at the mistaken notions of his role as patroon. One editor believed that he came to the colony in 1637. An accepted historian thought his colony a hamlet. A popular belief of the mid-eighteenth century was cited to the effect that "the manor" had originally been bestowed by King Charles because the old man had prophesied his restoration to the English throne ten years before it happened.[158] A Dutch visitor to Albany in 1827 noted the prominence of the van Rensselaer family but was led to think (mistakenly) that they were unrelated to van Rensselaers in Naarden and Vianen. The early-twentieth-century historian A. J. F. van Laer, who shared van Rensselaer's passion for tidiness, insisted in 1908 that he was alive three years after he had died.[159]

157. See The Hudson–Fulton Celebration, Albany, New York, October 7–8, 1909, Certificate of John E. Scopes [signed Henry F. Snyder, Mayor and Chairman], File 14847, NYSA; E[dmund] B. O'Callaghan, *History of New Netherland, or New York under the Dutch*, 1, 2 (New York, 1846), makes profitable but not extensive use of the collection.

158. Jeremiah Johnson, ed. of van der Donck's *Description of New Netherland*, CNYHS, 2nd ser. 1:126; John Doyle, *The English in America: The Middle Colonies* (London, 1907), 4:206; Journal of a trip to Albany, Cohoes and Mohawk town, Typescript SC11706, Folder, 2(3), NYSA.

159. See J. G. Swaving, *Reizen en Lotsgevallen*, II (Dordrecht, 1827), 29, and for van Rensselaers in Vianen, see "Introduction," VRBM, 38, and "Preface," *Corr JvR*, 7;

Yet seldom in colonial history does a figure emerge who was so determined to know the New World or so reflective of what that process involved. Without the least attempt at disguise – but also without success – van Rensselaer assumed a direct relationship between the capacity to interpret and the power to control. In a series of its later settings in New Netherland and New York, the relationship between the two will be ours to observe as well.

see "Introduction," *VRBM*, 31, and Van Laer, "Arent van Curler's Letter," 16; even Netherlands scholars think van Rensselaer died in 1644, and W. J. Van Balen, *Holland aan de Hudson: Een verhaal van Nieuw Nederland* (Amsterdam, 1943), 66, writes of a *"familielegende"* (family myth) that the patroon crossed to the colony.

2

Trading on the Land, 1652–1664

In 1659, the Company's officer at Beverwijck had to confront one of the most important traders in the land between the upper Susquehanna and the Connecticut rivers. He was John Pynchon, a man of formidable reputation. His name had already appeared on two Dutch maps depicting North America between 1647 and 1651. According to them, only the aborigines, the Dutch, and "Mr. Pinser" occupied all the land north of an east–west line drawn from the southern tip of Lake Champlain across to the Susquehanna River (about 325 miles). North of Pesquenock and east of the Connecticut River, they pictured Mr. Pinser's *cleyne val* (Mr. Pynchon's small waterfall) and, only fifteen milliaria Germanica Communia to Greenbos, Mr. Pinser's *handel huys* (Mr. Pynchon's tradingpost) (Figure 2.1).[1]

For Kiliaen van Rensselaer, Pynchon's name was a metaphor for a wave of Englishmen threatening to enter the fur trade. In 1639, his fear of William Pynchon led him to place his name before the States General, warning that the English would "soon take possession of the whole of New Netherland." He advised extending Dutch colonization east from Rensselaerswyck, even though it would mean direct confrontation with "Mr. Pinser's *handel huys*" at Enfield Falls. "I would not hesitate," he promised with considerable venom, "to force a certain master pingen, an Englishman who is nearest to me, to retreat across the Fresh River, whereby [with the westernmost tradingpost removed] the other Englishmen of the Fresh River will also be compelled not to come nearer to the Company."[2]

Van Rensselaer was unsuccessful in this suit, but his anxieties were well placed. In 1635, there were eight hundred residents in the four Connecticut Valley towns. More ominous, in 1640, Pynchon had sent an agent from Springfield west to Woronoco to intercept Mohawks with

1. I. N. Phelps Stokes, *The Iconography of Manhattan Island, 1498–1909* (New York, 1967 reprint), 1:143–8, and see Plates 7, 7a, 7b. Also see Stokes, *Iconography*, 2:119. *Millaria Germanica Communia* is Rhineland measure. See Note 4, Chapter 1.
2. KvR to Gerrit van Arnhem, January 29, 1641, VRBM, 526; 526.

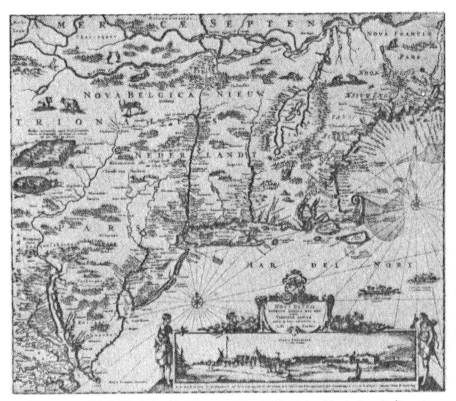

Figure 2.1. Belgii Novi Angliae Novae et Partis Virginiae Novissima Delineatio (The Janssonius Prototype). Courtesy of the New-York Historical Society.

furs. In 1647, Petrus Stuyvesant, as director of New Netherland, felt it necessary to warn Fort Orange of an "English trading-house" only "ten leagues" distant. But now, in the summer of 1659, William Pynchon's son was before the Beverwijck court with a direct proposal. Might he and William Hawthorn settle a community some five Dutch miles to the east, where they could farm and supply the Dutch with cattle and, presumably, draft animals?[3]

It is difficult for those of us who know the subsequent history of New Netherland to miss the effrontery of this request. Pynchon's profits in

3. J. H. Smith, ed., *Colonial Justice in Western Massachusetts (1639–1702): The Pynchon Court Records: An Original Judge's Diary of the Administration of Justice in Springfield Courts in the Massachusetts Bay Colony* (Cambridge, Mass., 1961), 17; Directors to Stuyvesant [extract], (December 1646 or early 1647), *DRCH*, 13:21; Ex. Sess., July 25, 1659, *CRB*, 208.

furs were declining after 1654, and he required contacts with tribes under the influence of Fort Orange. In fact, 1658 had been an unusually bad year. But the performance seems a particularly deceitful one because we know he was later involved in arming natives east of the Hudson as part of "plans for the eventual conquest of the Hudson Valley" by the English, that he was among the New Englanders who accepted the Dutch surrender in 1664, and finally, that he was quick to seize the position of Indian commissioner, a role always useful to a fur trader.[4] We can also consider his request within an ample history of New Englanders spuriously claiming parts of New Netherland: some claiming free passage on the Hudson to plant settlements; two generations of the Paine family scheming for land near Beverwijck; Pynchon later laying claim to Albany itself.[5] And yet Pynchon's court appearance made sense if we remember that, by 1659, the Dutch townsmen had brought him and other New Englanders into their trading world.

Pynchon saw that important traders of Beverwijck were desperate for cattle and horses in the summer of 1659. Because beaver pelts were scarce, Dutch farmers were in an unprofitable market and exercising the option of withholding livestock from sale, and in any case, the townspeople preferred New England farm animals. Merchants of New Amsterdam would have known – and therefore, as we shall see, those of Hartford and Springfield would have known – that even Petrus Stuyvesant had been waiting a full year for Kiliaen van Rensselaer's son, Jeremias, to find a New England-bred stallion to match the horse – an "Englishman" – already used for his carriage.[6] Van Rensselaer had tried Milford, Connecticut, traveling there himself to complete the transaction. But in the summer of 1659, he was still searching.[7] Jan Helmsz in Beverwijck disappointed him with inflated prices. Even Arent van Curler failed to procure the animals he required.

Pynchon envied the Beverwijck traders their economic alliances with the Mohawk, and their profits. Rumor of annual fur shipments from

4. Bernard Bailyn, *The New England Merchants in the Seventeenth Century* (New York, 1955), 54; 56; Francis Jennings, *The Ambiguous Iroquois Empire. The Covenant Chain Confederation of Indian Tribes with English Colonies from Its Beginnings to the Lancaster Treaty of 1744* (New York, 1984), 129.
5. Stuyvesant to Commissioners of New England and John Endicot (*sic*) of Massachusetts, October 27, 1659, SC16676–82, NYSA; Philip J. Schwarz, *The Jarring Interests: New York's Boundary Makers, 1664–1776* (Albany, 1979), 21, 22; 344, 250; "Memorandum, November 10, 1677," Victor Hugo Palsits, ed., *Minutes of the Executive Council of the Province of New York: Administration of Francis Lovelace, 1668–1673* (Albany, 1910), 30.
6. JvR to Stuyvesant, April 7, 1659, *Corr JvR*, 143; JvR to Anna van Rensselaer, May 8, 1659, *Corr JvR*, 156.
7. Stuyvesant to JvR, March 23, 1659, *Corr JvR*, 142.

New Netherland put the figure for the early 1630s at between 10,000 and 15,000 skins.[8] In reality, the number was higher – certainly for all New Netherland – and continued to climb. For example, 14,891 pelts were traded in 1635, and if we may give him credence, an *ondercommis* at Fort Orange estimated that he alone was floating 13,000 skins to New Amsterdam in 1634. In 1644, governor Johan Printz sent 2,124 skins (17,136 guilders) from New Amstel. Van der Donck estimated that 10,000 skins left Fort Orange in 1645.[9] In the two years just prior to Pynchon's visit to Beverwijck, 1656 and 1657, 46,000 pelts left the town. In 1658, the *Vergulde Bever* crossed the Atlantic with skins valued at gl 60,000. On a cautious estimate, the three weeks of trading that Jacob Eelkens conducted with natives outside Fort Orange in 1633 would have given him twenty times the amount of fur taken by Pynchon in 1632–3.[10]

The figures – and rumors – were signs of a hidden but elaborate and enviable trading structure. William Bradford had some sense of it in 1627. The New Netherlanders, he wrote, "have used trading there these 6 or 7 and 20 years and now have reduced their trade to some order." In the 1640s, trade expanded dramatically between the Low Countries and North America. A pattern of financing was developing that "enabled certain merchants to cut their costs, drive out their competition, and raise their profits." Bookkeepers were mastering "relatively complicated procedures of accounting." Dutch colonists were generally coping better with currency than their French or English counterparts, and Beverwijck townspeople were navigating the land from the town to points at 360 degrees around it.[11]

8. For John Winthrop's figure of 10,000, see Bernard Bailyn, *The New England Merchants*, 27; Capt. Mason to [Secretary Coke?], *DRCH*, 3:17, cites 15,000.

9. "The Beaver," *CHA*, 1:384; KvR to van Twiller, April 23, 1634, *VRBM*, 273; Amandus Johnson, "The Instruction of Johan Printz, Governor of New Sweden," *The First Constitution of Supreme Law of the State of Pennsylvania and Delaware, translated from the Swedish, with Introduction, Notes and Appendices, Including Letters from Governor John Winthrop of Massachusetts, and Minutes of Courts, Sitting in New Sweden* (New York, 1969 reissue), 107; Adriaen van der Donck, *A Description of New Netherlands (As the Same are at the Present Time;) Comprehending the Fruitfulness and Natural Advantages of the Country, and the Disirable Opportunities which it Presents...to which Are Added the Affairs of the Country, by the Council of the City of Amsterdam, the second edition, with a map of the Country* (1656), tr. Jeremias Johnson, *CNYHS*, 2nd ser. (New York, 1841), 1:97.

10. Sung Bok Kim, *Landlord and Tenant in Colonial New York: Manorial Society, 1664–1775* (Chapel Hill, 1978), 27; Oliver Albert Rink, *Holland on the Hudson: An Economic and Social History of Dutch New York* (Cooperstown, 1986) 257, on Eelkens's trade, see Examination of Bastiaen Janse Krol, June 30, 1634, *VRBM*, 303.

11. Bradford to Ferninando Gorges, June 15, 1627, Correspondence between the Colonies of New Netherland and New-Plymouth, 1627, from the *Letter-book of William Bradford*, *CNYHS*, 2nd ser. (New York, 1841), 1:367; Rink, Holland on the Hudson,

Pynchon's life was set within the cultural ways of New England. Frontier communities like his were basically agricultural, and as a consequence, the fur trade had never become an integral part of the economy. William Pynchon had repeatedly argued against that, demanding that the trade be carefully organized, that "one in a town . . . [be allowed] to trade in beaver." But no town, not even Mr. Pinser's *handel huys*, had dared to organize itself principally around the fur trade. The communities' texture was mediated in the statement of John Winthrop that "of all private occupations trade . . . [is] morally the most dangerous."[12] We can only conjecture, then, Pynchon's envy of his Dutch counterparts in Beverwijck, traders justified to call before them time and space and make them dance.

Time

For its people, Beverwijck was a town with two beginnings. First there was the beginning when the old fort was erected. No one had cared to say precisely when that was. When an English governor in 1685 wanted more accuracy about origins, Catelyn Trico was brought forward and provided a base for arithmetic calculations. She testified that she was now eighty-nine and had arrived when she was a child, so it must have been about 1612. There was a moment in 1647 when townsmen celebrated "with enormous libations of brandy" the first stone building erected outside the fort.[13] But this, like the rest, did not inspire a God's remembrancer: There was no founding hero to memorialize, nothing that required histories such as the Mathers gave New England. It is tempting to think that public memory arranged earlier time as sequences in the contests between van Rensselaer and the Company. We cannot know.

We do know that, to townspeople after 1664, the fort was a place of strong emotional force, holding its symbolic meaning long after crumbling into disuse. Publicly it was the place of celebrations, like the 4th of July in 1787. It filled out private meanings also. In 1734, a townsman bequeathed land in typical fashion, "in the city of Albany near the Old

200, *passim*; John M. McCusker, *Money and Exchange in Europe and America, 1600–1775: A Handbook* (Chapel Hill, 1978), 291.

12. Smith, ed., *Pynchon Court Records*, 10; Bailyn, *New England Merchants*, 20.
13. Deposition of Catelyn Trico, October 17, 1688, *DHNY*, 3:50–1; Johannes La Montagne, quoted in John W. Barber and Henry Howe, *Historical Collections of the State of New York containing a General Collection of the Most Interesting Facts, Traditions, Biographical Sketches, Anecdotes, etc. Relating to Its History and Antiquities, with Geographical Descriptions of Every Township in the State* (New York, 1842), 46.

Fort Joining to the Road that leads . . . to ye Said old fort."[4] Well before the passing of the first generation, it was cherished as much for the protohistory it gave the town as for its rich arable surrounds.

On April 10, 1652, the director general of the Company, Petrus Stuyvesant, put trading into time and space in a new way. He created the market town that soon became the envy of a trader like Pynchon, giving the area its second beginning. Provoked by a policy of the patroon to allocate house lots just outside the walls of Fort Orange, Stuyvesant claimed all land within a nineteen hundred foot radius of the fort. This included possibly twenty-nine house lots whose owners were now in effect invited to throw off *colonie* status and become free traders, that is, burghers of a new town. They were also made to move north, remaining within the nineteen hundred foot radius but building on lots plotted by Stuyvesant and lying in two rows later named Jonckheerstraat and Handlaarstraat. By 1655, seventy-five lots were patented to townsmen. In 1659, the palisades of the town were nine hundred feet north of Rutten Kill and encompassed twenty-four acres and about 127 houses – the population would have been close to one resident's estimate of "230 ablebodied men" or "1100 souls."[5]

Stuyvesant named the town Beverwijck. It was the first moment in the long separation of the town from the *colonie*. It was a time for a new court: the "Inferior Court of Justice erected . . . at the request of the burghers of the aforesaid fort and Beverwijck." The year 1652 did not make a clean slice in time – in March of 1654, for instance, the ever-peripatetic court of Rensselaerswyck was sitting in Beverwijck, and for several decades there was uncertainty about judicial boundaries. Yet by 1656, a start to separation was actualized in legislation. In that year, Stuyvesant announced that he would farm the excise on beer and spirits "first [from] the burghers and innkeepers of the Fuyck [Beverwijck] and then the innkeepers of the colony."[6]

For many, 1652 fixed a moment of biographical time. Two officers of Rensselaerswyck decided to become burghers, while a burgher who was a town magistrate resigned his magistracy in the town to take up a farm

---

14. City Records (1779), *CHA*, 1:294; Will of Jacob Staats, September 14, 1734, Van Vechten Papers, AQ7006, Wills No. 1, folder 18, NYSA.
15. Schaats to Laurentius, June 27, in Hugh Hastings, ed., *Ecclesiastical Records: State of New York* (Albany, 1901–1916), 1:383; for a study of the town's growth, see Merwick, "Dutch Townsmen and Land Use: A Spatial Perspective on Seventeenth-Century Albany, New York," *William and Mary Quarterly*, 3rd ser. January (1980), 37:53–78.
16. See Ord. sess., April 15, 1652, *CRB*, 15; for the court of Rensselaerswyck in Beverwijck, see Ord. sess., March 17, 1554, *CRB*, 125; JvR to Anna van Rensselaer (hereafter AvR) [October ?, 1656], *Corr JvR*, 33.

in Rensselaerswyck.[17] The year 1652 also rerouted the timeline of the fur trade. The town's use of time and space was, as Stuyvesant intended, its own determination. The merchants in furs were expected to be creators of the town's identity. Time and space would be essentially *burgerlijk*.

The Liturgical Year

The settlers' lives ran along several braided strands of time. For everyone, October was the eighth month of the calendar year, but it was also *wijnmont* in the cycle of agricultural events and the last month of the active trading season. Above all, time was dominated by the activities of trading on the land. However, order also came with the annual festivities marked by the church calendar.

Liturgical time drew townspeople to religious services on Sundays, Wednesdays, and occasions of special religious significance. The liturgies recorded for 1665 show that the Reformed church congregation attended services almost one out of four days a year. The festivals of December through March alone brought church members together thirty-five times.[18]

The days from early February to mid-April were richly celebratory. On Candlemas Day, February 2, the officials in New Amsterdam followed the tradition of Amsterdam and took office. It was a day when the church called the faithful to respect civil as well as religious authority: "We received your mercy, O God," went the liturgy, "in the midst of your temple." February 2 was not a day of civil ceremony in Beverwijck – where officials took the oath of office on May 1 – nor did the Reformed congregation observe all the medieval ceremonies of Lent, which ordinarily began in February. However, Shrove Tuesday (*Vastenavond*) was recognized as the moment of festive abandon immediately preceding the first day of Lent (Ash Wednesday), and merrymakers often seized upon it – to their undoing. One innkeeper, "not knowing what he was doing wrong," drank his way into serious charges of fighting and walking about in women's clothing. Herman Jansz van Valkenbergh apparently spent several hours in revelry with friends and then slandered the wife of the town's highest official, "rode the goose," "befouled" the servant of a leading citizen "on the public street," and finally got caught breaking into a burgher's home, where he started a fire that burned one of the doorposts and the floor. To the magistrates of New Amsterdam, "shrove-tide" was a detestable "pagan and popish feast," even though it was

17. Ex. sess., April 17, 1652, *CRB*, 17; 17.
18. I am discussing the Reformed congregation (not Lutherans) and using the *Deacons' Account Book* printed by Munsell in *CHA*, 1:1–57.

"looked at through the fingers in some places in Fatherland." Many in New Netherland looked through their fingers as well.[19]

Springtime brought Easter festivities, with liturgies for *boet predicatie* (Good Friday), Easter Sunday, and Easter Monday. In early summer, the triumph of Christ's resurrection was again savored on Ascension Day, a Thursday coming forty days after Easter. It was one of several feasts unmarked by church attendance but nonetheless religious in meaning. Townsmen used the special character of such a day as a mnemonic device, recalling occurrences "last year on Ascension Day." They also celebrated Whitsunday (Pentecost, *Pinkster*), commemorating the sending of the Holy Spirit to the Apostles. They did so to the fullest extent, even as the medieval church intended. The congregation met on Sunday and Pentecost Monday, probably kept Tuesday a holiday, and was conscious in some form or other of Whitsuntide, the festive octave of the pre-Reformation liturgical year. Whitsuntide also served as a completion date for work contracted in May or early spring. Summer and autumn were times of comparative quiet, even as they were for Roman Catholics. The feast of Saint Michael the Archangel on September 19 passed without celebration. In 1686, however, governor Thomas Dongan designated it as municipal election day, though residents seem not to have known its English significance as Lord Mayor's Day in London.[20] There was no liturgy for All Saints' Day on November 1. However, it was the termination date for countless rental agreements and other forms of debt. On All Saints' Day, religious belief and trading practice reinforced one another and exchanged values: It was the official end of *handelstijd*, the trading season that began on May 1.[21]

In December, the congregation celebrated the liturgies of Christmas,

19. *New York Historical Manuscripts: Dutch: IV, Council Minutes, 1638–1649*, ed. A. J. F. Van Laer and ed. Kenneth Scott and Kenn Stryker-Rodda (Baltimore, 1974), 466, 482; 489–96; Ord. sess., March 3, 1654, *CRB*, 118; Ord. sess., February 27, 1655, *CRB*, 207, 208. In "riding the goose" men rode on horseback at full gallop to try to pull off the head of a goose suspended by the legs; Minutes of March 2, 1654, *RNA*, 1:173. For Shrove Tuesday festivities in Dutch Flatbush, see William Mc-Laughlin, Dutch Rural New York: Community, Economy and Family in Colonial Flatbush (Ph.D. diss., Columbia University, 1981), 140.
20. See *Deacons' Account Book, CHA*, 1:26; for Ascension Day, see Minutes of May 20, 1658, *RNA*, 2:385; H. P. Phelps, ed., *The Albany Handbook: A Strangers' Guide and Residents' Manual* (Albany, 1884), 152.
21. See, as examples, Minutes of October 24, 1655, *RNA*, 5:304, and Minutes of October 12, 1660, *RNA*, 3:230; David Pietersz de Vries, in *Short Historical and Journal Notes of several Voyages made in the four Parts of the World, namely, Europe, Africa, Asia and America*... (1655), CNYHS 2nd ser. (New York, 1856), 3(Part 1):93 writes of All Saints Day as the end of summer; for Jeremias van Rensselaer's use of the term "trading season," see JvR to Jan Thomassen van Wely, May 22, [1657], *Corr JvR*, 47.

second Christmas (December 26), and a Communion Sunday. Depending on arrangements for preparation day, they might meet a fourth time, as happened in 1683. Christmas was an anticipated festival, announced as being "at hand" as early as December 13, and, following "the custom of our Fatherland," often calling for the suspension of ordinary court sessions for eight days after its celebration. Yet holy days were legitimately days of work. Kiliaen van Rensselaer, for example, worked steadily on December 25, 1633, and the magistrates of Beverwijck held court on Christmas Day, 1653. December 27 was Saint John's Day. Like All Saints' Day, it was a time when mortgage installments frequently fell due.[22]

On January 1, townspeople celebrated the feast of the Circumcision. As in the Netherlands, reflection was prescribed. Fathers wrote didactically to sons, and in 1656, even Stuyvesant's *commis* at Fort Orange sank into a suitably reflective mood. He shared with the director general his musings about the old year and hoped for divine blessings on "the assemblies of the burgomasters" in the New Netherland towns and the members of Stuyvesant's council in the new year. Finally, townsmen fired "a midnight gun" in honor of "the year of our Lord and Redeemer, Jesus Christ." It was a custom – allegedly full of abuses – that endured.[23]

It is the church records that give us the "book of hours" of religious lives in Beverwijck. Deacons kept them in formulaic style, for they made sense, as did religion itself, only if the men could see a regularity fixing the relations of men and women with God – only if their sums inscribed a regular collection, only if the consecutiveness of the recorded pages and the succession of scripts showed the recurrences of religious practice. It was religious time largely bereft of circumstance – washed clean of quarrels, nonattendance, levity, and censure. There were deliberate omissions in the records, but generally they looked to be and were a true account of keeping faith in time's small and large units of belief.

The account books of farmers also counted off regularities. Like van Curler's ledgers, they tracked seasons on the surface of paper, noting *wijnmont, hooimont* (July), weeks to harvest, and weeks to sell beans, peas, or corn. In the same way, the town's official records charted other dominant recurrences. Above all, they pointed to *handelstijd*, the season of trading on the land.

---

22. *Deacons' Account Book, CHA,* 1:7; 43; Minutes of December 13, 1655, *RNA,* 1:419, and see 274; KvR to Minuit and KvR to Planck, both letters written on December 26, 1637, *VRBM,* 389–92.
23. De Dekker to Stuyvesant, January 16, 1656, *ER1,* 238; see *City Records* (1867), *CHA,* 2:97, and, for firing of the gun in New Amsterdam, see Ordinance, December 31, 1655, *RNA,* 1:18.

Handelstijd

May 1 to November 1 was *handelstijd*. Merchandise coming inside the palisades doubled or tripled in bulk and value. There were New Testaments in French, pieces of eight, mirrors, seawan, gold rings, blankets, guns, velvet cloaks. Fifty thousand beaver pelts might have entered the town and fort in a single season as well. With each pelt probably weighing about 15 pounds, that would have amounted to something like 750,000 pounds of fur entering the town. Since it would have arrived largely in native canoes each capable of carrying as much as 4,000 pounds, conservatively 190 native craft would have lain along the riverside at some point during the season. Somehow the goods found space in about 127 houses.

In 1657, 40,940 beaver pelts were taken in trade. The value was gl 327,520. If only half of those pelts were purchased with seawan, then 39,320,400 black and white shells would have been strung in the customary lengths for the trade.[24] If the pelts were divided evenly among the 105 men and women claiming to be in the fur trade in 1659, each would have had 390, an earning of gl 3,120. Half of that was equal to six years' wages as a local farmhand. The furs and profits were, of course, not evenly distributed, for *handelstijd* was, above all, a time of competition. It rewarded a few but cheated the hopes of most and ruined others. It set all men gambling.

May 1 was a day when it profited an outsider to obtain a pass from the Company at New Amsterdam for upriver passage and to arrange lodgings or house rental. Rentals to transients were common, but an outsider could also purchase a house lot and earn the right to trade by swearing to build a dwelling – while actually squatting on a property by paying the first installment.

It was a time of strangers. They came to trade, sell seawan, bake, gamble at auctions, deliver merchandise, buy property, sue residents and other strangers for debt. The poor and the hopeful came. Youths arrived, contracting for house rental on May 1 and otherwise leaving no record of their existence. Agents like Robbert Orchard of Boston appeared, coming only once to take what profits they could. One man came to collect debts but had a pass allowing only three weeks' residence.[25]

---

24. Record of Dyckman, 1657, *ER1*, 244. Dyckman's figures are inaccurate. He may have added 3,300 beaver for the 300 otter not included, and consequently his sum should be 37,640; the figure of 39,302,400 is calculated on 1659 figures, when eight white or four black shells were valued at one stiver. In July 1664, Philip Pietersz Schuyler paid 91 beaver (i.e., gl 728) for seawan (*ER3*, 291), that is, 174,720 shells (black and white). In 1657, a good string went for gl 13.10, so he would have purchased about 56 strings (Ex. sess., June 16, 1657, *CRB*, 45).
25. Minutes of August, 25, 1653, *RNA*, 1:106; for Orchard, see Ord. sess., September

Wealthy men arrived: the wholesale merchants of New Amsterdam and Holland, Hartford and Boston. Some arrived precisely on May 1, making use of the court session ritually conducted on the first day of *handelstijd*. Thirty-two such figures appeared in court, suing or answering claims arising from ill-conceived business transactions. The merchant Johannes Withardt came from New Amsterdam in 1656 to collect a mortgage on a resident's house and lot. Paulus Leendertsz van der Grift, also a merchant of New Amsterdam, arrived in 1657. Withardt reappeared in 1658, as did Hendrick Hendricksz Obe, Asser Levy, Isaac de Foreest, Paulus Schrijk, Abraham de la Noy, and Barent van Marle (or his agent), all important wholesalers of New Amsterdam. Schrijk (of Hartford) and Jacob Steendam, Dirck Dircksz Keyser and Levy came in 1659. The burgomaster of New Amsterdam, Allard Anthyonij, came in 1660, along with Nicolaes de Meyer and Levy. In 1661, de Meyer, Levy, Johannes van Brugge, and the agent of van Marle returned. In 1662, Thomas Willet and Levy arrived. In August of 1663, Mr. John Willet, trader in New England, was in Beverwijck. Agents for Gerrit Suyck & Company of Holland and other "merchants at Amsterdam and vicinity in Holland," came in 1663. De Meyer made another appearance in *handelstijd* of 1664.[26]

The strangers' presence undoubtedly pleased townsmen who had wares to auction. At one sale held in July 1658, Abraham de la Noy bought an elk skin and two Englishmen bought a little coat and two new shirts. Strangers attended auctions together. Schrijk came with Robbert Engel and Willem Martensz More of New England. They also auctioned their own goods. Van Marle auctioned tobacco and Schrijk took bids on knives and a pistol.[27]

May 1 was a time for Beverwijck's outlivers to move back within the palisades. Some men, like Jan Dareth and Jan van Bremen, came away from their farms. Others came in from Schenectady. All added to the continual and unpredictable movement of people through the town gates. Natives arrived in the hundreds. They added to the elderly natives already camped nearby, fishing the Hudson with dragnets. It was a time of hastily

16, 1669, *CRA*, 99, and see 106; for Peter Neften [Nesten?], another agent, see Auction of sloop by Neften for Obe of New Amsterdam [sale incomplete], 1658, *ER4*, 28–9.

26. Data for this chapter are drawn largely from the public records of Beverwijck and New Amsterdam, such as notarial papers, court minutes and official correspondence. For genealogical evidence, I have used, among other references, the works of Jonathan Pearson and A. J. F. Van Laer, material in The Dutch Settlers Society of Albany yearbooks, and Carl Boyer, III, *Ship Passenger Lists: New York and New Jersey (1600– 1825)*, (Newhall, Calif., 1978).

27. Account of auction sales, July 22, 1658, *ER4*, 53; 54; 54.

erected sheds behind dwellings, of households sleeping natives, of little Indian houses reactivated outside the palisades. One trader asked the court's permission to erect an Indian shed on his property just for the three months of *handelstijd*. The wife of another simply allowed a tenant to do so. One burgher housed eight natives, whereas another allowed "a party of drunken savages" in his house. The disorder created by the interaction of natives with townspeople is for later pages, but the request of sachems in 1657 that they be allowed to bring women and children to Beverwijck and the report of four hundred natives settled in the area during *handelstijd* of 1659 testify to the movement and crowding that built up as the season got underway.[28]

Natives with furs ordinarily arrived in mid-June. In anticipation, townsmen organized the assets that might make them winners in the competitions of *handelstijd*. Gambling on a good season, they mortgaged properties for trading goods. Even Jeremias van Rensselaer, who had sufficient assets to prevent that kind of financial squeeze, shared the townsmen's anticipation and recorded their edginess in the early weeks of May 1658. "The situation up here is still fair, but we have no beaver trade as yet." In 1659, he again reported on the waiting game of May. "The Beaver trade... may turn out to be very good," he wrote, "for almost all the river Indians are out hunting."[29]

In the first weeks of *handelstijd*, the burghers engaged in a festivity that announced the season as one of heightened and potentially dangerous competition. They met in the combat of "shooting the parrot." It was a contest meant to discover and honor the best marksman among the town's burgherguard (*schutterij*) and was conducted by setting a wooden *papegaai* on a pole and taking aim from the edge of a wide circle. The competition was universal among the Dutch. At Table Bay in South Africa, for example, marksmen were awarded a variety of prizes for hitting the bird's left or right wing, head or tail, and then "the whole body of shooters" escorted the winner to his home "in state." He won the title King of the Marksmen.[30]

In Beverwijck, Hendrick Jochemsz directed the revels of the *papegaai-*

28. JvR to JBvR, [May 11, 1659], *Corr JvR*, 160; see Property auction [incomplete, n.d., ca. May 1663], *ER1*, 324; Ord. sess., April 17, 1657, *CRB*, 28; Lease of house, September 10, 1661, *ER3*, 109; Ord. sess., September 2, 1669, *CRA*, 96; Ord. sess. June 19, 1657, *CRB*, 47; JvR to OvCortlandt [August, 1665], *Corr JvR*, 381.

29. See, as examples, Mortgage and property auction, July 28, 1660 [incomplete], *ER1*, 266, and Property sale, May 1, 1655, *ER1*, 230; JvR to Jan Bastiaensen van Gutsenhoven [May 2, 1658?], *Corr JvR*, 86; JvR to JBvR [May 11, 1659], *Corr JvR*, 160.

30. Ord. sess., May 9, 1655, *CRB*, 220; F. C. Dominicus, *Het Huiselik en Maatschappelik Leven van de Zuid Afrikaner in de errste helft der 18de Eeuw* (s'-Gravenhage, 1919), 66, 67; see Ord. sess., May 9, 1655, *CRB*, 220 and 220, n. 45.

schoet in 1655. He was an innkeeper who frequently associated with the Company's soldiers at the fort and at whose house scenes of brawling and fighting occurred. So it is likely that the *schoet* was not only a ritual of some violence but that some of the contestants were men of violence as well. Certainly the community recognized this. The court, aware of past contests when "good order" gave way and "accidents" occurred, admonished Jochemsz to prevent disorder.[31] Yet it gave its permission, acquiescing in a ritual that allowed the burghers to fire weapons and, in that sense, conduct themselves in a way not otherwise sanctioned. The men undoubtedly played out the competition on the *plein* near the old fort and from there, full of drink and ready to cause accidents, escorted the victor through the south gate into town.

No man or woman in the game of *handelstijd* was unaware of its dangers. Natives came knowing that Dutch buyers would woo them but then brutalize and cheat them. Dutchmen entered the competition knowing they needed answers to some of these questions: At which of the several auctions of merchandise should one bid? Would prices of merchandise fall within the month? Could one gamble on the magistrates closing their eyes to selling liquor to natives? Would they be policing the Schenectady road? Would they enact ordinances protecting small traders against the large merchants, the *handelaars*? Would the court be severe on the practice of luring natives into private homes and shops? In 1658, the natives did not bring the usual number of pelts. Would it be so again?

The pace of competition was fast. Roman law, still in use among the Dutch, was the merchants' law. So cases of debt were settled with dispatch by a court that met twice – often thrice – weekly and recognized that the success of the town's trade depended on the movement of its citizens and their assets. Vendors at auctions wanted payment within twenty-four hours. In the agonistic moments of an auction, a house, a consignment of goods, a yacht, a canoe was lost. Success could also arrive suddenly, with a small trader unexpectedly having plenty of money.[32]

Trading became a frenzy. One woman betrayed her husband by trading away their household goods. Other burghers pledged "all their estates" for merchandise, and lost. Still others mortgaged houses and land, alienating their properties to both fellow townsmen and the powerful New Amsterdam merchants. During the *handelstijd* months of 1658 to 1664, twelve men (including eight leading traders) mortgaged properties to outsiders. Others simply got in way over their heads. Jan Michaelsz van Edan, for example, had purchased merchandise just before the season

31. Ord. sess., May 9, 1655, *CRB*, 220.
32. JvR to JBvR, July 11/21, 1668, *Corr JvR*, 407.

from two New Amsterdam wholesalers and Schrijk of Hartford, but July brought him no beaver. He was sued by all three creditors and had to mortgage his house.[33] There was desperation to get credit, fighting over profits, and gambling away of anticipated wages. Traders moved along the kills in "canoes, rowboats and other vessels," passing kettles of brandy "over the side . . . to the savages." Some went in twos and threes, fighting among themselves, carelessly running the risk of discovery and confiscation of sails and rudder. Others went alone, their dark activities betrayed only in testimony before the court that "he used the canoe many times last summer."[34]

Townspeople acted in unaccustomed ways. More than one townsman tested authority by plays of role reversal. Eldert de Goyer, who was continually in debt, did so by mimicking de Meyer and revealing an intensity of dislike that he would not otherwise have dared express. In fact, he physically attacked the New Amsterdam merchant, charging that he – "Mr. Captain Burgomaster" – owed him debts.[35] Other men and women traded and drank through the night. "Drunken women who all day long roam along the streets and make a vile spectacle of themselves" were imprisoned until "sober and slept out." Strangers cavorted in all-night brawls. Individuals never found before the court now appeared on charges of stealing from natives, and others were there for wounding native women. Ordinances regulating sealing and weighing were not only disregarded but "all memory thereof is forgotten."[36]

Ordinarily, inns, like individuals' houses, were well regulated. There was a place for drinking, and Dutch society accepted that at inns men would drink heavily – and gamble for high stakes (Figure 2.2). Although the authorities of Amsterdam denounced insobriety, they licensed 518 tapsters in 1613, one for every two hundred inhabitants. They were also tolerant of the drinking man, as were lawgivers elsewhere in the Low Countries.[37]

In Beverwijck, the court acted in accord with these practices. It farmed

33. Ex. sess., May 25, 1660, *CRB*, 253; Demand of Velthuysen, August 23, 1654, *ER1*, 190; Ord. sess., July 13, 1660, *CRB*, 277; Demand for payment, van Dyck, July 8, 1660, *ER1*, 265, and see 266.

34. For gambling with wages, see Bond of Hoogeboom, February 2, 1661, *ER3*, 53; Ord. sess., May 19, 1654, *CRB*, 148; Ord. sess., July 15, 1653, *CRB*, 74; Ex. sess., October 15, 1654, *CRB*, 183, and Ex. sess., June 19, 1653, *CRB*, 71; Deposition on theft of canoe, March 7, 1661, *ER3*, 57.

35. "Deposition . . . respecting a quarrel between Eldert Gerretsz Cruyf and Nicolaes Meyer," June 9, 1661, *ER3*, 67–9.

36. Ord. sess., September 30, 1669, *CRA*, 101; Ex. sess., July 16, 1670, *CRA*, 168–9; Ord. sess. May 9, 1672, *CRA*, 300.

37. A. Th. Van Deursen, *Het kopergeld van de Gouden Eeuw: Volkskultuur* (Amsterdam, 1978), 2:40, and see 46.

Figure 2.2. A. van Ostade, *The Dancing Couple in an Inn.* Courtesy of the Rijksmuseum, Amsterdam.

the excise on beer and spirits, well aware of the greater quantities tapped in *handelstijd* and the risk of brawling and uncontrolled insult to itself. In 1660, an abusive and intoxicated trader publicly "beat some of the magistrates," and, on other occasions, a magistrate's sayings were held up to public ridicule, the court itself abused as unlawful, and members of the council of New Netherland called "rogues" and "talebearers." As this sort of behavior was intolerable, the court multiplied its sittings, meeting in more frequent extraordinary sessions. In July 1674, it sat daily. Paced by the rushed momentum of *handelstijd* – hearing cases originating outside Beverwijck and serving New Amsterdam creditors suing within its jurisdiction – the court's control was as uncertain of holding as the unspoken rules of the season itself. Outside *handelstijd*, it was accustomed to moments of ritualized mockery and disobedience.[38] But in this season, the disorder moved toward defiance.

38. "The Governors Confirmacon . . . touching farming out ye Grand Excize at Albany, September 14, 1671," Victor Hugo Palsits, ed., *Minutes of the Executive Council of the Province of New York: Administration of Francis Lovelace, 1668–1673, Volume II: Collateral and Illustrative Documents 20–90 (Albany, 1910)* 551; Ord. sess., Sep-

For most townsmen it was enough just to stay in the game in Beverwijck. But for the principal *handelaars* – "the king of the marksmen" and the powerful runners-up – the risks of *handelstijd* were run in two locations: Beverwijck and New Amsterdam.

From late July to mid-October, a Beverwijck trader wanted his pelts at the Manhattans either for sale there or transshipment to Holland, for the beaver trade opened there in August, when the ships arrived from the Netherlands. Even more than the activities of preparing for the arrival of the natives and then bartering with them in Beverwijck, these functions required deft attention to timing. A man had to calculate the short turn-around time of the merchantmen berthed before Fort Amsterdam and satisfy the skippers who chafed at remaining more than five weeks and certainly expected to set sail by late October. A trader had to prepare goods for shipment and receive overseas merchandise, some of it for the next year's *handelstijd*. So, while the small traders of Beverwijck either bartered their furs there, consigned them to one of the town's *handelaars* for shipment, or in the case of a few, peddled them across Long Island and into New England, principal merchants found New Amsterdam to be a giant wharf with rituals that had to be mastered.[39]

Van Rensselaer had the best of both these worlds. When possible, as in 1657 and 1658, he lodged with Oloff Stevensz van Cortlandt in New Amsterdam, paying gl 18 a week while supervising the loading of cargoes on such vessels as the *Blue Dove*, the *Otter*, and the *Spotted Cow*. He was like his father: fussing about bottomry charges, checking captains' logs, and keeping records of it all.[40] He was able to reside in the port because his brother Jan Baptiste could manage the requirements of "the game" in the *colonie* and Beverwijck. In 1659, he again divided his time between Beverwijck and New Amsterdam, traveling downriver but arranging to be in Beverwijck in mid-July for an auction of valuable commodities.[41]

Upriver at Beverwijck, *handelstijd* peaked from mid-July to October. The elements that had made the marksmen's combat dangerous now

tember 14, 1660, *CRB*, 298; Memorandum [August 19, 1657], *ER1*, 246; JvR to JBvR, July 31, 1674, *Corr JvR*, 469; see Ex. sess., January 2, 1677/8, *CRA*, 288, for mockery of the court officials.

39. See, for example, JvR to David Becker, October [?], 1656, *Corr JvR*, 30; Ex. sess., August 8, 1658, *CRB*, 146, and see 148.

40. JvR to Jan T. van Wely, May 22, 1657, *Corr JvR*, 47, JvR to OvCortlandt, June 25, 1657, *Corr JvR*, 53, 54; Rychart van Rensselaer (hereafter RvR) to JvR, April 22, 1659, *Corr JvR*, 149.

41. JvR to AvR, May 8, 1659, *Corr JvR*, 156; see JBvR to JvR, August 9, 1657, *Corr JvR*, 53; Auction, July 16, 1659, *ER1*, 249. Jan Baptiste may have bid for him, of course.

multiplied in the contests of public auctions and a profusion of risky individual deals. For the competitors at auctions, there was the same gamble for prizes and reputation, and the knowledge that the contest would not come again for a year. For the onlookers, there was the chance to see them gambling on the knowledge each had of the other. The auctions focused, in time and space and staged performance, the contest of skills that made *handelstijd* – and the town – work.

The Auctions

Auctions were sales of merchandise with payment to be made in furs or seawan. They took place at taverns *(herbergen)*. In Beverwijck, any one of eleven houses might have been the venue.[42] Here townspeople lured to the auction played the role called for by the occasion. They were the *herbergvolk*, people of drink and derring-do, gossip and gambling, and contests of physical strength. Churchmen thought that the inns brought people to business transactions that were evil, foolhardy, prankish, and contemptible. But "the men," wrote one Dutch scholar, "liked to gamble, and always with money."[43]

Merchandise was often bulky and may have been displayed in the rear of the licensee's property. Or it may have been "exposed for sale" – as townsmen put it – where bidding took place, in the room reached immediately from the *stoep*. One innkeeper's place, that of Gabriel Thomsz, was able to accommodate more than one hundred men and women in 1689. However, the size of an inn was more likely 18 by 25 feet with easy room for thirty people, like the eight to ten persons playing ninepins, two at backgammon, fifteen or sixteen bowling or drinking in a New Amsterdam establishment in 1663.[44] Whatever the case, the *herbergier* plied the assembly with drink and billed the vendors. Costs could be high. One vendor faced either paying a bill for "gl 35 for auction fees, gl 13 for commissions, gl 12 for brandy consumed and gl 18 for beer" or submitting to "apprehension of his person." Perhaps such risks re-

---

42. For auctions in inns, see Auction [August 23, 1654], *ER1*, 191, 194, and 220, Ord sess., December 30, 1649, *CRB*, 102, and Ord. sess., September 2, 1669, *CRA*, 97; the eleven houses were those of Adriaen Appel, Hendrick Bierman, Pieter Bronck, Willem Fredericksz Bout, Long Mary (Goosens) Willem Gysbertsz, Marcelis Janse, Rut Jacobsz, Hendrick Jochemsz, Jan Joosten, Barent Pietersz, and possibly Cornelis Hendricksz. For Long Mary's Inn in New Amsterdam, see Kenneth Scott, "New Amsterdam's Taverns and Tavernkeepers: III," *de halve maen* (October, 1964), 39:13.
43. Van Deursen, *Het kopergeld: Volkskultuur*, 2:52; 45.
44. Auction, February 5, 1655, *ER1*, 221; At a convention, November 12, 1689, *DHNY*, II, 125; Gerald R. Baum, "The New Netherland Tavern: II," *de halve maen* XLVIII (January, 1974), 48:11, and see Minutes of June 26, 1663, *RNA*, 4:264.

minded participants of the popular Dutch axiom "Buy and sell in an inn but be prepared to pay the piper within twenty-four hours."[45]

A placard announced the auction and was customarily posted by the vendor three weeks before the sale. Roelof Janse and Lambert Cornelis, for example, announced the arrival of heavy clothing and building materials and its forthcoming sale at a tavern on August 23, 1654. They also arranged to have a placard displayed.[46] Beverwijck placards from the period have not been preserved, but they would have been similar in form to those of Amsterdam, though handscripted where those of the metropolis were generally printed. They described items for sale in the customary mix of detail and exaggeration – a ship "extraordinarily well-canvased," or a cloak "exposed for sale a second time." Some pictured the goods.[47] But all carried a formula that asked readers in Amsterdam and Beverwijck to further advertise the sale – pass it along! (*segget voort*). Auctions took place throughout the day. The house auctioned in Beverwijck on a Monday at "two o'clock in the afternoon" would seem unexceptional.[48]

On August 23, the actors assembled for Janse's and Cornelis's auction. The Company's *commis*, Johannes Dyckman, arrived to record the sales and confront the vendors with the Company's charges at the conclusion, that is, a tax on imports sold. At the appropriate time, the auctioneer (who was not always a vendor) probably followed the style of house auctions and read the conditions and terms of sale to the bystanders. Janse and Cornelis stipulated payment in beaver and within twenty-four hours. There were twenty-six successful buyers on sixty-one items or sets of items offered. Unfortunately it is impossible to know how many townspeople might have been present. However, the twenty-six buyers were one-quarter of the 105 men and women who designated themselves as traders in 1660. Janse and Cornelis realized gl 377.08 (47.5 beaver). Four other men, auctioning items like guns, a casket inlaid with ebony, and clothing and tools realized gl 514.17.[49]

At almost the same time, a placard was circulating for an auction at Pieter Bronck's tavern, and thirteen days later, Gerrit Teunisse van

45. Ord. sess., September 4, 1657, *CRB*, 72, 73; Van Deursen, *Het kopergeld: Volkskultuur*, 2:47.
46. See auction [August 23, 1654], *ER1*, 191 and 194; see also, Ord. sess., February 17, 1650, *CRB*, 106.
47. See Placards of July 30, 1660, and July 5, 1694, Handel en Nijverheid. Veilingen van Schepen, scheepsonderdelen, scheepsparten (Commerce and Industry. Public Auctions of Ships, ship accessories, ship fittings) File N51.01, GA.
48. See Placards for July 30, 1660, July 5, 1694, October 15, 1725, and March 2, 1733, ibid.; for examples in Beverwijck, see Ord. sess., December 30, 1649, and February 17, 1650, *CRB*, 102, 106.
49. Auction [August 23, 1654], *ER1*, 190–2.

Vechten auctioned household goods, including pictures and books as well as items of considerable expense. Unlike Janse's and Cornelis's auction, only leading merchants were successful competitors. Twenty-six men, including Cornelis Steenwyck of New Amsterdam, bought wares to the amount of gl 386.90 and paid "good whole beaver or half-beavers."[50]

During *handelstijd* of 1658, Pieter Pietersz van Nesten, Jan de Groot, and Bastiaen de Winter auctioned merchandise. Pietersz was in town to offer a fully rigged, fully equipped sloop on behalf of a New Amsterdam wholesaler. De Groot chose July 22 for his auction and wanted payment in beaver within eight days. He sold an ordinary assortment of merchandise – shovels, old coats, women's stockings, jugs, hats, and cravats – to thirty-eight men and women for gl 364.1. Prominent traders stayed away, but two Englishmen attended and bought clothing.[51] De Winter's auction on September 23 fell within Beverwijck's celebrations of· *kermis* (Amsterdam fair days). He sold furniture and clothing, netted gl 844.11 and demanded payment within twenty-four hours in seawan rather than beaver – perhaps because most pelts would by then have been shipped to New Amsterdam or bartered away. Forty to fifty leading traders bid against each other for a miscellany of wares. None of the small traders or artisans competed, perhaps because seawan was scarce in 1658.[52]

Auctions of merchandise after 1658 and into 1664 continued to pit townsmen against one another. On July 10, a Tuesday in 1659, Jan Claesz (Backer) sold black hats and furniture, leaving with pledges of gl 73.15. He was an unimportant man whose hats (if they kept them) sat on the heads of equally unimportant burghers.[53] Pieter Claerbout's auction was of a different sort. He arranged it for five days after Claesz's and about sixteen days after the arrival of his own merchandise from Manhattan. The delivery of the goods had brought its own difficulties. The captain of the vessel on which it arrived had allegedly let two chairs and a lamp blow overboard, and Claerbout had refused to pay the full freight charges. He had some reason to worry about the safety of his goods. First, his expenses were considerable, with auction and freight charges amounting to 22 percent of his gl 500.08 profit. Second, his wares were luxury items such as gold rings, porcelain, curtains with valances, pictures, expensive coats, and mantels. Twenty-one men bought his merchandise, but unlike those who bid for Claesz's, they were leading merchants. Jan de Kuyper

50. Public sales [September 2, 1654], *ER1*, 194; Auction, September 5, 1654, *ERI*, 206.
51. Sale of sloop [ca. May 1658], *ER4*, 28, 29; Auction, July 22, 1658, *ER4*, 54, 55; 53, 54.
52. Auction, September 23, 1658, *ER4*, 78–80.
53. Public sale, July 10, 1659, *ER4*, 112.

from New Amsterdam attended and successfully outbid Beverwijck merchants for three porcelain cups. Two years before, he had sent 2,000 beaver to the Manhattans, that is, fur valued at gl 16,000 in North America but gl 57,000 in Europe.[54] Abraham Staats was also in the competition. He remained the highest bidder on a black mantel, a picture, and a child's petticoat, pledging gl 48.05. In 1657, he sent to New Amsterdam twice the number of de Kuyper's pelts. He paid the export tax of two stivers on each of 4,400 pelts valued at gl 35,200 in New Netherland or gl 125,400 in Europe. Tuenisse Cornelisse (Bos) won the bid for a silk coat (gl 14) and an expensive black coat (gl 32). He was a prominent trader whose fortunes were already in jeopardy, and by 1664, he had died. The *handelaars* who were his associates in the trade, however, continued to participate in the auctions. In *handelstijd* of 1664, one of them conducted an auction for Dirck Janse Croon. Janse had received a large consignment and offered household goods of consistently high quality, such as copperware, pewter, pictures, and almanacs.[55] Twenty-seven burghers made successful bids, agreeing to pay whole beaver or beaver at gl 22 per beaver within thirty days. Janse received gl 427.05.

In structure, the *handelstijd* auctions were like others conducted throughout the year, those of a ship, a house lot, the slaughter excise, a deceased estate or "grain standing in the field."[56] Each of them made visible the power structure of the town and an individual's location within it. The auctioneer who opened the bid on a deceased townsman's estate effectually instructed everyone present about the rich and poor men of the town, the aspiring and the bankrupt. And it is clear that, in the cases we have been examining, auctions visibly sorted out the burghers of great and little substance. Those who were commoners stayed away from auctions like Claerbout's and de Winter's – or, more likely, attended but remained silent. On the other hand, the prosperous *handelaars* failed to grace Janse's and Cornelis's sales.

Auctions also taught the burghers that no man or woman was above the continual public examination – and occasional humiliation – that

54. Ex. sess., June 13, 1659, *CRB*, 196; Auction, July 16, 1659, *ER1*, 249–50; for Dyckman's recording of the pelts, see *ER1*, 244, and for the different purchase price of beaver pelts in North America and Europe, see David W. Mulholland, "Dutch Yankees and English Patroons," *de halve maen* (April 1984) 58:4, 48.
55. Auction of Claerbout, July 16, 1659, *ER1*, 249–50; Memoranda of Dyckman [1657], *ER1*, 244; Auction, August 15, 1559, *ER1*, 273; Auction [May 1–14, 1664], *ER1*, 350, 351. Staats and de Kuyper were captains of river vessels and may have been freighting the furs of others as well as themselves. Nonetheless, they were prominent traders.
56. See Ord. sess., September 4, 1657, *CRB*, 72.

town life generated. Van Rensselaer, for example, regularly put his movable property on the market. In 1654, the items were personal belongings,
that is, clothing of his brothers in Holland. One has to think of the "cloth
suits" of Nicolaes and Rychart "exposed for sale," commented on by
the *herbergvolk*, perhaps knocked down for a mean price, and worn by
a fellow townsman. In this sense, the same system that expanded acces-
sibility of goods also had a socially leveling effect – and this, in appearance
if not in substance, was what all traders wanted. Finally, auctions reinforced a *burgherlijk* society by bringing people into the central streets of
the town. Unlike auctions of farm stock, which, in agricultural communities, served to shift the focus away from the main streets of towns
to the rural peripheries, these sales marked the town itself as the site
where the risking of the town's assets and values took place.[57]

Taken solely as financial transactions, the auctions were small change.
The amounts spent were of little consequence, and even the sums realized
by the vendors usually ranged below gl 500. The large merchants relied
on their own brokers for merchandise. Their purchases at auctions were
useful but supplementary. For example, one week before Gerrit Teunise
realized gl 386.90 at his auction, Philip Pietersz Schuyler privately paid
gl 2,562 to Juriaen Thysen van Amsterdam for goods received.[58] Such
larger transactions and deeper risk takings had their own theater – in
private meetings, at the strand beyond the south gate, at the end of
journeys to Holland. "Walking in the woods" caught it all.

Walking in the Woods

Trading was risk in a more fundamental sense than the jeopardizing of
finances. Each man put his values at risk as he activated them in the
trade. The community did the same, risking its structure of values in the
annual enactments that corporately set it to trading in furs. In *handelstijd*
of 1660, the community did this as dramatically as it would at any time
in the seventeenth century. At one point in the twelve weeks that marked
the most violent period, one townsman called eighty of his fellows "a
rabble." They took him to mean that they did not "live decently." He
might have more honestly acknowledged that neither they nor his own
faction of twenty-five traders were living decently.[59] For each group was

57. AvR to JvR, December 26, 1654, *Corr JvR*, 14. For farm auctions, see John R. Walton,
    "The Rise of Agricultural Auctioneering in Eighteenth- and Nineteenth-Century Brit-
    ain," *Journal of Historical Geography* (January 1984), 10:16.
58. Receipt, August 29, 1654, *ER1*, 196.
59. Ex. sess., June 17, 1660, *CRB*, 267.

threatening the essential order of the trading town – which was what decent living was all about.

The court itself set the stage for the competition of what eventuated as two factions. At the commencement of *handelstijd*, it literally took bids on how the trade would be conducted during the summer. It put the fur trade to public auction. Should legal trading, it asked, continue to be conducted solely within the palisades, that is, conducted at licensed merchants' stalls and warehouses? As in ancient market towns, these were sites for which towns collected stallage fees and where competition was visibly ordered by the proximity of traders in a quarter or set of streets, even as it was along Handlaarstraat in Beverwijck. Or did "the majority of the community" wish to legalize walking in the woods, that is, the practice of traders and "brokers" – men and women hired to act for traders – bartering with native customers in the woods surrounding the town?[60] The matter involved the structure of trading and therefore called into consideration the structure of the town itself. It called for consideration of the balance between town and countryside. Townsmen were being asked what they wished to make of the marginal, and always dangerous, area just outside the palisades. They were being asked whether they wished to diminish the town by moving vital action outside its walls.

Two written responses came forward immediately. One was the petition of twenty-five principal *handelaars*, warning that "Christians" were "again about to run into the woods as brokers in order by subreptive [subversive?] and improper ways to get the trade entirely into their hands." This had to be prevented. The space around the town, they implied, belonged to them and under no circumstances was it to be a place of uncontrolled forestalling by Christians – that is, all manner of townsmen – who were determined to be in the trade. Actually, these were Christians still feeling the injustices of *handelstijd* in 1659, still plagued by poverty, and deeply resentful of the principal *handelaars*. The petitioners were well aware of this. So they made a bid, gambling that poverty would exclude all but themselves: Only Indians employed by traders as brokers should be allowed to barter outside the town.[61]

Within two days, forty-eight Christians had heard of the *handelaars*'s bid and offered their own. They signed a petition on behalf of themselves and thirty-two others. Let "everyone be allowed to do the best he can," they argued, with townsmen and native servants entering the trade. In that way, "many a poor person could earn a beaver and the community

60. Ex. sess., May 31, 1660, *CRB*, 256.
61. Ex. sess., May 25, 1660, *CRB*, 255; 255.

would be better served." As the court recorder put it, they requested "that the trade may be thrown open."⁶²

The magistrates had made the issue a public one. In fact, they had their own contest with the Company going on. The Company's standing rule about the trade of the staple (fur) was consistent with tradition: It would be carried on within the fort and the town, where surveillance (and profits) could be assured. Forestalling was bad for business, and Johannes La Montagne as the Company's *commis* and *schout* intended to prevent it. But it was not bad for the members of the court. They were principal *handelaars*, with as little respect for the Company's surveillance and profit taking as for the interloping and profit-snatching Christians. They wanted the town's control of the staple and were now gambling that the potential for violence for which they had provocatively set the stage would break the Company's will and give the town's magistrates control of the trade before the agitation seriously divided the community. The ruling that the five magistrates gave the community on May 31 regarding the two petitions further provoked unrest. They rejected the first petition, ignored the second, and put forward an opinion sought from the Company, with the knowledge that it would satisfy no one: All trade would be conducted within the town, with allowance for those who wished to beckon natives to their stalls by standing "on the hill" (Jonckheerstraat) or go "to the strand where the Indians arrive."⁶³

Within days of the court's ruling, the woods around the town exploded into violence as men and women made their own decisions about the conduct of the trade. In an area densely forested and bristling with *kreupelbosch* (thickets), townsmen "walked in the woods" or "roamed on horseback," moving "up and down" in the woodlands and along the Schenectady road. They ambushed natives, bribed them to trade or, more frequently, robbed them. They molested them by "kicking, beating and assaulting" them at will. Some they "beat severely with fists and... [drove] out of the woods." Breaking up the bargaining of a trader with a native, "ten or twelve of them [would] surround an Indian and drag him along, saying 'Come with me, so and so has no goods.' " At hidden trading places, natives robbed traders, while Dutch brokers violently drove natives "hither and thither" telling them lies about the merchants they "represented." Men went into the woods with guns and knives. They also went in with canoes, skiffs, and sloops. They enacted in the woods a lawlessness toward natives and each other that the magistrates

62. Ex. sess., June 17, 1660, *CRB*, 268; 267; 266.
63. Ex. sess., May 31, 1660, *CRB*, 256.

were barely managing to control within the palisades. The weeks became, the court acknowledged, "dangerous times."[64]

The violence of the woods immediately reached into the courtroom itself. By June 17, the magistrates had heard eight cases of illegal walking in the woods. It was an unprecedented rehearsal of lawlessness. Nothing like it had occurred in the previous eight years, and in 1659 – a year of mounting antagonism between small traders and *handelaars* – only three cases had arisen.

The court heard suits brought by the *schout*, La Montagne, against eight townsmen. Seven of them appeared on June 15, facing thirteen witnesses who had answered summonses and were now required to offer testimony. Four of the suits were against prominent townsmen. Eight townsmen testified against them, six of whom were also principal *handelaars*. Two of the signers of the second petition also acted as informers. But one of these, David Janse, was himself tried the same day. Four men who signed the petition of the small traders also faced La Montagne's suits and his demand for fines of gl 300 and suspension of trading rights for two months. Against them, La Montagne brought the testimony of ten informants, six of them wealthy *handelaars* and four lesser traders.

Yet if La Montagne won his fines, the court won the day; for, as was intended, the cases showed him that a wide cross section of the community was determined to break the law rather than comply with the Company's restrictive ordinances regarding the trade. Lawlessness existed in all directions and would continue to do so as long as the Company denied control of the trade to the town. The court, in fact, now prolonged and intensified the violent disorder. First, it accepted the innocence of six of the eight accused men, although there was strong evidence of their guilt, and it allowed the seventh man twenty-four hours to reconsider an earlier admission of guilt and "purge himself under oath." The eighth man, Jan Harmensz, had signed with the Christians and was the first man La Montagne had charged. He was carefully interrogated but refused to purge himself and was fined.[65] Only in his case could the community see justice done.

The court now decided to rule on the petition of the Christians. However, it handed down an overtly irresponsible judgment, one that was a further invitation to disregard the law. There were, it ruled, "dangerous consequences" to allowing men "to go into the woods as brokers." Consequently, it could not support the petition. On the other hand, the strict

64. Ex. sess., June 15, 1660, *CRB*, 269; 268; 269; Ex. sess., July 15, 1660, *CRB*, 285; Ex. sess., June 12, 1660, *CRB*, 262; Ord. sess., July 13, 1660, *CRB*, 278.
65. Ex. sess., May 31, 1660, *CRB*, 256; Ex. sess., June 15, 1660, *CRB*, 265; 263.

prevention of such practices was "causing greater mischief." "It is therefore left to the discretion of the petitioners to do or not to do it [fore-
stalling], the court protesting meanwhile its innocence of all mischief that
may result therefrom, the more so as some of the petitioners have said
that they would do it anyway, whether it was permitted or not."[66]

There is no doubt in my mind that, with this carefully worded ruling
of June 17, the court added significant pages to a record it had been
deliberately inscribing since May 25. There was now a carefully constructed, twenty-page narrative of the events that absolved the court of
responsibility for the uncontrollable chaos in the trade; it was its written
defense against the existence of disorder. The court had made concessions
to the commonalty but only to prevent greater mischief and because the
Company's ordinances were unworkable. When the level of current violence would become unacceptable and the Company, in the person of
Stuyvesant, be forced to investigate, then the carefully solicited petitions
and the court record would show that 105 townsmen opposed the Company's policy in one way or another, with 73 of them prepared to identify
themselves by name. It would also show the court's own "innocence of
all mischief" – and its unwillingness to enforce justice except on its own
terms, that is, by controlling the trade.[67]

By July 20, Stuyvesant was in Beverwijck. Some townsmen must have
known that he intended to meet natives at nearby Esopus in early July
and would continue on to Beverwijck, and in any case, his visits to the
town were predictable. Meanwhile, lawlessness had escalated, and its
record had lengthened. The minutes now contained the angry and threatening complaints to the court from representatives of the abused natives.
As expected, the "Maquas" spoke bitterly of their mistreatment in the
woods. The court secretary now had their detailed reproaches to inscribe
in the records. Equally important for the Company's official to read and
consider, the natives were questioning the authority of masters who allowed such ruthless treatment and threatening attacks like those being
carried out by another tribe near Esopus. The court placated them with
lies about imposing order.[68]

Stuyvesant read the records. He also heard and examined a wider set
of complaints. These were the accusations of La Montagne against ten

66. Ex. sess., June 17, 1660, CRB, 268.
67. The court also kept a "Minuytboeck" that is not extant (CRB 152, n. 26; Ex. sess.,
    June 17, 1668, CRB, 268; for the town's petitions to farm the excise, see March 17,
    1654, CRB, 127, and for conflict with de Dekker, Ord. sess., February 1, 1656,
    CRB, 249.
68. Appointment to accompany Stuyvesant, July 5, 1660, DRCH, 13:178, 179. For his
    predictable visits, see also JvR to Stuyvesant [April 7, 1659], Corr JvR, 143, and Ord.
    sess., January 6, 1654, CRB, 94; Ex. sess., June 17, 1660, CRB, 268; 268; 268; 269.

traders brought to trial on July 15 and the defendants' countercomplaints about trading under the Company's ordinances. Again the record would show the court to be the diligent but helpless auctioneer. On the morning of July 14, the secretary recorded that the court had authorized four of its members to make an inspection of the woods and fine all traders and Dutch brokers found there. That afternoon they discovered ten law-breakers who were tried the next day. Seven of the ten defendants were leading merchants, and two men, Rut Jacobsz and Andries Herpertsz, were members of the court. Taken as a whole, the day's hearings were a recitation of the complete disorder of the trading system, with each man setting his own rules.[69]

Some excuses for being in the woods were a mockery of the court. Paulus Janse said he was not in the woods to attract the savages with beaver but to pick blueberries. Cornelis Fynhout was looking for hogs. (In 1659, when tried for a similar offence, he was simply trying to catch horses.) Others offered explanations that held the court and the Company up to ridicule and showed that the trade was a free-for-all. Willem Brouwer, a leading merchant prosecuted by La Montagne on June 15, admitted sending a servant to forestall but blamed the crime on the corruption of the court and the council of New Netherland. Magistrate Rut Jacobsz, he charged, had assured him that La Montagne actually "did not wish to have anything to do with the matter" of forestalling and that "going into the woods was free." "I have already sent my servant into the woods," he reported Jacobsz saying: "You can do as you like." Others pledged they would break the law as long as violators among the wealthy *handelaars* went unpunished. So Marcelis Janse had sent his servant only to tell him "at once" if the "servants of Rut Jacobsz, Andries Herpertsz and Philip Pietersz Schuyler were in the woods." Adrian Janse van Leyden reminded the magistrates that they allowed the servants of those men to go "openly into the woods" and, on that grounds, he had sent his servant as well. Now the fear of being an informer was gone. Philip Pietersz coolly stated that he sent a man to the woods but "only to see what sort of Dutchmen were in the woods" and not "to get Indians with beavers." He was the trader who had summarized the ambiguity of the situation the year before: "Not a single beaver is bartered in the Fuyck but it is done contrary to the ordinances."[70]

In this cacophonous recital of wrongdoing, the town made Stuyvesant hear and read its latest bid for greater control over the fur trade. The

69. Ex. sess., July 15, 1600, *CRB*, 281; 278; see 278, 281.
70. Ex. sess., July 15, 1660, *CRB*, 278; 281; 280; Ex. sess., June 13, 1659, *CRB*, 192; 279; 280; 281; for fear of being an informer, see Ord. sess., July 17, 1657, 60; 281; for Schuyler's remark, see Ord. sess., June 10, 1659, *CRB*, 191.

gamble seems to have paid off. Publicly Stuyvesant published a placard reinforcing the past ordinances and reaffirming that "no one...shall... send any Christians or Indians as brokers into the woods." Trade in fur, he implied, would be conducted as trade in any staple was conducted in the Netherlands: within town walls and with a monopoly to the highest authority, customarily the municipality but, in this case, the Company.[71] However, in practice Stuyvesant's *commis* at Fort Orange brought no further prosecutions against principal merchants. La Montagne did bring three men to trial, but two of them were notorious trouble makers and openly contemptuous of him. The *stadhuis* (townhall) and not the fort was beginning to be the place where the business of trading in furs was being conducted. The independence of the town from the Company was closer at hand.

Everyone knew what walking in the woods meant: It was trading for the sake of one's livelihood. Paulus Janse was not in the woods to pick blueberries, and no one would have thought him to be. Janse was, in fact, a man convicted of smuggling brandy to natives two years earlier. He was in the woods, as he was into smuggling, for his livelihood. All would also have known that Jan Thyssen, during the same week when he was trading illegally with the natives, was forced to mortgage his house in default of a debt of gl 197. The four magistrates went into the woods on May 14 to get control of the trade for the town (and, consequently, themselves) and no one would have thought otherwise. The game was another round in the court's match with the fort's *commis* for autonomy. The cases of the previous five years make that clear. In one case, *commis* Johannes de Dekker had demanded a gl 1,000 fine and the court allowed gl 25; in another, gl 300 and the court determined on gl 10. In others, he asked for gl 100 and the decision was for gl 25, or he sought a sentence of whipping but the court preferred "leniency to the rigor of justice" and mitigation of the sentence.[72]

La Montagne raided into the woods to make his profits. Others made profits by taking cover and avoiding him. The *handelaars* walked in the woods (or sent servants) to maintain their primacy in an always shaky market. In their own words, they were indifferent to the plight of ordinary traders and wholly concerned for losses they would experience from what they called "the utter ruination of Fort Orange and the village of Bev-

71. Ordinance, July 22, 1660, *CRB*, 282.
72. Ex. sess., June 12, 1660, *CRB*, 261; Ex. sess., June 15, 1660, *CRB*, 265, 266; Ord. sess., November 30, 1655, *CRB*, 238, 239, 240, 244; "gratia voor rigour van justitie gekozen" was a common formula in the Low Countries (see Van Deursen, *Het kopergeld van de Gouden Eeuw: Volk en overheid* [Amsterdam, 1979] 3:38).

erwijck." Their intention was to retain the woods in its useful marginality. They needed ethically ambiguous spaces as much as others did.

The woods had its undiscoverable recesses but was never described as a place of terror. It was not the "wast[e] and howling wilderness" that New England ministers called up to arouse piety.[73] Rather, it was like the other hidden recesses that Dutch men and women made a place for in their lives: iron-bound money boxes, unfinalized figures in ledgers and municipal treasury accounts, "confused...pieces" of government, recurrent warnings in correspondence that "this is for your information," secret tables of interest, possession of New Netherland in notable quiet, and faces always half-turned away from the English after 1664. Moreover, Beverwijck's woods were like the liminal areas found just beyond walls of each Dutch trading city or town at home. There, anxiety about such places was expressed often enough to suggest that no city escaped the brigandage and violence they called forth. The magistrates of Haarlem, for example, recognized that just outside the northern defense canal there was "much disorder and mischief," not only by night, when the gates of the city were closed, but at all times. Earlier, the Catholics of Lille had looked on as close to a thousand Protestants held nightly meetings in the fields outside the walls and otherwise placid citizens menaced the gatekeepers for allowing such infidels to sneak back, one by one, within the walls.[74]

But 1660 was a season when participants were required to reflect on what trading in the woods meant. The *handelaars* were reflective in their petition. Their concern for its format – the listing of names carefully assembled along with the request and all set within margins where the word "fiat" would be written by an approving court – betrayed a desperate concern about trading. In its contents, they gave little away, obfuscating true intentions by use of invective. The Christians gave away more in their petition. The act of getting it drawn up was a daring move in itself, nevertheless, thirty-seven men wrote their names, twelve signed with a mark, and an additional thirty-one made it known that the petition represented them. In wording the petition, they reminded the court (and themselves) of the general rules of trading in the Netherlands: The fatherland existed because of the strength of its free (privileged) communities, where even the "least" burghers had as much right as others to freedom

73. Nadhorth to Morrice, October 26, 1666, DRCH III, 139.
74. William Temple, *Observations upon the United Provinces of the Netherlands* (London, 1673), 108; see JBvR to JvR, September 4, 1659, *Corr. JvR*, 150; Van Gogh to Estates General, November 7, 1664, *DRCH*, 3:80; Gerald L. Burke, *The Making of Dutch Towns: A Study in Urban Development from the Tenth to the Seventeenth Centuries* (London, 1956), 137; Robert DuPlessis, Urban Stability in the Netherlands Revolution: A Comparative Study of Lille and Douai (Ph.D. diss, Columbia University, 1974) 631.

from oppression.[75] They were, they argued, "the least burghers," and "the community would be better served" if "many a poor person could earn a beaver."[76]

In this statement, the disadvantaged burghers might well have meant what they said about the benefits of earning a beaver. Considering a single factor like diet, it is clear that a beaver mattered greatly. Like that of other commoners in the seventeenth century, the diet of Beverwijck's townspeople consisted largely of carbohydrates. Bread and beer were major components. An adult probably required between two to two and a half pounds of bread daily. In Beverwijck in the 1650s, the cost of one pound of baked wheat bread was 24 stivers in seawan, making the daily cost for one adult 5.62 stivers. At the same time, a "whole merchantable beaver" was worth gl 8, with choice pelts fetching 9. In seawan, a pelt was worth between gl 21 and gl 26. Using the figure of gl 26, a pelt would buy one adult's bread for ninety-two days. Four pelts would satisfy the cost for a year. Even in the case of a family of five, where the woman baked her own bread, a beaver mattered. In 1658, wheat was selling at gl 14 the muddle or gl 4.7 the bushel. One adult is thought to have required sixteen bushels a year. For him alone, the cost would be gl 75.2 or 4.12 stivers daily. The family's daily cost would be 14.24 stivers. A beaver pelt worth gl 26 (520 stivers) would have met the basic bread requirement for 36.5 days. Ten would have furnished bread for the year.[77]

Calculations regarding diet offer some understanding of what a beaver meant for a family's or individual's well being. However, it was all the performances involved in earning the beaver that gave it its full meaning. The disadvantaged traders were entering a plea for the right to work. Like their counterparts in any number of Netherlands towns, they were reminding their town council of their right to earnings. Amsterdam painters, in wording a petition demanding the right to engage in "the honest and necessary earning of their bread especially in these costly times," had used the same formula as the traders were now employing. One Dutch official along the Delaware River had heard the petitions of the "poor inhabitants of the colony" and agreed that, if they were not allowed

75. See, for example of "fiat", *ER3*, 20; the petitioners would have paid 20 stivers per page to a notary and 30 stivers for a judgment (Minutes of January 28, 1658, *RNA*, 2:317). Two men who did not sign the petition but presented it were Gerrit Slictenhorst and Lambert Van Neck.

76. Ex. sess., June 17, 1660, *CRB*, 267.

77. For a study of diet and carbohydrate requirements, see Bettye Hobbs Pruitt, "Self-Sufficiency and the Agricultural Economy of Eighteenth-Century Massachusetts," *William and Mary Quarterly*, 3rd ser. (July 1984), 41:342, and see 340; for data useful for calculations about Beverwijck, see *inter alia*, Ord. sess., November 27, 1658, *CRB*, 166, 167; JvR to JBvR [September 4, 1659], *Corr JvR*, 175; JvR to OvCortlandt, November 23, 1658, *Corr JvR*, 113.

to "sell or barter liquor to the savages for Indian corn, meat or other things, they would perish from hunger and distress."[78]

The small traders openly defined themselves as poor by explicitly identifying themselves in opposition to the principal traders. Discourse that openly tied the poor to the rich was common among the Dutch. The prosperity of a city or town was recognized to be dependent upon the efforts of those whom van Rensselaer called in 1661 "little fellows," and "big people." A commentator in the Netherlands caught this antiphonal sort of harmony in his definition of commerce. "Commerce is," he wrote, "a treasure which is enriched by the industry of each."[79]

All their lives, the least burghers of Beverwijck would have experienced townsmen applying the force of that maxim. The trade in furs was – like the town space that they knew so well, the woods, and the natives that came to trade – a resource divided inequitably, but properly so. A townsman saw his place in the community every time furs were packed in casks along the riverside and loaded onto sloops for shipment to New Amsterdam. During *handelstijd*, the common people consigned their pelts to larger merchants, paying a commission to a man like van Rensselaer, who would procure a sloop and arrange for the loading of pelts already layered in marked cases (Figure 2.3). Van Rensselaer usually included a list of the case's contents with the furs. He registered them by beginning, as he said, with "those on top" and then noting the exact number of skins as they lay carefully divided by white papers marked with the name or initials of the consignor. In 1661, he sent his brother in Holland, Jan Baptiste, 246 whole beaver and 4 half beaver.[80] On Jan Baptiste's account were 151 whole and 2 half-beaver. Forty-eight were the property of trader Jan Hendricksz van Bael; 39 whole and 2 half pelts were those of trader Volkert Janse Douw, 5 belonged to Jan Thyssen, and three to Hendrick Ruer. Jan Baptiste's cargo was about 3 times that of Janse and Hendricksz, 30 times that of Thyssen, and 50 times that of Ruer. Hendricksz's was 9.6 times that of Thyssen and 16 times that of Ruer. Janse's was 7.8 times Thyssen's and 13 times that of Ruer. Averaging Hendricksz's and Janse's goods at 43.5 and Thyssen's and Ruer's at 4, Janse's and Hendricksz's consignments were 10 times the value of Thyssen's and Ruer's. The relative values of the consignments were not even close.

78. John Michael Montias, *Artists and Artisans in Delft: A Socio-Economic Study of the Seventeenth Century* (Princeton, 1982), 72; quoting J. J. Becker, "Preface," *ER3*, 19.
79. Ex. sess., June 17, 1660, *CRB*, 266; JBvR, October 17, 1661, *Corr JvR*, 272; Conversation of the Duke of Albermarle and Van Gogh, July 1664, cited in John Beresford, *The Godfather of Downing Street: Sir George Downing, 1623–1684, An Essay in Biography* (Boston, 1925), 182.
80. JvR to JBvR, August 25, 1660, *Corr JvR*, 231; JvR to JBvR, October 17, 1661, *Corr JvR*, 270, 271.

Figure 2.3. Nieu Amsterdam, engraved on copper. I. N. Phelps Stokes Collection, Miriam and Ira D. Wallach Division of Art, Prints, and Photographs, the New York Public Library. Astor, Lenox, and Tilden Foundations.

The white papers that so visibly divided the pelts into lucrative and seemingly insignificant bundles would, however, have made visible the divisions of economic power already known. Any one of the exporters, if asked to insert white papers at the proper places between the consignments, could have made a good approximation. For (setting van Rensselaer aside momentarily) Hendricksz and Janse were prominent traders and their known transactions over recent years would have put them well above Ruer or Thyssen. Indeed their combined assets would have been close to ten times the value of Ruer's and Thyssen's.[81]

81. For Thyssen and Douw, see List of contributions pledged to Stuyvesant for defense against the Mohawk, Ex. sess., June 18, 1654, *CRB*, 161–4. Douw was expected to contribute gl 160, whereas Thyssen's contribution was gl 12. The late 1650s were years when Thyssen had "no means of paying [debts] on account of his serious accident and prolonged illness" but was sued by ten burghers nonetheless. Still indebted, he mortgaged his house in 1658. See Ord. sess., June 25, 1658, *CRB*, 119, and Ord. sess., July 9, 1658, *CRB*, 126. Hendrick Ruer was in his early career in 1661 and inhabiting a house he had allowed to go unfinished in its construction for four years (see Ord. sess., November 27, 1657, *CRB*, 81).

Those smaller traders who sent only a few pelts, however, elaborated on their three or ten skins and made investment plans for them in the same way as the leading traders. The five pelts of Jan Thyssen were to be sold in Amsterdam and the profit laid out as passage for one or two farmhands. Jan Baptiste was to arrange it. If that option failed, Thyssen would expect Jan Baptiste to send linen, if it could be purchased at "13 or 14 stivers a year." Both Jeremias and Jan Baptiste added further elaboration to the transaction. Jeremias wrote Jan Baptiste a lengthy identification of Thyssen, suggesting the man might be someone he would remember – he had married a certain widow, he was diligent but beset by misfortunes, he "asks you to be kind enough" to give assistance. Jan Baptiste saw to the sale of the five pelts, at 6.25 Holland money the beaver. Paying 15.6 stivers the yard, he sent forty yards of linen. It left Holland in the spring of 1662, this time in a case with Jan Baptiste's "specified list ... at the top."[82] The linen was a small item among a more substantial consignment, just as his five pelts had been six months earlier. But then it would have been on a vessel in which, as smaller traders would have known, their merchandise "filled in the extra spaces," that is, those not booked to the larger firms and traders (*hoofdbevrachteren*).[83]

When the eighty burghers stated in 1660 that every man should be allowed to earn a beaver, they may have meant it in the literal sense, as we have seen. However, it also expressed the right of poorer townsmen like Thyssen to engage in the skills and pleasures the trading provided: the opportunity to exercise memory, the chance to send and receive consignments along the strand, the challenge of envisioning and manipulating a portfolio of investments. It meant waiting, comparing, complaining, fighting, appearing in court, marrying, farming, and finally, writing a will, all in terms of the trade.

The Season's End

During September, the whirl of trading continued as the natives spent their last weeks before preparing to depart. They were the burghers' cheap labor force but only the background, of course, in all the records of *handelstijd*. Although their culture intersected with that of the Dutch and although they created *handelstijd* as surely as the Europeans, their place in September of this chapter can be no more accurately constructed

82. JvR to JBvR, October 17, 1661, *Corr JvR*, 271; JBvR to JvR, [March 24, 1662], *Corr JvR*, 281; 281.
83. Rink, Merchants and Magnates, 270.

than it can be in any narrative about the town. How the natives were appropriated into Dutch settlers' understanding is virtually unrecorded.

Some parts of the record are explicit about the natives' presence in September. Especially their dependence is described, with concern about drunken savages expressed by both the court and themselves. Natives stressed their reliance on the Dutch because September and October were times when they conjured the Dutch for favors that would take them through to the next *handelstijd* – the ransom of a son from the French, the repair of castles, the provision of powder and guns. In return they shamed themselves for drinking: "we drink ourselves drunk; we cannot fight." They argued that, "when any one of . . . [our] people dies and one of the Dutch is his partner, he ought to give to the relatives of the deceased one or two suits of cloth." Yet in striking a note of accord, they had the sociology of European commerce all wrong. The magistrates listened. But in 1659, they responded to the natives' propositions with a provisional answer and gave them "50 guilders in seawan" – the value of one male adult's bread requirement for half a year.[84]

In the third week of September, the town celebrated Amsterdam *kermis*, a fair held in Amsterdam on the first Sunday after the feast of Saint Lambert and continued for two weeks for outsiders and three weeks for inhabitants. It was a "spectacle of wondrous strange things" to one self-styled, nineteenth-century wanderer, and a carnival of fools and drunks, freaks and tricksters to another. Its essence was danger and "time and money" (*"tijd en gelt"*).[85] We have no record of ordinances regulating townspeoples' activities during Amsterdam *kermis* in Beverwijck, but a placard of 1668 declaring that they were "sin[ning] badly" suggests parallels with Holland, where there were "abuses against good order . . . [with] gambling, loitering, rope-dancing . . . and other vanities."[86] In Beverwijck, the whole of *handelstijd* was something like the inversion that fairdays enacted in the great European cities. They became open cities where the walls, charters, and markets that ordinarily marked them as enclosed spaces now became invitations to participate. Beverwijck did not become an entirely open city during *kermis*. If it had, John Pynchon might well have arrived then and been a welcomed merchant rather than a pariah trying to parlay usefulness into trust. *Kermis* was not an invi-

84. See Ex. sess., September 6, 1659, *CRB*, 212, and also Ex. sessions of July 15 and July 28, 1660, *CRB*, 286, 288, 289; Ex. sess., September 6, 1659, *CRB*, 213.
85. *De Twee Beschouwende Vrienden, als Wandelaars op de Amsterdamsche Kermis, 1820* (Amsterdam, 1820), 1, 8; *De Amsterdamsche Kermis of Kluchtige Brieven over dee-zelve* [1] (Amsterdam, 1823), 6, 5.
86. Sale of house, May 1, 1655, *ER*1, 230; Van Deursen, *Het kopergeld: Volkskultuur*, 2:48.

tation to all strangers, but it was a period meant to be anticipated. In a carnivalesque way, it allowed a burgher to be levitous and rude while simultaneously reminding him of serious financial responsibilities. The court in 1654 gave a man "until [Amsterdam] fair" to build on his lot, whereas vendors expected second or third installments "next Amsterdam Fairday" and merchants extended credit "until the fair at Amsterdam."[87]

By mid-October, time was running out on the trade. The town began to have fewer residents. Most of the natives had gone. Beaver pelts were at their thinnest in autumn, so hunting would wait until the following spring. The New Amsterdam creditors whose names appeared with regularity in the records of earlier months had gone as well. Sloops were less available. A baker moved off to work as a farmhand in Schenectady until next *handelstijd*. Transients also paid their rents and moved away by November 1. A few men who had gambled on the viability of the town now requested house lots. Several burghers made journeys to the Netherlands. Between 1651 and 1665, forty-seven townspeople returned there at least once, with eight making more than one trip. Most traveled in August and September, but several waited until October.

The winter months of November through early spring left most of the trade behind. The season when the full range of the burghers' resources was tested was over. Now there was sleighing and skating, and one neighbor visiting another. Van Rensselaer described such visiting, but in words that merely conferred quiet on a practice that had occurred at a frenetic pace during *handelstijd*. The rituals of *handelstijd* made sense because they elaborated upon those of winter, when visiting was a practice within the ordinary rules of conduct, but when bartering beaver, auctioning, drinking, and "tap[ing] the whole night in spite of" the court went on as well.[88]

The economy was one of two seasons as well. Winter certainly closed in but not as dramatically as portrayed. Townsmen simply used the rivers and kills in different ways. The Hudson did not freeze over for long periods of time, not even for all of January and February. Nineteenth-century figures show that temperatures fluctuated considerably. Five days of freezing weather occurred one February, but otherwise mild weather often caused the melting of ice on the river and kills. Figures for 1845 to 1856 show that ice on the river broke up any time between February 24 (1845) to April 11 (1856). Often the adverse weather made river

---

87. Ord. sess., May 12, 1654, *CRB*, 145; see Announcement of auction, May 1, 1655, *ER1*, 230, and Announcement of auction, January 19, 1662, *ER1*, 299; Minutes of March 13, 1663, *RNA*, 4:213, and see 259.
88. Ex. sess., December 30, 1660, *CRB*, 312.

transport to New Amsterdam impossible in December, as it did in 1653.[89]
But the frozen waters and melting ice were eagerly utilized for logging.
By the first week of April, skippers expected to be hauling boards on the
river to New Amsterdam again.[90]

The braiding of liturgical, agricultural, and mercantile time was perhaps most noticeable in the winter and spring days. Each townsman
turned to his own multiple work tasks, traces of which were present even
during *handelstijd* – farmers traded while merchants attended to their
investments in sawmills, farms, sloops, woodlands, and pastures. Winter
also meant the building of houses and barns. The magistrates of 1657
thought that January offered "good and suitable" weather for erecting
a warehouse. Others preferred February: One contractor wanted a house
completed in three weeks; another stipulated that a builder use his own
sleigh and horses to begin a barn; a third offered a bonus of one whole
beaver if the builder completed a house in town by May l.[91] The building
activity of winter followed logically from the lively property auctions of
the previous November, but properties were taken up for the first time
by buyers in wintertime as well.[92]

Spring meant preparations for *handelstijd*. In early April of 1662, the
farmer of the excise arranged to be sent an extra seventy-eight barrels
of beer from New Amsterdam. In the same month, Jan Tomassz built a
shed to house the coming summer's native traders. In May 1655, local
bakers foresaw the influx of nonresident, seasonal bakers and (unsuccessfully) requested permission to form a guild to exclude them. Creditors
made the usual arrangements to be present for the first week of May.
Arent van Curler, whose peregrinations were often elusive, was in Beverwijck on May 7, 1658, suing for the recovery of a canoe. The court
tried to anticipate the crowds and disorder. In 1670, it ruled that no
more than "20, 25 or 30... [natives] may be lodged at one time" in the
trading season. It was time again for the extraordinary court session of
May 1, when the new magistrates would take their seats at the *stadhuis*
"after having been congratulated," and those retiring would be "discharged from their oaths and thanked for their good services."[93]

89. City Records, 1867, *CHA*, 2:73; Notes from the Newspapers, March 1865, *CHA*,
    3:237; JBvR to JvR, December [?], 1653, *Corr JvR*, 11.
90. Memoranda of Dyckman, 1657, *ER1*, 245.
91. Ord. sess., January 7, 1653, *CRB*, 47; Contract, February 28, 1679/80, *ER3*, 471;
    Contract, October 18, 1678, *ER3*, 463; Contract, November 27, 1683, *ER3*, 566.
92. See, for example, Ord. sess., January 6, 1654, *CRB*, 94.
93. Check the following for Teunisse: Contract, May 20, 1673, *CRB*, 407; Contract, April
    6, 1662, *CRB*, 150; Ord. sess., April 17, 1657, *CRB*, 28; Ord. sess., May 9, 1655,
    CRB, 219; Ord. sess., May 7, 1658, *CRB*, 111; Resolution to draft a revival of the
    ordinances, Ord. sess., May 26, 1670, *CRA*, 148; Ex. sess., May 1, 1660, *CRB*, 250.

Handelstijd made the year *burgerlijk*. It is true that, alongside the liturgical, agricultural, and trading year, men and women had countless devices for marking time. One man made use of comparison, matching his first year in the valley with his present circumstances. Another man gained a sense of continuity with the 1630s from the annual practice of paying rents in January and February. A third man used his association with a fellow townsman as a device for segmenting time. He knew the man, he said, "many years in his youth at Houten, in the bishopric of Utrecht, having been brought up with him in the same neighbourhood."[94] Still, the demands and pleasures of trading dominated classifications of time. Account books that were carefully specified as *dagboeken, montboeken,* and *jaarboeken* were a principal device for dividing time. In them, a man who thought it unnecessary to remember his child's birthdate took care to record the moments of business transactions with exactitude.[95] Women measured time in their own small account books, called *tafelboeken* (table books). All the records brought time under proper control. It was *burgerlijk*.

Space

To the disdain of nineteenth-century American commentators, the Dutch conquered the West not with the ax or plough, but by drawing it to them as fur trade in the Indians' great canoes. Their organization of space was as the reception places for this traffic and as the waterways and *entrepôts* to sustain this mode of domination. In significant ways, the system pointed back to the Netherlands where the commerce was supplied and capitalized.

From the streets of the *handelaars* outward, Beverwijck's expansionism was a start at subduing a riverine system not a landmass, and it was accomplished by navigating over the land. The town's merchants extended the trading system westward, but they also moved it east into New England, north to Nova Francia, and south, to the river towns, to New Amsterdam, and from there, to the Netherlands. There was nothing contradictory in this. In fact, a presence in Hartford, Boston, Springfield,

---

94. John Romeyn Brodhead, "Introduction" and "Notes," *A Short Sketch of the Mohawk Indians in New Netherland, Their Land, Stature, Dress, Manners and Magistrates, Written in the Year 1644 by Johannes Megapolensis, Junior, minister there.* Revised from the translation in Hazard's Historical Collections, CNYHS 2nd ser. (New York, 1857), 3(Part 1):150; Crt. sess., Livingston v. Melgert Abramsz, 1684/1685, Court of Sessions, Canvass of Votes, 1820, OCCA; Deposition, October 28, 1660, ER3, 41.
95. Arthur B. Gregg, *Old Hellebergh: Historical Sketches of the West Manor of Rennselaerswyck* (New York, 1975 reprint), 80.

Montreal, or Amsterdam signified a good sense of direction. Expansion did not require possession of the land. It did not entail conquest or strategies of dispossession. It meant reaching a terminus of trade but not necessarily possessing it. The Beverwijck traders, then, are the historian's moving targets.

Spaces in the Town

Beverwijck was a diverse set of spatial elements. It was the fort, a riverside strand, inns, palisades, and gates, fenced properties, a surrounding woods, a marketplace, and burial sites. Each of these had multiple uses and meanings so they could, at different times, be part of a religious, familial, or political moment. The *stadhuis* and the inn of Gabriel Thomsz had intensely political meaning in 1690 when townsmen, divided over the role of lieutenant governor Jacob Leisler, excluded the mayor from the *stadhuis* and met in raucous sessions at Thomsz's inn. But Thomsz's rooms would more ordinarily have meant entertainment, the gambling of auctions, the thrill of politics limited to gossiping. And the *stadhuis* – or so it seems from the records – was more generally a symbol of economic power. Collating some of the spatial elements of Beverwijck to describe a trading structure is, therefore, partial and selective. Yet it allows us to see that such a structure – in this case, trading – was, in fact, a process. Individuals continually used elements – including those more commonly called religious, political, or familial – to construct a set of relationships that they understood as the town's economy.

In the widest sense, the townspeople understood the town through its adjacency to the old fort. They also understood it by calling upon the dominance of two streets, Jonckheerstraat and Handlaarstraat. The most significant line of local traffic and trade followed Handlaarstraat from its intersection with Jonckheerstraat to the south gate and on to the fort. Along this street of commerce and trade, the town's public buildings were erected, just as they would have been in the Low Countries. At the intersection stood the church built in 1657. Its door was arranged to open south, so that exiting churchgoers faced the *stadhuis* and south gate. Directly against its east wall was the marketplace. This meant stalls adjacent to the church and, even as in a city like Zutphen today, a widening of the street to accommodate them. The *stadhuis* was 3,500 feet south of the church, facing Handlaarstraat. Everyone had an opinion about its design when it was built. All thought it made "a strong, commodious and handsome structure."[96] Almost immediately south, a bridge

---

96. For discussion of the *stadhuis*, see "Preface," *CRB*, 11; Jonckheerstraat and Handlaarstraat are now State Street and Broadway.

carried Handlaarstraat over the Rutten Kill, which flowed at a right angle to it and emptied into the river within some 250 feet. The kill was never referred to as a *gracht*. But it was treated as such in ordinances requiring that it be diked with wooden planks by owners whose properties abutted on it.

Outside the gate, the strand lay along the Hudson River. Sloops and native canoes were expected to dock there, undergoing inspection of cargo by the impost master and occasionally the *commis*. The strand was a special rendezvous point for traders as well as a commodious place for off-loading planks and grain. It was the only place where burghers could legally conduct trade outside the palisades of the town and the walls of the fort. It seems that an inn, such as was customarily located near principal city gates in the Netherlands, was operating here after 1654.[97]

North of the fort were private gardens, laid out in order and numbered. Jan Martensz's garden was marked W7 in 1653; numbers 11, 16, and 14 were also owned in that year. They were drawn by lot. Some were the properties of burghers who made the fort their residence as late as 1661; others belonged to men and women residing in town. They were not places frequently visited by day.[98]

The fort, like the men who lived in it, signified the identity between military and commercial purposes. The *commis* was the highest-ranking military officer but also something like a supercargo, insofar as he arranged all trading matters for the Company. Under him were the men whose careers also gave the fort its proper role as a drydocked and armed merchantman. They were ships' officers and marines. Andries Herpertsz, Abraham Staats, and Jan Labatie, all of whom played leading roles in Beverwijck as magistrates and traders, were originally a *konstabel* (junior officer of the marine), a ship's surgeon, and a ship's gunner respectively. They were employed in the merchant fleet of the West India Company and privileged to trade with natives or other Europeans at the Company's trading stations. By the 1650s, men like them had left the Company's employ. Nevertheless, some of them, acting as free traders, continued to maintain a house inside the fort and retain a garden lot allocated around its outer walls.

Fort Orange and its surrounds were not the area of orderly trade that might have been anticipated. The fort was a neglected structure and the area around it a hangout for the soldiers. A soldier sexually molested a child there in 1659, and in 1658, the court recorded the illegal conduct of two soldiers smuggling brandy to natives by lowering casks "over the northeast bastion" of the fort, loading them into canoes, delivering the

97. For the inn, see Ord. sess., June 17, 1654, *CRB*, 159–60.
98. Ord. sess., January 14, 1653, *CRB*, 48; Ord. sess., April 29, 1653, *CRB*, 64, and see 273.

brandy to natives on the nearby island, and exchanging it for pelts.[99] In 1659, Jeremias van Rensselaer wrote that townspeople considered the fort to be "no more than a nest.... No business is to be done there and not many people go there." He was trying to sell a house located within the fort, for which the family had paid gl 2,325 in 1655 but for which he could get neither a buyer nor a tenant.[100] The decay of the fort was the architectural evidence of Company's loss of control over the trade. Beginning in 1655, the *stadhuis* and Handlaarstraat controlled it. The story was revealed in the court minutes of the disputes over walking in the woods.

On Jonckheerstraat were houses for traders. Possibly named after Jonckheerstraat in Amsterdam, it was a street that crossed Handlaarstraat at level ground but then ascended a steep incline that dropped to ravines on both sides before leveling off.[101] In time, there was a gate to the north that, unlike the south entrance, opened directly onto the woods. When Stuyvesant laid out the town, men drew lots for properties on Jonck-heerstraat, and soon it was a double line of small *handelshuizen*.

A town property was a kind of *pied-a-terre*, a space sufficient to keep "hearth and light" and thereby qualify the owner to trade. The house lot was not kept intact or necessarily added to. On the contrary, properties were subdivided. Dense construction of housing was as Dutch as the architectural elements that marked the buildings. Houses were set so close that deeds frequently contained clauses protecting an owner from neighbors who might cram buildings on the entire width of their lots. Gysbert Janse had just such a house "twenty-two feet broad" on a front-age of exactly the same measurement. A more acceptable one was put to sale with "six inches free on both sides of the lot for drip." In 1657, a townsman sold part of his house lot but agreed (as continuing occupant) to keep closed "the door and windows on the south side of ... [his] house" so that the buyer might enjoy all his space. Houses were cramped by small houses erected in the back gardens, by shanties and outbuildings encroaching on neighboring plots, and by dwellings like Janse's with a street frontage considered "very restricted" in medieval towns.[102] How-ever, they gave the appearance of conforming to a Dutch aesthetic and, equally important, were suitable for trade.

99. Deposition, August 20, 1658, *ER4*, 69; Ord. sess., July 16, 1658, *CRB*, 135.
100. JvR to Johan van Wely, July 9, 1659, *Corr JvR*, 164; 164.
101. For the street name, see *De Wandelende Beschouwer: Gedurende de Amsterdamsche Kermis, Behelzende het meest merkwaardige daar op te zein geweest, zoo in de Speelen-Nacht-Huizen; als op openbare plaatzen-en de afloop derselve* (Amsterdam, [1820]), 5.
102. For the data, see Donna Merwick, "Dutch Townsmen and Land Use: A Spatial Perspective on Seventeenth Century Albany, New York," *William and Mary Quar-terly*, 3rd ser. (January 1980), 37:60.

The most valued properties were those that caught the flow of trade. The movement of traffic was affected by the natives' habitual ways of reaching the fort and town, and after the erection of the stockade in 1659, the placement of three gates. Properties just inside the south gate were the object of vigorous competition. This was less the case with the others, but the advantages of forestalling at all were obvious. Townsmen were well aware of what we would call main streets and side streets. As in Amsterdam and other Dutch towns, houses facing sidestreets were *dwarshuizen.* They were generally not the dwellings of important townsmen. When Jan Verbeeck requested a house lot that would take him off a "street where there is no business," he reflected the burghers' association of good streets with profitable activities. Verbeeck received a better house lot but was still not on Jonckheerstraat. Lambert van Valkenbergh, on the other hand, was a tailor and was specifically denied a small lot on the hill, probably Jonckheerstraat. He was given one "along the street toward the north" that is, a *dwarsstraat.*[103]

To know Beverwijck now from the early maps – John Miller's or Colonel Wolfgang Römer's – is to form a certain kind of mental image. The palisades, represented in strong lines drawn between tidy square blockhouses, form an octagon and seem to give shape and order to the city (Figures 2.4 and 2.5). The streets, *stadhuis,* and south gate appear unnoteworthy. Perhaps after the palisades were erected in 1659, they shaped the town into a dominant geometry for the burghers as well. Certainly they provided defense, summoned the burgher guard into being, and allowed people to refer to the enclosed space as a "city."

Yet the burghers' first mental map of the town was as "*de fuyck.*" They saw an animal trap shaped like an anchor. Probably, they derived it from taking a perspective on the town from across water. Partly because our maps give us a static view of Beverwijck, or, more likely, because we cannot take that perspective, we have to rummage around to make sense of their image. To them, the very name of the town connoted the movement essential to a Dutch market town: It pointed to the river.[104]

The River

Water was the *sine qua non* of the trading system. The rivers and kills were essential sources of energy and transport. They were also sources

103. Ord. sess., March 17, 1669, *CRB,* 135; Ex. sess., July 20, 1670, *CRA,* 170, 248–9; 170.

104. For *fuyck* derived from *wildfuik,* see W. J. van Balen, *Holland aan de Hudson: Een verhaal van Nieuw Nederland* (Amsterdam, 1943), 69, and for Danckaerts's account of the inhabitants' explanation of *fuyck,* see Bartlett Burleigh James and J[ohn] Franklin Jameson, eds., *Journal of Jasper Danckaerts, 1679–1680* (New York, 1913), 216.

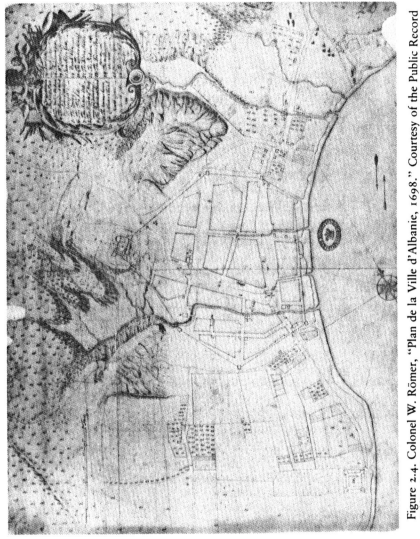

Figure 2.4. Colonel W. Römer, "Plan de la Ville d'Albanie, 1698." Courtesy of the Public Record Office, U.K.

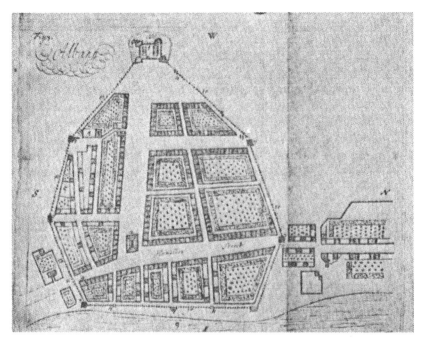

Figure 2.5. Map. Fig. 3. "Albany," in John Miller, *New York Considered and Improved*..., held in British Museum, Add. Man 15490. Courtesy of the British Library.

of imagination and self-referentiality. They were full of power and meaning. Normanskil, two miles south of town had its murderous *Lorelei* – *het poelmesie* (the maiden of the pool) – and the lads who were her victims gave the town some of its folklore, even as similar tales did in towns at home. The Hudson, too, was present in the gothic folktales of the town. Aboard a sloop in the river, the story went, Robert Livingston drew up the will of the town's only teller of destinies, Nicolaes van Rensselaer. Other men were remembered as drowning downriver in the Hudson, "battling with the spirit of the waters."[105] Horses perished in the river and men threw themselves into it to end their lives. Drowning one's enemy was a ready image. "I shall tie a stone with a rope around his neck," one burgher threatened, "and throw him into the *kil*." Natives

105. Van Cleaf Bachman, Alice P. Kenney, Lawrence G. Van Loon, " 'Het Poelmeisie': An Introduction to the Hudson Valley Dutch Dialect," *New York History* (April 1980), 51:161–86; episode cited in Carl Carmer, *The Hudson* (New York, 1939), 62; Martin Roth, *Comedy and America: The Lost World of Washington Irving* (New York, 1976), 140.

identified the Dutch with the water. They once said of their God, "There cannot be one God. If your God were our God we too would have known how to build ships."[106]

Townspeople knew the town as lying on five kills: Normanskil, Beverskil, Rutten Kill, Vossen Kill, and Patroon's kill. The town was its gorges, islands, and "gardens extending down to the river"; later it was Dock, Water, and Marsh streets. Property owners near Rutten Kill knew their responsibilities for diking its sides – "sheeting" it – and all knew as readily how to buy and sell water rights as they did how to deal with the square rods of town land or acres of farmland.[107]

The Hudson River was the essential waterway in the town's economy. Isaac Jogues, himself a man of travel and distances, captured its value splendidly in 1646 because he construed it operationally. He wrote simply: "It passes by the Dutch" at Fort Orange.[108] The townspeople harnessed the river and in doing so gave themselves two town spaces. ·

The burghers had Beverwijck and, like Kiliaen van Rensselaer much earlier, New Amsterdam. All had access to the city and some took out its great *burgerrecht*. The records show that, for twenty-five men, the river provided passage to properties owned there. It took three others to houses or farms owned on Long Island.[109] For a further ninety-nine residents (55 percent of the adult male population), it was a link to business associates. It tied another eighteen men and women (10 percent) to thirteen New Amsterdammers who represented them in court.

The Hudson was a trader's river. Court records capture some of its

106. Ex. sess., April 14, 1657, *CRB*, 26, and see 32; B. A. Botkin, *New York City Folklore: Legends, Tall Tales, Anecdotes, Stories, Sagas, Heroes and Characters, Traditions and Sayings* (Connecticut, 1976 reprint), 13.
107. Ord. sess., May 5, 1654, *CRB*, 141; see Agreement of Jeremias van Rensselaer and B. A. Bradt, February 24, 1671/2, Ledger, 1666–1708, VRMP, SC10643, NYSA; Acknowledgment of indebtedness, November 15, 1671 *ER1*, 491, and Grant of water rights, March 9, 1693/4, *ER2*, 353, 354.
108. John Gilmary Shea, ed. and tr., *The Jogues Papers*, CNYHS 2nd ser. (New York, 1857), 3(Part1):218.
109. I have used the public records of Beverwijck and New Amsterdam to compile the investment portfolios of the burghers. Each is the name of a Beverwijck burgher whose name appeared specifically related to a resident of New Amsterdam, either as partner, broker, or creditor. Thus Abraham Staats and Pieter Bogardus, as skippers of river craft, would certainly have done business on Manhattan Island, but no known associates are in the records, and therefore their names are not included here. The twenty-five men were Jan Juriaensz Becker, Francois Boon, Evert Jansz Bout, Albert Andriesz Bradt, Claes Carstensz, Johan de Dekker, Johannes La Montagne, Sander Leendertsz Glen, Pieter Hartgers, Cornelis Pietersz Hoogenboon, Rut Jacobsz, Rem Janse, Jan Jansz [Flodder], Thomas Janse [Mingael], Jan Labatie, Teunis de Loper [Quick], Evert Pels, Philip P. Schuyler, Cornelis Teunisse Slingerlandt, Willem Teller, Storm van der Zee, Goose Gerritsz van Schaick, Lambert van Valkenberg, Evert Janse Wendell, and Hendrick Willemsz; the three men who owned Long Island property were Jan Cornelisse Cleyne, Rem Janse, and Willem Teller.

frenetic vitality. Just after *handelstijd* began in 1654, the Company director at Fort Orange, Johannes Dyckman, admitted that he had lost
control of the river traffic and that residents were on the river in "canoes,
rowboats or other vessels" sailing to Esopus or the Catskills and selling
spirits to natives. In order to freight boards to New Amsterdam, one
yacht owner attached a raft to his vessel and set sail through the ice at
night. Other skows were hastily loaded and yachts offered for quick sale.
In mid-*handelstijd*, there was speed and organization. A retailer in wines
at New Amsterdam agreed in 1662 to "make a delivery" to Jan Gerritsz
in Beverwijck "by the sloop every week or 14 days" and expected the
immediate return of the empty casks. Two partners meant to work their
sloop continually in 1664, sharing the expenses "of the skow and of the
men whom they may put [to work] thereon."[110] Such continuous and
possibly profitable use must have been every skipper's intention.

Between 1652 and 1664, at least forty men owned yachts sailing between Beverwijck and New Amsterdam, and four others were nonowning
skippers. Twenty-four were burghers of Beverwijck; sixteen resided in
New Amsterdam. Three Englishmen owned vessels, and at least one
Holland vessel operated on the river as well. By my calculations, fifty-
three privately owned vessels would have been on the river between 1652
and 1664. The *Oak Tree, Unity, Jan and Mary*, the *Seahorse*, the *Princess
Royale*, and *Glowing Oven* were some of their names. They carried flags,
and one was notably political, flying the colors of the Sea Beggars. Others
married religion and trade in *Abraham's Sacrifice* and *Saint Marten*.
Probably none looked as lovely as the yachts drawn on the Duke's Map
of 1664 and resembling, to our twentieth-century eyes, graceful water-
borne insects (Figure 2.6).[111]

110. Ord. sess., May 19, 1654, *CRB*, 148; Ord. sess., March 26, 1658, *CRB*, 107; Ord.
    sess., July 1, 1659, *CRB*, 196, and Conditions of sale, [incomplete, ca. May 1, 1658],
    28; Quitclaim, September 3, 1661, *ER3*, 282.
111. The forty owners of yachts were Hendrick Andriesz, Luycas Andriesz, Harme Jacobsz
    Bamboes, Claes Bordingh, Albert Andriesz Bradt, Hans Carlsz, Symon Claesz, Jacob
    Clomp, Cornelis Janse Coele, Paulus Cornelisz, Dirck Janse Croon, Abraham de Trieu,
    Cornelis de Vos, Jacob Janse Flodder, A.(?) Hermann, Rut Jacobsz, Pieter Marius Ja-
    cobsz, Gerrit Janse, David Jochimsz, Jan Joosten (may be only a skipper), Thomas Lod-
    wicksxz [also Lewishon?], Pieter Lourensz, Marite Meyndertsz, Merten Ottsz, Evert
    Pels, Reindert Pietersz, Pieter Ryerson (may be skipper only), Philip P. Schuyler, Abra-
    ham Staats, Jacob Staats, Jan Janse Stol, Dirck Wessels ten Broeck, Claes Thysz, Jan
    Martensz van Alsteyne, Jan van Bremen, Jan Cornelisz van der Heyden, Cornelis van
    Langveld (half-owner with A. A. Bradt), Dirck Teunisse van Vechten, (half-owner with
    J. Clomp), Johannes Verbrugge, and Reinert Wisselpennigh.
    The three Englishmen were Thomas Davidsz, Willem Martensz, and Willem Moor.
    The Holland vessel was skippered by Arien (*sic*) Claesz. In addition, there were an un-
    specified number of yachts owned by the Company and the *colonie*. A score of Dutch
    men – like Jan de Caper, Michiel de Kaarman, Adrian Janse de Vries, (?) Reucke, and
    Jan van St. Aubin – were in the records as skippers but cannot be identified as owners.

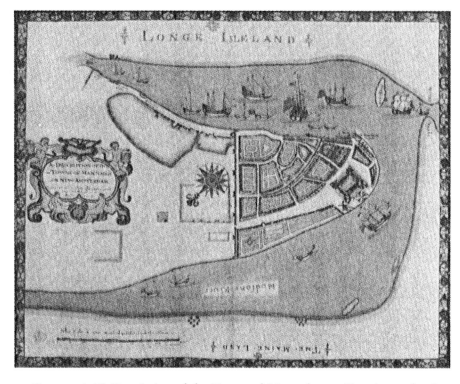

Figure 2.6. "A Description of the Towne of Mannados on New-Amsterdam"
(The Duke's Plan, date depicted 1661, issued 1664). Courtesy of the New-York
Historical Society.

Note 111, *cont.*
I have calculated the figure of fifty-three by assuming that the Company had the use of six
vessels and Rensselaerswyck three. These data are drawn from *RNA; CRB; CRA; ER14;
Calendar of State Papers;* Stokes, *Iconography,* vol. 2; Collier, *A History of Old Kinder-
hook from Aboriginal Days to the Present Time; Including the Story of Early Settlers,
Their Homesteads, Their Traditions, and Their Descendents; with An Account of Their
Civic, Social, Political, Educational and Religious Life* (New York, 1914); David Thomas
Valentine, *History of the City of New-York* (New York, 1853); *Corr JvR,* and official cor-
respondence in major document collections.

The owners of yachts were generally neither the wealthiest nor the poorest burghers. The cost of a yacht was high. A man might expect to pay gl 275 to gl 400 – sums that would buy an average house – or as much as gl 1,130.[112] Partnership was a way around expenses. For example, Philip Pietersz Schuyler, Andries Teller, Thomas de Lavall, and Jeremias van Rensselaer had one-quarter or one-eighth shares in the *Margriet* of Albany in 1671. Yet multiple ownership was the exception during this time, and present data suggest that, unless a man had considerable assets or was of a family of ship owners and sailors – like the Staats and the Bradts – he was unlikely to be an owner. Nor was it common for a leading burgher to own a vessel or act as skipper. Philip Pietersz Schuyler and Hans Hendricksz Obe owned ships but only as the result of suits of attachment for debt. Rut Jacobsz owned two vessels over time. But they were meant for the use of his (unreliable) agent and seem to have been unwelcome properties. Abraham Staats sailed his own vessel and exemplified how a man of ingenuity and connections could become wealthy. But most prominent merchants preferred to hire a rivercraft, paying according to the value of the cargo.[113]

How well river transport accommodated one of the twenty-five men who owned property in New Amsterdam or, to put it another way, how good his chances might have been of boarding a yacht departing daily or weekly from Beverwijck during *handelstijd* may never be known precisely. Clearly, we have nothing like schedules of departures and arrivals. But there is one moment in 1657 when the flow of river traffic can be caught. It confirms the hypothesis that, on average, a sloop departed from Beverwijck twice a week or about every three days. Johannes Dyckman recorded eighteen skippers making thirty-two departures from Beverwijck between June 20 and September 27 of that year. We cannot be certain that his record is complete, but it yields an average of one sloop every three days, although the departures were not evenly distributed. For example, 53 percent left on Sundays and Wednesdays, while none departed on Saturdays. On one Sunday, three sloops left together. On two occasions, two sloops left on the same day. From July 10 to 27, nine vessels set sail; from August 1 to 14, eight left Beverwijck. Three skippers made three departures during the time – for example, Jan de Kaper left on June 20, July 12, and September 3. Seven set sail twice – Claes Bordingh sailed on July 2 and was back on August 6, while Hans Carlsz

112. See Ex. sess., July 25, 1653, *CRB*, 74, and Settlement of accounts, August 18, 1661, *ER3*, 92; Bond of Cornelis Teunisse, May 16, 1658, *ER4*, 26.
113. For Jacobsz, see Ex. sess., September 4, 1652, *CRB*, 35; Van Rensselaer, for example, used Rensselaerswyck yachts and those of J. Staats and L. Andriesz (see JBvR to JvR, August 9, 1657, *Corr JvR*, 53, and see 113).

also set sail on August 6 and was ready for another departure on September 1. Abraham Staats's sloop made the speediest journey, returning within fifteen days. Luykas Andriesz's departures on July 2 and 18 meant he had completed his first journey in sixteen days.[114]

The situation was complicated by the practice of Hudson River yachts running along the Delaware as well. The yacht owned by Bordingh and Jacobsz certainly did. Dirck Janse Croon may have sailed his yacht to Virginia. Such trips would clearly lessen the availability of transport on the Hudson itself. The captains customarily called in at the landings, and this too would have affected the rate of river traffic. Skippers like Bordingh, Pieter Jacobsz, Pieter Ryersz, Staats, and Willem Albertsz acted as agents for wholesale merchants and did the same for farmers or villagers at the *raks* along the river. Jochim Staats, whose family operated sloops from 1650 through the eighteenth century, was reported to have constructed his journey in this way: Sailing downriver from Albany, he arrived at Kinderhoek Creek and "went ashore to the house of Joh[nes] Staats and brought on board bread, eggs and milk." Staats was getting provisions in this instance, but masters also anchored alongside mills to load grain.[115]

Nevertheless the demand for frequent and reasonably regular river transport from Beverwijck to New Amsterdam continued to increase after 1650, and figures from decades after 1664 strengthen the view that Beverwijck's inhabitants had easy and fast access to Manhattan Island. Scattered data from the 1670s and 1680s show an Albany townsman making the round trip to New York in thirteen days and another in nine.[116] A New York resident reached Albany – leaving at night – in seven days, and two Dutch visitors, Jasper Danckaerts and Pieter Slyter, left New York on a Friday at 3 o'clock P.M. and reached Albany at noon the following Monday, despite a day of adverse winds.[117]

114. Records, June 25 to September 27, 1657, *ER1*, 244.
115. See *ER3*, 231, n. 3; for Croon, see Conditions of sale, June 16, 1659, *ER4*, 111; see Collier, *History of Old Kinderhook*, 158, Henry C. Murphy, ed., *Journal of a Voyage to New York and a Tour in Several of the American Colonies in 1679–80, by Jasper Dankers and Peter Slyter of Wiewerd in Friesland, tr. from the original manuscript in Dutch for the Long Island Historical Society* (Brooklyn, 1867), 359, and for landings at "Apjes Island" to exchange goods for seawan, see Collier, *History of Old Kinderhook*, 16; see Elinor Robinson Bradshaw, "Philipsburg Manor at North Tarrytown, New York," *de halve maen* XLIV (January 1970), 44:16, for a mill "adjacent to the North-River."
116. George S. Roberts, *Old Schenectady* (Schenectady, n.d.), 140, and Paul Wilstach, *Hudson River Landings* (New York, 1969 reissue), 75.
117. "Abstract out of the Journal [*sic*] kept by Coll. Nicholas Bayard the 11th June, 1689 in New-York" [1689], *DRCH*, 3:604; Murphy, ed., *Journal of Dankers*, 358, 359.

Possessing New Amsterdam:
The Great Wharf of the Manhattans

The sloops gave Beverwijck residents a second town. They bore passengers to a city where residents had invited the river in, constructing slips that served as canals and inlets that were generally a city block long before becoming the streets and paths of the port. One of the canals, the Heeren Gracht, was originally navigable to Wall Street where it became the Princes Gracht (Figure 2.7). Sloops did not sail amid streets as in Netherlands cities, but they took advantage of the five-foot tides to sail down the slips and canals, reaching markets and warehouses lying well within the shoreline.[118] And in these places of commerce and merchant housing, Beverwijck settlers owned properties.

Twenty-five men retained forty-seven properties in New Amsterdam, while residing in Beverwijck. They were one in seven of the 178 men active in the town's affairs. Thirty-four of the properties were houses, that is, 17 percent of New Amsterdam's dwellings in 1660. The others were six undeveloped lots, one tobacco warehouse, and one brewery. Three men disposed of properties before moving to Beverwijck. Dirck Bensingh, a corporal with the Company, conveyed his house and lot to domini Megapolensis; Evert Janse Wendell released one of two houses; and Goose Gerritsz van Schaick sold a large property. But others retained properties or bought them when their fortunes improved. Most properties were under single ownership, but the Dutch preference for joint ownership operated as well. The Red Lion Brewery belonged to Johannes La Montagne and Daniel Vermullen. Rut Jacobsz and William Teller came to own van Schaick's property "just outside the water gate." Cornelis Teunisz Slingerlandt and Storm van der Zee each held two-eighths ownership of a house rented in 1662 to New Amsterdam's burgomaster Allard Anthonij. One Beverwijck resident owned a third of a lot and a garden; another owned half a lot.[119]

The properties were distributed in all parts of New Amsterdam. Jan

118. John W. Barber and Henry Howe, *Historical Collections of the State of New York Containing a General Collection of the Most Interesting Facts, Traditions, Biographical Sketches, Anecdotes, etc. Relating to Its History and Antiquities, with Geographical Descriptions of Every Township in the State* (New York, 1842), 286. J. F. Watson notes that there were markets at every slip (see his *Olden Times, Researches and Reminiscences of New York City, in 1828, appendix in Annals of Philadelphia, Being a Collection of Memoirs, Anecdotes and Incidents of the City and its Inhabitants from the Day of the Pilgrim Founders* [Philadelphia, 1830] 23).
119. For the twenty-five men and women as well as the properties in New Amsterdam, see note 109 this chapter.

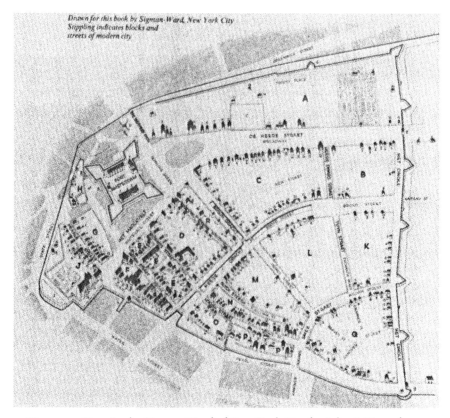

Figure 2.7. Drawing by Sigman-Ward of New York City for John A. Kouenhoven, *The Columbia Historical Portrait of New York: An Essay in Graphic History.* Copyright 1953 by Doubleday, a division of Bantam, Doubleday, Dell Publishing Group, Inc. Reprinted by permission of the publisher.

Evertsz Bout and Teunis de Loper owned houses near the fort. Evert Pels's was on Broadway near the North River, next to Stuyvesant's orchard and about one-third of a mile from the Jacobsz-Teller property "outside the wall" (that is, beyond Wall Street). On the East River, Jan Janse Flodder owned a house at Smits's Vly and Albert Andriesz Bradt held fifty acres nearby. However, there was a significant clustering of properties in the blocks bordered by Herre Dwars Straet, Broadway, Brower's Straet, and the paths facing the Princes Gracht and Herre Gracht. Bevers Gracht and Markvelt Steegh bisected this sixty-five acres of land. Twenty-seven of the fifty-nine dwellings had access to the *grach-ten*, and all residents were within 1,480 feet of the wharves below Fort Amsterdam.[120]

A substantial number of Beverwijck's traders knew the city well enough to own a piece of Manhattan and do so with the sureness of the local resident. They felt possessive enough to select among the available prop-erties. Hendrick Willemsz, whose lot was on Winkelstraat, knew as well as any inhabitant that the street of the "Five Stone Houses" opposite his own was a choice one.[121] In a moment we shall see the great number of Beverwijck residents who had contractual but non-property-owning ties with New Amsterdam. And we cannot be certain that they were disadvantaged by not investing in real estate. Certainly by 1660, New Amsterdam offered the investor real estate in a promising city. But it also rewarded knowledge. Any point of entry, any opportunity to put a toe into the eddying waters of the business community added to one's account. Moreover, it is unlikely that the propertyowning Beverwijck merchants shared a face-to-face community with their merchant neigh-bors, certainly not in the sense of sustained interaction. Philip Pietersz never lived in New Amsterdam nor were the others year-round residents.

Real estate gave the twenty-five Beverwijck property owners a highly visible stake in the commercial success of the Manhattans. But properties could be static, and in the Dutch world of trade, stasis of any sort had little place. Nor was high visibility of wealth desirable. Dynamism, the gamble and risk of fluctuating investments, movement – these, and not occupancy, mattered. Knowledge of the waterfront and participation in its demanding activities gave mastery too.

This mode of possessing New Amsterdam by knowing its ways was shared with an even larger number of Beverwijck residents. Records show 103 Beverwijck men and women (including the 25 property owners) who knew the slips and *poortjes*, warehouses and markets well enough to use them as points of exchange, places of auction, and depots for their planks, beaver, cattle, and cereals.[122] In a court case of 1669 involving

120. For the Bout, de Loper, Pels, Jacobsz-Teller, Janse, and Bradt properties, see "Top-ographical, Biographical, and Historical Data [pertaining to Afbeeldinge van de Stadt Amsterdam in Nieuw Neederlandt (The Castello Plan)]," Stokes, *Iconography*, 2:275, 248, 226, 339, 326, and 333. Jacobsz also owned properties closer to the fort, 302.
121. See Stokes, *Iconography*, 2:257.
122. The 103 residents with business ties to New Amsterdam were Stoffel Janse Abeel, Pieter Andriesz [Sogemakelijke], Teunis [beer-carrier], Francois Boon, Pieter Jacobsz Bosboom, Gertie Bouts, Albert Andriesz Bradt, Barent Albertsz Bradt, Catelyn Bradt, Storm Bradt, Pieter Bronck, Willem Brower, Frederick Carstensz, Thomas Chambers, Pieter Claerbout, Leendert Philipsz Conyn, Pieter Cornelisse, Dirck Janse Croon, Elbert Gerbertsz Cruyf, Johannes de la Montagne, Andries de Vos, Cornelis de Vos, Teunis Dircksz, Volkert Janse Douw, Cornelis Dyckman, Maria Dyckman, Jan Janse

lost merchandise, the magistrates needed an account of occurrences on the dock during a disturbing commotion. The scene described was one of a dockside cluttered with consignments of cloth intended for Beverwijck and a partner of one of its traders desperately trying to keep her forty-four yards of haircloth separate from other merchandise newly arrived from Holland. The woman had bought and paid for her trading goods in Holland, but a substantial number of townsmen bought merchandise from New Amsterdam wholesalers, some contracting impossible debts in the process.[123]

Sixty-two of the 103 townsmen had contracted debts with one or more of the New Amsterdam wholesalers. Generally the obligations were in respect to goods purchased for the upriver fur trade. Townspeople might use a sequence of suppliers, juggle as many creditors as reputation would allow, and pay the most recently acquired debt first rather than (as in Holland) those of long standing. Jan Verbeeck, to select an example, was receiving merchandise from Dirck Claesz Bout in 1652. In 1658, he used Dirck Dircksz Keyser. Three years later he turned to Barent van Marle. In 1662, he was still dealing with Keyser – owing gl 255 and giving him mortgages on houses and lots in Beverwijck – but in 1664, he was buying merchandise from Gerrit Hendricksz van Rhys. Rut Jacobsz, whose fortunes went dramatically downhill after 1659, bought merchandise from Withardt, Keyser, and Steenwyck in 1658 and 1659. In 1661, he accumulated more debts by purchasing from Pieter Symonsz van Oostsanen. In 1662, he was dealing with Jacob Gevick, owing gl 1,200.[124] Mean-

[Flodder], Harme Gansvoort, Hendrick Gerritsz, Sander Leendertsz Glen, Symon Symonsz Groot, Albert Gysbertsz, Dirckien Harmensz, Pieter Hartgers, Claes Hendricksz, Jacob Hendricksz [Maat], Marten Hendricksz, Cornelis Hoogboom, Baltus Jacobsz, Rut Jacobsz, Anthony Janse, Marcelis Janse, Paulus Janse, Rem Janse, Stephen Janse, Willem Janse [Schut], Hendrick Jochemsz, Jochim Kettelhuym, Uldrick Klein, Jan Labatie, Jacob Lookermans, Teunis de Loper [Quick], Jan Mangelsz, Jan Martensz, Marten Mouritsz, Jan Nack, Helmer Otten, Fran Pietersz [Pastoor], Gillis Peitersz, Johannes Provoost, Pieter Quakenbos, Daniel Rinkhout, Pieter Ryverdingh, Catherine Sanders, Jacob Schermerhoorn, Philip P. Schuyler, Gerrit Slectenhorst, Cornelis Teunisse Slingerlandt, Gerrit Swart (of the *colonie*), Roelof Swoutwout, Adrien Symonsz, Michael Tades, Jan Thomasz, Jan van Aeckelen, Arent van Curler, Wynant van der Poel, Jan Frasz van Hoesem, Jan Baptiste van Gutsenhoven, Jan Gerritsz van Marchem, Dirck van Ness, Adrian Gerritsz van Pappendorp, Jeremias van Rensselaer, Goose Gerritsz van Schaick, Aukes van Slyck, Lambert van Valkenberg, Cornelis Teunisse van Vechten, Teunis Jacobsz van Wemp, Gerrit Hendircksz van Wie, Harme Vedder, Jan Verbeeck, Isaac Vermullen, Arnout Cornelisse Viele, Poeter Vrooman, Evert Janse Wendell, Reynier Wisselpennigh, and Jan Hendricksz Westerkamp.

123. Ex. sess., August 4, 1669, *CRA*, 91, 92.
124. For Verbeeck, see Ex. sess., August 7, 1652, *CRB*, 30, Acknowledgment of debt to Keyser, August 29, 1659, *ER1*, 257, Acknowledgment of debt and mortgage, August 2, 1661, *ER1*, 376, Acknowledgment of debt to Keyser, August 15, 1662, *ER1*, 307, and List of debts which Arent van Curler is to collect, October 13/23, 1664, *ER3*,

while the others used each of the prominent New Amsterdam merchants.[125]

Beverwijck's residents made choices at their own risk. Even on incomplete figures for 1652 to 1664, one out of five men could expect to
mortgage his house and lot (or other immovable property) to a New
Amsterdam creditor in the course of business transactions. When Jan
Labatie and Hendrick Westerkamp pledged all their estates to Schrijk,
Labatie was forced to sell Schrijk his New Amsterdam house in 1654
and mortgage or liquidate his investments in Amsterdam. Fran Barentsz
was more fortunate, but the wife of Johannes Dyckman was not. In 1657,
Barentsz owed Jan Peeck, an innkeeper of New Amsterdam, ten beaver,
perhaps a debt arising from animals purchased at one of Peeck's fairs.
Peeck sued Barentsz for the beaver in the Beverwijck court. Found guilty,
Barentsz turned to collect the pelts (or equivalent goods) from Pieter
Bronck to whom he had paid them to cover a debt but who had already
handed them over to Johannes Dyckman to cover his debts. Dyckman's
wife, herself a trader, paid Peeck on the court's order.[126]

Such adventuring was emblematic of the Manhattans. Another thirty-
eight burghers had business associations with less prominent New Amsterdammers but were also part of the volatile trading scene, bargaining
for merchandise and accepting brokerage at 5 percent or whatever the
market demanded. Labatie, Westerkamp, and Croon had dealings with
the Gerardy brothers. Westerkamp frequented Philip's tavern and owed
gl 64 in 1662. Labatie acted as his lawyer and debt collector in Beverwijck
in *handelstijd* of 1652; in 1659 Croon held credits from Jan Gerardy for
gl 470 in Virginia tobacco. Arent van Curler went down to New Amsterdam to trade rye for a horse with Sixt vander Stichel. In the summer
of 1662, Jan Gerretsz van Marcken was purchasing wine and beer regularly from Jacob Kip. In 1653 and 1654, Andries de Vos was freighting
boards downriver to his New Amsterdam partner, Hendrick Andriesz.
The planks typify the spread of simple commodity production based on
a largely self-subsistent economy. But in this instance, the marketing of

304. For Jacobsz, see Acknowledgment of obligations to Withardt (October 17, 1656,
ER1, 3), to Keyser (August 29, 1659, *ER1*, 257), to Steenwyck (Copy of statement,
August 24, 1660, *ER1*, 279), to Simonsz (September 10, 1661, *ER1*, 384) and to
Gevick (March 3, 1662, *ER1*, 330, and see 355.

125. In addition to the two burghers cited, eight residents chose to do business with de
Meyer, five with Withardt, five with Ebinck and Keyser, three with van Marle,
Anthonij, and Levy, two with Schrijk, Gevick, Steenwyck, and Jan Harmensz Wint-
dorp. At least one townsperson selected Jacob Vis, Paulus Leendertsz van de Grift,
Jacob Steendam, Johannes van der Meulen, Symon Janse Romeyn, Gillis van Brugge,
Govert Lookermans, and Margaret van Hardenbroeck.

126. Settlement between Schrick, Labatie, and Janse [Westerkamp], August 20, 1654, *ER1*,
188; Ord. sess., January 9, 1657, *CRB*, 10.

the product does not seem to have canceled out debts both men had with Leendertsz van der Grift, doubtless for trading goods.[127]

The business activities of Beverwijck townspeople in New Amsterdam make an archive of townspeople's careers and lives that were continually intersecting and crisscrossing with those of men and women outside Beverwijck. They had a stable community, but it did not depend upon a covenanting mentality. There was no desire to make contracts excluding oneself from other communities. Nor did community rest on the compactness that such practices as perambulating the bounds reinforced in New England. Men moved from New Amsterdam to Beverwijck without feeling obliged to dispose of properties or terminate business associations there. Some had only gambled on Beverwijck, renting for a season or year but then deciding to take up permanent residence. In all of it, they brought to an understanding of community a spatially inventive imagination that entertained many variations on inclusiveness.

The Land Beyond: The Low Countries

Beyond Manhattan Island lay the Netherlands. It was reached by "the summer ships." These were the eight to fourteen vessels that annually disgorged cargo and then awaited freighting for the return voyage, usually undertaken from early August to November. For forty-nine townsmen and women – slightly over one-quarter of Beverwijck's adult male population – the ships carried bonds, receipts, wages, notarized accounts, and letters that tied them to families and business associates in patria, belittling the distance of almost 5,000 miles.[128]

At least nineteen of the forty-nine residents had business dealings with brokers, partners, agents, notaries, and family members in Amsterdam. Some were selling beaver or goods; others were purchasing merchandise, arranging bills of exchange or bottomry charges, paying debts, or calling

127. Seventeen other men and women made use of thirteen representatives before the court of New Amsterdam. The residents were Pieter Andriesz [Sogemakelijke], Albert Andriesse Bradt, Pieter Bronck, Dirck Janse Croon, Jan Barentsz Dulleman, Sander Leendertsz Glen, Harme Thomasz Hun, Rut Jacobsz, Helmer Otten, Michiel Teunisse, Jan Thomasz, Jan Coster van Aecken, Harme Thomasz van Amersfoort, Storm Albertsz van der Zee, Jan Fransz van Hoesem, Lanbert van Valkenberg, and Isaac Vermullen. The thirteen New Amsterdammers were Claes Bordingh, Andries de Haas, Nicolaes de Meyer, Asser Levy, Govert Lookermans, Johannes Provoost, Symon Janse Romeyn, Paulus Schrijk, Oloff van Cortlandt, Hendrick van de Water, Adrian van Laer, Tielman van Vleeck, and Thomas Willet.
128. JBvR to JvR, [January 18, 1664], *Corr JvR*, 345; for the figures on vessels, see C. H. Jansen, "Handel en scheepvaart van Amsterdam op Noord-Amerika, in het Bizonder op New York van 1664 tot 1690" [unpublished paper] (Amsterdam, seminar, 1961), 10, who lists eight in 1661, eight in 1662, nine in 1663, and fourteen in 1664; I am considering those with direct contacts in the Netherlands only.

in credits. One colonist was claiming 6,000 Carolus guilders on a merchant's account and 10 percent interest (ca. gl 12,000 New Netherland money). Each man had a known contact, of course, but it is difficult to say anything more specific about the meaning of Amsterdam for them. Of the nineteen men and women, fourteen were born in the Netherlands. Like most colonists, they would have sailed to New Netherland from Amsterdam, leaving in their late teens or early twenties. Claes Cornelisse knew of Amsterdam's Orphans' Hall. Philip Pietersz Schuyler had some knowledge about local streets. Frederick Carstensz sold beaver through a relative and might have known his home. Stoffel Janse Abeel seems to have known a clerk in one of the commercial houses. Jeremias van Rensselaer, of course, knew the city well. Interests of the other thirty-one townsmen suggest close relationships with people outside Amsterdam. At least eighteen were born in the Netherlands. Of these, ten were still retaining land or estates. They held properties in Vianen, Velthuysen, Friesland, Utrecht, and Nykerck. Fifteen others were involved in estates of deceased relatives in Swoll, Hoorn, Brabant, Naarden, Schoenderwoort, Rotterdam, and elsewhere in Holland.[129]

The summer ships also took Beverwijck townspeople to patria. From 1651 to 1665, forty-seven residents made return voyages. Eight men made the trip more than once. From 1651 to 1659, the annual number of men and women journeying to the Netherlands never exceeded four. From 1659 to 1665, however, the average was six men a year. Thirty-seven journeys were undertaken during *handelstijd* – three in July, twenty-five in August, seven in September, and two in October. Generally townsmen undertook the journey for purposes of trade. Three traders, for

129. The nineteen men and women were Stoffel Jansz Abeel, Hans Conraeta, Claes Cornelisz, Maria Dyckman, Carsten Fredricksz, Arent Janse, Philip Pietersz Schuyler, Harme Thomasz [Hun], Evert Thys de Goyer, Pieter van Alen, Gerritz Wynant van der Poel, Storm Albertsz van der Zee, Gertruy Andriesz van Doesberg, Jan Bastiansz van Gutsenhoven, Jeremias van Rensselaer, Goose van Schaick, Willem Janse Stol, and Arnout Cornelisse Viele. All were born in the Netherlands, except Hans Conraetsz and Carsten Fredericksz, who were born in one of the German principalities, and Claes Cornelisse and Arnout Cornelisse Viele, who were born in New Netherland; Demand for payment to Claes Cornelisse, August 16, 1659, *ER1*, 274; Power of Attorney from P. P. Schyler, August 26, 1660, *ER3*, 38; Bond of Carsten Fredericksz, July 28, 1663, *ER3*, 232; Bond to Stoffel Jansz Abeel, September 12, 1663, *ER3*, 249. The thirty-one residents were Jacob Andriesz, Jan Barentsz Dulleman, Sweer Barentsz, Harme Bastiaensz, Francois Boon, Cornelis Brantsz van Nijkerck, Tierck Claesz deWith, Claes Claesz, Catelen Claesz, Ludovicus Cobes, Gysbert Cornelisz Bogaert, Jan Dareth, Eldert Gysbertsz Cruyf, Gerrit Hendricksz van Rhys, Anthonij Janse, Dirck Janse Croon, Pieter Janse van Hoorn, Carsten Meyndertsz, Jan Nack, Pieter Ryverdingh, Cornelis Teunisse Slingerlandt, Teunisse Cornelisz Slingerlandt, Roelof Swortwort, Harme Thomasz van Amersfoort, Jan van Aeckelen, Arent van Curler, Jan Cornelisse van der Heyden, Claes van Elslant, Cornelis Hendricksz van Ness, Gysbert Philipsz van Velthuysen, Evert Janse Wendel.

example, accompanied pelts intended for sale, eight went to collect debts, seven went as agents for fellow townsmen.

What these "colonials" experienced in cities like Amsterdam and mercantile houses like West India House is another matter. We know that they entered an economic community structurally like their own. Their travel on the Hudson, for example, was like that of the Amsterdam businessmen, who, as a group and just to speak of Leiden, left "their homes several thousand times a year to board *trekschuiten* for overnight trips." Some, at least those with beaver, may have timed their departure to coincide with Amsterdam *kermis* and intended to experience its festivities. Harme Vedder was an agent for a wealthy Amsterdam merchant family and probably welcomed. Jan Juriaensz transacted business in Amsterdam with Jan Baptiste van Rensselaer in July, 1664 and may have been welcomed also. Others may have felt the sense of dislocation in Amsterdam that even Jan Baptiste expressed on his return in 1659. But it remains hypothetical.[130]

They entered a world rich in communication. It was, first, a world of speech, of the pleasures of illiteracy, if you will. There were the skills of managing talk, remembering, making mental computations, using endless idioms of trading. The Manhattans and Dutch cities like Amsterdam were places thick with communications about commerce and rewarded such skills. But Beverwijck's trading structure, though diminutive by comparison, was, of course, the same. So the townsmen, whether as itinerants or at home, were *cognoscenti* to the placards and auctions, fairs and *trekvaarten*, forts and ships, market stalls and city walls – in short, the ways of all Dutch towns, to one degree or another. They were *cognoscenti* to discourse as well. William Temple noted in 1673 that the skill and wit of Dutch merchants was sharpened by the conversation that city life afforded, and, whether in Amsterdam or New Amsterdam, a Beverwijck man could comfortably place himself within such conversations and use the local patois of trading.[131] Any number of accounts left by Beverwijck merchants in New Amsterdam testify to such a sharpening of skills or business sense. It was the "entertainment" expected in New Amsterdam. Arent van Curler, for one, anticipated it. In a letter to Jeremias van Rensselaer, he deliberately divided the "entertainment" of conversation – his afternoon "at the honorable general's" – from the

---

130. Jan de Vries, *Barges and Capitalism: Passenger Transportation in the Dutch Economy, 1632–1839* in *Afdeling Agrarische Geschiedenis Bijdragen* (Wageningen, 1978), 21:119; on Vedder, see Oliver A. Rink, *Holland on the Hudson, An Economic and Social History of Dutch New York* (Ithaca, 1986), 90; Power of attorney, June 17, 1664, *ER3*, 288; Power of attorney, August 30, 1654, *ER1*, 197; 197; JBvR to JvR, February 20, 1659, *Corr JvR*, 133.

131. Temple, *Observations*, 137.

tasks of letter writing. He also listened to news of the sailors (*de heeren van zes weken*) and remembered detail.[132]

Being part of a Dutch trading town also meant participating in a world of words in script and print. After nine years in New Netherland, van Rensselaer, for example, wanted to write about commerce in New Netherland and apparently produced the *Neu Nederlands Marcurius*, presumably something like the *Haarlem Mercurius*, which informed merchants about European and overseas affairs (Figure 2.8). The trader Volkert Janse Douw wrote either so troublesomely or copiously that he was considered "too quick with a pen." Even Hendrick Janse "the cowherd" could write and "make a lampoon" of the *schout*. All townsmen had to skill themselves in reading and writing to some degree. There were placards and trading regulations to be read, notices circulated by merchants planning to leave town, and announcements of auctions. Above all, there were account books and receipts to be read, leases to be annotated, certificates and invoices to be scrutinized. All required some literacy and numeracy if one were not to be continually duped. It is not surprising that one had to "write reasonably well" to be a smith or that, in 1655, two men in Beverwijck taught night school and one man day school.[133]

The world of conversation and script in a great trading city like Amsterdam was enriched by a world of print. Since that was also the case in New Amsterdam and Beverwijck, residents traveling abroad were not confronted by an entirely strange world. True, it was vital in New Amsterdam to have conferences about trading restrictions, and it was important to get advice from the last arriving *handelsschips* by talking with skippers about inspection regulations – *praatjes*, the yarns and fables of mariners, were essential to trading, and gossip was "one of the most common and daily activities of . . . [urban] life."[134] But merchants were also putting print to commercial advantage. They were using bills of lading, and these were perhaps the earliest common artifacts in print in New Amsterdam and Beverwijck. Obviously not every trader needed to

132. A. van Curler to JvR, [April 1661], *Corr JvR*, 252; the nickname for sailors is in G. M. W. Acda, *Voor en Achter de Mast: Het Leven van de Zeeman in de 17de en 18de Eeuw* (Amsterdam, 1976), 15.

133. JvR to JBvR, August 7, 1663, *Corr JvR*, 325 and 325, n. 697 and see JvR to AvR, September 12, 1663, and JvR to JBvR, September 14, 1663, *Corr JvR* 329, 332; JvR to AvR, [June 8, 1660], *Corr JvR*, 230, 231; 231; JBvR to JvR, October 8, 1659, *Corr JvR*, 181; Ord. sess., February 8, 1656, *CRB*, 251; for a carpenter's literacy of some sort, see Ord. sess., December 5, 1556, *CRB*, 304; Indenture, February 1, 1685/ 6, *ER3*, 585; Ord. sess., February 2, 1655, *CRB*, 200.

134. See Deric Regin, *Traders, Artists, Burghers, A Cultural History of Amsterdam in the Seventeenth Century* (Amsterdam, 1976), 57; for van Curler's conference, see AvC to JvR [April 1661], *Corr JvR*, 251; see Power of attorney, August 30, 1654, *ER1*, 197; for *praatjes*, see de Vries, *Short Historical and Journal Notes (1655)*, 128.

Figure 2.8. Anthony Leemans, *Still Life*, 1655. Courtesy of the Rijksmuseum, Amsterdam.

handle them, but many must have seen them and become aware of new efficiencies in commerce as well as a mode of communication in which repeatable images were taken for granted.

A packet of thirty-three such bills of lading among the van Rensselaer Manor Papers offers some idea of what these meant. They are dated from 1655 to 1749. Some are now torn, but all were once uniformly on paper now measuring 5.75 by 9.75 inches. Those dated before 1664 bear the seal of the West India Company and the words "Nieu Nederlandt." Otherwise they are all alike. They were obviously printed off one plate in Amsterdam and meant for use by merchants forwarding goods to New Netherland. However, the New Netherlanders, lacking printing presses, bought them in bulk and made use of them to record consignments simply and efficiently. One had only to fill in seven blanks, affix a date, and get the signature of the ship's captain. A merchant had only to cross out "Nieu" in "nae Nieu Amsterdam" (to New Amsterdam) to have Amsterdam as the proper destination (Figure 2.9).

> I _____ skipper next to God of my ship, named _____ as she now lies ready on the tide at _____ and with the good wind which God may grant shall sail to New Amsterdam, in New Netherland, where my duties shall be discharged, record and avow that I have received under the deck [*overloop*] of my aforesaid ship from you _____ to wit _____ [goods] all dry, satisfactory and in good condition and denoted with this mark [*woorstaende*, that is, a marginal emblem of the Company]. All the which I promise to deliver (if my God grants a safe trip) with my aforesaid ship to New Amsterdam, in New Netherland aforesaid to the Honorable _____ or to his factor or one so deputed, with payment for freight of this above-written goods _____ guilders, and from the same for average [three stivers per guilder]. [dated and signed.][135]

The bill of lading was an accepted closure of print around script. It closed the impersonal around the personal, the wider world around the narrower. It was what the experience of enclosure within the rich communications networks of a city must have been for burghers from smaller towns like Beverwijck. Something of the pleasure of this is implied in the letter one young Dutch friend sent to another delayed in Virginia before sailing for Amsterdam. He thought the days must be tedious "because you have or can make few acquaintances there owing to the fact that the people live so far apart."[136] In the bill of lading, print, script, and illustration jostled each other on paper, even as merchants, sailors, and artisans did in a Dutch city. Each was pleasurable and imparted the positive meaning of trading.

Possessing New England

The objective of all this commercial activity was to have a portfolio of readily negotiable investments. Some were movable feasts; others were lean fare. Investigation of them reminds us that our economic histories

135. Bills of lading and Receipts, 1655–1749, Numbered (18–51), *VRMP*, SC7079, Box 13, folder 6, NYSA.
136. Brandt Schuyler to Kiliaen van Rensselaer [son of Johannes], December 30, 1696, *VRBM*, 803, 804.

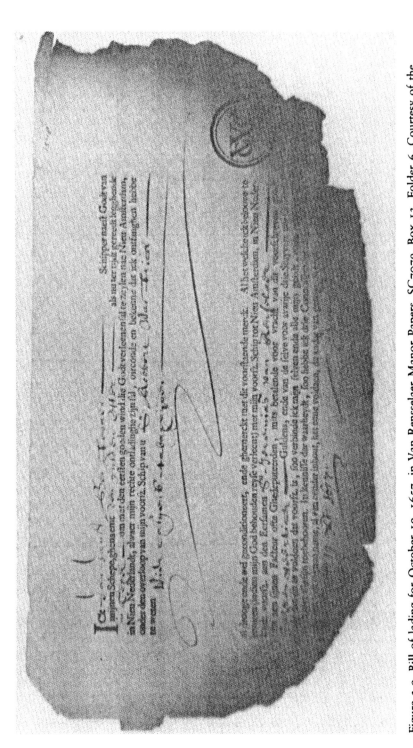

Figure 2.9. Bill of lading for October 19, 1657, in Van Rensselaer Manor Papers, SC7079, Box 13, Folder 6. Courtesy of the State University of New York Library, Albany.

were their webs of relationships, our regional geographies were their *handelshuisen*, that is, networks of mercantile houses with which they traded. This was the way Beverwijck's townsmen knew New England. They traded with *handelshuisen* there, seeking multiples of Mr. Pinser's *handel huys* and, in doing so, rejecting our geographies of solid planes for theirs of point-to-point trajectories.

Dutch men in Beverwijck generally called the land east of the Hudson River either "the northern section [*kwartier*]," or "the north." In this, they were applying geographical categories used at home, and by implying that the northern section was part of New Netherland, were signaling that Dutch claims to land east of the river were by no means unrealistic before 1664.[137] The northern section, however, was not all of New England, but rather, its trading towns or, better, its trading houses. Trading with New England meant knowing Harrfort (Hartford), Sprinckvielt (Springfield), New Haven, Milfoort (Milford), and Boston. Beverwijck was a place within that network of towns, and commerce with New England frequently meant dealing with a Dutch resident in one of the communities. So while Hartford and Boston stood for turn-around points in journeys to arrange trade, repair a yacht, or peddle merchandise, they also meant Paulus Schrijk (Hartford), Samuel van Goedenhuysen (New Haven), and Andries Teller (Boston).

Until the English occupation, townsmen piloted their way into New England: down the Hudson, across Long Island and up the Connecticut River or around the coast to Boston. In August 1658, seven Beverwijck traders made such a trip, sailing downriver and peddling beaver pelts or goods across Long Island, sleeping in a garret at Southhold and quarreling about the thievery of one among them, then making for the north by ascending the Connecticut River probably as far as Hartford. Such peddlers were coming to be resented by the Yankee Long Islanders, but their procedures were little different from those of the "ocean-going peddlers," the great families of Vanbrugge, De Wolff, and Van Rensselaer.[138] After 1664, the "Great New England Path" provided an overland route to Springfield and the Connecticut River. By 1670, travel on horseback "from Sprinckvielt...to Albany" was commonplace.[139]

Beverwijck was linked to trading towns in New England, first, because of commercial structures that had already allowed the penetration of its trading world by outsiders. Third-party debt was an accepted practice and automatically meant possible indebtedness to individuals outside

137. See Kieft's use in *Jogues Papers*, CNYHS, 2nd ser. 3(Part 1):227, and "to the north," in Ord. sess., May 9, 1672, CRA, 300.
138. Ex. sess., August 8, 1658, CRB, 147; Rink, Merchants and Magnates 270.
139. Indenture, May 23, 1670, ER3, 373.

one's choice. Second, Beverwijck was tied to the area because freedom
to trade with New England was part of an unspoken belief that the
exploitation of any hinterland for trading purposes was beyond criticism.
Finally, the town was connected to New England through local townsmen
of English (or Scottish) origin whom the Company had hired as soldiers
in the 1630s and 1640s and who established mercantile ties with New
England more readily than Dutch-speaking burghers.

Individual situations, though naturally episodic, illuminate the structure. When young Adam Hendricksz Vrooman apprenticed himself as a
millwright to Cornelis Willemsz van den Bergh, a farmer of Springfield
in 1670, he stepped in the world of John Pynchon but not out of the
Dutch world of Beverwijck. Willemsz – or Cornelius Williamson as Pynchon or his assistant wrote his name – was deeply in debt a year after
Vrooman's arrival and pursued by Asser Levy, one of the same New
Amsterdam merchants who had foreclosed mortgages and demanded
other payments in Beverwijck over the previous twenty years. He was
also indebted to an unspecified number of Beverwijck traders and to
Pynchon himself. To write off the farmer's obligations to him, Pynchon
called in Willemsz's debts in Beverwijck and used the services of townswoman Gertruy Hieronimus to do so. Pynchon's ties with Beverwijck
were many by 1670, but even in 1661, he was able to record "Mohawk
Bever" which he had acquired "of[f] ye Dutch men."[140] The notation is
a fragment of evidence, but it explains Vrooman's choice of Springfield
as a place to gain farming experience and suggests an interpenetration
of Springfield and Beverwijck that makes sense of later ongoing ties
between the two towns.

The relations of Jeremias van Rensselaer are easier to reconstruct. In
1658, he made, as he put it, "a little trip to New England" and saw the
country for the first time. His plan was to buy stock at Milford, Connecticut, but he and three or four companions traveled as far as New
Haven. A Dutch merchant resided in the town nine years later, so a
handelshuis may have been available to him then. He had consciously
taken "the opportunity to see something of the country" but admitted
that it did not "appeal to ... [him] very much." At the same time, he was
being directed by the family in Holland to include New England in his
business enterprises. He might, they urged, arrange with some acquain-
tance to sell a set of guns there. There had been no purchasers for them
in New Netherland, but New England, where "there are more people,"

140. Ibid., 372; Pynchon Record Books, 1664–1667, 3:312 (editor's pagination), Pynchon
Papers, John Pynchon's Account Books, 1661–94, 6 vols. in Connecticut Valley
Historical Society, Springfield, Mass. Ord. sess., April 13, 1671, CRA, 236; for his
dealing with "ffort Albany" in 1668, see Pynchon Record Books, 3, 143, Vol. 2:
370.

promised a larger market. Some months later, he hired an English farm-hand. All the while he must have been aware that a relative, Andries Teller, was a licensed trader in Boston and that his father-in-law took Teller's usefulness seriously.[141]

But not until 1669 did van Rensselaer consider continuous trading arrangements with Boston or, more specifically, Teller. In that year, he tried "an experiment." He took a small shipment of wheat to Boston and, making comparisons with conditions in New Netherland, got a surprisingly good price. As a result, he chartered a sloop that would again voyage from Rensselaerswyck to Boston with grain, this time eight hundred bushels. He was learning that each year he could get a return cargo and barter it for furs. He was also learning that the *Margreit* of Albany, the sloop in which he had one-eighth share, could be used for the trade and refitted more cheaply in Boston than New York.[142] His operations in Beverwijck, New York City, and Holland no longer made sense without Boston. In using Boston's wharves, he was perhaps beginning to see it as a city, rather than a *handelshuis*.

Van Rensselaer's contact in Boston was Andries Teller. The twenty-eight-year-old man was the eldest son of Willem Teller, a prominent merchant of Beverwijck. Willem Teller was "of Holland" and in every respect *burgerlijk*. He was a violent man – twice charged for manslaughter – and strongly distrusted by some townsmen, but he was not a marginal man in the community and never treated as such. Yet his career was thick with relationships with Englishmen; his affairs consistently related things English to Beverwijck before 1664. He chose an Englishwoman, Margaret Dongan, as his first wife. Her sister Catheryn married Sander Leendertsz Glen, a Scot also in the employ of the Company. Leendertsz and Teller were often partners. In 1658, they used the services of an Englishman, skipper Willem Thomassen (William Thompson), to send beaver to Holland. Thomassen resided in New Amsterdam and owned a property next to Schrijk after 1654. Charles Bridges (Carel van Brugge) held the patent. Neither Glen nor Teller put themselves in the debt of Levy, de Meyer, or the range of Dutch merchant-brokers operating in New Amsterdam. Their associate was John Willet, a man who held the great *burgerrecht* of New Amsterdam and was prominent among the English merchants. In *handelstijd* of 1663, Willet was in Beverwijck buying beaver. The court ignored his residence in New Amsterdam, recog-

141. JvR to JBvR, October 2, 1658, *Corr JvR*, 112; Deposition, October 28/November 7, 1667, *ER1*, 425; JvR to AvR [May 8, 1659], *Corr JvR*, 156; RvR to JvR, April 22, 1659, *Corr JvR*, 148; OvCortlandt to JvR [January, 1665], *Corr JvR*, 372. I believe Andries is the merchant referred to.
142. JvR to AvR, November 16/26, 1669, *Corr JvR*, 416; 424; 419.

nizing him as a "trader from New England." Willet's partner from Boston, Andries Teller, was also present for *handelstijd* that year.[143]

When Margaret Dongan died, Willem Teller married a Hartford woman, Maria Varlet, the widow of Schrijk. This gave him mercantile connections in Boston, Hartford, and New Amsterdam. His relationships with the English multiplied, of course, after 1664, but he was actually living out a process of socialization to English ways well established by that time. He could, for example, make differentiations others could not or did not make. He could distinguish a good map of England from a useless one and do this in a way that left a reasonably well trained merchant like Jeremias van Rensselaer very much in his debt. On one occasion, he even alleged "his ignorance of the Customes of Albany" before the English governor. He also had English, or at least non-Dutch, terms ready to hand. In 1660, he used the word "rabble" to abuse a number of townsmen disgruntled about trading restrictions during *handelstijd*. The word had seldom been used and was now received with disproportionate agitation. Its intent was interpreted as people "living indecently" or "rebel[ing] against the law of the public authorities or mak[ing] a law against the authorities." It may have carried the meaning of peddlers who lacked the *burgerlijk* quality of the established merchant.[144] The townsmen took Teller to court for using the word and required him to explain it; they made it the centerpiece of a lengthy petition against trade restrictions.

Teller's instinct to reach for a foreign rather than a Dutch word was out of the ordinary in Beverwijck in 1660. Hearing English was not extraordinary. For those trading into New England or regularly spending time in New Amsterdam where scores of Englishmen resided, it was inevitable. For some, listening to English was the result of Dutch–English marriages: the Glens married into English families; Rut Jacobson van Woest's sister-in-law was an Englishwoman. But speaking English was exceptional. Van Rensselaer had more opportunities than most to learn another language and was a reasonably curious man. Yet he regretted the obligation to learn English, which he felt the conquest required. In New Amsterdam as in Beverwijck, the Dutch population came from all the Netherlands provinces but had no apparent difficulty communicating

---

143. See, for example, Ord. sess., July 4, 1656, *CRB*, 281; Deposition, May 17, 1658, *ER4*, 26, 27; Conveyance, August 19, 1654, *ER1*, 188; see Power of attorney, August 23, 1660, *ER3*, 33; Bond August 7, 1663, *ER3*, 239; Bond of John Willet and Andries Teller, August 3, 1663, *ER3*, 236. The public records might equally be used to reconstruct the relationships of townsman Thomas Powell with New England.

144. JvR to JBvR, October 17, 1661, *Corr JvR*, 273; Deposition of William Teller, July 6, 1698, *DRCH*, 4:352; Ord. sess., June 8, 1660, *CRB*, 260; 267; 260; for Dutch society's abhorrence of peddlers as dishonest, see Temple, *Observations*, 137.

across dialects. Yet English and French were apparently unmanageable. On one occasion in New Amsterdam, a public conversation conducted in French caused a mob to collect. "As they spoke French to one another," declared an observer, "everybody stopped." Testimony offered to the court in English regularly required translation into Dutch.[145]

Trading with New England, then, had its own kind of sociology. Burghers, however, also compiled portfolios by investing in the Delaware River area, the Catskills, the far reaches of Normanskil, and Esopus. A study of each of those relationships is beyond the scope of this book. However, a moment's attention to their enterprises in Canada will perhaps make the case for each and reinforce a point made at the beginning of this chapter: In trading, the burghers did more than establish and construct business relations. They moved into the religious, political, familial, in fact, all the aspects of other cultures. In contacting the French settlers, the Beverwijck townsmen met people who were a mirror image of themselves. Both used space in much the same way. The men and women of Nova Francia traded out of company forts that were like merchantmen riding along the Saint Lawrence; they sought an economy based on furs and, like the Dutch, made the natives a working population. *Habitants* farmed close by the fortified *handelshuisen* and almost all lived within a mile of the river. Many were "floating traders," traveling north and south on "the busy fur route." The New Netherland connection was easy and existed because they too managed portfolios for a wide range of purposes other than farming.[146]

The signs of French Canadian contact with Beverwijck were read by traders in their account books. Robbert Sandersz was inscribing his records in the eighteenth century, when the English had proscribed the trade. He coded the names of Canadian clients in such symbols as clay pipes and roosters.[147]

Another sign of the French in Beverwijck argues that there was a more complex contact between the two cultures than such fragmentary evidence suggests. In 1668, Daniel Rinckhout left Beverwijck "in his canoe on the trip to Canada." He would have made his way north to Lake Champlain, then up the Richelieu River as far as Le Prarie de la Mag-

---

145. JvR to AvR [June 10/20, 1668], *Corr JvR*, 403, Minutes of January 28, 1662, *RNA*, 4:19; for translations, see Minutes of February 16, 1654, *RNA*, 1:163.
146. Richard Colebrook Harris, *The Seigneurial System in Early Canada: A Geographical Study* (Madison, 1968), 11, 12.
147. Entries from 1752 to 1755 cited in Jean Lunn, "The Illegal Fur Trade out of New France, 1713–1760," *Canadian Historical Association Report* (Ottawa, 1939), 63.

daleine. There he might have traded merchandise for furs with men and women who, like those in Schenectady, intended to forestall the trade, in this case, goods coming up from Beverwijck and heading for Montreal, just across the Saint Lawrence. Rinckhout journeyed as a trader but also as a deacon of the Reformed congregation. He had gl 1,100 with him and deposited part of it with the Beguine convent "to be sold to advantage" for "silver and gold." It was an investment that fellow deacons later validated by a receipt "from a Jesuit" and that may have been prompted by worries about the value of the guilder following the declaration of war between England and the Low Countries. Whatever the reasons, the Calvinist congregation, that is, the majority of burghers, would have known of this transaction with a Catholic institution.[148]

Both the convent and Beverwijck's deaconry were urban institutions. Both regularly invested and loaned considerable sums of money. The transaction of 1668 was fleeting, but it was an expression of structural resemblance and raises the possibility that the burghers may have understood Canada in ways we have not appreciated. Certainly, the way of life at Montreal legitimated Beverwijck's own culture. It was a place of walls and defenses, watergates and merchant ships, markets, and fairs. One visitor noted that the Montreal markets "burst into frenzied activity briefly in the spring when a great fleet of Huron or Ottawa canoes brought in the winter's peltry collection, and subsided back into normal routines during the rest of the year."[149] The comparisons are enticing, but the full impact of seventeeth-century Canadian culture upon the Beverwijck burghers' sense of themselves is another study.

Like time and space, the land around Beverwijck was *burgerlijk*. The farmland had not been turned into the well-ordered places for husbandmen found in seventeenth-century New England townships. An inventory of van Rensselaer's farms in 1651 showed no uniformity. Far from giving the rural lands the look of agricultural community, farms were as widely dispersed and unevenly profitable as in Kiliaen van Rensselaer's days. They averaged about sixty-six acres, but "one was as small as six,

---

148. Ord. sess., November 26, 1668, CRA, 37, and Ord. sess., October 19, 1668, CRA, 28.
149. Francis Jennings, *The Ambiguous Iroquois Empire. The Covenant Chain Confederation of Indian Tribes with English Colonies from Its Beginnings to the Lancaster Treaty of 1744* (New York, 1984), 69. For the visit of Baron LaHontan and the 1703 fair in Montreal, see Ruben Gold Thwaites, ed., *New Voyages to North America by the Baron LaHontan: Reprinted from the English edition of 1703, with facsimiles of original title-pages, maps, and illustrations, and the addition of Introduction, Notes and Index Vol. I* (Chicago, 1905), 92–5.

and one as large as seventy morgens, with diverse sizes in between." In 1668, there were twelve farms. If a farmer managed to get ten bushels of wheat to the acre, he considered it a good yield. Breeds of cattle were poor and pasturage scarce and insufficient. Cattle commonly ranged the forests and were inevitably thin, sickly, and scrawny. "Many died mysteriously, possibly poisoned by laurel. Often cows were lost in the woods, and dried up quickly, not being regularly milked. Sickness, insect pests, poor food meant cows gave but a quart or two of milk per day. Butter made from the cream of such browsing cows was of the lowest quality." Sheep raising amounted to little, and breeding was impossible; hogs were wood hogs – "long-legged, short in the body" and allowed to feed in the woods all winter.[150]

No orderliness or promise was there to compete with the promise of the market town. Certainly there was no emerging gentry to create a town-and-country dialectic. Agricultural land was real estate. It was static and, as such, a commodity subject to the burghers' higher valuation put on sloops, beaver, properties on Manhattan Island, or consignments of merchandise. Pynchon's name was on a European map by 1651 because he owned land. No Beverwijck resident looked for that distinction.

150. Inventory of animals in the colony . . . and memorandum of farms in the colony [1651], VRBM, 732–3; JvR to JBvR, July 11/21, 1668, Corr JvR, 406, 407; Ulysses Prentiss Hedrick, *A History of Agriculture in the State of New York* (Albany, 1933), 68.

3

Surrendering the Land, 1664

New Amsterdam Contrives Capitulation

[d'Engelsen] komende met eenige Oorlog schepen voor Nieu Amsterdam in Nieu Nederlant die so dwongen haer die plaets (wijl geen
ontset voor oogen en d'Engelsen wel 20 tegens 1 Nederlander waren)
sick me Accost der 8 September ober te geven zonder eenige tegen-
weer te doen.

[The English] arriving with some warships at New Amsterdam in
New Netherland so forced that place (because no relief was in sight
and there were twenty Englishmen to every Dutch man) on the dawn
of the 8th September to surrender without putting up any resistance.[1]

The *Hollantz Mercurius* chronicled the fall of New Amsterdam. It presented the surrender as a European happening. The news item was about
the world of Europeans and one of their overseas cities, in this case a
daughter city of Amsterdam.

The year 1664 was midway in what Dutch historians have called, for
its wars, "the long seventeenth century." Cities were reduced, invested,
held as pawns, exchanged, pillaged, and razed. Their magistrates looked
from ravelins, blockhouses, and parapets as armed foes operating vast
protection rackets negotiated ransoms. Dutch men of Petten paid eighty
guilders to buy off the Sea Beggars; inhabitants of Spijk handed over an
"annual tribute" to avoid pillaging by Spanish-backed forces in 1621.
And so it went.[2] Each city was responsible for its own survival (Figure
3.1). None thought to be exemplarist in its survival strategies, any more
than the *Hollantz Mercurius* thought to depict the fall of New Amsterdam
as an event in some synchronized social movement. In its description, it
had located the meaning without providing a simile: The surrender could

1. *Hollantz Mercurius, Vervaetende de voornaemste geschiedenissen. voorgvallen in 't
gantza Jaer 1664 In Christenrijck: Het Vijftiende Deel* (Haarlem, 1665), 154.
2. A. Th. Van Deursen, *Holland's Experience of War during the Revolt of the Netherlands,*
in A. C. Duke and C. A. Tamse, eds., *Britain and the Netherlands, VI: War and Society:
Papers Delivered to the Sixth Annual Anglo-Dutch Historical Conference* (The Hague,
1977), 27, 36.

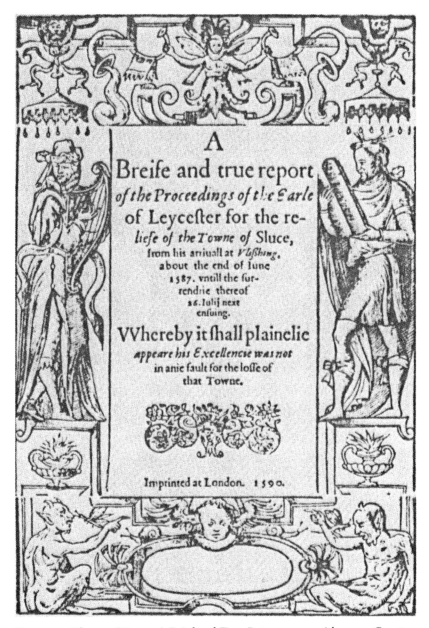

Figure 3.1. Thomas Digges, *A Brief and True Report*, 1590, title page. Courtesy of the British Library.

be known without an analogue to the capture of another city. There was
a nominalism in cities not yet leeched of their singularity by the nation-
state and in chronicles not yet disdained for their alleged interpretive
thinness by professional historians.[3]

New Amsterdam was another city isolated in its defenses and meeting
its fate. We may see the events of 1664 as the surrender of a province
or an ethnic group. But the structure within which it actually occurred
was that of the late medieval European order when great cities, each
acting as singular centers of political power, played dominant roles. New
Amsterdam acted within that order. Beverwijck did as well. Ironically,
however, Beverwijk's seizure by England and involvement in her subsequent wars against France for hegemony in North America meant living
the long seventeenth century into the seventh decade of the eighteenth
century. It meant having a markedly longer European experience than
most North American settlements.

When Colonel Richard Nicolls sailed into the great sound of New
Amsterdam on August 27, he undoubtedly had considerable intelligence
about the design of the city he was commissioned to "reduce...to an
entire obedience." The military operations had been planned in some
detail in London. There, vagaries of wind and weather were foreseen,
and the possibility of making for New England before going "first upon
Long Island." Any gaps in strategic information would have been closed
by Samuel Maverick, who, if he did not accompany the fleet directly to
New Amsterdam, crossed the Atlantic with it from London.[4]

Nicolls wrote many letters about the conquest of New Netherland and
his subsequent experiences over the next four years. They are distinctly
pleasurable to the twentieth-century Anglo-American reader. Even as
set out in the print chosen by Weed, Parsons & Company in 1853 for
the bulky volumes *Documents Relative to the Colonial History of the
State of New York: procured in Holland, England and France* or as encountered on the slightly transparent paper used for *The Documentary*

3. For other events in New Netherland presented as chronicle, see *Hollantz Mercurius*
(January 1666), 17:16. M.E.H.N. Mout, "Turken in het nieuws: Beeldvorming en
publiek opinie in de zestiende-eeuwse Nederlanden," *Tijdschrift voor Geschiedenis* (3,
1984), 97:3, 65, substantiates the noninterpretative character of *couranten*; R. B.
Walker, "The Newspaper Press in the Reign of William III," *Historical Journal* (1974),
17:708, argues that, at least in England, pamphlets were decidedly interpretive, while
"real issues and feelings were ignored by the newspapers."
4. Private instructions to Nicolls, April 23, 1664, *DRCH*, 3:57; Mavericke (*sic*) to Hon.
William Coventy (*sic*), July 21, 1664, *DRCH* 3:65–6. Details may also have been
supplied by John Scott, an English Long Islander who despised the Dutch and with
whom Nicolls consulted aboard Scott's sloop. See Bernice Schultz, *Colonial Hempstead*
(Lynbrook, N.Y., 1937), 78, and Lilian T. Mowrer, *The Indomitable John Scott: Citizen
of Long Island, 1632–1704* (New York, 1960), 117.

History of the State of New-York published in 1849, they are compelling. As a conqueror, Nicolls appears to have done everything right. He is reputed to have been "very nearly the perfect man for the delicate assignment," with Dutch people soon realizing that "they had a better and kinder government than ever before."⁵ While his co-commissioner, Robert Carr, allowed his men to pillage the Dutch settlement on the Delaware in the late summer of 1664, and the other commissioners, George Cartwright and Samuel Maverick, needed only months to be considered bullies in Boston, Nicolls seldom revealed himself as menacing the populace or arousing disfavor.

Nicolls often described himself as spending time coming to like the natives. "They will prove better subjects," he wrote of the Dutch, "than we have found in some of the other Colonyes [that is, Massachusetts]." Myth has it that he became "an intimate friend" of Stuyvesant, dining frequently at the Bowerie, and generally learning the inhabitants' ways. By spring of 1666, he could remind the English secretary of state, Lord Arlington, that to succeed one had to know "the knacke of trading here to differ from most other places" and appreciate New York as a prospering city.⁶ He was using "burgemasters" properly, referring to the city as "a factory," and receiving praise from his superiors as "prudent."⁷ Like van Twiller, van Curler, Jan Baptiste, and Jeremias van Rensselaer, he expressed an aesthetic appreciation of the land, making statements of

5. Allen W. Trelease, *Indian Affairs in Colonial New York: The Seventeenth Century* (Ithaca, 1960), 175; Montgomery Schuyler, *Richard Nicolls, First Governor of New York, 1664–1668,* Number 24, *Publications of the Order of Colonial Lords of Manors in America* (New York, 1933), 14; for similar views, see Randall Balmer, "Anglo–Dutch Wars and the Demise of Dutch Reformed Power, 1664–1682," *de halve maen* (1983), 58:5–8, Edward T. Corwin, *A Manual of the Reformed Church in America (Formerly Reformed Protestant Dutch Church) 1628–1902* (New York, 1902), 47, John Fiske, *The Dutch and Quaker Colonies in America* (Boston, 1899), 2:2, 4, who wrote of Nicolls as "one of the most genial and attractive figures in early American history," a man of "very different stuff" from Carr, and who excluded Nicolls from the "English Autocrats" in chap. 10. Oliver Albert Rink, Merchants and Magnates: Dutch New York, 1609–1664 (Ph.D. diss., University of Southern California, 1976), 355, uses "peaceful surrender" rather than "conquest" to characterize 1664; Schuyler, *Richard Nicolls,* 11; William Smith, Jr., *The History of the Province of New-York, from the First Discovery, to which is annexed a Description of the Country, an Account of the Inhabitants, their Trade, Religious and Political State, and the Constitution of the Courts of Justice in the Colony* (London, 1756), 36.

6. Nicolls to Arlington, April 9 [1666], *DRCH,* 3:114; Schuyler, *Richard Nicolls,* 16; Nicolls to Arlington, April 9 [1666], *DRCH,* 3:114; Jan Wagenaar saw the city as beginning to "prosper" in 1662. See Extract from *Wagenaar's "Beschryving van Amsterdam," Relating to the Colony of New Amstel, on the Delaware,* tr. John Romeyn Brodhead, CNYHS, 2nd. ser. (New York, 1857), 3 (Part 1), 291.

7. Schuyler, *Richard Nicolls,* 7; Philip J. Schwarz, *The Jarring Interests: New York's Boundary Makers, 1664–1776* (Albany, 1979), 27; Nicolls to Arlington, April 9, [1666], *DRCH,* 3:114.

delight well before landscape became scenery. Only a man who saw beauty in the "Manhatoes" would have had Jacob van de Water's map of the city reproduced for himself shortly after arrival and copied – with flags altered – for the Duke of York[8] (see Figure 2.6).

In all of this, it is forgotten that England and the Netherlands were not officially at war until March of 1665. New Amsterdam was the only city along the eastern coast of North America threatened with sacking in the colonial period. However marvelously self-possessed in bearing, Nicolls represented a plundering royal family, making him a predator as well.

Nicolls's actions and words need to be disentangled from his reputation, for together with other accounts in English, the record he left has been our main source for understanding this first significant contact between Dutch and English culture in North America. And it seems to suggest that coming to understand another culture is relatively easy. Yet as read from a Dutch perspective, or simply read with an appreciation of the difficulty of putting the scattered practices of another people into proper contexts, it is clear that the years after 1664 were filled with violence and resentment, much of it arising from cultural misunderstandings.

As a case in point, Nicolls's written communications with the Dutch may, at a distance, seem indistinguishable from theirs. Letters exchanged with Albany's magistrates were, after all, written in the same alphabet, divided into paragraphs, and enclosed in conventional salutations and complimentary closings. They softened harsh content with something like the same dissimulating phrases. Only when one reads something like "Mr Ryvan, Be pleased to translate these 3 letters into Dutch, as soon as you can conveniently...y^r aff^{ne} freind, R. Nicoll," or "I shall write to you [the magistrates of Albany] in Dutch...yet I suppose everyone of you can read English, at least Capt. Baker can assist you at any time," or when one examines calligraphy and sees an English signature on a page otherwise filled with characteristically seventeenth-century Dutch script is one reminded that the parties did not speak or understand the same language.[9] Some Dutch men may have been getting the notation correct, but if they could not read English well enough to get meanings and the contexts for meanings off the pages, then it is doubtful that

8. The Duke's Map, as it is called, was probably based on Jacques Cortelyou's 1660 survey. See I. N. Phelps Stokes, *The Iconography of Manhattan Island, 1498–1909* (New York, 1915), 1:207–10.
9. Nicolls to Gerard Swart, Sheriff of Albany, January 5, 1666/7, *DRCH*, 3:145, and Nichols to Commissaries of Albany, August 17, 1667, Livingston Papers, BW 10272 Group B (2), NYSA; for Fort Orange misunderstood by Englishmen to be "Fort Ferrania," see Carr to Nicolls, October 15, 1664, *DRCH*, 3:74.

Nicolls's Dutch correspondents were receiving communications well at all.

The Dutch and the English lacked a knowledge of the processes by which the two cultures reproduced and reinvigorated themselves. Each misinterpreted the other's actions. One such incident occurred during Nicolls's program for settling the capitulation of New Netherland. The negotiating meetings did not go off properly. His arrangements must have seemed faultless to him. The burghers were being deliberately and stubbornly thick-headed. In fact, he was both wrong and right. He was wrong because the Dutch meant to make only the most accommodating moves. There is nothing in the documents, at any rate, to suggest deliberate recalcitrance. He was correct, however, in judging the Dutch dense. They did not know how to capitulate his way. They knew their way, but as we shall see, he did not understand that.

For the participants, such misunderstandings added to the many instances of violence that occurred after 1664. For us, they give a richer picture of the conquest than we have had. The incidents document a significant difference between Dutch and English culture, indeed between continental European and English ways.

Proprieties of Surrendering a City

On Friday, October 14, the burgomasters of New Amsterdam complied with Nicolls's instructions to summon "the Magestracy of this City and some of the principal inhabitants" to the *stadhuis*. There, on the thirty-sixth day after the surrender of New Netherland, they and other city officials were meant to take the oath of allegiance to the English crown.[10] After assembling, they received Nicolls "with his Secretary at this City Hall." Immediately they heard him demand an explanation for the absence of Petrus Stuyvesant, secretary Cornelis van Ruyven, and "the preacher." In response, the Dutch officials assured him that they had not realized "that they should be sent for." They were then "invited" and immediately came. The city court's secretary put all of this in the records.

Having managed to convene the burghers, burgomasters Paulus Leendertsz van der Grift and Cornelis Steenwyck heard Nicolls's proposed formula for oath-taking. They and "divers other" then began debating until "finally all in the meeting *roundly* declared they could not take such an oath." Unless Nicolls added to the formula, "conformable to the Articles concluded on the Surrender of this place," they had to reject it. They stated their fear "that by taking such oath, they might nullify or

10. Minutes of October 14, 1664, *RNA*, 5:142.

render void the articles." Domini Johannes Megapolensis and van Ruyven, two of the initially uninvited men, argued that they "saw no impediments" but debate continued. Finally, Nicolls and his secretary angrily departed without the oaths of fealty.[11]

On the next Tuesday, Leendertsz and Steenwyck walked to the fort where Nicolls waited to examine or take possession of the city's Treasurers' Books. He was there with Cartwright and Thomas Willet. The "old burgomaster," that is, the senior one who would be the next rotated out of office, would have presented the key of the Chest of Deposits. But again the issue of oath taking arose. Now the burgomasters heard Nicolls threaten that the "commonalty" of the city might rise against them for refusing the oath. They persisted that they knew nothing of that and still "could not take the oath."[12] Finally Nicolls declared that he would put in writing that those refusing the oath would be considered "disturbers of the peace," that is, liable to criminal action in the form of prosecution for "mutiny." It might result in banishment or execution.

Thursday, two days later, was one of the usual weekly court days. The burgomasters again convened a meeting of principal men in the *stadhuis* and put before them "all proceedings, including what passed in the fort." Either Leendertsz or Steenwyck now read "the writing of Governour Nicolls" and asked whether "the oath could not now be taken, inasmuch as Mr. Nicolls [has] stated in writing that the articles of surrender are not broken in the least, nor intended to be broken." They debated the matter at length. This time it was *"universally* resolved in the affirmative, provided the above named Governor Nicolls shall seal his given writing." The next day, 251 New Netherlanders, including 30 men from Beverwijck, took oaths of allegiance to Charles II.[13]

These proceedings seem to indicate trivial breaches of protocol. In some inexplicable way Nicolls apparently first erred in assuming Stuyvesant, van Ruyven, and Megapolensis were principal inhabitants of New Amsterdam and would therefore be among those witnessing the officials' oath taking. He had seemingly neglected another trifling protocol by requiring an oath of allegiance in the form presented or by offering it without stating its conformity to the articles of surrender. Yet the Dutch leaders' persistence on this point – their actions in "roundly" refusing and then resisting his intimidation in the fort – shows that something

11. Ibid., 143, 144 (my italics).
12. Minutes of June 26, 1663, *RNA*, 4:268; Minutes of October 14, 1664, *RNA*, 5:144.
13. Minutes of October 20, 1664, *RNA*, 5:145 (my italics); *A Catalogue Alphabeticall of ye Names of such Inhabitants of New Yorke, Etc. as tooke the Oath to bee true subjects, to His Majestie, October 21st, 22nd, 24th and 26th dayes, 1664*, DRCH, 3:74-7.

more fundamental than etiquette was at stake. At stake was saving the substance of their political authority.

Before an enemy like Nicolls, Dutch burgomasters and principal men were representatives of an autonomous city, and there were complex rituals by which a city of the seventeenth century surrendered itself to the enemy. In the rituals of surrender, a city confronted its own autonomy and took measures to salvage it. In the Low Countries, it might negotiate strenuously for assistance from other cities, the province, or the *stadhouder* serving the States General, but it would intend to retain its independence. Without that, there was no political order within the commune or in the country. It was the balancing act that Utrecht's *vroedschap* (burgomasters and selected principal men) played out in 1674, when the city's autonomy was compromised by William III's dismissal of the magistrates. The *vroedschap* assembled and (falsely) announced that "several of the leading citizens" had requested the *wetsverzetting* (change of magistracy). In an attempt to create a legal fiction, they alleged that the burghers had never lost authority.[14]

This same delicate process was being undertaken in New Amsterdam in the first months of occupation. It was threatened by Nicolls's ignorance as much as by his policies. First, his procedures were blurring the distinction between the West India Company and the city. In that respect, there were two surrenders required, as he should have known. The city magistrates wanted a separate surrender, and they wanted it fully documented. Nicolls had failed to assist in this. At a future time the city might be restored to the United Provinces or to Amsterdam. (In fact, it was returned in 1673 and the conventional "restitutio view" later executed [Figure 3.2]. The restitution was considered a possibility as early as 1666.) It would then need to be shown that the burgomasters and *vroedschap* had surrendered only in the face of impossible circumstances. All of this had to be in writing.[15]

By 1664, New Amsterdam was proudly separate from the Company. The independence that it had achieved by 1664 was perhaps the most dramatic change in New Netherland preconquest history. By the time of

14. D. J. Roorda, *William III and the Utrecht "Government-Regulation," background, events and problems*, in *The Low Countries History Yearbook* (1979), 12:105.
15. For expectations of separate surrenders of the fort and city by Cornelis Evertsz de Jonge and Anthonij Colve when they captured Fort James and New York City in August, 1673, see *De Zeeuwsche Expeditie naar de West onder Cornelis Evertsen den Jonge 1672–1674; Nieuw Nederland een jaar onder Nederlandsch Bestuur* ('s-Gravenhage, 1928) xxxviii; for Monsieur J. B. Talon's proposal that Louis XIV negotiate a Dutch–English treaty in 1666 "stipulant la restitution de la Nouvelle Holland," see Talon to the Minister (Quebec), November 13, 1666, in *DRCH*, 9:56; for the "restitutio view," see Stokes, *Iconography*, 1 (Plate 8b): following 1:115, and see 220, 221.

Figure 3.2. "Nieu Amsterdam" (the Restitutio-Carolus Allard Map). I. N. Phelps Stokes Collection, Miriam and Ira D. Wallach Division of Art, Prints, and Photographs, the New York Public Library. Astor, Lenox, and Tilden Foundations.

Nicolls's arrival, the city, which had described its own condition in 1653 as "the weak state of this just-beginning city," had come to have a charter. Repeatedly it had pushed Stuyvesant to the wall, aggressively demanding independence from the Company.[16] By 1664, its privileges were daily and multiple enactments of the city's strength. They were the customary ones. The burghers could farm the excise on beer and wine, regulate bakers, control the slaughter and grain markets as well as the ferry and weighhouse, and collect fees at quays and the *stadhuis*. And all of this was amplified by taking the city of Amsterdam as an analogue. It helped inhabitants make sense of their experiences and enriched them. Traders measured merchandise according to "genuine Amsterdam ells, measures and weights." Bakers produced loaves of bread according to the customs of Holland, whereas farmers of the excise called on "Amsterdam's ancient charters" (*handvesten*) for their practices. Creditors pursued suits against bankrupts "according to the edicts and statutes of the Laudable City of Amsterdam in Holland," and burghers faced prosecution by the *schout* acting "according to the custom of the renowned City of Amsterdam." In instances beyond counting, New Netherlanders referred to New Amsterdam as simply Amsterdam.[17] It was the only seventeenth-century North American city that consciously strove to imitate a European city.

"Amsterdam" shaped the power slowly wrenched from Stuyvesant. It constructed an urban political style that governed time and civic courtesies. As in old Amsterdam, afternoons were the proper time to issue excise permits. When Tomas Fredericksen resigned as operator of the weigh scales, he appeared in the *stadhuis* where the court secretary carefully recorded the formalities. Fredericksen "thank[ed] the Magistrates for their favour; who accept it, thanking him for the service." Even the power to impose fines allowed the opportunity to enact Amsterdam's rituals for punishing citizens misbehaving "in the presence of a magistrate" or before his stoop. Although the acquittal of an Englishman who had failed to pay an excise fee because he was "unacquainted with the custom" was not uncommon, strangers in the city remained ignorant of its ways at their peril.[18]

The city controlled land development like any medieval commune. Its regulations governed the margins of the city – the gates, the wall, the riverbanks – and the land itself. It owned the strands by collecting wharf-

---

16. Minutes of March 3, 1653, *RNA*, 1:56.
17. Ordinance of July 19, 1649, *RNA*, 1:12; Minutes of February 8, 1661, *RNA*, 3:263; Minutes of August 22, 1662, *RNA*, 4:122; 1:283; see, for example, Oloff van Cortlandt to JvR, May 5, 1659, *Corr JvR*, 155.
18. Minutes of November 25, 1653, *RNA*, 1:130; Minutes of September 9, 1659, *RNA*, III:43; Minutes of October 2, 1663, *RNA*, IV:310.

age fees, regulating the selling of yachts, and determining trading procedures along the rivers. Having erected a wall, the burghers by 1656 could define themselves as those "within the walls of this City." The city disposed of public and private lands. Jacques Cortelyou's survey of its 342 houses in 1660 formed the basis of van de Water's map. Employees of the city roamed its streets, with the payment of "beneficies" to public servants calling forward a medieval world. By 1664, it had overawed not only the English in a place like Maryland but, to a considerable degree, Stuyvesant himself. From the distance of the twentieth century, it was part of "the recommencement of Europe" in America.[19]

Above all, the *stadhuis* stood as the primary symbol of New Amsterdam's privileges. Here the court held ordinary sessions on Tuesdays and Thursdays following Amsterdam practice. It was a body of inferior jurisdiction, referring capital crimes to the Company. But it was consummately confident of its own authority. Repeatedly its decisions made it a surrogate of the court of the "laudable City of Amsterdam." Much of its power was defined in opposition to that of the Company. The *stadhuis* and the fort symbolized that opposition. The *burgerwacht* (citizen militia of the city) seems to have exercised at the fort on occasion, lacking a *doelen* (archery ground) of its own in the city. But the separation was guarded. For example, Stuyvesant's *schout* put his petition for a divorce to the director-general and council of the Company at the fort. Yet this was only after completing the courtesy of appearing "before the [city] court," which had sent him on to Fort Amsterdam, "regard being had to the quality of the petitioner." "Burghers' prisoners" were held in the *stadhuis* and those offending against the Company were restrained in the fort. The opposition was acted out in posting placards on walls of the *stadhuis*, which was occasionally done without Stuyvesant's authorization, in contrast to displaying all public notices at the fort.[20]

Most dramatically, the careful opposition was maintained in the care with which Stuyvesant, his secretary, and *schout* refrained from entering the *stadhuis* and the city officials remained outside the fort. Stuyvesant entered the courtroom in the *stadhuis* only once yearly, to administer oaths of office. In 1661, he entered it twice, on the first occasion seeking approval for his *schout* to vote with city officials. The magistrates refused; they called on a precedent of "the City of Amsterdam in Europe" but

19. Notice, September 25, 1659, RNA, 1:44; Minutes of October 4, 1661, RNA, 3:377; 1:44; 2:52; 1:151; Fernand Braudel, *The Expansion of Europe and the "Longue Duree,"* in H. L. Wesseling, ed., *Expansion and Reaction: Essays on European Reaction and Reactions in Asia and Africa* (Leiden, 1978), 18–19.
20. Minutes of February 15, 1661, RNA, 3:267; 1:334, 339; Minutes of December 9, 1659, RNA, 3:90; 2:289; 1:174.

were overruled. On the second occasion, Stuyvesant went to settle a dispute between the burgomasters and *schepenen*, undoubtedly summoned by one party or the other. Never, at least as far as the records show, had he and his secretary together entered the courtroom. Similarly, if the magistrates went to the fort, it was always after deliberations and as a delegation. All other communications were strictly in writing.[21]

Never over the years of winning privileges from Stuyvesant would city magistrates have convened such a meeting in the *stadhuis* as that which they were ordered to call and at which they debated the Nicolls on October 13. It was unprecedented that the officials of the Company and the city, together with the *vroedschap* should be convened and meet in the *stadhuis*. This was especially so in circumstances affecting surrender. Consequently, the burgomasters made the intentional mistake of failing to summon Stuyvesant, van Ruyven and Megapolensis, men responsible to the Company and not the city. Without doubt the *vroedschap* was angered not only at Nicolls entering the court chamber with another outsider (probably Willet) but also at the insolence of Megapolensis and van Ruyven who, as the court secretary designedly put into the record, spoke out for easy acquiescence in taking the oath but were two of the only three men present with as great a stake in the Company's future as the city's.

Enactments of Republican Politics

The *vroedschap* was determined to ensure a proper surrender. None of their actions were out of confusion at the arrival of an unexpected enemy. On this and at least six occasions during the previous fifteen years, New Netherland had prepared for an English attack. Each time, the survival of the Dutch enterprise was in the balance. Yet each time, the Company's director general and the *vroedschap* (or the burgomasters acting on their own) behaved, at least to our eyes, as though it were an auction. They engaged in the dangerous gamble of haggling over the price of safety, while an enemy made possible fatal preparations. On each occasion, Stuyvesant was forced to concede privileges to the city in return for promises of military aid.[22] One year before the surrender, the magistrates and Stuyvesant enacted, in an eerie sequence of dramas, some of the

21. Minutes of February 1, 1661, and September 10, 1661, *RNA*, 3:257, 351; for data on written communications, see Minutes of February 1, 1661, and January 25, 1661, *RNA*, 3:257 and 252; for further examples, see Minutes of May 29, 1654, *RNA*, 1:201; Minutes of September 9, 1659, *RNA*, 3:45, Minutes of October 21, 1659, *RNA*, 3:60; Minutes of February 11, 1664, *RNA*, 5:19; Minutes of May 2, 1665, *RNA*, 5:233.
22. See Minutes of November 19, 1653, *RNA*, 1:128, 201.

formalities of 1664. Under fear of English attack, the magistrates gathered thirteen leading burghers "in the manner of a *vroedschap*" and inaugurated two days of deliberations regarding defenses. Stuyvesant wanted men for the fort and "other places." Gambling on his desperation, they bargained, threatening that, if he did not give them "forever... the income of the weighscales," he could be provoking *oproer*, the rioting of the populace.[23]

Such negotiations were not actions taken by politically irresponsible men. Nor was New Amsterdam, by the fact of its notable tolerance of non-Dutch people, merely what one Anglo-American historian called a *"colluvies omnium gentium,"* a gathering of people lacking organic ties with one another. It was the politics of a republic federation. New Amsterdam's maneuvering to defend its autonomy against the incursions of the Company was structurally similar to that taken by any number of municipalities in the Low Countries against the Estates General, or provinces against the States General. The magistrates and Stuyvesant would have understood it. When he wrote that, if "hostile movements of the English" did not convince the Company directors to make firm decisions regarding boundaries, "we had better make a move *both for your and our vindication*," he simply called upon a basic understanding of republican politics.[24]

In 1658, New Amsterdammers had also expected the troops of the English to "plunder" the city. And it was a European devastation imagined. The villages of the "out people" would be burned unless they paid bribes, *lantsmannen* (countrymen) would flock into the city where, if it could not be defended or tribute raised, all would face fire or wait, "closed in" to be "sold, betrayed and murdered."[25] The image of siege was not new. In 1652, Stuyvesant had been warned by the Company to help "the merchants and inhabitants convey their valuable property within the forts." In September 1659, townsman Jurrian Janse was cautious enough to write into a rental contract with *lantsman* Willem Bredenbent that he would "let him the house [in the city] on condition, if any war occurred, he [himself] may move in to dwell there."[26]

After such a siege, a court like that of New Amsterdam would have

23. Minutes of July 3, 1663, *RNA*, 4:273.
24. J[ohn] A. D[oyle], "Richard Nicolls," *Dictionary of National Biography, XIV*, ed. Sir Leslie Stephen and Sir Sidney Lee (London, 1921–2), 498; Minutes of February 11, 1664, *RNA*, 5:19.
25. Minutes of February 11, 1664, *RNA*, 5:21; Minutes of September 14, 1658, *RNA*, 3:15.
26. Arthur James Weise, *The History of the City of Albany, New York, from the Discovery of the Great River in 1524, by Verrazzano to the Present Time* (New York, 1884), 100; Minutes of September 23, 1659; *RNA*, 3:55.

expected its records to be examined. In the ordinary course of events, the books would have been inspected by subsequent burgomasters and *schepenen*. Should a city fall and later be restored, however, the records would certainly come under scrutiny by authorities looking to vindicate or punish the *vroedschap* in power at the time of the capitulation. It was essential that the records be complete and show that the leading men who were eligible to be members of the *vroedschap* and were under scrutiny, were deserving of future trust and merited reinstatement.[27]

A large part of the play surrounding the capitulation of New Amsterdam's authorities was of their contrivance. The debating and delaying tactics of October 14 to 17 confounded and angered Nicolls. However, the Dutch, in managing the two sessions and recording them, had got Nicolls to play his part properly in the account they needed for future examiners. They had literally controlled the written history of the event, showing that they had negotiated the best possible terms.

Moreover, oath taking had occurred only after the Englishman had put his word behind the threat that "the Commonalty of the City might rise against them." This possibility was the nightmare of the Dutch towns. It conjured such dread as to justify any reasonable preventative action. Fear of any hint of complicity in *oproer* led the New Amsterdam burgomasters of 1653 to defend themselves in advance of any possible disturbances. "We are guiltless," they recorded, "of any mischief [which] may hereafter (which God forbid) come... [from] the Commonalty." So it was well that the 1664 burgomasters could record themselves saying they "knew nothing of that." It was still better that they had it on record as the reason for swearing obedience to an English king. They had also got Nicolls to put in writing his pledge that the oaths did not contravene articles of surrender, which allowed the city its autonomous (privileged) status.[28]

Presumably the book with the minutes was placed in the cases ordered to be constructed in a room of the *stadhuis* in 1661.[29] It was possibly the first library constructed in New Netherland. The minutes were certainly one of the first constructed histories of the city.

27. See Joost de Damhouder, *Practycke In Criminele Saecken ghemaecht door Joost De Damhouder van Brugge,...* 1642 (Rotterdam, n.d.), 113, 122; for an example of Beverwijck's magistrates interrogated by the local court for their previous decisions, see Ord. sess., June 16, 1654, *CRB*, 158–9.

28. Minutes of November 25, 1653, *RNA*, 1:129; when he helped recapture the city in 1673, the Dutch commander Jacob Binckes "dealt very severely with people" because he thought "no one [had earlier] stipulated any privileges," as quoted in JvR to JBvR, November [1]4, 1673, *Corr JvR*, 453.

29. Berthold Fernow, ed., *Minutes of the Executive Boards* (sic) *of the Burgomasters of New Amsterdam* (New York, Arno Press reprint, 1970), 2:90.

Jeremias van Rensselaer and Richard Nicolls:
Land and Political Power

Surrendering the land was like a play. It was a series of performances
from which the actors took meanings of the surrender and themselves.
It is important to try to represent how some New Netherlanders living
outside New Amsterdam experienced it. Jeremias van Rensselaer, who
was then acting as director of Rensselaerswyck, and the burghers of
Beverwijck were actors in scenes of misunderstanding and violence. Fundamentally, the conflicts arose because the English expected the Dutch
to share their notions about the proper occupancy of land. When these
expectations were not met, the Dutch were taken to be somehow
uncivilized.

Five months before the capture of New Amsterdam, Jeremias van
Rensselaer attended the *gemene lantdagh*, a meeting of two leading men
from each of the New Netherland towns (and Rensselaerswyck) convened
in New Amsterdam to consider its parlous state. Predictably he approached the sessions presupposing that the essentially dispersive nature
of political power would determine their decisions. Each town would
hear arguments – beginning with those offered by the town with the
most ancient privileges – but would decide according to its own self-
interest. Intending to make certain that the order of precedence was
correct, he opened "a great dispute" regarding it. As Dordrecht did in
Holland, he demanded "the right [of Rensselaerswyck] to preside . . . as
being the oldest colonists." The *lantdagh* accepted him as presiding officer
but gave New Amsterdam precedence, allowing its representatives to
speak first.[30]

In the process of surrender that spanned the ensuing years, van Rensselaer continued to construe power as fundamentally divisible. He expected the surrender to be reversible, laying plans in 1668 "not doubting
but that we should again come under the jurisdiction of their High Mightinesses."[31] From 1664 to his death ten years later, he followed the fortunes of patria by remarking on the changing fate of its cities. In 1674,
he wrote home, "I should like to know how Naarden was fortified."
Later he asked for confirmation that the king of France had "again
withdrawn from all his conquered cities [in the Low Countries] except
Maestricht." Thirteen years earlier he seemed to assume that England,

30. JvR to JBvR, April 25, 1664, *Corr JvR*, 353; E[dmund] B. O'Callaghan, *Register of
New Netherland, 1626–1674* (Albany, 1865), 147; for New Amsterdam's counterclaim
to being "the oldest and most considerable" city, see Minutes of October 22, 1663,
RNA, 4:319.
31. JvR to JBvR, June 10/20, 1668, *Corr JvR*, 399.

too, could be grasped by knowing its cities. "Send me," he wrote to an elder brother, "another map of England...but the country must be set off better by cities, for...the other map was no good, there were no cities shown on it."[32]

English mapmakers, of course, were still reprinting Humphrey Lhuyd's 1570 map of England and Wales. There urban settlements were represented with "little differentiation between larger and smaller places." Englishmen were learning their country as counties. Cartographically and politically, England was not its cities. So van Rensselaer was mistaken.[33] But he was especially in error in expecting the English conquerors to share his assumptions about political authority and how civilized men used it.

Dispersed Power: Family and State

Van Rensselaer had exercised a good deal of power in his life before September of 1664. His authority came from being a reliable merchant, a professional man for whom custom reserved the salutation "the honourable, pious, and very discreet." His education as a merchant came principally from Jan Baptiste, an older brother who was, on one occasion, unequivocal in identifying the key to success for his now twenty-four-year-old brother: Discipline yourself to make countless decisions wisely by meticulous and daily organization. "If in my time I could have settled down to writing [accounts and letters] as regularly as I do at present," Jan Baptiste advised, "it would have been worth a thousand guilders to me."[34] But Jan Baptiste provided more than advice. He appointed him director of Rensselaerswyck in 1658.

Jeremias's life took its contours from the structure of seventeenth-century Dutch life. At least in the northern Netherlands, the chances were overwhelming that a wealthy man like his father would be a city merchant and that he would start a family late in life. It was the convention that he or his wife would apprentice sons at an early age to merchant-relatives or merchant-friends. The children would learn that parental authority was meant to be dispersed through an extended family. This splintering of authority did not deny the endurance of special ties, particularly those

32. JvR to RvR, July 3, 1674, *Corr JvR*, 465; JvR to Vastrick, August 28, 1674, *Corr JvR*, 471; JvR to JBvR, October 17, 1661, *Corr JvR*, 273.
33. Norman Thrower, *Maps and Man: An Examination of Cartography in Relation to Culture and Civilization* (New York, 1972), 58.
34. JvR to AvR, [October? 1656], *Corr JvR*, 32, see also 82, 83, 84, 143; JBvR to JvR, April 23, 1660, *Corr JvR*, 215.

of father with sons and mother with daughters.³⁵ But parental solicitude showed chiefly in providing children with a numerous cousinry, one so widely dispersed that offspring could expect sustenance at any one or several of its geographical extremities. This meant keeping up an elaborate correspondence, writing references, procuring apprenticeships, arranging proper marriages, lending money and housing, and training relatives' children.

It was a role for both parents. The children would know their mother's shared role in as small a token as the retention of her family name. For Jeremias, for example, his mother's letters were not always reminders of his father because she frequently signed herself Juffrow Anna van Wely. The father's role was not merely parenting, even in the legal sense. Roman law made that clear. *Gebroedered* (brother-ed) captures this well. He was to give sons brothers, to generate relationships as strong as the parental one. He was also to assume a major role in educating his grandchildren, so that they too learned to recognize the family as a pool of beneficiaries.³⁶

Englishmen misunderstood this. In 1665, a pamphleteer satirized that "the Father and the Son" among the Dutch were surely created simultaneously as "there is not to be found ... any Demonstration of Duty or Authority to distinguish them." In fact, the place of the eldest son was recognized but primogeniture, for example, was not the rule. Jeremias would have expected that, in his deceased mother's estate, "everyone is to share equally in everything" and that family members would draw lots for certain articles in the estate. This was the *lantdagh* played out on the family stage. Anna van Rensselaer's caution to Jeremias, "Respect your brother as the eldest," would have echoed the call for respect due to Dordrecht and New Amsterdam as the oldest political communities in Holland and New Netherland.³⁷

Within this structure van Rensselaer experienced and exercised authority. He was young and untrained coming to North America at the age of about twenty-five yet he would have known that he was sent into

---

35. See *Schoolboekjen van Nederlandsche Deugden, uitgegeven door de Maatschappij tot Met van 't Algemeen* (Amsterdam, 1788), 18–23, and Bruyn Harmensz, *T'samenspraeck tusschen Vaden Ende Soon over de Deucht van Weynich Spreechen* (Delf, 1619), 1–8.
36. Patrick M. Colquhoun, *A Summary of the Roman Civil Law, Illustrated by Commentaries on and Parallels from the Mosaic, Canon, Mohammedan, English and Foreign Law* (London, 1849), 1:448.
37. *Quaeries, or a Dish of Pickled-Herring Shread, Cut and prepared according to the Dutch Fashion. For the squeamish Consciences of English Phanaticks, who pray for the New building of their Old Babell. Printed at Amsterdam for the use of the High and Mighty States of Holland, and printed at London,* 1665, 4; JBvR to JvR, May 9, 1671[?], *Corr JvR*, 437; AvR to JvR, December 26, 1654, *Corr JvR*, 15.

a cousinry of at least eight men and women from whom he could expect to derive support and with whom he could also expect to share authority. Jeremias, for example, was never more than manager of the patroonship. Both he and his young cousin Jan Bastiaensz van Gutsenhoven were clearly sent to Rensselaerswyck to gain administrative experience and earn a more solid place in the family's enterprises.[38]

In van Rensselaer's experience of familial, commercial, and political life, no one could have been seen exercising sole authority, either in the Rensselaerswyck venture or earlier enterprises at home. His father made independent decisions but effected them within changing sets of partners. His own decisions were closely tracked by family and a range of partners. Jan Baptiste, Anna, Uncle Johannes van Wely, and another brother, Rychart, all tutored him in a structure that subjected power to collegiality.

The Netherlands did the same. It was an age when the captain of a ship carrying an English ambassador (or his wife) expected passing Dutch vessels to dip their colors because the emissary was thought to bear the king's person. The States General entertained no such fictions. The *stadhouder* Frederick Henry wrote to a Dutch ambassador in 1625, "not I, but *messieurs les Etats* are the sovereigns of these provinces."[39] Ambassadorial missions were "entrusted to a multiple embassy," and even the admiralty could not bring itself to function under a single admiral-general. In the cities, groups of burghers held power. They were the orphan masters, marksmen, and trading company directors who sat for Rembrandt's or Hals's group portraits.[40]

New Netherland also taught van Rensselaer the excellence of dispersed political power. Stuyvesant was merely "the general," not a governor. As Jeremias and every colonist knew, he was one of the Company's soldiers, paid about gl 3,600 a year. His authority lay in competently administering the trading station and not in embodying the state in his person or lands. He was liable to recall without explanation and could

38. The cousins and siblings were Willem Teller, Jan Bastiaen van Gutsenhoven, Robert Vastrick, Cornelis van Schel, Arent van Curler, Philip P. Schuyler, Brandt van Slectenhorst, Jan Baptiste van Rensselaer; I am translating van Rensselaer's role as *directie* as "manager," whereas Van Laer uses "administrator." See JvR to Oloff van Cortlandt, September 12/22, 1665, *Corr JvR*, 382, and W.J. Van Balen, *Holland aan de Hudson: Een verhaal van Nieuw Nederland* (Amsterdam, 1943), 66 who uses "bewindvoerder" for someone in a managerial role.
39. P.J. Blok, *The Life of Admiral De Ruyter*, tr. G. J. Renier (Connecticut, 1975), 171, 172, quoted from "Archives de la Maison d'Orange-Nassau," Deuxieme Serie, tome III, 3302, in Baronesse Suzette Van Zuylen Van Myevelt, *Court Life in the Dutch Republic* (London, 1906), 15.
40. Rowen, *John de Witt: Grand Pensionary of Holland, 1625–1672* (Princeton, 1978), 244; Robert Fruin, *Geschiedenis der Statsinstellingen in Nederland tot den val der Republiek* ('s-Gravenhage, 1901), 200.

expect all his decisions to be approved in Holland except in extreme emergencies. The kinds of decisions he could make, moreover, were often military ones, and they diminished rather than enlarged his prestige. As commander, Stuyvesant conducted foreign affairs and did so remarkably well, despite New Netherland's vulnerable status in North America. However, these tasks were enacted within the general Dutch distrust of soldiers and armies, an anxiety once expressed by a tough man like Kiliaen van Rensselaer: "There is no place for the military in government."[41]

Some men and women affirmed Stuyvesant's unexceptional place in New Netherland visually by writing his name, unadorned, over and over again in their ledgerbooks. Frequently it appeared in accounts with no title whatsoever. Evert Nolden recorded that he bought French wines *"met Sander [Leendertsz Glen?] en met Stuivesant."* A loose account in Jan Baptiste's hand had the director-general simply as "Stuijvesant." In a promissory note to Jeremias van Rensselaer for gl 290, the commander himself signed only his patronymic. In Maria van Rensselaer's accounts for 1660, "Pr Struijvesant" was inscribed simply, while Abraham Staats was "Mr Abram" on the same page. Gerret Swart put him down as "P. Stuyvesant."[42] All of this helps explain why Stuyvesant could never intimidate van Rensselaer and why the young director could boast of winding the general "around ... [his] little finger."[43]

The Governor and the Director:
The Nicolls–Van Rensselaer Letter

It is against this background that one of the most revealing letters of seventeenth-century New York may be placed. It was written to van Rensselaer by Nicolls. Set in context, it reveals expectations about political power significantly different from those of van Rensselaer and suggests the notional distance separating the two men on this issue. I am not the first to consider the letter remarkable. Obviously I mean to place it in the context I have been constructing, but it has been used in folklore,

41. JvR to JBvR, September 14, 1660, *Corr JvR*, 239; KvR to A. vander Donck, March 9, 1643, *VRBM*, 641.
42. Bill of Evert Nolden, 1657, on Jeremias van Rensselaer, Papers VRMP, SC7079, Box 13, Folder 45, NYSA, Notes and Bonds (5–17), VRMP, SC7079, Box 13, Folder 5, (1657–1669), 13–16 [Dated 1/10 April, 1665], NYSA; Clad Reecken boeck voor Maria van Rensselaer, 1658–1665, [Memorandum, Book of Accounts Kept by Maria van Rensselaer, 1658–1665], VRMP, SC7079, Box 41, n.p., NYSA; Account of G. Swart against P. Stuyvesant (1660), VRMP, 7079, Box 13, NYSA; Clad Reecken boeck voor Maria van Rensselaer, 1658–1665, VRMP, SC7079, Box 41, n.p., NYSA.
43. Account of G. Swart against P. Stuyvesant (1660), VRMP, 7079, Box 13, NYSA.

local history, and other narratives since Nicolls inscribed it in November 1666.[44]

"Monsieur Renzelaer," the letter opened. "By the date of y^r letter from Renzelaerwicke in Albany October the 25th I percieve that you conclude the Towne of Albany to be part of Renzelaerwick; I give you friendly advice not to grasp at too much authority, and you may probably obtain the post more to y^r profitt." He went on, "If you imagine there is pleasure in titles of Government I wish that I could serue your appetite, for I have found only trouble. You see me," he continued, "to plead for a succession to y^r brother Baptista as of right belonging to you, I will make answer in a Latine verse which in some sort you may apply, Filius ante diem Patrios inquirit in annos." Nicolls concluded, "Let there be no Controversies of this nature betweene you and mee who will in all reasonable things serue you. Sett y^r hearth therefore at rest to bee contented with the profitt not the government of a Colony till we heare from His Royall Highness. In my letter to the Commissaries you will find Theunis Cornelis Spitsenberg confirmed. My service to y^r wife, y^r brother and Mon^r Curler. I am Y^r aff^{te} freind R. Nicolls 6/16 9ber, 1666."[45]

The letter is a harsh one. But Nicolls had often treated van Rensselaer harshly and, on the issue of the future of Rensselaerswyck, treacherously. He knew in April of 1666, for example, that all land west of the Hudson River was either already ceded away by the Duke of York to Lord Baltimore and Carteret or was in jeopardy as to ownership. And in May he was following private instructions to "continue Jeremias van Rensselaer [in office]... *for the time being.*" He was denying the legality of all *grondbrieven* (patents) issued before 1664 on the fiction that the Dutch had never established rightful claim but was, at the same time, personally upholding the validity of Dutch patents on Long Island and arguing that such instruments were legal.[46] He patented land within the *colonie* to

44. See, for examples, Edward A. Collier, *A History of Old Kinderhook from Aboriginal Days to the Present Time: Including a Story of the Early Settlers, Their Homesteads, Their Traditions, and Their Descendents; with an Account of Their Civic, Social, Political, Educational, and Religious Life* (New York, 1914), 7; Maunsell Van Rensselaer, *Annals of the Van Rensselaers in the United States, Especially as They Relate to the Family of Killian K. Van Rensselaer, Representative from Albany in the Seventh, Eighth, Ninth, and Tenth Congresses* (Albany, 1888), 19; Sung Bok Kim, *Landlord and Tenant in Colonial New York: Manorial Society, 1664–1775* (Chapel Hill, N.C., 1978), 12–13.
45. Nicolls to JvR, October 6/16, 1666, *Corr JvR*, 389, and reprinted in *DRCH*, 3:143–4. This letter is deposited in the British State papers but not VRMP.
46. See S[amuel] G[eorge] Nissenson, *The Patroon's Domain* (New York, 1937), 269; Nicolls to Arlington, April 9 [1666], *DRCH*, 3:114, and Confirmation by Nicolls of the privleges [*sic*] enjoyed by J. V. Rensselaer, May 8, 1666, VRMP, SC7079, Box 13, Folder 18, NYSA (my italics); Schwarz, *Jarring Interests*, 13.

townsmen, and when he returned to court in 1668, was reported as being "no friend" of the van Rensselaers. Jeremias found that "strange" because, before his departure, either his brother or the *colonie*'s secretary had heard Nicolls "promise to show [them] every friendship and favor."[47]

By the autumn of 1666 when he rebuked van Rensselaer, Nicolls had endured twenty-seven months of trying to impose royal authority upon the king's North American plantations. In an irritable letter of 1665 to the Massachusetts authorities, he and the other commissioners had, in fact, denounced that colony's expansionism and recalcitrance with a rebuke remarkably similar to that directed to van Rensselaer: "Striving to grasp too much may make you hold but a little." Only that spring he had been complimented for signs of success. The royal court's jealous watchdog, Edward Hyde (Lord Clarendon), had praised him for "doing good" for his country, and Charles II had sent him £200 and agreed that he might return to court "at [his] Liberty." But little progress had been made. The New England colonies remained, as he put it, "in contempt of the monarch's authority." Military force was not an option but neither were economic sanctions. Late in 1666, Nicolls had suggested that Whitehall chastise Boston by a "temporary Embargo on their Trade." New York could receive Boston goods "and from hence [see them] carried into England." The measure was not adopted, and later threats that "his Mat^{ies} arme will...be strecht forth [against] usurpation" affected nothing.[48]

Nicolls wrote despising the disloyalty of the New Englanders and resenting time spent with them and away from New York. But he knew them down to the last iota. He not only knew their disobedience but how it would be expressed. He could have anticipated that their sedition would be publicly voiced on muster fields, that Bostonians would mock the commissioners by blowing trumpets outside their lodgings, and that they would start rumors of increased taxes.[49]

With the Dutch it was different. The protocols of surrender at New Amsterdam had tripped him up. Capitulation by the upriver communities was also marked by violence and misunderstanding. There had been rebellion in Esopus (Kingston), and news of it had already reached Bos-

47. Nissenson, *Patroon's Domain*, 269, 279; JvR to JBvR, May 12/22, 1669, *Corr JvR*, 413; JvR to JBvR, August 8/18, 1668, *Corr JvR*, 411.
48. Commissioners to the Governor and Council of Massachusetts, July 16, 1665, *DRCH*, 3:99; Clarendon to Nicolls, April 13, 1666, *DRCH*, 3:116; Nicolls to Secretary Morrice, October 24, 1666, *DRCH*, 3:136; Nicolls to Council of Massachusetts, June 12, 1668, *DRCH*, 3:171.
49. Report of the King's Commissioners concerning Massachusetts, n.d., *DRCH*, 3:110, and Carr and Maverick to Secretary of State, November 20, 1665, *DRCH*, 3:107.

ton. It arose from the misconduct of soldiers, their contempt of the burgherguard and violations of privacy as men quartered on the populace. People feared the town would be fired.[50]

The uneasy surrender of Albany was also still going on. The disposition of Rensselaerswyck was a major component in the new order of things, but Nicolls and van Rensselaer were in conflict about it, particularly its political relationship to the town of Albany. Also, in the early months of occupation, Nicolls had needed van Rensselaer's cooperation and particularly solicited his help in avoiding "a war" – as van Rensselaer described it – presumably rebellious actions taken by the natives and some local inhabitants. Yet he found him looking to his own interests, showing bad faith by not exacting oaths of allegiance from tenants, and continually falling short of delivering the agreed tribute of wheat and planks.[51]

Van Rensselaer's recalcitrance in the first two years of the occupation was more than clear. He now sought a northern boundary of "one mile above the *vlackte*" for the colony whereas he reckoned it at half that distance before the conquest. He was secretive about activities conducted on behalf of the Company and failed to acknowledge that certain of his town properties were actually owned in Holland.[52] He was no man's fool. He had the political sense to send Stuyvesant documents allegedly proving that the English had encouraged two Mohawks to burn a burgher's house early in 1664 and to see that Nicolls's plan to combine the courts of Beverwijck and Rensselaerswyck was a change of fundamental law – "*hij [Nicolls] heeft de wet hier heel verstelf*" (he has entirely altered the law here).[53]

Some time in 1666, probably in August when Nicolls was in Albany, he and van Rensselaer clashed. It was the summer when the town was still recovering from floods caused by the breaking up of the ice on April 7. Damage had been extensive, with as many as forty houses swept away, animals lost, and crops so badly destroyed that "many farmers" had "no grain for seeding or for making bread." Others were worse off than van Rensselaer, but his barn and brewery were "carried away" together with

50. Cartwright to Nicolls, April 19, 1665, DRCH, 3:94; *The Papers that Concern ye Esopus Mutinys with ye Death of Henrick Cornelius, DRCH, 13: 410, 409;* "Testimonies sent to Nicolls [1667]." *Second Annual Report of the State Historian of the State of New York, transmitted to the Legislature, February 22, 1897* (Albany, 1897), 203.
51. JvR to JBvR, October 21/11 (sic), 1664, Corr JvR, 365; JvR to Nicolls, November 15/25, 1664, Corr JvR, 369; JvR to JBvR, October 21/11 (sic), Corr JvR, 365.
52. JvR to JBvR, April 25, 1664, Corr JvR, 354, and see 366; JvR to SvCortlandt, August 5, 1664, Corr JvR, 359, and JvR to JBvR, [July 11/21, 1668], Corr JvR, 405–6.
53. JvR to Nicolls, November 15/25, 1664, Corr JvR, 356, and JvR to OvCortlandt, September 12/22, 1665, Corr JvR, 382, 382 n. 782.

his house, which contained two rooms full of oats and wheat, including some 250 schepels (195 bushels) that were tribute demanded by Nicolls. He wrote to the governor, claiming that flood damage had "released [him] from that obligation." Nicolls rejected his claim and before November 4 had ordered him to pay "in full." On November 16, he wrote the response to a letter of van Rensselaer's in which he construed him to have claimed "the Towne of Albany to be part of Relselaerwijk." The English governor had then offered his "freindly aduice [sic]" not to "grasp at too much authority."[54]

Before November, the relationship between Nicolls and van Rensselaer had begun to be a reasonably constant, if sometimes tense, one. They had met at least three times and corresponded with regularity, discussing the quartering of soldiers, the Indian trade, imports and exports at New Amsterdam, the recent business affairs of Jan van Gutsenhoven, family affairs, news, and the weather. Nicolls had more than once met Jeremias's brother Rychart, his cousins van Curler and Schuyler, his close friend Abraham Staats, and possibly his cousin Andries Teller in Boston. On one occasion, he addressed a warm and newsy letter to "his loving freind [sic] Mr. Jeremias van Renzlaer at Albany," and, at another time, the two men exchanged hopes for the blessings of peace.[55] The letter of November 16 makes it clear, however, that Nicolls simply did not understand van Rensselaer, the meaning of the patroonship, or the structure of Dutch life.

Nicolls brought to his considerations of Rensselaerswyck the model of an English manor. He assumed it to be an estate that reflected and advanced social and political aspirations of the highest sort, as it did in England. This was not the Dutch way of construing landownership and certainly not the way Jeremias looked upon Rensselaerswyck or his role in its administration. Nicolls rebuked van Rensselaer for seeking "titles of Government" and "the government of a Colony." Yet it is inconceivable that he would have entertained such aspirations. Even if the colony survived English rule intact, he could not have thought to be patroon. Kiliaen van Rensselaer's eldest son, Johannes, was marked for that, and even he would make decisions about what Jeremias called "our patrimonial lands" with Dutch shareholders and, always, with the family. And if he had somehow thought to be patroon, it was in any case not a significant determinant of one's political power or social status. An investment in land could become an unprofitable one. It was for the director

54. JvR to JBvR [October 25/November 4, 1666], *Corr JvR*, 388; SvCortlandt to JvR, [1665?], *Corr JvR*, 386; Nicolls to JvR, October 6/16, 1666, *Corr JvR*, 389.
55. Nicolls to JvR, January 7, 1667/8, File No. 11346–2, NYSA; Nicolls to JvR, January 7, 1667/8 File No. 11346–2, NYSA.

of an estate to bring it to full utilization, report on its profitability, and counsel further action. Should its profits fail, the good manager counseled the alienation of marginal lands and, if necessary, the disposal of the entire enterprise.[56]

Six years before Nicolls's denunciation of his "appetite" for power, Jeremias began encouraging the family in Holland to sell properties within the colony. He showed no sense of the tactics taken by English ruling families to preserve manorial estates intact. If they could sell more of the farms, he pleaded, "it would be far better." "In my opinion," he wrote elsewhere, "it would be better to sell some farms and to send over the money" [to Holland]. And again to Jan Baptiste, "I shall await your answer whether we should sell some farms, as at Bettelem [Bethlehem], which yield little revenue anyway." With and without permission of the family, Jeremias pursued a policy of disposing of the colony's land. He sold properties "often for a trifle . . . in fee Simple." He was, as one scholar has put it, "a consistent advocate of land sales."[57]

The metaphor of profit and loss made sense of "lord" and businessman for him. He mused on his real "appetite": desire for success in ventures of his own choosing. "When I busied myself only with my own affairs," he reflected, "I always had money and was content, but now I sit with empty hands and . . . cannot even pay for the goods which I ordered. One may think oneself to be a great lord, but it does not amount to much." He was then residing in a house 20 feet long by 22 feet wide and awaiting a good farm for himself.[58]

In the initial months of surrender, Cartwright had assumed that an estate like Rensselaerswyck belonged to one man and could be negotiated in Jeremias's name. But van Rensselaer told him authoritatively that he "could not do that, the colony was jointly held." Elsewhere he insisted, "even if it [the anticipated patent] were issued in my name, I should not for that reason claim the right of patroon."[59] He was acting in a managerial capacity for the family and, in fact, expected to complete his years in North America well before the English came. If he had pleaded "for a succession to . . . brother Baptista" as Nicolls accused, it could only

56. For van Rensselaer's counsels in this vein, see Nissenson, *Patroon's Domain*, 50.
57. JvR to JBvR [June 3–6, 1660], *Corr JvR*, 225; JvR to JBvR, September 154, 1660, *Corr JvR*, 239; Memorandum Book of John G. Van Schaick, March 29, 1782, Van Schaick Family Papers, EQ 10837, NYSA; Nissenson, *Patroon's Domain*, 49.
58. JvR to JBvR, October 17, 1661, *Corr JvR*, 270.
59. JvR to JBvR, October 21/11 (sic), *Corr JvR*, 366. Van Rensselaer was at times imprecise in citing his title. On one occasion he signed himself "Colonie pastor and director" [trans.] [Ledger, 1666–1708, August 25, 1677], but three months later "patroon" [Ledger, 1666–1708, October 30, 1677]. VRMP, 10643, NYSA; JvR to JBvR, November 16/26, 1670, *Corr JvR*, 431.

have been to retain the directorship. Jan Baptiste had never held any other position.

All of this puts particularly wide of the mark the Latin verse Nicolls inserted in his letter of November 16 in order to drive home his point about greed for land and power: "*Filius ante diem Patrios inquirit in annos*" (The Sonne his Fathers hastie death desires).[60] The line was taken from Ovid's *Metamorphoses*, a classic prescribed in English schools in the seventeenth century and well known to men of letters. The statement was meant to castigate greed and had particular application in a society like England whose ruling ethos was that of a rural aristocracy. It related power unequivocally to paternity, locating virtue in filiopietism and defining vice as the envy a son might feel for his father's continuing power over lands and flocks that would be his inheritance.

Some would argue that Nicolls's use of this classical text was an unconscious attempt to depersonalize his criticism of van Rensselaer by universalizing the evil of his greed. However that may be, the passage is, even on its own, a cruel one. Set in its original surrounding text, the cruelty is thickened. Ovid describes the fourth of a series of ages that had come upon man: an "iron age" of unsurpassed wickedness. With iron had come "Deceit, violence, criminal greed and war."

> All live by spoyle. The Host his Guest betrayes;
> Sons, Fathers-in-lawe: 'twixt Brethren love decayes,
> Wives husbands, Husbands wives attempt to kill:
> And cruell Step-mothers pale poysons fill.
> The Sonne his Fathers hastie death desires:
> Foild Pietie, trod underfoot, expires.[61]

Nicolls's abstraction reduced to seven words a wide range of English experiences, all of which had patriarchalism and primogeniture as the cornerstone. The filiative model was a telling motif permeating English life in the sixth decade of the seventeenth century. The restoration of Charles II had meant the ritual restoration of the murdered king-father Charles I as well. The romance of his escape from England to Europe and return to the throne changed simple genealogy into melodrama. The younger Charles wrung the allegorical motifs of his father's assassination and his own picaresque escapes for every drop of their romance "for the rest of his life."[62]

60. George Sandys, *Ovid's Metamorphoses Englished* [Oxford, 1632] (London, 1976), 4.
61. Sandys, *Ovid's Metamorphoses Englished*, 4. Mary M. Innes, tr. and ed., *The Metamorphoses of Ovid* (Harmondsworth, 1955), 33, translates the passage as "and sons pried into their fathers' horoscopes, impatient for them to die."
62. Christopher Falkers, *The Life and Times of Charles II* (London, 1972), 35, 68.

Certainly in New York there were curious instances of such romantic Toryism. Officials there, as in England, backdated official instruments to the year of the regicide rather than the coronation of Charles II. The year 1664 was "the sixteenth year of our Reigne." Congregations prayed specially for the king on his birthday, May 29, and also on the day of his father's execution, January 30. These were among the first royalist rituals imposed on Boston by the commissioners in 1665.[63]

In Nicolls's correspondence, the peculiarly English motif of father–son helped him make sense of the conquest of New Netherland. He was aware of the role Charles II meant to play as executor of his father's projects. Part of his commission was to present the king's reminder to the rebellious brethren of Massachusetts that they held their charter "from Our Royall Father of blessed memory." Filiation appeared again in the king's private instructions in which "our Royall Father" and "our father and ourselfe" doubled the claim to his control over English plantations in North America. Even the cagey Puritans could appreciate the appeal of the image to the Stuart court and therefore its efficacy for them. To disarm the court's complaint against lands seized from Sir Ferdinando Gorges and to mark their reluctant acquiescence, they invoked the biblical injunction, "The rightful commands of political fathers ought to be obeyed."[64]

In London, one of the king's closest relationships was with Edward Hyde, Lord Clarendon, the courtier who had taken on a foster father role toward him. With fatherly – and often sinister – effectiveness, Clarendon sought to distance the young man from unacceptable associates with the wedge of his paternal advice. He did the same with Nicolls on one occasion – though the soldier was then in his early forties – implying that his "friends in Rowhampton" merely wanted to welcome him home, whereas he could see that Nicholls had set an example that would encourage others to "looke a little abroad, and employ themselves in doing good for their Country."[65]

In making variations on the theme of filiopietism, Clarendon and the court were enacting a metaphor that masked the realities of monarchical

63. Instructions to Nicolls and Commissioners, April 23, 1664, *DRCH*, 3:56, Nathaniel B. Shurtleff, ed., *Records of the Governor and Company of the Massachusetts Bay in New England* (Boston, 1854), 4:212; see Patrick Morrah, *Restoration England* (London, 1979), 25.
64. Instructions to the King's Commissioners to Massachusetts, April 23, 1664, *DRCH*, 3:51; Private instructions to Nicolls, April 23, 1664, *DRCH*, 3:57; Special General Court Meeting [Boston] August 9, 1676, Shurtleff, ed., *Records of the Governor and Company of the Massachusetts Bay*, 5:100.
65. Morrah, *Restoration*, 25; see Richard Ollard, *The Image of the King: Charles I and Charles II* (London, 1979), 131; Clarendon to Nicolls, April 13, 1666, *DRCH*, 3:116.

power. It was a mask that Nicolls pulled over political actions as well. In New York, he played out the violence that all unlawful seizure and occupation is. In some ways, the patriarchal image leeched his actions of that violence. It helped structure his attitudes toward his soldiers and the inhabitants – and, more important, his sense of his own and England's purpose in North America.

Nicolls described his struggle as sole provider for his soldiers and the Dutch populace in a letter to James, the Duke of York, written in the summer of 1666. He put before James the picture of an old man fathering his soldiers and the Dutch people in an outpost desperately awaiting relief by sea. He drew attention to the "care" he had "taken for their reliefe" and the relative indifference for his "owne ruine in point of fortune." He wrote of his own mortality. Juxtaposing the recent loss at sea of a close friend and his own uncertain future, he imagined himself "dead" or "recalled" from New York. And he imagined the duke soon receiving a copy of laws he had drawn to bring "one frame [of government] and policy" to the North American plantations.[66]

Coded Understandings of Land and Men

In mid-August 1666, Nicolls went upriver to Albany. He was not un-known there, but neither was it a town where he lingered longer than necessary. So his "suddaine Resolution" to visit a town cleaning up from floods and still openly disgruntled at the occupation may have come as a surprise to the townspeople. In fact, he had come in the hope of meeting an emissary sent to the magistrates of Albany by Alexandre de Prouville, Chevalier Siegneur de Tracy, commander of the king's forces in Quebec. The messenger, as it happened, had already left.[67] As a result he remained in Albany and composed the first in a series of letters to de Tracy. They are remarkable when set alongside those to Dutch residents of New York.

In the first letter, Nicolls wrote that the English had no part in a recent Mohawk ambush of three French farmers. As he phrased it, nothing except the invasion of "His Majesties of England's dominions" could persuade him to side with "the heathen in America" against Christians like the French. The remarkable affability arose from Nicolls's discovery that de Tracy was a comrade in arms from soldiering days in the con-tinental wars. The final nine lines of his letter burned with the pleasure of having found a gentleman-soldier like himself. Quickly he introduced

66. Nicolls to Duke of York, November [?], 1665, *DRCH*, 3:104, 104, and see Nicolls to Secretary of State, October [?], 1664, *DRCH*, 3:69; Nicolls to Duke of York, November [?], 1665, *DRCH*, 3:106.
67. De Tracy to Nicolls, April 30, 1667, *DRCH*, 3:153.

himself as someone who could bear "testimony" to the nobleman's reputation because he had attended the "Duke of York and Albany a few yeares in the french army" and knew of his "great civilities" to James and "all his servants in their low estate and condition of Exile."[68]

On April 30 of the next year de Tracy responded, writing about affairs between the French and English and between their respective native allies, the "Alqinqins" and the Mohawk. He then turned to Nicolls's reference to their soldiering in Europe. Though he had fought with French forces in Germany, he explained, it was his son who had served as cavalry officer in Flanders and whom Nicolls would have known. He confirmed his son's respect and willing service to the Duke of York at that time and assured Nicolls of similar courtesies on his own part. He regretted that Nicolls had voyaged to Albany in vain.[69]

De Tracy had allowed eight months to intervene before answering Nicolls. But the Englishman wrote his response within days, perhaps seizing the opportunity to send a letter with van Curler, who was leaving for Quebec. Whatever its prompting, it shows a man taking pleasure in corresponding with a person of "quality" and military "reputation." He wrote of the present state of war between England and France, regretting its effect in North America and promising every effort to avoid hostilities. On one level, the correspondence allowed him to verbalize ideals of a European world he thought to be still feudal. It was one of chivalrous liege men like themselves, men still medieval in their intention of observing "the Peace of God" here among the savages of North America. He described the ideals in the rhetoric of courtly life in which moral categories like dutifulness and forbearance were realized in a range of performative styles. And now, as the virtue of the courtier required, he had a proper audience in de Tracy. He identified himself and the *chevalier* as men of "integrity" and "passion" for justice. Each was, he was sure "a person of ... Quality, and a good Christian."[70]

On another level, the correspondence located power within the father–son relationship. Whatever might come of present hostilities, de Tracy should know that his English counterpart was a gentleman of dutiful, indeed filial, affection. Nicolls made an unnecessarily pointed reference to his "pardonable mistake" in writing "to the father of a son so highly exteemed." He now recognized his confusion and assured the older man that he would find all his declarations of "respect towards ... [his] son

68. Nicolls to de Tracy, August [?], 1666, *DRCH*, 3:133, 134.
69. De Tracy to Nicolls, April 30, 1667, *DRCH*, 3:154, 153.
70. Nicolls to de Tracy, May 28, 1667, *DRCH*, 3:157; Nicolls to de Tracy, August [?], 1666, *DRCH*, 3:133; De Tracy to Nicolls, April 30, 1667, *DRCH*, 3:153, and see 133, 157.

converted to . . . [his] service and satisfaction." With a schoolboyish bra-
vado he told him not to worry for the inconvenience of his recent trip
to Albany. "The voyage," he wrote dismissively, "was of no great consequence . . . and our rivers are pleasant enough at that season of the
year." At another point he also boyishly criticized his own prose style.
"It may be my weakness but not my fault," he apologized, "that I cannot
fashion my words into a style more proportionable to y^r merit and my
own sincere meaning." Yet he hoped for "a good time and occasion . . .
not farre remote" when he could express his respects more adequately.[71]

This sense of comparability was never present in his correspondence
with Dutch men. Although he was open with de Tracy and prepared to
enlarge on a subject he never raised with Dutch men, that is, his earlier
life as a soldier in Flanders, his correspondence with the Dutch was brittle
and certainly impersonal. He had the gentry's condescension that unconsciously yet accurately measures out the exact amount of affability
required.

But there is a curiosity in the whole situation. Even leaving aside an
invasion of New York by the French in the winter of 1666 – something
about which de Tracy had complete knowledge and to which he gave
wholehearted approval – from January of that year to June of 1667,
France and England were officially at war. The English and Dutch were
also, but the Dutch of New York were neutralized by the garrison. Nicolls
was right in writing to van Curler, letting him know "how little good
will Monsr de Tracy hath for the Dutch and when time serves he will
make use of those pretenses to colour his ambition of Ingrossing the
Beaver trade by destroying and interrupting ours in Albany." De Tracy
was so minded.[72] It is surprising, then, to find this remark written four
months after his first fulsome letter to the nobleman and two months
before the second.

Nicolls's letter to de Tracy was not a conscious deceit. De Tracy had
drawn from him the realization that they were both ornaments in the
crowns of Christian kings and performing tasks that called upon their
own courtly *virtu*. Together they could make the kind of abstractions
that subordinated the present "hostilities" and rival "ambitions" to the
understanding that the long-term goal of all Christian princes was justice
and peace. Dutch men could not make such abstractions. Among other
things, they did not have the same sense of time. Even van Curler would
only understand the present events in the concrete. De Tracy's "Ingrossing

71. Nicolls to de Tracy, May 28, 1667, *DRCH*, 3:157.
72. Nicolls to Van Curler, January 11, 1666, *DRCH*, 3:147.

the Beaver trade" – of which Nicolls was quick to warn van Curler – was the sort of ambition he would understand.[73]

Nicolls was not lacking in good will toward the Dutch. Rather, with them there was no shared social order whose stylization could transcend local controversies. His words to Jeremias van Rensselaer, "Let there be no controversies of this nature between you and me" remained a curt order because he could not appeal to the values of a culture like his own. Although he assumed that van Rensselaer would share his belief that landownership had primarily to do with the relationships of fathers and sons, he was forced, for the same reason, to acknowledge that he did not understand his correspondent's culture well enough to know how his "Latine verse" about it might be applied. It would be done by van Rensselaer "in some sort" of way.

Between the Dutch and the English there was no immediate understanding of how political power operated. Nicolls saw van Rensselaer maneuvering to retain a large landed estate. Among Englishmen, such a man's machinations, however contemptible, were nonetheless judged not only to be shrewd but essential if he were to obtain "titles of Government." Since his arrival in New Netherland, Nicolls had been authorizing large land grants to a number of Englishmen whose expectations about hereditary lands and titles he would have shared. He recommended that the "houses and land belonging to the Dutch principal officers" in Delaware be conferred on Sir Robert Carr, his son and a subordinate officer. Carr had already granted "all that tract of land" at "the head" of the Delaware River hereafter "called by the name of the mannour of Grimstead" to two officers and "their heyres and assignes for ever." One was empowered to "erect and establish a Court Leete for himselfe and himselfe to bee Lord of ye same mannor and court." By December 1665, Carr had a "desire to settle upon" a tract of land in the Narragansett country and sought a patent in England. The land was eventually for his son, but meanwhile he would fulfill the desires of "the people in the Eastern parts" (of Long Island?) and "be their Governor." Nicolls's role was that of a gentrified real estate agent. He wrote that an estate in the wilderness might cost £20,000 before yielding a reward, but that the patentees' "children's children may reap the profit."[74]

It is impossible for us to conceive that van Rensselaer's strategies to retain Rensselaerswyck would be outside the rules of this power game.

73. Nicolls to Van Curler, January 11, 1666, *DRCH*, 3:147.
74. Nicolls to Arlington, April 10, 1666, *DRCH*, 3:115; Carr's Grant to Captain Hyde and Captain Morley, October 10, 1664, *DRCH*, 3:72; Carr to Secretary of State, December 5, 1665, *DRCH*, 3:109; Nicolls to Duke of York, n.d., *DRCH*, 3:105.

It was a time when the rules were so obvious. In New York, one English officer took land named Prudence Island (near Rhode Island) and raised it to manorial status. Another took 25,000 acres on the north shore of Staten Island and raised it to the "Lordshippe or Manner of Cassiltown," intending to erect a proper manor house and hunting lodge. Still another took possession of a large Dutch house near Esopus, and by redescribing it as a mansion house called Fox Hall, paved the way for its erection as "a Manor." Land was status made visible. It symbolized a meaningful cosmology and was therefore outside costing procedures. Jeremias van Rensselaer costed the patroonship. In innumerable ways he paraphrased a definition of the colony once put to his mother in April of 1664. It was "our patrimonial goods which have cost father, deceased, so many thousands." He did not understand the English rules that even John Evelyn's five-year-old eldest son had right. Dying, the young boy assumed "a more serious manner than usual" and, as the father recorded it, told him, "I should give my house, land, and all my fine things to . . . [my] brother Jack."[75]

Van Rensselaer's role as director of Rensselaerswyck continued to be misunderstood. In April 1670, Nicolls's newly arrived successor, Francis Lovelace, was expecting to organize a local militia upriver and approached van Rensselaer with the proposition that he be an officer. He expected that van Rensselaer would understand that he should be captain of the horse as he was the largest landowner in the Albany area. He had apparently not anticipated either van Rensselaer's ignorance of a county militia or his possible distaste for the idea. At any rate, van Rensselaer responded cordially, beginning, "I see your honor would like *us* to proceed with the formation of a troop of horse." But, he insisted, he did not really know how "to proceed in the matter." He offered fumbling excuses about being "all ready" and "favorably disposed," but somehow the organization was stalled. Finally and in words that must have baffled Lovelace as coming from a country magnate, he added disingenuously, "We shall now await until your honor, please God, shall come up the river yourself to instruct us a little. Many" – it must have infuriated Lovelace to read – "have their saddles and bridles all ready."[76]

75. Schwarz, *Jarring Interests*, 19; Dorothy V. Smith, *Staten Island: Gateway to New York* (New York, 1970), 31; "A Privilege granted to Capt Thomas Chambers, for ye Erecting Fox Hall into a Mannor," October 16, 1672, *DRCH*, 13:468; JvR to AvR, April 24, 1664, *Corr JvR*, 350; William Bray, ed., *The Diary of John Evelyn* (London, 1907), 1:329.
76. JvR to Lovelace, [April, 1670?], *Corr JvR*, 417, 418.

Jeremias was both dense and devious in this – like the New Amsterdam *vroedschap.* In England, an affluent landowner knew the system inside out and might protest such an appointment, that is, being rated for the cavalry rather than the infantry. Jonathan Ivie did so in 1715. "I am not willing," he insisted, "to be to the horse but to the foot. So I hope you'l Please to Grant it." Jeremias's recourse was otherwise. It left Lovelace's request in its particularity. He could not place the request within a political system and, therefore, could not debate the request on an abstract level.

Quartering was an epistemological problem for the Dutch in this sense as well. In England there was a long and violent debate about quartering soldiers on the populace. In the discussions, Englishmen moved from the particular – the point that infirmaries and barracks, for example, would be cheaper in the long run – to abstractions: soldiers or sailors quartered in private homes tempt people to debauchery and infringe the basic rights of Englishmen. The Dutch could not do this. So, sustained opposition to quartering was frustrated both because such resistance was dangerous and because they did not know the forms of discourse in which to attack it.[77]

In his letter to Lovelace, van Rensselaer turned to the two hundred schepels of wheat already sent on the governor's account to New York City. Circumstances had prevented him shipping a further hundred but he promised their dispatch "at the first opportunity." Whenever it arrived, it would be tribute paid not of an English manor but, as he said, "of the *colony.*"[78]

Becoming "Albany"

In July 1673, Jeremias van Rensselaer had to defend himself to his brother Rychart and his own conscience on a matter he had never before had to consider. He was writing after experiencing nine years of English rule and at a time when the United Provinces had regained New Netherland – only to lose it permanently to the English in some two years' time. Now van Rensselaer was assuring Rychart and himself that he was not a man of public violence. Townspeople full of taunts and mockery, he described, had gathered to see the English soldiers march out of Albany.

77. Quoted in Frances Wood, Merchants and Class: The Social Identification of Merchants in Exeter, 1680–1760 (M.A. thesis, Monash University, Melbourne, 1977), 140; see Entry for February 20, 1666, Bray, ed., *Diary of Evelyn,* 2:3.
78. JvR to Lovelace, [April 1670?], *Corr JvR,* 418 (my italics); as "director of the colony" see ibid. and Stuyvesant to JvR, March 23, 1659, *Corr JvR,* 143.

"As to my farewell to the English," Jeremias wrote defensively, "I showed them nothing but friendship, but they were uncivilly treated by some."[79]

In Albany, the military occupation that began in 1664 had, from the start, jostled all the relationships that made up the burghers' lives. Thirty years before, a single crew of Englishmen under Jacob Eelkens had come up the Hudson and, with the connivance of Hans Hunthum, been allowed to camp at Fort Orange for three weeks, illegally trading with the natives. Even that limited episode had caused a ripple effect. In the colony, amicable relations with the natives were disrupted and questions arose in colonists' minds about the effectiveness of the prescriptive trading regulations then in force. In Amsterdam, Kiliaen van Rensselaer hounded Hunthum in committee rooms of the Company and the States General. He began to reevaluate his own relationship with the Company and thereafter gave Rensselaerswyck a more recognizably military posture. Another discordance was played out in the London law courts. There, the airing given to Eelkens's suit for damages against the Dutch simultaneously raised questions about the relationship between the United Provinces' monopoly on trade and the rights of other European states to free markets overseas. The courts also sought to define the scope of English law in places like Amsterdam and Fort Orange. Nearby, the court of Charles I became privy to the proceedings in London and the rough treatment of Eelkens by the Dutch. It sent an angry letter to the Noble High Mightinesses demanding explanation and apology. Stung by the breakdown of a reasonably cordial relationship, the States General brought uncharacteristically strong pressure to bear on the West India Company to remedy the affair.[80]

When Eelkens intruded upon the *plein* near Fort Orange, he was like the army malingerer who nudges into line after it has formed up at parade and causes a shift in the relationships of every man to the other. In this sense, the presence of the conqueror changed everything in Albany after 1664. It will require this and following chapters to understand that process. Relationships of time and space changed. Religious, political, social, and economic meanings did as well. The small community of Lutherans, for example, saw in English rule the opportunity to secure greater freedom of worship, and put itself on a new footing with the Reformed congregation. The conquest also reopened the matter of boundaries with Rensselaerswyck. Van Rensselaer, seeking reconfirmation of the patroonship, claimed lands including Albany and the Catskills. Some landowners in

79. JvR to RvR, July 3, 1674, *Corr JvR*, 465.
80. See Examination of Bastiaen Jansz Krol, June 30, 1634, *VRBM*, 302, 304; and Oliver A. Rink, *Holland on the Hudson, An Economic and Social History of Dutch New York, 1609–1664* (Ithaca, 1986), 110, 120.

the Catskill area later lost their properties. They may have been among the townsmen who made "revelations" to the English commander that van Rensselaer had deliberately dallied in administering the oath of allegiance to his tenants. Meanwhile the colony's lands, now suspended in uncertain title, were available to opportunists. Men who could not procure certain lands from Stuyvesant – for example, islands above or below the town – now got them from Nicolls.[81]

The basis for political advancement changed. Burghers with skills to fit the strangers into the systems of native trade and land distribution found particular favor. Rivercraft owners, like Abraham Staats and Jan Janse Flodder, offered obvious services and were rewarded. Staats was one of Nicolls's first appointments as magistrate, and Janse was soon the owner of six acres of land near Apjes's Island and the partner of captain John Baker in other land purchases. Those who spoke English and the natives' languages had an edge. Christofel Davidsz (Christopher Davidson, an Irishman) got special jobs from governor Lovelace because he spoke English and made gunlocks, skills that went unremarked before 1664.[82] Those who knew the lands that might serve as speculative properties were of heightened usefulness. Often they were men living at Schenectady, the beachhead between the natives' lands and the trading post at Albany.

Nicolls immediately singled out Arent van Curler. A leader in Schenectady and an entrepreneur welcomed in Montreal and Quebec, he was Corlear to the natives and a trader who shared much of their own knowledge of the lands. And he was not a half-breed. He was van Rensselaer's cousin and held office within the colony. Something of a scholar and cartographer, he was now about forty-eight and could find welcome in Canada, New York City, and Nykerk in Gelderland, where he held property. He must have seemed a man of some civility. Nicolls appointed him to the magistracy of Albany and clearly expected to establish a special relationship with him. In 1666, he wrote as patron to client, "S[r] I am so abundantly satisfied with y[r] care and conduct in these troubles [Canada] that I shall now only desir you to continue in well doing, whereby you have and will extremely oblige, very aff[te] freind."[83] He imagined him as the link in a chain of command reaching downward from himself. It was the form of political authority as the English knew it. Van Curler drowned

81. Alice P. Kenney, *The Gansvoorts of Albany: Dutch Patricians in the Upper Hudson Valley* (Syracuse, 1969), 24; see, for example, the lands granted within Rensselaerswyck to Volkert Janse Douw and Jan Thomasz Witbeck in JvR to Johan van Rensselaer, September 3, 1659, *Corr JvR*, 172, and Nissenson, *Patroon's Domain*, 270.
82. Lovelace to Magistrates at Esopus, February 24, 1668/9, *DRCH*, 13:423.
83. Nicolls to Van Curler, January 7, 1666, *DRCH*, 3:145.

before the expectations of such leadership could be played out. Twenty years later, the same expectations fell on Philip Pietersz Schuyler's son, Pieter. It would be his sorest burden.

The military occupation dislocated the relationship of the burgher-guard to the town and the fort. Before 1664, the guard stood in an accepted opposition to the Company's soldiers. The duties of each were casually, often carelessly, performed, but the place of each was clear. Among the burgherguard, codes governed the requisition of candles, firewood, and powder as well as the wearing of swords and organization of the watch. Soldiers and burgherguards enjoyed an unruly cameraderie toward which the town's authorities turned a blind eye. The guard were the organizers of the *papegaaischoet*, men in roles of civic significance. However, with the old fort now a monument to the Company's dispersed soldiery and operating in English hands, the role of the burgherguard changed. It was more than ever one of opposition to the soldiers, and the rules were gone. Finding their way with the Englishmen proved difficult. The dislocation led to tragedy in Esopus in 1666 and 1667, whereas in Albany it meant coming to share status with militia units organized north and south of the town. We hear no more of the *papegaaischoet*, though it may have persisted. Perhaps the lone account of natives performing as marksmen on May 1, 1684, registers a festivity lost to the Dutch and adopted into native rituals.[84] Whatever the case, the fort and its *plein* were places of foreign soldiers until the English left in 1673. When they returned in 1675, they built a new fort; the burgherguard's status came to depend on the growing identification of its officers with those of the fort.

The relationships of the town with outsiders were also jostled in the aftermath of the conquest. Only certain features can be noted here. Patterns of trade altered radically. One scholar has argued that, although 1665 was a particularly disastrous year for overseas shipping to New York, the commerce of the Albany merchants with the natives continued unaltered because they had anticipated hostilities and hoarded enough merchandise to see them through until transatlantic trade recovered in 1666.[85] It was, if true, a short-term solution. Trade with Holland never recovered. Dutch colonizing efforts in North America were "destroyed." In New York City, the van Brugge family abandoned its properties and its role as broker for Albany traders. The family's home on Stone Street was confiscated and sold at about one-third its value to two Englishmen, Captain John Needham and Mathias Nicolls. Pieter Hartgers's house was

84. Ord. sess, May 6, 1684, CRA, 446.
85. For hoarding, see Jan Kupp, "Aspects of New York–Dutch Trade under the English, 1670–1674," *New-York Historical Society Quarterly* (April 1974), 58:142.

bought by Ensign Sylvester Salisbury for gl 100, about one-tenth its value. All confiscated properties in New Amsterdam went to Englishmen. By 1674, imported merchandise was taxed at 5 percent; it was 10 percent in 1683. The tax was considered high because a further duty fell on exported goods when they reached England. By 1687, those trading with the natives paid an annual tax of 10 percent on the value of the trade.[86]

Above all, the management of the fur trade upriver was in the conqueror's hands. Before 1666, there was no way of knowing that war between England and France would be conducted intermittently for over a hundred years. But de Tracy began to reconsider Canada's relationship with Albany's burghers as soon as the English came. He was quick to let them know that he now viewed with suspicion the neutrality of a community professedly interested only in trade. It was unrealistic to hope for a continuation of the cordial relationship with Quebec and Montreal and the relatively well regulated commerce with the native tribes.[87]

The Dutch burghers soon became spectators to English rituals designed to control their native clients. On the day they officially claimed the town, three English officers also assumed command over the town's trading partners, the Mohawk. The rituals of their surrender were a ceremonious affair. On September 24, five Englishmen received eight natives at "Fort Albany," called them "Indian Princes," and made assurances that the chain of friendship would not be broken. The natives asked that walking in the woods be continued, along with free trade and the right to be "lodged in houses as formerly."[88] They signed a treaty which was drawn up under New England's flag and later archived among its papers. The Dutch onlookers might not have been surprised.

Reactions to Conquest

Townspeople had expectations of what defeat and occupation would mean. There was some anticipation that New Netherland would be restored to Dutch control. Even Lovelace foresaw that eventuality in 1673, when he cautioned a subordinate to treat the New Netherlanders reasonably because "the Game . . . [might] shift and wee and Holland shake hands."[89] At the same time, the burghers were fearful from the start that

86. Trelease, *Indian Affairs in Colonial New York*, 218.
87. De Tracy to Commissioners at Albany, July 22, 1666, and Commissioners at Albany to de Tracy, August 20, 1666, DRCH, 3:131, 134–5.
88. Articles between Cartwright and the New York Indians, September 24, 1664, DRCH, 3:67, 68, and see Further transactions with the Mohawks, June 5, 1674, DRCH, 13:480.
89. Lovelace to Salisbury, January 27, 1672, Victor Hugo Paltsits, ed., *Minutes of the Executive Council of the Province of New York: Administration of Francis Lovelace,*

violence would be inflicted upon them if defeated. Especially, they expected the "Yankees at Hartfort" to play a treacherous role in the capture of Beverwijck. The fear had dominated the scenes surrounding the defeat of New Amsterdam, where predictions that the English would fire the city were supported by the threat of one English Long Islander to burn Hempstead, by the plan of another to cut off the feet of anyone "declaring for the Estates General," by rumors that Dutch families would be at the mercy of the English just as they were left "naked and plundered" by the Portuguese in Brazil, and by fears that "English neighbors" would make good their threat of "removing all Dutch magistrates."[90] A Dutch eyewitness testified that the English invaders were assisted by New Englanders manning six hundred privateers and coming "with a desire to pillage the place."[91]

The same motif shaped rumors of imminent attack on Beverwijck in the days preceding Nicolls's landing on September 8. The New Englanders were feared as a "threatening concourse" of "evil-disposed neighbors," and now the burghers had documented proof that they had encouraged natives to burn the farmhouse of Abraham Staats two months earlier. The attack may have been particularly frightening, as Staats was one of the few men with military expertise, and powder for defense may have been in his home. It may have called up a vision of the complete devastation that a later historian believed the articles of surrender prescribed, namely, that "fort Aurania [Orange] should be levelled." Certainly Philip Pietersz Schuyler sensed imminent danger when he petitioned Stuyvesant for land at Half Moon (Cohoes) "to keep the English away."[92]

The fear of losing control of the fur trade to Yankees like Hawthorn, Pynchon, and Paine was real as well. In the 1670s, the burghers were well aware of a claim by "Boston" to ownership of land as far west as

1668–1673, Volume II, Collateral and Illustrative Documents, 20–98 (Albany, 1910), 2:757.

90. See Benjamin H. Hall, "The Tale of the Whale," Webster's Calendar, or the Albany Almanac for the Year of Our Lord, 1874, Number 91 (Albany, 1874), n.p.; Schultz, Colonial Hempstead, 78; N.C. Lambrechtsen, A Short Description of the Discovery and Subsequent History of the New Netherlands, A Colony in America (at an Early Period) of the Republic of the United Netherlands (Middleburg, 1818), CNYHS, 2nd ser. (New York, 1841), 1:110; Directions of Stuyvesant, December 19, 1656, DRCH, 14:375.

91. Samuel Drisius to Classis of Amsterdam, September 15, 1664, DRCH, 13:393.

92. Weise, History of the City of Albany, 141; see JvR to OvCortlandt, July 17, 1664, Corr JvR, 356; on the storing of gun powder, see Ord. sess. August 11, 1654, CRB, 175; William Dunlop, History of the New Netherlands, Province of New York and State of New York to the Adoption of the Federal Constitution in two volumes (New York, 1970 reprint), 1:117; Petition of Philipp Pietersen Schuyler and Goose Gerritsen for leave to purchase the Half Moon from the Mohegans, in order to prevent its purchase by the English, May 27, 1664, DRCH, 13:387.

Schenectady. As it happened, anxieties about Yankees moving solidly into Albany would have been misplaced. English governors had no intention of sharing New York's fur trade or lands with them. Nevertheless, Paine's insistence to Lovelace in 1672 that Massachusetts men deserved free passage up the Hudson for the "settlement of Plantacons" in order to increase the number of "his Majes" good Subjects" and as payment for assisting in the conquest of New Netherland was a warning to all.[93]

Downriver from Albany, the inevitable resistance to English occupation occurred. Anticipating popular disturbances, Dutch magistrates dealt quickly with anything that savored of rebellion, but many refused to submit. In New York City, rioting broke out in June of 1665, and the first exchange of shots between a soldier and a civilian was recorded. Although all burghers had been disarmed, a Dutch man fired a weapon and an English soldier "ran after him with a gun and discharged it." There was *oproer* in Bergen and Esopus. Bergen had to be quieted by soldiers of the garrison, and its magistrates made to act as guards against rioters. In Esopus there was a mutiny in which "60 or 70" burghers took up arms. In a town where forty-three house lots were owned in 1664, that represented more than one male from every household.[94]

The record of public occurrences in Albany between 1664 and 1668 is nonexistent. Nicolls, however, alluded to a war there and was confronted by serious disturbances as late as 1667. Some men were publicly banished, like Johannes de Dekker, a former *commis*, who was tried and given ten days to leave. He was charged with promoting armed resistance at Beverwijck and "other places upon Hudson River" – undoubtedly referring to Esopus, a fortified trading station with "interests" he had served as a member of Stuyvesant's council over the previous eight years. He had apparently urged the Beverwijck burghers to repel the invaders on more than one occasion. Because he had been a man of some distinction in Holland and then commissary at Fort Orange, his "discourses" must have been such as to "alienate the minds of H.M. Dutch subjects," as the English later asserted. In November of 1665, the Mohawk around Albany were also offering resistance. Nicolls had to increase the garrison

93. For the claim, see Letter rec'd on November 10, 1677 from Albany by Claes Luck and two Englishmen from Boston . . . who declared that they did not say Schenectady belonged to Boston, *New York State Library Bulletin 58, March, 1902, History 6: Calendar of Council Minutes, 1668–1783* (Albany, 1902), 30, and see JvR to AvR, April 24, 1664, *Corr JvR*, 349; Address of John Paine, agent of Massachusetts, to Governor Lovelace, September 9, 1672, *Report of the State Historian* (1896), 1:342.
94. Minutes of June 22, 1665, *RNA*, 5:262; [Nicolls's] Order directing the magistrates of Bergen, N.J., to receive and quarter a garrison of soldiers, n.d., *DRCH*, 13:395; Complaints against Capt Broadhead (*sic*) in the proceedings and sentences of the court held in Esopus, April 25, 26, 27, 1667, *DRCH*, 13:410, 414.

because burghers of Albany and Esopus refused to march out against them.[95] Other acts of resistance were real but less dramatic. Philip Pietersz Schuyler wrote a contract warning that he might "resolve to depart with his wife and children from here to Holland" but would give notice "one month or six weeks in advance." Francois Boon got a pass to Martinique, sold out, and never returned.[96]

Any of the aspects of military occupation might have caused trouble. Certain features of being an occupied town, however, seem to have been anticipated and accepted. It was expected, I believe, that all rights in property would have to be reconfirmed. English denunciations of Dutch claims of New Netherland had long been abroad in the colony, so more than ordinary difficulties might have been anticipated. In New Utrecht, two parties to a land transaction in 1665 agreed that "in Case that the English ... might take away and propitiate the Land to themselves then the bargain ... should be void." Elsewhere the elderly feared their lands would be sequestered and they would be made to move on.[97] A number of Beverwijck's burghers invented subterfuges to delay submission of *landbrieven*, and in many cases Nicolls did not examine them until 1667. The town, however, had to accept that properties would be confiscated. Nine houses, five yards and a barn were sequestered when war with the United Provinces was officially declared by England in 1667 and may have been used to house soldiers.

The town would also have expected to quarter soldiers. Netherlanders' hostility toward garrisons was always intense, with animosity shown by harassment of troops and recalcitrance in providing housing even under great pressure. New York City's magistrates were defiantly uncooperative in quartering Nicolls's soldiers. As late as April 1665, they were instructing him that they would "contribute" rather than lodge men, and by May of 1666 were paying a "weekly assessment on behalf of the soldiery" to a Frenchman who seems to have farmed it for the English.[98]

On the matter of quartering, as in most issues related to the occupation, English commanders worked through local magistrates. In Albany, the magistrates acted as a buffer between resentful residents and possibly sixty soldiers. But they were incapable of containing violence, at least in

95. Conveyance, May 31, 1657, *ER1*, 29, and see 29, n. 1.
96. "Indenture [of apprenticeship] 13/23 March [1665]," *Dutch Settlers Society of Albany IV: Yearbook, 1930–1931* (Albany, 1931), 14; E[dmund] B. O'Callaghan, ed., *Calendar of Historical Manuscripts in the Office of the Secretary of State, Albany, New York, Part II, English Manuscripts, 1664–1776* (Albany, 1866), 60.
97. Minutes of August 22, 1665, *RNA*, 5:286 Magistrates of Amersfoort, Brevckelen, Midwout, Utrecht, and Boswyck to P. Stuyvesant, n.d., *DRCH*, 2:375.
98. See Du Plessis, *Urban Stability in the Netherlands Revolution: A Comparative Study of Lille and Douai* (Ph.D. dissertation, Columbia University, 1974), 660; Minutes of April 7, 1665, *RNA*, 5:212, and Minutes of May 8, 1666, *RNA*, 6:4, 5.

the first eleven months. Nicolls retaliated by inspecting Albany in August 1665, changing the command, and investigating charges exchanged between householders and soldiers. Over the next months, he accused the magistrates of quartering most of the soldiers with commoners. In the summer of 1666, the burghers were still refusing blankets and bedding to troopers. Such supplies, the magistrates reported, had been embezzled, presumably by officers like Baker, and they added, even New York City was not as heavily burdened by quartering as Albany.[99]

Townsmen would not, I think, have expected surrender of the town to entail the loss of its name. On the continent, a vanquished town was likely to retain its name or suffer its foreign equivalent. In North America, Europeans had, of course, renamed native settlements but otherwise set no precedent. What the Dutch might have understood by "Albany" is difficult to say. The final syllable might have offered the pleasure of the popular Dutch diminutive *ij*, but confusion was widespread. At one point, van Rensselaer thought he was living in the "duchy of [New] Albany." Jan Baptiste thought his brother was now in New England, north of Virginia. In 1679, a Dutch overseas visitor assumed he had anchored "before de Fuyck, and Fort Albany or Orange." At the same time a knowledgeable resident, Robert Livingston, thought himself living in "New Albany" but two days later in "Albany." Even Nicolls (or his secretary) confusedly put the burghers "within Beverwijck att Albany."[100] Well into the eighteenth century, whether out of habit or reproach, residents continued to locate themselves in "Beverwijck" or "de Fuyck."

Civilizing the Land

There were seriously frustrated expectations both for the burghers and for Nicolls. Two sets of disputes make this clear: those occurring over the proper use of land and those attached to the proper administration of law, that is, political authority.

The English and Dutch envisioned a town differently. In Albany, the English took over land north and west on the hill, beginning in 1666 when Nicolls reconfirmed the land of early settlers and allocated small house lots to soldiers. It was not highly desirable land, falling to a deep

99. Weise, *History of the City of Albany*, 147; Nicolls to Commissaries at Albany, June 22, 1666, *DRCH*, 3:117.
100. JvR to AvR, October 21/11 (sic), 1664, *Corr JvR*, 367; Henry C. Murphy, ed., *Journal of a Voyage to New York and a Tour of Several of the American Colonies in 1679– 80, by Jasper Dankers and Peter Slyter of Wiewerd in Friesland*, Vol. 1 in *Memoirs of the Long Island Historical Society* (Brooklyn, 1867), 297; Conveyance, July 1, 1678, *ER*2, 18; Patent of Nicolls to Gerrit Bancker, April 26, 1667, *Report of the State Historian* (1896), 1:185.

ravine nearby where tanyards were just starting to be established in these decades. A path leading north, to Greyenbosch and Half Moon (Watervliet and Cohoes), separated the tanyards from the Hudson River and was eventually improved by the English for military forces going north to combat the French.

More significantly, the English moved directly into the area of the old fort (Figure 3.3). The townspeople's sentiments enhanced the importance of the fort and pastures here. It was, like Pirenne's medieval town, a site chosen by commercially minded men whose good fortune with a staple – in this case, furs – had resulted in the creation of a viable town. The fort, then, was not in opposition to the town. Though the Company's soldiers there were not always burghers, it was not a military installation of outsiders. Generically it was the town. By 1664, New Amsterdam was a far more successful objectification of this evolutionary process than Beverwijck. There a group of merchants had won a city charter and were already making their own distinctive marks with the pen of their accumulating privileges, while those in Beverwijck were still where they were in 1660, when they were forced to harass La Montagne for autonomy. Two months before the surrender, however, Stuyvesant assumed they could summon a *vroedschap*.[101] These were early days, but a charter must have seemed a certainty.

On September 24, the English took Fort Orange. They confiscated more than the fort itself. Captain Baker assumed that land around it also belonged to the crown and hence to the officers and soldiers. Consequently he ejected occupants of lands held under the earliest grants, many of them owners of the house lots and gardens proper to the old fort. Nicolls reprimanded Baker for his manner in executing such removals, denying a man like Thomas Janse land he had "peacefully possessed... all of his natural life," and collecting rents for his own profit. He rebuked the harshness; he did not question the propriety.[102]

The English military in North America were, like the Dutch, a defensive force. The forts they built before the revolution gave a lasting shape to the landscape of New York. But their concept of security also made them, unlike the Dutch, a mobile, offensive force that expected to move out over the land. Even the local militias in England, New England, and Virginia were armed forces of the countryside not, like the Dutch, those

101. See Minutes of July 8, 1664, *RNA*, 5:88.
102. In 1762, the provincial attorney general accepted the legality of Governor Dongan's action in 1686 reserving to the Crown only the land on which the fort was built and his right to sell off the surrounds (see Chalmers Papers, 2:55–9, NYPL); for a detailed discussion of this issue, see Merwick, "Dutch Townsmen and Land Use: A Spatial Perspective on Seventeenth-Century Albany, New York," *William and Mary Quarterly*, 3rd ser. (January, 1980), 37:53–78.

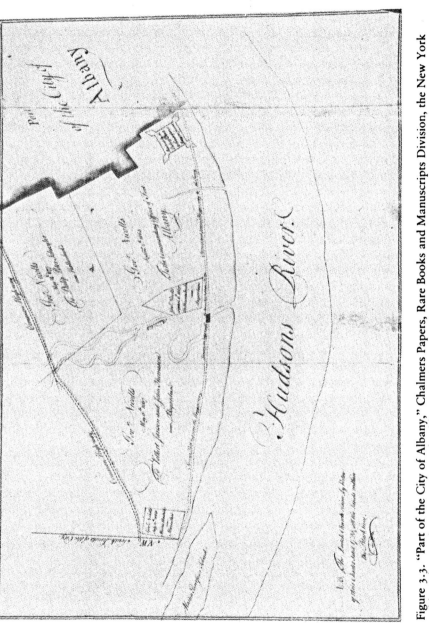

Figure 3.3. "Part of the City of Albany," Chalmers Papers, Rare Books and Manuscripts Division, the New York Public Library. Astor, Lenox, and Tilden Foundations.

of fortified cities and towns. Excepting the trainbands of London, citizen-soldiers mustered on fields and meadowlands, not in target ranges (*doelens*). The military history of seventeenth-century Anglo-Americans is one of expeditions by militiamen and British armies against native peoples and other Europeans.

Perhaps a concern for effectiveness as an offensive force as much as security explains the appearance of references in seventeenth-century records to anxiety about natives owning horses. Authorities assumed that armed encounters with natives would be a matter of both sides covering distances and ordered that horses be "retrieved" from natives. Every trooper, as from 1665, was to "keep and maintain a good horse." Horses were apparently found in such numbers when the Dutch squadron reconquered Fort Orange that adequate pasturing was a problem. Baker, then, may have expected and needed enough land around the fort to accommodate horses, carts, and caissons. From his point of view (and that of later British commanders) it was inconceivable that possession of the fort would not mean ownership of sufficient land to muster and to accommodate animals and equipment. From the Dutch burghers' viewpoint, it was inconceivable that they should. In fact, many may not have understood on whose part claim was being made, for on September 25, 1665, Nicolls "gave the pasture and marshground at Albany [almost 60 acres] near the then fort to John Baker" for "his Sole Use and Behoof, during the time of his said Command and so for ever to the Sole Use and Behoof of such Person, or Persons, as shall, from time to time, Succeed in the Command of the said Fort." These lands included "several small tracts ... very Valuable, from their Vicinity to the City of Albany ... some parts of them were in Actual occupation holding under the Original Patentees."[103]

Baker's actions were soon condemned by claimants and Nicolls alike. The commander understood that he had violated titles to property, and he must also have realized that the south pastures were the townsmen's only available arable, other than islands. He may not, however, have understood that his occupation of the fort and the land trod upon the

103. Schultz, *Colonial Hempstead*, 87; Earliest English Colonial Laws [1665], Article 18, *Second Annual Report of the State Historian* (Albany, 1897), 1:152; "The Pasture," *AA*, 1:97, and for Arent van Curler's pasturing of horses on "the south pasture," see *ER1*, 292; Abstract of Mr. Santen's memoranda and of Governor Dongan's answer [ca. October, 1687], *DRCH*, 3:494, and for the figure of sixty acres, see "The Pasture," *AA*, 1:99, 100; Opinion of William Smith [Jr.] on the grants for the pasture land near Albany, February 23, 1762, Chalmers Papers, 2:44, NYPL, and see "A List of the Houses and Land ... Confiscated ... September 26 [?], 1667, *Second Annual Report of the State Historian* (Albany, 1897), 1:188, where the land is "Captain Bakers (*sic*) Pasture."

town's genealogy, and that it made uniquely contentious a landscape in which the inhabitants read their hidden mythologies.

Nicolls was not continually involved in the dissensions surrounding property rights on the south pastures. However, he commented on them often enough to show his wider misperception, that of the town itself. To him the *plein* was unsuitably low for habitation and offered no advantages for individuals' house lots, gardens, or farming. "I would wish those people [to be made to live] on the hill," he wrote the magistrates in 1666, and "this be [made to be] a common."[104] Dutch settlers, however, invariably chose river flats (*broekland*) for dwellings and farms. They were unlike their New England counterparts in this respect, and Beverwijck's inhabitants were no exception. But more important, a common was not a feature of land just outside the walls of Dutch cities. As in England, it was integral to "an agricultural system" and played a part in the lives of villagers (*dorplingen*). But Beverwijck's was an urban economy. The establishment of a common within such a town's immediate surrounds was avoided because it necessarily foreclosed expansion.

For Nicolls the arrangement he proposed seemed to legitimate the community by creating something like a proper English township – dense habitation on the hill, "places for husbandmen" nearby, and larger holdings for gentrymen (like van Rensselaer) at a greater distance. This model would have given outlying woods to gentlemen and a common to the poorer sort. Nicolls's sense of such communities as primarily concerned about an adequate agricultural base makes sense of his reference to Schenectady's traders, on one occasion, as "paisants."[105] The proposed arrangements also would have provided the geographical foundation for the kind of English local government that later commentators wanted to think Nicolls had "carefully and slowly" introduced across New Netherland. Meanwhile, on at least one occasion, English administrators convened themselves on what they thought was the "Common . . . East of ye South Gate" in Albany. To residents, the space continued to be *het plein* (the pasture).[106]

104. Nicolls to Commissioners of Albany [ca. October 26, 1666], DRCH, 3:143.
105. For a description of the model, see Darrett Rutman, *Winthrop's Boston: Portrait of a Puritan Town 1630–1649* (New York, 1965), chap. 4, and E.C.K. Gonner, *Common Land and Enclosure* (New York, 1966 reprint), 6, and Christopher Hill, *The World Turned Upside Down: Radical Ideas during the English Revolution* (Harmondsworth, 1975), 52, 53; Nicolls to de Tracy, May 28, 1667, DRCH, 3:156.
106. William Smith, Jr., *The History of the Province of New-York, from the First Discovery, to which is annexed A Description of the Country, an Account of the Inhabitants, their Trade, Religious and Political State, and the Constitution of the Courts of Justice in the Colony* (London, 1776), 36; Council Minutes, September 6, 1672, Paltsits, ed., *Minutes of the Executive Council of the Province of New York: Admin-*

Although Nicolls continued to promote Albany as the leading fur-trading town in North America, he and other seventeenth-century governors believed that towns like it in New York should stand within a jurisdictional framework that would subordinate them to a ruling landed class. A dissection of the Duke's Laws of 1667 would show English images of the province ordered in this way, but often a fragment of documentation will serve as well. When Lovelace raised Thomas Chambers's house and land at Esopus to manorial status, he created a territorial unit that would fit into what we would call county government in England. Chambers was a man of "long presence in the colony and service" and Lovelace counted on him and his "house" for military leadership or, as he put it, support "against any sudden Incursion." He gave him superior political status by explicitly placing the manor beyond the jurisdiction of the nearby town of Kingston (formerly *Wiltwijk*).[107]

Meanwhile, the towns that began to fill out the landscape alongside such gentlemen's estates were not the market towns I have been discussing but essentially the townships established in seventeenth-century New England. A. J. F. van Laer, the New York state archivist in the early twentieth century, labored long and honorably in Albany's early records but remained puzzled by the word "precincts" in the charter drawn up for the city by the English in 1686. The instrument referred on more than one occasion to the "af'd City, Liberties and Precincts thereof." He needed to examine New England's archives in which precincts were essential territorial units in the evolution of the town. The town was an association of husbandmen. "These persons," one Englishman described in 1670, "settle the place, and take in what inhabitants to themselves they shall see cause to admit of, till their Town be full." The farmers then "make a division of the Land suitable to every mans occasions... the rest they let lie in common till they have occasion for a new division." Invariably, the undivided agricultural lands went to sons who formed adjoining towns or, strictly speaking, precincts, until properly incorporated.[108]

With such a rural model in mind, the Dutch towns of Bergen (New Jersey), Kingston, Fordham, Kinderhook, and Schenectady were given incorporation. In 1665, Nicolls expected that in reconfirming lands he

---

istration of Francis Lovelace, 1668–1673 (Albany, 1910), 2:146, and, for *plein* see Ord. sess., August 15, 1676, and July 4, 1676, *CRA*, 141, 130.

107. Privilege granted to Capt. Thomas Chambers, erecting Fox Hall into a manor, October 16, 1672, *DRCH*, 13:468.

108. Van Laer, Notes for articles in Dutch Settlers of Albany, MS 11779, NYSA; Charter of the City of Albany [1686], *AA*, 2:66; Daniel Denton (1670) quoted in Cornell Jarey, ed., *Historic Chronicles of New Amsterdam, Colonial New York and Early Long Island* (New York, 1968 reissue), 17, and see 18.

would be examining grants and patents to "town shipps, lands or Houses."[109] Lovelace called Kingston a parish on one occasion. Under the English, a town might be entrusted to a single individual. John Winthrop, Jr. and his heirs, for example, were granted the "privilege and Right of ordering and disposing all [the] publick buildings and affairs" of Pequot in 1650.[110] Governors of New York also entrusted new towns to trustees, that is, associations of five, seven, or twelve freeholders who held political authority. The system was entirely foreign to Dutch residents. When it was imposed on Schenectady, rivalries arose that lasted three generations.

The English were experts with land. It provoked and justified their talents and mythologies, just as cities and arteries of trade evoked Dutch skills. In his patent of the Nevesinks' land to two countrymen in 1664, Nicolls synthesized the topography of the area as no Dutch man had, inscribing a vision of agricultural settlements that would be fruitful and where some men would enjoy "hawking and fowling" while others settled in to "manure and plant" the soil. The land enticed him into seeing metes and bounds; it evoked his knowledge of tenements and hereditaments.[111]

Nicolls and Lovelace were at ease in fusing political power and landownership. Power would lie with men like Chambers and, if he would, with van Rensselaer. As a ruling squirarchy, they would be justices of the peace enjoying deference from sheriffs, townspeople, and fellow or junior officers in militias now organized by townships. The provincial laws of 1667 already required that one-third of the town militias be "mounted, armed and ready for service at all times." The remainder were to be alert "near their plantations." Towns would go to each other's assistance. Commanding officers, those above the rank of captain, would be men of the king's household or local gentry.[112]

England was replicated. There, too, towns were politically weak alongside the central government and local gentry. "By 1700 the gentry [even] progressively dictated the social diversions and intellectual life of towns." Country houses, not municipalities, were the fountains sprin-

109. Earliest English Colonial Laws (1665), Article 17, *Second Report of the State Historian* (1897), 1:152.
110. Order for Laying Out Highways and Common Roads in Kingston, Hurley and Marbleton, 24 September, 1669, *Second Report of the State Historian* (1897), 1:275; Richard Dunn, *Puritans and Yankees; the Winthrop Dynasty of New England, 1630–1717* (Princeton, 1962), 75.
111. Patent for the land at the Neversinck, New Jersey, April 8, 1665, DRCH, 13:396, 397.
112. That Chambers was a justice of the peace by 1671, see *New York Historical Manuscripts: Dutch, Kingston Papers, 2 volumes [revised and reedited by Peter Christoph]*, eds. Kenneth Scott and Kenn Stryker-Rodda, tr. Dingman Versteeg (Baltimore, 1976), 1:xiii; Schultz, *Colonial Hempstead*, citing the Duke's Laws, 1667.

kling the English and Anglo-American countryside with the waters of manners, taste, and virtue. "Nothing contributes so much to the civilization of a country," sighed one of James Fenimore Cooper's eighteenth-century Anglo-American New Yorkers, "as to dot it with a gentry." Theirs was the virtue spilling over and saturating commoners with civility. "You cannot fully imagine the effect produced by one gentleman's family in a neighbourhood, in the way of manners, taste, general intelligence, and civilization at large."[113]

"Civilizing" Law Enforcement

Nicolls needed to establish a civilian chain of command in Albany. He had to anticipate that, when the striking force of soldiers would fall back from encounters with the French in Canada, it would lay in garrison in Albany. He needed civilians in authority who could impose English law and collect the taxes that would pay for the needs of the new provincial government. He found, to his pronounced dissatisfaction, that the magistrates, far from being decisive in administering law and order, were lax, procrastinating, and evasive. The English ambassador at The Hague had encountered such indecisiveness in 1664 and dismissed it as a vile discourtesy, "their way of treating others." The Duke of Alva attributed it to magistrates who were untrained in the law and basically venal.[114] In his nineteenth-century parodies of Dutch decision making, Washington Irving presented a process fogged in long hours of pipe smoking, multiple levels of babble (or doldrums of silence), and the arrival at decisions for which no one in particular needed, or cared, to take responsibility.

One of Nicolls's complaints to the magistrates was of their inability to recognize the line between his lawmaking powers and those within their discretion. By June 1666, he clearly felt that such discriminations had been adequately laid out and ought to have been understood. He brought to their attention cases in which his "directions" took precedence and those "wholly left to yourseules." Yet misunderstandings continued to arise. He had made it clear, when he inspected Albany, that the town retained the staple of fur and the power to regulate such local issues as the cost of bread. However, the magistrates had "either undervalued or

113. Peter Clark and Paul Slack, *English Towns in Transition, 1500–1700* (London, 1976), 13; James Fenimore Cooper, *The Chairbearer or the Littlepage Manuscripts, Works of J. Fenimore Cooper* (Boston, n.d.), 451.
114. See, for example, Nicolls to the Commissaries at Albany, June 22, 1666, DRCH, 3:117; Sir George Downing quoted in Henri and Barbara Van Der Zee, *A Sweet and Alien Land, The Story of Dutch New York* (New York, 1978), 436; Duke of Alva quoted in Robert Fruin, *Geschiedenis der Staatsinstellingen in Nederland tot den val der Republiek* ('s-Gravenhage, 1901), 119.

not understood these points." As a result, traders and bakers were coming to him for licenses that the magistrates should have been granting. He was willing to entertain the magistrates' complaints about the expenses of quartering and the breaking of seals on his letters by an officer, but most issues should have been handled locally. "You are appointed," he charged, "to make such orders as conduce to the benefit of the Inhabitants."[115]

On the other hand, the town leaders went beyond their jurisdiction and waded into matters that Nicolls judged his own. They meddled in affairs with the French. Characteristically, their role was one of indirection, the *croupier* to French and English players. They had assured de Tracy in 1666, for example, that the English presence had not put the Mohawk in an aggressive mood but one that would see them suing for peace. But the information was inaccurate. An attack occurred in which French lives were lost, and Nicolls reproached the magistrates for interference. He commanded them to accept the blame, which they did, writing de Tracy that "since you have not well comprehended . . . our good interests, we shall not for the future intermeddle with your affairs, which Comand [as we have received it from Nicolls] we shall obey." They complied with Nicolls's warning, "Do not over much rely upon your sense and judgements hereafter."[116]

In Nicolls's view, the magistrates not only failed to comprehend the authority they retained, but also were dilatory in applying the law. It was a carelessness he addressed in 1665. He sent a curt letter to captain John Manning and van Rensselaer ordering them as Indian commissioners to arrange that the Seneca or Mohawk surrender natives he thought guilty of murdering settlers. The events had come to his attention in July, and this was only August, but he was writing for the second time about the matter and clearly suspected that the Albany burghers would let the "extraordinary occasion" pass without punishing the offenders. Within the next ten months, he ordered that another sort of criminal prosecution be brought. This time the court was expected to bring charges against "Cobus the Loper." Earlier, as he accused, they had "demurred." Rather than making a "ready complyance with . . . [his] direction," they had set about prosecuting de Loper only when "he gave you a particular new occasion." It was the same "sloth" he had encountered in New York City.[117]

115. Nicolls to Commissaries of Albany, June 22, 1666, *DRCH*, 3:117; 117.
116. Commissaries of Albany to de Tracy, August 20, 1666, *DRCH*, 3:135; 117.
117. Nicolls to Manning and van Rensselaer, August 4, 1665, MS11346, NYSA; Nicolls to Commissaries of Albany, June 22, 1666, *DRCH*, 3:117; Minutes of May 2, 1665, *RNA*, 5:211.

Nicolls was not meeting a court bent on protecting Cobus the Loper. The man is not easily identified, but a "Cobus de loper" who does appear in the town records was a known troublemaker. He may have resided in New Amsterdam, perhaps directly opposite the fort. Jeremias van Rensselaer was trying to collect a debt from him there in October 1666.[118] Whatever the case, he was not in himself worth the price of disobeying the English governor.

Nicolls's encounter was not with an isolated instance of the court's obstructionism. He was meeting the proper procedures of law and order, formalities that for years had kept Beverwijck as harmonious as any equivalent New England town. Precipitousness, confrontation, show of force, exposing oneself as the "bad one" among other officials – these were diminished in favor of contextualization.[119] What Nicolls construed as the court's inability to pinpoint its authority was its unwillingness to do so. Anything other than minimalism made the court itself a prick to the censoriousness it was meant to control. Only on rare occasions (and then by indirection) did the burghers of Beverwijck, for example, know exactly how each of the six men on the court voted in individual cases. When they were informed, as in the summer of 1660, it was in order to cause disturbance. Generally no single person should be known to have had the decisive vote. But more than that, no individual should have a decisive vote or role, if it could be prevented. What was true of the councillor-pensionary of Holland – in the 1660s the most influential man in the United Provinces – held generally: He had "no right of command, only the duty of persuasion."[120]

Debating, postponing, reconvening, sitting as court in busy inns, discussing town matters after church services – all were formalities that met that duty. The court continually masked its power by rotating functions in complex ways and generally leveling its prominence downward by such devices as convening in inns. It appointed nonofficial adjudicators ("good men") in certain cases and regularly withdrew itself in others. For instance, in a manslaughter case it allowed the assailant and victim's kin to determine restitution and then shake hands in a residual

118. Deposition of Jacobus de Louper [Jacob Teunisse de Loper Quick], November 1, 1660, ER3, 42 n. 3; Power of attorney from Jeremias van Rensselaer to Notary Mattheus de Vos to collect money due to Jacob Teunisse, alias Cobus de Looper to Johan van Twiller, October 16/26, 1666, VRMP, SC7079, Box 13, Folder 23, NYSA.
119. For vander Donck's failure to collect tithes promptly because "he did not want to be the bad one among" the *colonie* tenants, see Nissenson, *The Patroon's Domain*, 75.
120. See Colve to New Orange, January 15, 1674, *DHNY*, 1:609, who writes that the court is "not [to] publish ... [any minority opinion] in any manner out of the court on pain of arbitrary correction"; Herbert Rowen, *John de Witt: Grand Pensionary of Holland, 1625–1672* (Princeton, 1978), 141.

enactment of the ancient *bloedwraak*. Settlement by "honorable reparation" (verbal apology and pecuniary compensation) was the rule.[121] Mitigation of sentences, even those handed down to natives, was customary.[122]

There were legal niceties for the court to exploit. Dutch law, for example, filled the space between murder and manslaughter with multiple gradations. Assault also had an intricacy of categories. But in practice, law smothered rather than adjudicated conflict. There was no place for lawyers or divines. So, to take an example, whereas Bostonians often expected ministers to explain the appearance of comets or other supernatural occurrences, Dutch settlers (following Roman law) turned to civil authorities for such interpretations, who, in turn, "imposed silence on public clamour" as they had in Roman times. The burghers did this when they sighted the comet of 1680.[123]

Some verdicts were never intended to be executed, and that was understood. On countless occasions in New Netherland, individuals convicted of crime were banished. Fine gradations governed the duration of banishment, for six weeks, six years, or *voorgoed verbannen* (in perpetuity). This agreed with criminal procedures in Gelderland, the province from which many Albany residents emigrated. There, between 1590 and 1694, the court banished 419 of the 730 individuals charged. The guilty were banished for thieving, manslaughter, unlawful behavior in inns, kidnapping, conspiring with the enemy, and criticizing magistrates. Like New Netherland, the duration of banishment was as wide as the range of offenses. An offender might be banished for two, five, ten years, or permanently. A criminal might be banished *uit Veluwe* or *uit Veluwezoom* (beyond the Veluwe, beyond the borders of the Veluwe). When one of the banished returned, he was ordered away again.[124]

Cobus de Loper, then, was receiving the due process of law as much as Jacob Janse Schermerhoorn, who was banished and returned, or Philip Pietersz Schuyler, who was fined and never paid. In the same way, the magistrates were more obedient than befuddled in not licensing nonburghers. Stuyvesant had rigidly retained that right; they could not grant the small or great *burgerrecht* without charter privileges. The same legal

---

121. See Ord. sess., July 13, 1660, CRB, 276.
122. Minutes of August 7, 1683, CRA, 377.
123. See Ord. sess., December 17, 1648, and ex. Sess., July 18, 1650, CRB, 51, 123;
    Magistrates to Capt. Anthony Brockholes, January 1, 1681, CRA, 57, 58.
124. Hof Criminele Processes, 1544–1599, M.S. Inventaris No. VII-E [door H. L. Driessen,
    A. J. Maris, R. Wartena], RG; Archief van het Hof: Criminele Processen, 1600–1629,
    M.S. Inventaris No. VII-E.1 [door F. F. J. M. Geraedts, April 1971], Archief van het
    Hof: Criminele Procesdossiers, 1630–1694, M.S. Inventaris No. VII-E.2. [dewerkt
    doot J. den Draak, July 1971], RG (Arnhem).

constraint applied to licensing bakers.[125] The magistrates were men of "sense and judgements," but not to the English strangers.

In any situation of dominance, the conqueror will deny that the vanquished operate from abstract principles of jurisprudence. Their application of law will appear wholly particularized. Authority will look to elicit too little reverence, command too little respect, and continually contradict its own dignity. It will need to be brought into line with "civilized" jurisprudence.[126] The victor need not be mindful that he too is continually contextualizing law. He knows that his abstractions are in place and that particularizations are merely temporal and nonthreatening excursions away from their substance. This was Nicolls's position in dominating the burghers of Beverwijck. He observed the Dutch making necessary applications of law but could not find the law itself, although his entire administration was a continual particularization of law as well.

The fact that English law was being administered by military men to secure an act of conquest necessarily meant that it was not English justice as practiced at home in courts leet, quarter sessions, and borough government, in short, in all the outlets of immemorial law. English law, for example, did not permit an entire village to be put on public trial in order to solve a problem of petty theft. Yet in New Utrecht, Nicolls ordered a constable to "assemble all [the] townsfolk in the square" of the village, to report the theft that had been committed, and to remind them that "no strangers had been in the village" so "some of the inhabitants must be guilty." Houses were searched until neighbors began to inform.[127]

In reality, the presence of England in the upriver communities was only a military one. The English there were fighting men, and, though the protection they gave had certain benefits, it also meant an increased possibility of residents being involved in court-martial proceedings. The conquered had no experience of English common law as it related to marriage, inheritance, torts, or contracts. At times Nicolls and Lovelace were aware of these and other ambiguities that the conquest presented. In 1670, for example, Lovelace knew that his court should have heard the suits brought against Baker by Albany burgher Joachim Wesselsz. But he transferred them to the magistrates. They might well have wondered what principle of jurisdiction was being applied in the decision, but Lovelace knew he was making an exception because the case was "too tedious to decide."[128] Law had to be adjusted to circumstance.

125. For bakers, see Ord. sess., November 27, 1658, *CRB*, 166, 167.
126. For a study of the "civilizing" process, see Norbert Elias, *The Civilizing Process*, tr. Edmund Jephcott (London, 1978).
127. Minutes of August 22, 1665, *RNA*, 5:287.
128. Lovelace to Dudley Lovelace, April 11, 1670, Victor Hugo Palsits, ed., *Minutes of*

Similarly there was martial law. Military handbooks regulated against such injustices as the seizure of booty, mistreatment of women, and violation of citizens in their homes. However, the Articles of War that constituted English military law were little more than "a curious cabinet of antiquities" even in the eighteenth century, and there was grave uncertainty as to who fell under its jurisdiction.[129] Violators of the articles were meant to receive swift punishment. When it was not meted out to the soldiers who sacked Fort Amstel or to the men who violated the homes of the Esopus inhabitants or to the noncommissioned officer who used a sword to wound a Dutch boy after kicking him, it was not for lack of military justice. Discretion had dictated a lax interpretation.

As the conquerors, the English had the power to recover law from its varied performances. They could enact the rule book. They could construct rituals of how the law was meant to be applied. This was done on at least two occasions. Each was a performance occasioned more by a determination to teach the Dutch and the natives lessons in the essentials of English justice than by a commanding officer's conviction that wrong done to an individual had to be righted.

In the first instance, Nicolls arranged the drama of a court-martial in Esopus. His sensitivities to the semiotics of the trial were too many to be analyzed here. In secret directions to the justices, he instructed that they avoid impaneling a jury and allow only a limited number of burghers into the room as witnesses of the proceedings. "Take up the Fisher murder case first," he directed, "and hear the evidence patiently, etc., You will conclude him guilty of manslaughter."[130] Whether English justice was communicated to the Dutch onlookers during the trial is open to question, but that is not the point here – rather it is taking notice that the power to constitute law in moments of ritual was one of the ways in which the conquest worked.

In the second instance, the power to constitute law was again formalized in a premeditated way, but the determination to make the spectacle instructive was more explicit. Both the formalities of the occasion and its didactics were known to be disproportionate to the crime committed. In 1672, an English soldier of the Albany garrison, John Stuart, was found slain, and eventually two natives were apprehended and

---

the Executive Council of the Province of New York: Administration of Francis Love-lace, 1668–1673, Vol. I: Minutes, Collateral and Illustrative Documents, I-XIX, 1:384.

129. Frederick B. Wiener, *Civilians under Military Jurisdiction: The British Practice since 1689, Especially in North America* (Chicago, 1967), 3.

130. "Regulations and Procedure for Holding the Court of Oyer and Terminer" [1669], *Second Annual Report of the State Historian* (1897), 235.

charged with the crime. Lovelace wrote to a fellow officer that Stuart was a man whom he knew would "dye some violent death" and had been involved illegally in the fur trade. Nevertheless the trial of his alleged murderers occasioned a timely enactment of English justice. Lovelace ordered Captain Sylvester Salisbury to obtain a warrant for a Court of Oyer and Terminer to try the natives. He was to seek out Mathias Nicolls, the provincial secretary, and furnish himself with a "modell as to the formality of it." His instructions were to have "Cap Renslaer and his troop drawn up" not only to enhance the proceedings as participants in the drama but, like the natives, to be observers "attend[ing] the solemnity of that day." The dramatization of dominance and the law that legitimated it was consciously staged. They were procedures, reminded Lovelace, "in accord with our laws and customs."[131] In this instance, one day's solemnities would serve to overawe two conquered peoples, the Dutch and the aborigines. Earlier, Nicolls had told the General Court in Boston that an unfortunate symbiosis existed between the natives and the Dutch. "The spirit of the Dutch" was disorderly as a result of native contacts but, he thought, he had finally got both parties "orderly." But Lovelace, continuing that ordering, was orchestrating procedures with care: "Power and solemnity commonly strikes as great a terror in Spectators" as in the prisoners. The natives were hanged. Salisbury later reported that each had confessed. One was a "younger fellow (which is but a lad)," he wrote. His elder companion claimed the younger man had struck the first blow, and he then "cut...[the] neck bone in two with an axe."[132]

The youth was the only son of Chickwallop (as the Europeans called him), a sachem of the Monotucks and a "friend" of John Pynchon and English settlers near Springfield. The Monotucks, revealing a different sense of law and retribution, begged that he might be spared, "one being enough to die for one." To them the double executions remained a reason for continued "resentment," whereas to Pynchon they were a "favor of God" and fulfillment of his expectation that "justice will be executed." To Lovelace, however, they were proceedings undertaken in "accord with our laws and customs," a spectacle that acted out the "especial grace, certaine knowledge and meer motion" of the sovereign. To the Albany

131. Lovelace to Sylvester Salisbury, January 27, 1672/3, Palsits, ed., *Minutes of the Executive Council*, 2:756–757.
132. Nicolls to General Court of Boston, July 30, 1668, DRCH, 3:172; Lovelace to Salisbury, January 27, 1672/3, Palsits, ed., *Minutes of the Executive Council*, 2:757; Pynchon to John Winthrop, February 10, 1672/3, in Carl Bridenbaugh, ed., *The Pynchon Papers, Volume I: Letters of John Pynchon, 1654–1700* (Boston, 1982), 113.

burghers the hangings, whatever meaning they gave them, were the first ceremonious execution of natives carried out in the town.[133]

The lesson about the merits of dealing out summary justice did not take, as with so many things, where the burghers were concerned. They resisted English ways – or negotiated their own path among them – by employing obfuscation, conciliation, and always, delaying tactics. In the summer of 1693, two natives, this time Mohawk, were in custody in Springfield and charged with murdering settlers at Deerfield. Pynchon wanted immediate trial and execution, but a delegation of Dutch officials from Albany had come to Springfield with pleas for delay. Against all the evidence, even that of dying victims, the Dutch men, reported Pynchon, "would have been glad [if] we would have discharged ... the two." He strongly demurred, and "so they left [the town] ... *desiring that we would deliberate* and [wait to] hear again from Albany before proceeding to their trial."[134]

After waiting several weeks for such counsel, Pynchon received John Schuyler, the eldest son of the mayor of Albany. He arrived with "full expectation to have obtained the discharge of the two Indians." When that was not forthcoming, Schuyler put up arguments with such insistence that even Pynchon was amazed. "He (though a very moderate tempered man)," wrote Pynchon to Massachusetts governor Sir William Phips, "in some passion expressed himself that all the Five Nations would look upon us as breaking with them, and for his part he said he would not stay an hour in Albany if we proceeded against these Indians, positively asserting their innocency." Schuyler clearly wanted the peaceful relations that would allow navigating the land to go forward. He exerted himself to the utmost. He could not be "pacified" by an explanatory letter "writ in ... [Pynchon's] handsomest way" to governor Benjamin Fletcher of New York and offered for his inspection. His vehemence even shook the New Englander's faith in his own judgment on the case. On July 27, the natives escaped from jail, at least indirectly abetted by the delaying tactics. They were "gone," Pynchon wrote flatly, "probably unrecoverably ... to Albany."[135]

133. Bridenbaugh, ed., *Pynchon Papers*, 1:113; Lovelace to Salisbury, January 27, 1672/3, Palsits, ed., *Minutes of the Executive Council*, 2:757, and see Charles II to Massachusetts, *DRCH*, 3:64; in each of two known earlier instances, a native was executed by the Dutch around Fort Orange, but we have no reason to think that ceremony would have been made of the executions (see Weise, *History of the City of Albany*, 114, and Jennings, *Ambiguous Iroquois Empire: The Covenant Chain Confederation of Indian Tribes with English Colonies from Its Beginnings to the Lancaster Treaty of 1744* (New York, 1984), 52.
134. Bridenbaugh, ed., *Pynchon Papers*, 1:270 (my italics).
135. Bridenbaugh, ed., *Pynchon Papers*, 1:274, 275, 276.

4

Occupancy of Land under English Rule, 1674–1690

In the years from 1674 to 1690, Dutch values continued to be symbolized in the landscape around Albany. In fact, they were to be read in two symbol systems regarding land: in the topographical features of the land and in the notarized papers and court minutes in which they were inscribed again and again on paper. English policy introduced changes to both systems. Among other things, it bent the residents' gaze to a landscape jurisdictionally redefined along county lines and to forms of property recordation that were valid because they were trans-local, or provincial.

During the first of these years, Jeremias van Rensselaer died. His burial came a short four weeks before the permanent English occupation of New Netherland and was one of the last all-Dutch, public moments in Albany. It was a moment when the land was made to play its role in the small dramas of one death. It is an illuminating beginning, nonetheless.

The Funeral of Jeremias van Rensselaer: Spaces for Mourning and Death

Jeremias van Rensselaer died at the age of about forty-five. Friends would have thought that death caught him at an early age. In Dutch lore, the sixty-third year was the one to be feared. Whoever could "round this corner" would live long. At about the age of sixty-five, a man might begin to call himself old and seek such privileges as concessions on municipal taxes.[1] Jeremias predeceased older and younger brothers. His younger brother Rychart lived another twenty-one years, retaining an administrative role in Rensselaerswyck's affairs for part of that time.

Jeremias's problems in the months before his death had been pressing ones. The United Provinces had retaken New Netherland, and Jeremias

---

1. Paul Zumthor, *Het dagelijkeleven in de Gouden Eeuw* (Utrecht, 1962), 1:137; see, as examples, Minutes of January 19, 1654, *RNA*, 1:151, Conveyance, 5/15, 1668, *ER1*, 442, and Minutes of March 18, 1661, *RNA*, 2:88.

shared the pride of it all, convincing himself that New Amsterdam was now "so strongly fortified that our neighbors ... [are] afraid of us and that one single vessel [*De Zeehond*] ... [would keep] the entire country to the north [New England] in awe." The familiar forms had returned. Commanders Evertsz and Colve had again structured the communities into "town[s] ... and the farms and settlements *thereto belonging*": Space disposed under the old rubric of *"stad en jurisdictie"* was again in place.[2] There were rumors, however, that the lands might be returned to England. Jeremias wanted more reliable information and requested the family to send works by Adrianus Cocquius "about this war with England." He feared that the cause of England's blessings might lie in prayers for King Charles offered inadvertently by men like himself. "It is true," he examined himself, "that we prayed for him to Almighty God, but mostly on the regular days of prayer and not in secret, and that we did not count on such a blow [as recapture by the English] God knows."[3]

Some time before October 17, van Rensselaer died, and the age-old rituals of burial were set in motion. The *aanspreeker* (inviter to funerals) wrote his "List of Those Who are Invited to the Interment, Bearing Mourning, of the Corpse of Mr. Jeremias van Rensselaer, Deceased, Director of the Colony Rensselaerswyck: on Wednesday Next, in the Afternoon, at One O'clock, Being the 17/7 October 1674."[4] His list was on paper that could have been removed from any one of dozens of extant account books. The *aanspreeker*, who was Hendrick Rooseboom, wrote 151 names. Below the names of Jeremias's two sons, Kiliaen, aged thirteen, and Hendrick, aged eleven (but leaving out his daughter Anna, aged nine), he inscribed the names of twenty prominent townsmen. He also devised a "List of Those Who Will Carry the Corpse of the Hon. Mr. Rensselaer, Director of the Colony of Rennsselaerswyck, Deceased." It included the names of fourteen burghers of the town and farmers of the *colonie*. Their average age was about forty-seven, close to that of Jeremias. The *aanspreeker* bid the wives of the pallbearers to the funeral also, but their names were not included on his list. Grouped together were four of the oldest men of the town, but beyond that, the list suggests no discernible ordering.[5] Mourners' names were not collated alphabet-

2. JvR to JBvR July 3, 1674, *Corr JvR*, 465; Order allowing Elizabethtown, Newark, etc. New Jersey to send delegates to surrender their towns, August 12, 1673, *DRCH*, 13:473 (my italics).
3. JvR to RvR, July 3, 1674, *Corr JvR*, 467; JvR to JBvR, June 29, 1674, *Corr JvR*, 461.
4. List of those who are invited to the interment ... being the 17/7 October, 1674, 54 OV, AIHA.
5. It is impossible to establish the age of Jeremias van Rensselaer and the participants and with accuracy confirm the assertion of Gertrude Lefferts Vanderbilt, *The Social History of Flatbush, and Manners and Customs of the Dutch Settlers in King's County* (New

ically nor by family or occupation. Neither was it a translation onto paper of the *aanspreeker*'s movements in some system as he went around the settlement delivering his invitations up and down the river. Nine names were inserted at different points in the list as afterthoughts. Some were the names of young men, but there is nothing to suggest a pattern.

Whether the list was the result of Maria van Rensselaer's dictation or the composition of the *aanspreeker* with her revisions, it was, in any case, a selective one. In inviting 151 mourners, the *aanspreeker* reached a slightly larger number of males than were members of the Reformed congregation nine years later. It exceeded by five the number of burghers required to repair the town's stockades in 1679. But many were not included for reasons we cannot hope to know. Two of the five magistrates who choreographed the walking-in-the-woods episodes of 1660 were dead by 1674. Possibly a third was as well. The fourth, Evert Wendell, was invited; the fifth, Jan Verbeeck, was not, though he was alive and mentioned as a grandfather in the court records of 1679.[6] Of the eight men whose auctions we looked at most closely from 1658 to 1664, only Gerrit Teunisse van Vechten and Bastiaen de Winter received invitations, four men having disappeared from the records and one residing elsewhere. Another man, Pieter Claerbout, predeceased van Rensselaer in 1674. He might otherwise have been bid to attend as his name was in Maria van Rensselaer's account book more than once, certainly in 1667. Hendrick Jochemsz, who organized the *papegaaischoet*, was not invited but neither was his name in the town records after 1669.[7] Paulus Janse, who busied himself lowering brandy from the fort and picking fictitious blueberries in the woods, was alive in 1677 but, not surprisingly, uninvited.

Jeremias would have hoped to embrace death publicly and with the composure he had admired in seeing Jacob d'Hinse die three years earlier. The man died, he noted, "conscious till the last minute and in a peaceful frame of mind." Dying set the expiring person the task of playing the joyful transient. Jeremias's family had expected him to make sense of his mother's death by considering that metaphor. Their letter assured him

York, 1899), 354, that pallbearers were as close as possible in age to the deceased; the four names are Cornelis van Slyck, Andries de Vos, Cornelis van Ness, and Albert Andriesse Bradt.
6. See Alice P. Kenney, "Patricians and Plebians in Colonial Albany: Part II: Aggregation," *de halve maen* (July 1970), 45:11; Ord. sess., March 4, 1678/9 [Ordinance enacted March 5], CRA, 396, 397; those dead were Andries Herpertsz and Rutger Jacobsz. Frans Barentsz Pastoor has disappeared from the records; for Verbeeck, see Ord. sess., May 6, 1679, CRA, 410.
7. The four men who disappeared from the records were Jan de Groot, Lammert Cornelisse, Jan Claesz van Oostsanen and Rem Janse; Dirck Janse Croon left Beverwijck in 1664; for Claerbout, see entry of January 12, 1667, Reecken Boeck Van Den Outfanck Ende Uitgift voor Maria Van Rensselarer, VRMP, SC7079, Box 19, Folder 33, NYSA.

that "she took her departure with great piety from the Church Militant here to the Church Triumphant above." For its success, the metaphor needed a mise en scène: a dying person, like Anna van Rensselaer, enunciating wishes "to be set free and to be [with Christ] who has taken her soul so mercifully." Together with the dying person, attendants made both poles of belief real: With a church militant so dramatically real – Anna died "in the presence of all ... [Jeremias's] brothers and sisters in this country" – could the church triumphant be less so?[8] With the space of death composed so sweetly, how, they might well ask, could the space of life everlasting be anything less?

Jeremias and his friends were diviners of Providence in the gestures surrounding the moment of death. They read death in other natural signs as well. The fiery comets of 1665 were read for God's displeasure. The tails required close attention because they pointed to the human objects of His anger. Just as folk in the Low Countries devoured *planetboeken* and read the skies for the comets and eclipses that meant war or public calamity, so Jeremias minuted his observations in 1665. He noted the comet's tail was "at least 12 feet long, later 24 feet long, but very pale." The tail of a second comet "extend[ed] behind toward the east." A third had a tail "threatening toward the south." He hoped Jesus Christ would "be merciful." The face, the piety, and the peace of the dying were a comparable text. A death, like that of Hendrick Fredericksz in 1677, held out improper signs and was recorded with an uncharacteristic redundancy: He died "all by himself, without anyone being present." The unease was not that the community had failed to extend him charity but that, in his dying, the inexplicable had gone without the protocols that made it credible.[9]

From records and folklore we can reconstruct Jeremias's funeral fairly confidently. After death, relatives washed the body, clothed it, and laid it on the bed with the head somewhat raised. Mirrors, like the one Jeremias owned in 1660, were turned to the wall. Like maps and lenses, they made a man or woman the recipient of a special kind of knowledge. They gave the world of illusionism: the inside of truth, reversals, the devil seen as a clown. Now the silvered plates that organized so much of life were deadened. Most furniture was removed from the room. The body was displayed in a coffin resting on supports, with the feet facing the door. Visitors remained standing.[10] Only if a child died would children view the corpse.

8. JvR to RvR, August 21, 1671, *Corr JvR*, 441; 422.
9. JvR to JBvR, April 5/15, 1665, *Corr JvR*, 375, 376; Ex. sess., December 24, 1677, *CRA*, 285–6.
10. For Dutch attitudes toward mirrors, see Svetlana Alpers, *The Art of Describing: Dutch*

Meanwhile the *aansprekker* earned his wages. In a place like Amsterdam, he would have belonged to a guild and written elaborate invitations for a prominent family like the van Rensselaers. In Albany, the role was undertaken by sextons of the church, generally the Roosebooms and Bradts. When he was seventy-eight in 1765, Barent Bradt remembered the day in 1712 when Jochim Staats died. His father was *aansprekker* and "sent him . . . to invite on both sides of the River, as far as Coeyman's" (Bethlehem)."

At one o'clock on Wednesday, October 17, those invited to the funeral arrived at Jeremias's home at Watervliet. Domini Gideon Schaats read appropriate verses from the Bible. The coffin was closed and decked with black linen, perhaps with the family's coat-of-arms embroidered on the cloth. A procession of townsfolk formed, walking in pairs, somberly but without outward signs of mourning, and following the coffin now on a bier and carried by fourteen men, who, like the others, would have covered their heads. In a Netherlands town, a *rouw-steller* or *luyck-steller* might have been hired to order the funeral. It is likely that Rooseboom carried out that function in Albany. How he arranged the funeral procession we do not know. There are paintings of Dutch countryfolk – men and women together – forming up in lines of carts at some distance behind pallbearers and mourners on foot. Such wagons may have been used in van Rensselaer's cortege as the family home was some four miles from the place of interment. More probably, most mourners walked.

The place of interment is lost to memory. Evidence suggests that the body was buried in a plot "to the northward of the old Fort at Albany." Here Jeremias's eldest son, Kiliaen, directed his remains to be buried in 1720. He identified the location as a burying place in the possession of a tenant but retained and bequeathed separately from the "Manor of Rensselaerswyck."¹² In a letter of 1682, Maria referred to the "patroon's garden," using a phrase reminiscent of numerous *grondbrieven* men-

Art in the Seventeenth Century (Chicago, 1983), 178, 179, and A. Th. van Deursen, *Het kopergeld van de Gouden Eeuw* (Amsterdam, 1978) 1:59.

11. Deposition of Barent Bradt, August 7, 1765, Staats Family Archives, 1654–1910, MG15250, Box 2, Folder 4 (Testimony of Witnesses), NYSA.

12. Extract from the will of Kiliaen van Rensselaer, Esq., proved May 10, 1720 [from a copy in VRMP], No. 11346 (7), NYSA. In 1652, the van Rensselaer plot was next to that of Cornelis de Vos, whose land was "near the bridge" over the Rutten kill (Ord. sess., June 16, 1654, *CRB*, 158). For conveyancing papers that help place the van Rensselaer property north of the fort, see Reconfirmation of land to A. Staats, April 25, 1667, Van Vechten Papers, AQ7006, Patent No. 1 (Folder 27), NYSA; Grant of land to A. van Ilpendam from Stuyvesant, October 16, 1653, HM9724 [Ms from Huntington Library], Box SC16676–8, NYSA; Transport from Kiliaen van Rensselaer to Robert Sandersen and Myndert Harmensen, June 25, 1692, Staats Family archives, MG15250, Box 3 (3–1), NYSA.

tioning "gardens" just north of the old fort and in the possession of burghers like van Rensselaer and Abraham Staats. A will of 1734 also specified that private land there was a burying place.¹³ Wherever his bones were interred, the marker would have been simple. There may have been none at all. Dutch graveyards of upstate New York do not resemble those of New England. Soul effigies "are not found here," nor are burial sites marked with "inflated epitaphs." Rather, it was noticeable in the late nineteenth century that a large majority of tombstones gave name and age only. One commentator noticed at Hurley that simple initials on stones sufficed, even as they did on householders' casks, kegs, fire buckets, and packets of letters.¹⁴ An Albany resident wrote in 1854 that his aunt was buried without "a tomb-stone to designate her grave."¹⁵

The markers announce a characteristic of New Netherlanders that we who study colonial New Englanders and later Americans cope with badly: their lack of didacticism. Undeniably van Rensselaer's grave is lost because later generations became New Yorkers, that is, men and women of Dutch and (dominantly) English culture. It was a change that everyone knew would come but few knew how. Four months after van Rensselaer's death, for example, two Dutch men and two Englishmen were approached by a group of "Mahicanders" mourning his death and insisting that he had "helped make the peace between themselves and the Maquas." The Dutch had let them live in peace and "remain" on the land, they said, but they now feared changes. They were assured, however, that there would be none, despite the fact that "we are English now."¹⁶

The natives were the wise ones in the encounter. Changes would come. Had New York remained Dutch, surely greater care would have been given to preserving the relics of the earliest Netherlanders. But in any case, the recovered tombstones of men like van Rensselaer would not have given promise of evolution into the elaborate designs we are familiar with in New England, for the notable feature of the carved headstone there was its publicness. It was more than a biographical notice. It was the church gone "out-of-doors" two hundred years before Ralph Waldo

---

13. MvR to RvR [January, 1682?], A[rnold] J. F. Van Laer, ed., *Correspondence of Maria van Rensselaer, 1669–1689* (Albany, 1935), 57; see, Deed of sale of "The Pasture" from mayor of Albany to Rev. Dellius, November 1, 1687, *AA*, 1:99–100; Will of Jacob Staats of the City of Albany, September 14, 1734, Van Vechten Papers, AQ7006, Wills, No. 1, Folder 18, NYSA.

14. Vanderbilt, *The Social History of Flatbush*, 160, 159; for lettering, see Crt. sess., October 14, 1865, *City Record, CHA*, 1:161.

15. Sketch [1854], *AA*, 5, 112.

16. Lawrence Leder, ed., *The Livingston Indian Records, 1666–1723* (Gettysburg, 1956), 37; 38.

Emerson. The gravestone was a New England townsman's last polemic to his neighbors, one which insisted upon their gaze. It was his last evangelization in towns where orthodoxy had a crucially self-defining role. New York had its gravesites in the seventeenth century, and they undoubtedly evoked the memories, regrets, and resolutions aroused by all places of the dead. But they were not classrooms on the landscape. Some were family spaces, though the melancholy visit to a cemetery was an unknown act. The Bronck family burial ground is an example. It is some thirty yards from the farmhouse and seventy yards from a kill, sluggish and half-hidden in bowing saplings and tangled brush. The graves are like those in the small Dutch graveyards in Hurley, quite hidden by foliage. In the seventeenth century, theology carved on stones received as little priority as orthodoxy imposed on natives.[17]

Jeremias van Rensselaer's family would have placed themselves closely around the open grave when they arrived at the burial site. They would have ensured that the corpse faced east and that the bearers received a gift (*fooi*), perhaps a scarf. After it, the bereaved returned to the house of the deceased, where they received condolences for the remaining hours of the day and night. At the end, the family retained a few friends, sharing a lavish meal in the final hour of friendship (*de laaste eer*) given to the dead man. Revels could go beyond bounds. It was at the funeral of a child that Cornelis de Vos talked his way into a fine by concocting nicknames for the houses of prominent men.[18] The festivities that followed a funeral held "at the close of the day" in eighteenth-century Albany lasted far into the night: "A pipe of wine, stood in the cellar some years before for the occasion, was drunk; dozens of pipes of tobacco consumed; grosses of [clay] pipes broken; scarce a whole decanter or glass left; and, to crown it all, the pallbearers made a bonfire of their scarves on the hearth."[19]

The observer of this occasion was someone who misunderstood that the consuming flames of a bonfire (*lijkstroo*) were signs of the fragility (*broosheid*) of life and generally considered that Dutch funerals were barbarism.[20] However, his observations about the expenses of funerals and their unrestrained conviviality were not amiss. One worried Albany burgher specified in 1694 that his funeral expenses not exceed "thirty

17. Edward V. Lucas, *A Wanderer in Holland* (New York, 1924), 9, observed that "the cemeteries are minute [in Holland] and the churches have no churchyards, and Alpers, *Art of Describing*, 172, briefly discusses the "self-effacing manner" in which death was commemorated in funerary art within Dutch churches.
18. See Ord. sess., February 2, 1655, *CRB*, 198.
19. Egbert Benson, *Memoirs Read before the Historical Society of the State of New York*, December 31, 1816, CNYHS, 2nd ser. (New York, 1848), 2 (Part 1): 110, 111.
20. See Jacob Van Lennep and Johannes ter Gouw, *Het Boek der Opschriften* (Amsterdam, 1869), 140; Benson, *Memoirs*, 110.

pieces of eight at the most," and in 1720, the deacons of the Reformed church paid a townswoman who had offered her home for the funeral of a pauper 10 guilders for the disturbance to her house.[21] Generally funeral expenses in Albany were borne directly by the family or by neighbors contributing through the Reformed church. Over the years, the congregation paid townsmen for cakes, pipes, tobacco, linen shirts, tablecloths, napkins, spiced wine, coffin nails, boards, beer, and rum. It reimbursed townspeople for services: digging the grave of a Christian native, making shrouds, and providing nails for coffins. The deacons received payment for the use of the church's pall, expecting gl 6 to 8 for the large pall and gl 1.5 to 4 for the child's small pall. Hendrick Rooseboom recorded gl 101 for some of the expenses of van Rensselaer's funeral.[22]

Van Rensselaer's funeral was one of the last public moments in Albany before the permanent English occupation. It embraced his obvious friends and associates, but also Lutherans, publicans, tax gatherers, and men who had abandoned the *colonie* for burgher status or disagreed with Jeremias over the years. There were no Englishmen. Soldiers and resident English merchants – men like Jan Connell, William Parker, William Penniman, and Samuel Nottingham – were excluded. Yet a moment's thought will suggest that "things English" could not have been bleached out of the event any more than they were absent from all the public and private moments of the next sixteen years.

From 1674 to 1690, the younger men at the funeral, those below the age of forty, shared in possessing Albany. At the end of those years, they also directly participated in what we call Leisler's Rebellion, that is, the events precipitated in New York by the accession of William III to the English throne in 1689. Those were months of violence, and for us, provide dramatic testimony of how deeply English ways had penetrated the townspeople's lives. Yet cultural change had been in process before that time, though less well recorded. Burghers were coming to interpret the land out of two cultural systems. They were recording and talking about it differently, they were struggling with new definitions of the town, and they were perceiving landownership as clientage.

21. Will of Jan Juriaensen Becker, August 31, 1694, ER4, 136; "To Ragell Ratlif...for the funeral and the disturbance in her house" [October 1720], in Deacons' Account Books, No. I, 1716–1762, p. 27, in Burial Record, First Dutch Reformed Church, Albany N.Y., 1654–1862, copied and arranged by Willian Vanderpoel Hanney, *The Dutch Settlers Society of Albany VIII and IX: Yearbook, 1932–1934* (Albany, 1934), 1–145.
22. Deacons' Account Book, *CHA* 1:33 passim; Memorandum, Hendrick Rooseboom, October 17, 1674, VRMP, 7079, Box 49 (59), n.p.

Landownership: The English Threat to Privacy

Two groups of men at van Rensselaer's funeral were involved with land-ownership in the 1670s and 1680s. The first was five men – Adriaen van Ilpendam, Jan Juriaensz Becker, Ludovicus Cobes, Johannes Provoost, and Dirck Wesselsz ten Broeck – who were the town's notaries or clerks of the court. They kept the formal record of property ownership in Albany. The second group was fifty-seven men, who were under the age of forty. Taken together, they owned 115 properties.²³ Both sets of men followed customary Dutch practices with respect to land. Above all, they protected the privacy of its ownership.

Landownership was not meant to be a precise reflection of social real-ities. There were no moments in the town's earlier history when mag-istrates had summoned a town meeting about property distribution, commissioned a survey, or drawn attention to land ownership.²⁴ The paperwork surrounding land use was undertaken with a respect for pri-vacy as well. The *protocols* (notarial registers) of a man like Adriaen van Ilpendam were meant to be an intimate archive of the business and family relationships that surrounded land transactions. They were kept at his home and opened for the inspection of clients, not the public. The notary was traditionally an urban man, and his conveyancing papers were civic as well – housed inside city walls and available after a short walk or, as in the Netherlands, a convenient *trekschuit* journey for the merchant or artisan. They were urban in another way. They were *narratives* of a civic occurrence. The notary began the episode, "Appeared before me," and then narrated the story of a private meeting at his home, naming himself

23. The estimated fifty-seven landowners were Jan Janse Bleecker, Pieter Bogardus, Jan Bricker, Hendrick Bries, Maes Cornelisse, Hendrick Cuyler, Evert Janse Cuyper, Mar-ten Gerritsz, Sander Sandersz Glen, Jan Gouw, Gerrit Gysbertsz, Willem Gysbertsz, Andries Hansen, Dirck Hesselingh, Paulus Jurianensz, Thomas Davidsz Kikebel, Pieter Lansingh, Anthonij Lespinard, Hendrick Maesz, Jan Mangelsz, Jan Outhout, Harme Rutgers, Albert Ryckman, Gerrit Ryersz, Hendrick Jacob Sanders [Glen], Johannes Sandersz [Glen], David Schuyler, Pieter Schuyler, Jacob Staats, Andries Teller, Dirck Wesselsz ten Broeck, Hendrick Coster van Aecken, Laurens van Alen, Jan Hendricksz van Bael, Cornet Janse van Bael, Paulus Martensz van Benthuysen, Marten Cornelisse van Bergen, Ripse Claes van Dam, Jacob Abramsz van Deusen, Cornelis van Dyck, Jan van Eps, Gerrit van Ness, Hendrick van Ness, Pieter van Olinda, Sybrant Goose van Schaick, Abraham van Tricht, Cornelis Teunisse van Vechten, Dirck Teunisse van Vechten, Gerrit Teunisse van Vechten, Sweer Teunisse van Velsen, Arnout Cornelisse Viele, Tierck Harmensz Visser, Jacobus van Vorst, Teunis Willemsz van Woutbergh, Adam Vrooman, Johannes Wendell, "Young Jan." I am excluding Hendrick and Kil-iaen van Rensselaer.
24. On one occasion, there was a "survey" of town lots, but this was clearly information for Stuyvesant, not the town (see Ord. Sess., November 7, 1656, *CRB*, 300); see William McLaughlin, Dutch Rural New York: Community, Economy and Family in Colonial Flatbush (Ph.D. diss., Columbia University, 1981), 54.

as a sort of family attorney, the vendor, one or two sureties, and the purchaser. The setting insured that the business of this clutch of men transferring a property was surrounded with privacy. And like the notary's house, his carefully guarded books treated landownership as a matter of professional discretion.[25]

Beginning in the 1680s, however, English forms of conveyancing appeared in Albany registers. The wording of such deeds carried landownership outside the civic episode. It carried the assumption that settlements affecting land were matters of the crown – and the crown's bureaucrats. They concerned not just the present but the future. Above all, landownership was subject to public scrutiny. The conveyancing paper was a message to the public about individual ownership. It addressed "all Christian People to whom this present writing shall come" and allowed them to "*know*" that a farm or house, tenement or meadow was newly possessed. In 1683, Albany's burghers were informed that the proper depository for titles to property was no longer the home of the notary or court secretary. It was the office of the county clerk and subsequently that of the king's provincial officers in New York City.[26]

The function of the Dutch notary was at an end. Van Ilpendam, perhaps recognizing this, committed suicide on the day that Albany received a city charter stipulating that recordation would henceforth be in English. His resistance to English ways lived after him. For fifteen years the burgher to whom he entrusted his registers protected them from public access despite threats of prosecution.[27] By 1700, there were no functioning notaries in Albany.

Property was given meaning in two symbol systems: in the notations made on the pages of notarial registers and, of course, in the practices of townspeople using the environment of Albany. If we consider the practices of each of the fifty-seven men at the funeral with regard to land ownership, we see that they also sheltered the full value of their property ownership by maintaining properties both in and outside the town's bounds. They owned fifty-two properties in town as well as fifteen holdings distributed on the pastures south of it and twenty-five parcels of land to the north. Beyond that, their landholdings were further scattered to places like Schenectady, Greenbush, Half Moon, Bethlehem, the Catskills, and Kinderhook. They were properties in investment portfolios

25. The notaries' papers of Beverwijck and Albany are collected in four volumes edited and translated by Jonathan Pearson and A. J. F. Van Laer. I have cited them as *ER1*, *ER2*, *ER3* and *ER4*. For a brief introduction to them, see "Preface," *ER3*, 3–23.

26. "Preface," *ER2*, 8; for examples, see Will of Marten Cornelissen and his wife Maeycke Cornelis, January 12, 1676/7, and Antenuptial contract between Gerrit van Ness and Maria Pieters, February 14, 1676/7, *ER3*, 359, 355 (My italics).

27. "Preface," *ER3*, 17; 17.

selected to satisfy each man's diverse – and changing – interests. Out of
these shifting expectancies, Albany's land was made an ill-defined patch-
work that purposely hid as much as it showed about the accumulation
of wealth.

Predictably, visitors translated these practices into evidence that Dutch
men and women were willing to live with disorder. They could find no
pattern in the uses of agricultural land and no care for its appearance.
Residents lived amid woods, bogs, and swamps, while hogs and cattle
ran wild.[28] Soils were not improved, and taken altogether, the land, and
particularly the woodland, was "not worth much."[29]

In fact, of course, the landscape was not meant to be read by outsiders
nor to reveal everything to insiders either.

In the 1670s, land became a more attractive commodity for all the
burghers of Albany. The fur trade continued to be the basis of the town's
social order well into the eighteenth century, but pressure on available
land began to increase as families were forced to find their subsistence
and, if they could, profits in agriculture as well as trading in fur. However,
Albany's burghers confronted serious difficulties in acquiring parcels of
good land. Competition for properties on the pastures south of town was
especially keen but frustrated by the magistrates' determination to parcel
out a good deal of it among themselves. *Handelaars* like Philip Pietersz
Schuyler were in a favored position to make acquisitions. By the 1680s,
the Schuyler family had extensive holdings both south and north of town.
South of the palisades and on the *plein*, Schuyler had woodland and fields
adjacent to those from which others had been dispossessed. North of
town, the family's properties were less extensive, but they were more
valuable than those of the van Rensselaers. In the 1670s, Schuyler had
acquired three properties. The first was "the great flat," the farm so
highly prized by Kiliaen van Rensselaer and extending for two miles
along the Hudson on a fertile and beautiful plain about four miles north
of Albany. He also possessed the extensive lands of Bastiaen de Winter.
Finally, he owned a property lying immediately across the river from the
great flat and acquired from a man probably acting as his dummy when
he took ownership. Farther north of Schuyler and on the Hudson's west
bank, the van Schaick in-laws had three valuable properties at Half Moon
and Cohoes. Here too, Schuyler's son Pieter had acquired grazing land

28. Jonathan Tenney, *New England in Albany* (Boston, 1883), 20, 21; Victor Hugo Paltsits,
     ed., *New York Considered and Improved, 1695, by John Miller, Published from the
     original MS, in the British Museum* (Cleveland, 1903), 42; 43.
29. Henry C. Murphy, ed., *Journal of a Voyage to New York and a Tour in Several of
     the American Colonies in 1679–80, by Jasper Dankers and Pieter Slyter of Wieward
     in Friesland, Memoirs of the Long Island Society* (Brooklyn, 1867), 1:336–7.

in 1681. Then, in 1683, Pieter and Sybrant van Schaick received large tracts of Indian land along the Mohawk River and adjacent to land also purchased from the Indians and owned jointly by their fathers.[30]

Undeniably, Schuyler was, although still buying geographically dispersed lands, beginning to consolidate his holdings in certain areas. This was obvious to Maria van Rensselaer, but even she, when referring to his activities, called him only an "interloper," leaving her correspondent to surmise her meaning and certainly saying nothing specific about the amount of land he held.[31] Landownership, like other ventures, was a private affair. Just as the magistrates continued to find no reason to survey the town, so individuals like Schuyler apparently felt no necessity to accompany *grondbrieven* with survey maps that might have given greater precision about boundaries. The Dutch believed that maps, like mirrors, conveyed a special kind of knowledge, that they brought objects before the eye in a way different to words. Perhaps for that reason the *grondbrieven* were uniformly without sketches, although there was a man with surveying skills residing in the town. Whatever the case, the English patent transferring land just north of Albany to Mathias Nicolls is remarkable among the hundreds of others in this period because it stated that the land had been surveyed.[32] Men knew the genealogies of properties and gathered information about land, but all in private conversations. These took place in houses, at *herbergen*, around wells, on streets, and on *stoeps*. There an individual's landholdings might well suffer the close scrutiny and disfavor of townsmen but remain the subject of private speculation.

The subject of landownership had no place in official or public discourse. The court case brought in February 1684 against the old man Jan Clute is a case in point. "Being very drunk" one evening, he had "shouted across the street, 'Oyes! Here is to give notice.... They [the assembly and perhaps the governor] buy up all the land. I have money too; I can pay for it too, even for the choicest land. The devil take them all.'" Brought to court, he faced the magistrates who handed down a curiously lenient verdict. But more pertinent here are actions of neighbors and the sheriff, all of whom sought to quiet Clute before charges could be laid. None of the witnesses showed disagreement with Clute's remarks about English authority, but each sought to prevent his remarks being made in public. Two men and one townswoman tried to force him into his house, one of them offering protection by putting "his

---

30. See, Merwick, "Dutch Townsmen and Land Use: A Spatial Perspective on Seventeenth-Century Albany, New York," *William and Mary Quarterly*, 3rd ser. (January, 1980), 38:74.
31. MvR to RvR, October 12, 1683, *Corr MvR*, 125.
32. See Ord. sess., July 6, 1680, *CRA*, 27.

hand over his [Clute's] mouth." A third man conducted him "to the corner of [Backer's] house," where Clute blew out the candle used for direction and said, "I am not as drunk as I make out to be. Let me go; I know what I am saying." Even the Dutch sheriff warned him, "Go into the house."[33]

Certainly the town's various efforts to save Clute from possible committal for contempt charges are significant in this affair. Only eight months before, a more prominent townsman than Clute had been summoned "to go to New York [City] to answer the charge of having made remarks to... [the acting governor's] prejudice." Clute had not only endangered himself but others who privately shared his sentiments. So his desperate neighbors and the town behaved as they did.[34] But in making landownership the subject of a nightwatchman's public outcry he also flaunted the venue for such discourse, and those involved reacted instinctively to that as well.

Clute's case arose at a time when privacy about landownership was being more severely threatened than at any period since the first English occupation. We might know less about this but for scattered occurrences like that at the *stadhuis* one month after his arraignment. Forty burghers and ten farmers were made to appear at two "extraordinary" court sessions for arrears of provincial taxes. A number of them were simply evading payment of a property tax by demurring, but the nature of the tax was also misunderstood. At least one farmer seemed genuinely confused that nonlocal officials could "take away his money" and "give... [it] away." One female trader thought that the sheriff, rather than the governor, had authority to levy taxes. The confusion is understandable. The city was expected to be the object of one's care. Words still in common use tied taxes to local needs. A license to tap, for example, was a *"spinhuissedeel,"* that is, a charge for supporting the local workhouse.[35]

Behind the matter of defaults there also lay deep resentment of a structure of taxation that governor Edmund Andros had introduced in 1675, replacing the traditional system of excise payments. The old system tapped personal wealth through a cohort of collectors. The demands were continual and often harsh. But in its multiplicity, the system actually defended individuals against the exposure of their total wealth to recurrent public scrutiny.

33. Ord. sess., February 8, 1683/4, CRA, 416; 419; 418.
34. Ex. sess., June 18, 1683, CRA, 365; for court cases that make this motivation clear, see Ord. sess., April 1, 1684, and Ex. sess., April 15, 1684, CRA, 435, 439.
35. Ex. sess., March 10, 1683/4, CRA, 429–31, 434; 429; Ord. sess., April 1, 1684, CRA, 435; Ord. sess., May 2, 1676, CRA, 97; Ord. sess., November 12, 1668, CRA, 36.

The English were collecting property tax. It required precise assessment of property and laid that measurement open to public view. So for the first time burghers appeared in court stating their total assets or, rather, stating sums below the estimates reached by assessors but totals nonetheless. In 1675, the new system forced Barent Coeymans to state publicly that his capital (*commende goederen*) was gl 8,000. Hans Hendricksz was forced to disclose that his was gl 13,000. Six weeks later the court heard Philip Pietersz Schuyler say that his assets were gl 24,000. Such disclosures were understandably few, and delinquency was common, with English officials prosecuting townsmen in late 1677 for debts going back to 1675 and employing soldiers to enforce collection.[36]

On one occasion, four months after Clute's outburst, the town magistrates tried to reverse the English manner of paying "the public expenses of the town and county" by reintroducing a tax on "a list of [arriving] Indian goods," that is, an excise tax. Andros rejected this maneuver as unlawful.[37] In late 1684, the townspeople acquiesced in dividing the town into *wycks* (wards). They introduced a structure whereby each burgher's real property would be known by only one resident assessor who in turn would know only the assets of those in his *wyck*.[38] An annual property tax remained. But this system at least likened the paying of taxes to a contract between two individuals and, in doing so, made the experience somewhat like that of the *schout* collecting his fines from individual offenders or the excise man taking his fees on beer and spirits from individual licensed retailers. It went some way toward veiling landownership. Prosperity and ambition were hidden as well.

But this was to change. Over the coming decade, the English instructed the burghers as to the appropriateness of making landownership highly visible. A man who would qualify for local leadership might be expected to answer the governor's requirement for a property extensive enough to shelter up to fifty families of Indian allies. Land was the visible reward for loyal service: Enemies were "those who had considerable estates" into whose ownership they had "screwed" themselves, favorites were those who were expected to covet land and watch it appreciate over that of others.[39] Those exercising English authority had to be notably landed men, whether of Dutch or English origin.

36. Ex. sess., September 30, 1675, *CRA*, 34; 30; Ord. sess., November 2, 1675, *CRA*, 48; for some prosecutions, see Ord. sess., March 14, 1675/6, and Ord. sess., September 5, 1676, *CRA*, 88, 160, but see also 186, 264, 267.
37. Ex. sess., June 11, 1684, *CRA*, 461; 461.
38. Ord. sess., December 2, 1684, *CRA*, 489–90.
39. For Governor Benjamin Fletcher referring to Robert Livingston and quoted in Carl Carmer, *The Hudson* (New York, 1939), 63. For governor Bellomont's similar dis-

Inside New – and Public – Boundaries

This "civilizing process" first required boundaries. Boundary making ordered men properly, that is, according to the land. Moments of orientation arose from a series of direct orders from successive English governors and marked the years after 1674. People experienced those moments in ways beyond calculating. However, we can consider them as experiences of self-identification that followed as new boundaries were set out, as existing ones were altered, and finally, as those pertaining to the identity of the city itself underwent change.

In 1675, during the first month of Andros's occupation, residents were reminded that Albany was now "an English place." Soon each inhabitant was located according to his place along "the king's highways" and ordered to see to their maintenance "each as far [along the highway] as he is concerned." For the first time, the passageways on land rather than water received emphasis, and from that time forward scores of men were identified with strips of roadway leading to and from the town. They and the "road-master" and "surveyors" of the king's highways were now identified as men of "the county." A phrase like "the town and such places under its jurisdiction" was retained but, for the first time, the town was identified as the physical center of a community and economy essentially rural.[40]

Precision about bounds partitioned residents in new ways. For example, the sequence of ordinances governing highways made it clear that the town was set within pastures and farmlands. For anyone who cared, the directives constituted a new social mapping of the area and thrust certain of its residents into unavoidable prominence as husbandmen. Boundaries and the location of men and women along them were all important. The highway from Catskill ran "from Dirck Teunise' house" through "the great flatts or Plain" to Coxackey and then "to Barent Gerritse at Bethlehem, but Barent Pieterse [Coeymans] is to assist s^d Barent Gerritse at Bethlehem." Inhabitants of Bethlehem were to keep the highway to the "gate of the So[uth] end of the Great Pasture," and then keeping the highway lying "on this [the city] side of Bethlehem, along the [Hudson] River," the inhabitants were to be "assisted by inhabitants of Nefions Island [that is], Teunis Slingerlandt, Gerret Bancker,

paragement of Nicolaes Bayard, see Bellomont to DePeyster, April 5, 1700, DePeyster Papers, 1695–1710, NYPL.

40. Ord. sess., August 24, 1675, CRA, 16; Ord. sess., January 6, 1684/5, CRA, 503; Ord. sess., February 3, 1684/5, CRA, 515; for references to the rural surrounds, see, as examples, Ord. sess., August 24, 1675, Ex. sess., September 7, 1675, Ord. sess., December 3, 1678, Ord. sess., April 6, 1680, CRA, 16, 22, 377, 493.

Jurian Callie [Callier?] each from their respective houses." Finally the highway reached the city and called upon familiar landmarks. It was to be kept in repair from the south to north gate of the "great Pasture" by owners there and then it was the city's responsibility to the northernmost limits.[41]

The ordinances, in order to describe the highway, carried visual images of the lands outside Albany leading to it. But this was an inversion of the customary relationship of the city and the countryside. Previously it was the city that served as a descriptive starting point: Now it was far distant lands. In phrases like *"from* Saratoga" to "the bounds" of the city, the descriptions of outlying lands were subtly beginning to redefine the city itself. The highway placards located scores of men at farms and mills. Those for Roosendale, Schenectady, Kinderhook, and Greenbush conjured up a new order of places and inhabitants as well. Together the descriptions made the whole area a solid of joined farms, *pleins*, gates, and arable lands. They placed a visualization of status based on land occupancy alongside the one still provided by the layered cases of furs seen in the summer months awaiting departure from the strand. Both were relatively imprecise – the highway repair placards certainly were – but inhabitants were now directed to self-identification by placing themselves inside a geometry of landholdings, and that was something entirely new.

The presentation of names on the highway placards was cognate with other modes of listing. On militia registers and occasional accounts listing contributors to the dominie's salary, the classification of men and women as occupants of land recurred. Men were still drawn into the town's center for auctions and other civic occurrences, but the new mappings of space, like those persistently executed in the ordinances governing highway repairs, could not be ignored. The slow sorting out of yeomen and merchants, of civilized men and women who occupied the land and those who simply navigated it for trade, was underway. Imperceptibly, emphasis was shifting from the dynamism of trading to the stasis of husbandry. Words – in ordinances, muster rolls, and governor's orders – were helping to shape the emergence of another English country town.

Inside the town boundaries, the burghers also had to accept English directives regarding space and bounds. In 1684, the city was divided into four *wycks*. Basically the reorganization facilitated the taxing of real property. But residence also became the base of the magistracy. Formerly

41. Highway repair placard, December 4, 1688, in Court of Sessions, 1685–9, Canvass of Votes, 1820, volume in English, 50–7. Office of the County Clerk, Albany, New York.

marriage alliances, profession, and service qualified a man for the magistracy. Now landownership was a fourth determinant, because the aldermen, unlike the earlier magistrates, were representatives of a specific *wyck*. Until the charter of 1686, they took direction of local affairs together with the justices of the peace.

It was governor Thomas Dongan who formally ordered New York's landscape into the dominant counties (and chartered cities) of the 1680s. Generously, one might allow that a reduction of New York to such jurisdictional units may have allowed him to recognize it as a plausible replication of England. More cynically, however, it meant opportunities to line his purse by literally selling boundary lines to town fathers eager to settle disputed perimeters. Whatever his purposes, Dongan's legislation creating Albany county in 1683 gave the city not only a highly public moment but a new definition. In his perception of it, the countryside (called a county) "*contain*[ed] ... the town of Albany."[42] In an English way, the city took its meaning from that of a county, which in turn was a proper areal unit because its adjacencies with other counties constituted an unbroken domain of authority – and military control as well.[43]

With the county outlined on parchment, Dongan was in a position to see Albany as a county seat three years later. In the charter of 1686, he visualized it managing the trade "with all the Indians living within [the county] and to the eastward, northward and westward of the said county of Albany." He saw it managing municipally owned land as well, and brought an English courtier's expertise to the matter. He immediately cut away claims of the van Rensselaers to municipal lands and established in detail the city's jurisdiction over them and a range of other properties. He gave it the roadway to Schenectady, land along the Hudson to low water mark, and even property that he would have known very well was the king's, namely that of the old fort and its *plein* south of town. He pocketed £300 for executing the charter and secretly retained a substantial expanse of land for himself.[44]

---

42. "Charter of Liberties and Privileges, Passed October 30, 1683," *AA*, 4, 39; for Dongan's surreptitious acquisitions of valuable real estate, see, with reference to New York City, Dongan to William Penn, December 12, 1683, *Pennsylvania Archives, selected and arranged from Original Documents in the Office of the Secretary of the Commonwealth ... by Samuel Hazard, Commencing 1664* (Philadelphia, 1852), 1:81; Governor Dongan's Report on the Province of New-York, 1687, *DHNY* 1:181. For land personally acquired as a result of passing Albany's charter, see S[amuel] G[eorge] Nissenson, *The Patroon's Domain* (New York, 1937), 303.

43. For the Stuarts' recognition that only the control of counties assured them military superiority, see Leonard Hochberg, "The English Civil War in Geographical Perspective," *Journal of Interdisciplinary History* (Spring, 1984), 14:750, 734–5.

44. "Charter of the City of Albany" [1686], *AA*, 2, 80; 67; see Nissenson, *Patroon's Domain*, 303.

What the townspeople made of these moments that first gave them their principal geographical bearings in English New York is difficult to know. Probably only one or two townsmen saw the "Charter of Liberties and Privileges" that created county government, and this may explain why Clute's behavior – the first public outburst of anger toward English land policy – occurred just months after its passage. The city charter, in contrast, was received in Albany with some degree of public ceremony. It was immediately published (presumably in a Dutch translation) and would have afforded townsmen a rare and unfamiliarly public overview of the land base of the city. In another break with the past, it gave precision to the magistrates' control over land. They were proprietors, with the power of trustees over real estate such as "the said town hall or stadt house with the ground thereunto belonging; the said church or meetingplace, with the ground about the same; the said burying place; the watch house, and the ground thereto belonging."[45]

We generally read that the charter was received in Albany with "joy and acclamations." Actually these words were a marginal insertion in the original court records written by a partisan of the burghers who had advised Dongan about the charter and who were now its principal beneficiaries. Their acclaim was seriously contested. The charter made that conflict public, and even after its radical changes no longer provoked public comment, it directed concern toward land. For example, it compelled those men who were disputing the magistrates' right to dispose of the "pastures" to give uncharacteristic attention to land, that is, to put time into seeking clear titles to properties and determining precise boundaries.[46] Seen from our perspective, they were being initiated into the small rituals that confirmed the Englishman's reverence for land.

At the same time, the local court was being introduced to the fact that its jurisdiction over property matters was now limited and its ways of discoursing about them obsolete.

The Court and Land: More Words and Less Jurisdiction

Much of the discourse about land began to move beyond the competence of the magistrates and Dutch-speaking litigants. Increasingly, the court became involved in suits in which one or other of the opponents had the aid of an English-speaking counselor. Questions about land at the disposal of the Crown were at the heart of this dislocation. The practice of

45. "Charter of Albany," *AA*, 2, 89; 64; 62; 63.
46. For details of this conflict, see Merwick, "Dutch Townsmen," 74, 75.

the court at Beverwijck had been to hear cases regarding land disputes but not to enlarge on them. On one occasion the magistrates had demurred in a decision regarding property wishing "to remain out of it . . . in order not to burn our fingers."[47] As such aphorisms do, the statement caught nicely the political ideology of the court. Rulings did not refer backward to precedent or call upon comparison.

But within its own room in the *stadhuis*, changes to the court were evident, certainly after 1682. Two cases will make the point. In the first case – a curtain raiser, as it were – the court heard Christopher Skaife, a soldier of the garrison, make a plea on Jonathan Walker's behalf to act as his attorney. An attorney introduced into a case involving a mere twelve schepels of wheat and one hat was a sign of the times. In the second case, the magistrates, directing a jury, heard Marten Cregier (the son of an English-speaking New Yorker) proceed against Philip Pietersz Schuyler in a suit regarding attachment of a debt in New York City. Schuyler's defense consisted of an appeal to third-party debt as practiced by the Dutch. He had "proceeded in the matter according to the old custom and . . . [was] ignorant of any other form."[48] The jury found in Cregier's favor, and the court upheld its decision. But Robert Livingston, acting for Schuyler, immediately attacked the insularity of the jury's knowledge and that of the magistrates. He harangued them for failing to recognize that he had already attended proceedings in New York pertaining to the case. He also confounded them with a word used in English law and now prevalent in New York City: Cregier had been "nonsuited." Livingston offered to prove his claim and pledged £500 as security, a sum equivalent to gl 5,500 and one of the largest ever offered in the courtroom, as far as the records tell us. Three days later the court and jury again heard Livingston's aggressive courtroom language: Cregier was nonsuited and he (Livingston) had a "certificate thereof" and an "affidavit . . . [was] expected from New York" as further proof. The court reversed its decision.[49]

Two months later Cregier was again in court, and again his case chanced to have a curtain raiser involving an Englishman. Robert Gardner, who was an associate of the soldiers and New England traders now in Albany, stood accused of enclosing land possessed by Wynant Gerritsz. His defense was also cast in novel and arrogant language. It was a rejection of Gerritsz's claim because his transport was vague – as was customary among the burghers – and did not constitute clear title. Gerritsz's declaration, the court heard, was "a demand and claim of such

47. Ord. sess., November 5, 1678, *CRA*, 369.
48. Ex. sess., April 3, 1683, *CRA*, 338; 336.
49. Ord. sess., May 1, 1683, *CRA*, 346.

general character that no one is able to make answer to it, for he claims some ground, but in what part of the county this ground is situated he does not know. Therefore," the astonished court was told, "he [Gardner] does not find himself bound to make answer and demands a nonsuit." The court refused and, following Dutch custom, recommended the parties settle their dispute by arbitration.[50]

The court then turned to Cregier's dispute regarding property ownership. It turned on a similar point: Testimony under oath was insufficient proof of ownership. Only a county court deed carried legal authority. The plaintiffs were Gerrit Bancker and Jan van Eps, each of whom had been joint owners with Cregier of a house and lot derived from a deceased estate. But they had no deed of title. In proving two-thirds ownership they proceeded as was customary, calling witnesses and allowing the court to hear familiar phrases like "Some years ago she heard" and "Further she knows not." They were simple but accepted phrases that traditionally collected and communicated information.[51]

Cregier then put limits upon actions that might be taken during the customary time allowed for arbitration. He compelled the court to order that, if after the parties showed each other all relevant documents "in the presence of four referees ... at a neutral place ... any papers [that is, the deed] should be accidentally found, the party finding them shall not be able to derive any advantage or profit from them."[52]

Van Eps and Bancker used the adjournment to place a further witness before the court, fruitlessly enacting a procedure of traditional but diminishing value. Jacob ten Eyck's testimony narrated one of the folksy episodes that the court was accustomed to hearing. "Many years ago he was in conversation with Marte Cregier about the lot in question ... and asked Marte: 'How about the lot, have you got it yet?' Whereupon Marte Cregier said: 'No, but I have a large account with ... [the deceased]. I'll get the lot some time anyway.' " Ten Eyck swore an oath to the truth of his statement.[53]

On March 3, the hearing was resumed, and – as an outsider can see it – the two cultures met again in the courtroom. Van Eps and Bancker called upon the testimony of one of the city's most respected burghers, Barent Pietersz Coeymans. The customary recital ensued: "Being in discourse [with the previous owner, now deceased] ... she answered 'No, they [Van Eps, Bancker, and Cregier] were all equally entitled to it' [the property] ... and further he knows not." Cregier answered this by moving

50. Ord. sess., February 3, 1684/5, CRA, 509; 511.
51. Ibid., 510.
52. Ibid., 511.
53. Ibid., 516, 517; 517.

entirely away from episodes, sworn witnesses, oaths, dialogues, and indeed from the local court and Dutch law. He made the plaintiffs adversaries on a new level of meaning by calling solely on "the laws & acts of the General Assembly" to show that they "should not have brought suit in the court." He further declared that "this court can not try any cases regarding title to land, a freehold not being subject to appraisal at any price." In effect he was arguing that land was not subject to the merchants' customary law but was a tenure received from the crown. Having delivered his lesson to the magistrates, he requested release from the plaintiffs' demands and costs. The court felt compelled to uphold him.[54]

These cases show that a new language about land was appearing and diminishing the role of the municipal court. The magistrates now faced a "civilized" legal system intruding into their own liturgies. Criminal justice, to take one example, had previously been dispensed in a continual procession of disputes played out before the court by the *schout* and alleged offenders. Yet after 1681, Livingston, as secretary, replaced Richard Prettij in that capacity,[55] and by September of 1687, words that had once expressed a Dutch structure behind criminal prosecutions – "The honorable *schout* of the colony of Rensselaerswyck, plaintiff" or "Johan de Dekker, commissary and officer [*schout*] here, ex officio plaintiff" – were dropped in favor of "John Doe vs. Meus Hoogeboom." After 1686, the court reduced its meetings to monthly sessions. Its hearings now began, "Hear ye, hear ye."[56]

The wording of documents pertaining to land outside the palisades was teaching the court a lesson as well. Legally, land grants were now gratuities of the crown. Land was vested in the king, not contracting parties. For a variety of reasons, governor Dongan authorized a series of feudal holdings in New York. They would create a set of loyal retainers along the borderlands, with tenants useful as work forces and fighting units. They gave new meaning to the land. The van Rensselaers and Livingstons, in accepting their lands as manorial, helped introduce them. Whereas the first patroon had contracted an *akkoord* (agreement) as an equal with fellow directors of the Company for the right to develop a patroonship and followed proper republican procedures – "Kiliaen van renselaer," it

54. Ibid., 520.
55. Ord. sess., March 1, 1680/1, *CRA*, 89.
56. For "John Doe" see Crt. sess., September 6 [?], 1687, Court of Sessions, 38–9, Office of the County Clerk, Albany, and also the City Records, 1686–1695, *AA*, 2:95.

read, "declares himself *cum suis* from now on as patroon on the North river of New Netherland"[57] – manorial rights were those of a client.

Yet, again, the meanings behind this traffic in large land grants eluded the magistrates. They were ignorant of Dongan's overall plans for New York and ignorant of the process by which property ownership was beginning to be political power. Clute was enraged at assemblymen buying up "all the land" because the clamor to do so was not customary and because he could not see the purpose or end result of it all. The magistrates admitted to their ignorance in a different way. When they had the opportunity to take a decisive role in Dongan's negotiations to acquire the "entire Susguehalla [Susquehanna] valley," they gave "the businesse" of the cession over to his subordinate, John Graham.[58]

Burgerlijk Ways: Constricted but Continued

The seventeenth-century records of Albany were like so many nets that trapped the names of townsfolk. But the same names that were caught in land papers got snagged in merchants' account books and the records of the collector of public revenues. Some of Robert Livingston's papers collected the names of men identified as property holders. The same individuals, however, were also named in his other papers as merchants, innkeepers, traders, owners of sloops, bakers, investors in saw mills, interpreters, and tanners.

Taken together, the records of the burghers' activities allow three generalizations. First, Albany was still a market town, with the fur trade and, less so, agriculture dominantly structuring self-images and social values. At the same time, the rituals that sharpened the identity of the city as a *handelshuis* for furs – those like the performances of *handelstijd* – were being impoverished by the declining fur trade and English rule. Second, most householders continued to engage in multiple occupations, while the *lantsman* who simply farmed or was a tenant remained a person without status. Third, houses constructed on the landscape functioned like the scattered parcels of the land itself: They continued to shelter the socio-economic realities of the city and make it Dutch.

The city's gates and walls still created the proper geographies of residence and trade. In 1684, burghers identified residents south of town as in "the ward of the south gate"; those above were in "the ward of the

---

57. Agreement between the directors and chief participants of the West India Company, June 21, 1623, *VRBM*, 126; Registration by Kiliaen van Rensselaer, November 19, 1629, *VRBM*, 157.
58. Magistrates to Dongan, September 24, 1683, *DHNY*, I, 1:395, 396.

north gate."⁵⁹ They performed the *ratelwacht* each evening by getting
the keys to the gates from the house of the "president" (presiding magistrate) and "an hour after the clock ringing, [they] close[d] the gates
[*poorten*] returning the keys to ... [his] house."⁶⁰ Within the walls, men
had a stake in an economy distinctly urban. Of the fifty-seven young men
at van Rensselaer's funeral, twenty-four were recognized retail merchants
and traders. Another six men were deeply involved in the fur trade, often
dealing with English soldiers and New Englanders. Six men were brewers.
The same number of men owned river sloops, combining those activities
with other skills as a glazier, brickmaker, and ferryman.⁶¹

The case of Jan Hendricksz van Bael makes the point well. In 1672,
he received land "lying on both sides of Norman's kil" including unspecified woodland, islands, and meadows that "lay in a square." The
deed, however, identified him as *koopman* (retail merchant) and he appears to have set up a *herberg* (inn) there. In short, the townsmen
undertook agricultural tasks as by-employments, retaining their identification as burghers. Even those whom the records catch as *lantsmannen*
are frequently unmasked as traders. Certainly it was the case with Teunisse Willemsz. When his apparently sudden death made an inventory
of his effects necessary, it was shown that this man, who came out as a
farm laborer in 1660 and then took to farming along the Mohawk, was
not a *boer* but a trader. The assessors found not only ordinary household
goods among his belongings but also "27 pistoles" and enough trading
goods to suggest his regular relations with the natives.⁶²

Earning a beaver was still a way of life though trading was now "a
Prerogative Royall."⁶³ *Handelstijd* continued to be a time of contest and

59. Ord. sess., June 3, 1684, CRA, 458.
60. "Conditions under which the Commissaries & the Commander, etc., set up the Ra-
   telwagst (*sic*), May 1, 1677–May 1, 1678," Robert Livingston: General Correspondence, 1667–1728, L-RP.
61. The merchants were Jan Janse Bleecker, Marten Gerritsz, Sander Sandersz Glen, Dirck
   Hesselingh, Anthonij Lespinard, Jan Mangelsz, Hendrick Jacob Sandersz [Glen], Johannes Sandersz [Glen], David Schuyler, Pieter Schuyler, Jacob Staats, Andries Teller,
   Dirck Wesselsz ten Broeck, Hendrick Coster van Aecken, Jan Hendricksz van Bael,
   Jan van Eps, Pieter van Olinda, Sybrant Goose van Schaick, Cornelis Teunisse van
   Vechten, Dirck Teunisse van Vechten, Sweer Teunisse van Velsen, Teunis Willemsz
   van Woutbergh, Arnout Cornelisse Viele, Johannes Wendell.
       The six men were Jan Bricker, Andries Hansen, Laurens van Alen, Hendrick van
   Bael, Paulus Martensz van Benthuysen, and Tierck Harmensz Visser; the brewers were
   Hendrick Cuyler, Pieter Lansingh, Harme Rutgers, Albert Ryckman, Sybrant Goose
   van Schaick, and Jacobus van Vorst; the river craft owners were Pieter Bogardus,
   Thomas Davidsz Kikebel, Jan Outhout, Laurensz van Alen, Jacob Staats, and Pieter
   Schuyler.
62. Sale of land to Jan Hendricksz van Bael, July 18, 1672, SC16676–30, NYSA; Inventory,
   November 12, 1682, CRA, 404–8, and, for sale of his possessions, 428.
63. Council in New York, May 6, 1679 reported at Ex. sess., May 15, 1679, CRA, 412.

risk. Walking in the woods continued, and the "cunning methods" customarily used to entice natives into shops and houses were retained as
practices defying the traditional ordinances. The marginal land just outside the gates also remained dangerous at nighttime.[64] Yet many of the
rituals, whose full meaning depended on their sequential enactment and
that gave the trading season its dramatic force, were gone. May 1 no
longer announced *handelstijd*. The magistrates, as we have seen, sub-
mitted to a London custom and took office in October rather than May.
May 1 was not a court day after 1675. There was no notice of the
papegaaischoet. There were strangers in the city, but they were predom-
inantly New England traders and their agents, men whose arrivals and
departures did not coincide with *handelstijd*.[65] The English legislated
against the presence of outsiders from Manhattan Island, and their business would have been greatly diminished in any case. In the middle of
handelstijd 1678, Andros expressly denied trading rights to "the several
persons, who doe come up from New York hither, and dryve a great
trade with the Indians."[66] The strangers disappeared as did the summer
auctions. Even the public vendue of houses was no longer common, for
reasons not entirely clear.

The English erected "Indian houses," insisting the natives be prevented
from entering the palisades and, it was feared, spying on fortifications.
The houses were less the appendages of a *handelshuis* – where customers
came to trade under a surveillance that reflected the social order as much
in the breaking of rules as in their keeping – and more the outbuildings
of the Englishmen's "fortres Albany."[67] The detailed specifications drawn
up by English commanding officers regarding the houses reveal an explicit
determination to isolate them. It was only reluctantly shared by the
burghers whose concern was to repeat the successes of earlier trading
seasons and to "induce the Indians to come here in the summer in large
numbers." They were as unsuccessful in this as in providing an open
market town to the "divers Frenchmen" who were "daily [arriving] by
water as well as over land" to trade in *handelstijd* 1679.[68]

64. See, for example, Ex. sess., June 11, 1684, *CRA*, 461; Ex. sess., August 4, 1683, *CRA*,
    369, 370.
65. See Merwick, "Becoming English: Anglo–Dutch Conflict in the 1670s in Albany, New
    York," *New York History* (October, 1981), 62:396.
66. Ord. sess., July 2, 1678, *CRA*, 336.
67. Anthony Brockholes's letter to Livingston, September 26, 1682, L-RP, is directed to
    him "at fortres Albany"; for stricter regulations of natives, including measures taken
    to prevent them coming inside towns, see Agreement between Nicolls and the Esopus
    Indians. October 7, 1665, *DRCH*, 13:399.
68. See Order for the constables, Ex. sess., May 26, 1676, *CRA*, 106; for specifications,
    see 106, 107 and also 244. Ord. sess., July 5, 1681, *CRA*, 143; Ord. sess., June 27,
    1679, *CRA*, 422.

The decline in the fur trade did not occur because of the English conquest. Yet because of it, the burghers were not free to choose among the traditional forms to cope with it. By 1705, the structure of *handelstijd* as a six month event was gone. Natives, it was then ordered, must "lay in Indian houses from April to October 14." At other times, presumably when they were far fewer, they might be received into burghers' homes and shops. Long before, the space of *handelstijd* had disappeared, for in the 1680s, parties of traders had begun to go out on lengthy expeditions to trade. It was necessary, wrote Dongan, "for us to encourage our young men to goe a Beaver hunting as the French doe." The traditional places of trade, the stalls of the *handelaars* inside the walls, and the places of smuggling just beyond the walls were gone. The traders were physically beyond the local court's control, or better, a large part of its jurisdiction over commerce was cut away. Dongan issued the licenses for the expeditions, and at least in 1687, an English soldier was in command.[69]

Handelstijd had always meant knowing the Manhattans. That was still the case. It now meant reading the intentions of a bureaucracy that looked to strengthen the military position of the whole province and to organize the geographies of the two river cities for trade. New York City and Albany, however, were not trusted to determine the scope of their markets, even though Dutch cities like Dordrecht and Amsterdam did so, while still contributing to the strength of the province of Holland. There each could trade internally and overseas if it had the talent and resources. It was the sort of competition envisaged in the continual maneuvers of the Albany merchants for permission to mill, package, and ship overseas the cereal products that were now replacing fur as a profitable export commodity. Andros and Dongan could not understand such political and economic decentralization.

On the contrary, New York City and Albany required autocratic control. When the merchants explained to Andros in 1679 that "many of the inhabitants have made their arrangements and preparations to ship flour, wheat and other grains across the sea," they were simply calling upon "the ancient privilege of the inhabitants of this place to trade over seas" and upon a way of seeing their town as a node along a long-distance trade route. But Andros "resented" the petition, called it "mistaken," and gave the burghers a choice that expressly denied the right to manage their own trade: They could have the staple of furs or elect to trade

69. Proclamation relating to the Indian trade, April 25, 1705, the City Records, 1705, AA, 5, 120; Dongan quoted in John H. Kennedy, Thomas Dongan, Governor of New York (1682–1688) (Ph.D. diss., Catholic University, 1930), 93; David Arthur Armour, The Merchants of Albany, New York: 1686–1760 (Ph.D. diss., Northwestern University, 1965), 17.

overseas and forfeit that privilege.[70] The burghers yielded. The framing of the petition and subsequent deliberations on its rejection were moments when those involved saw themselves conducting a commerce that no longer took them to great distances or required an understanding of patria, Boston, and Canada. Dependent entirely on "those of New York ... pleas[ed] to buy" the fur and flour, they needed no knowledge of Europe or transatlantic shipping, navigational skills, or bills of lading. In short, the spatial orientation of the burghers and the pleasure taken in the skills needed to know and possess distant landscapes were disappearing. Yet this sort of knowledge was still prized. Into the 1690s, small traders, artisans, and female householders still exported small quantities of fur, "some sending as little as one packet."[71]

Centralization under military rule constricted the burghers' need to know about distant places and a complex commercial world. By 1690, in effect only Livingston needed to know provincial affairs. He was the chief broker to the city, and in times of war with France, he alone knew the fit between military policy and trade, that is, war contracts. In this sense, the "Account of Sundry Disbersements for ... [the] Reliefe of Christian Prisoners" forwarded to Dongan by Pieter Schuyler on March 12, 1688, can be read as an epistemological one. Here, Schuyler's knowledge was, like his effectiveness, regional at most. It was that of the marginal man, of Corlear, the intermediary. It was also knowledge of a new set of elements in the meaning of Albany: military installations and the traffic of soldiers. His words situated the trade within others that stood for redoubts, forts, and military highways. They offer some insight into the kinds of trading practices that the burghers had to learn. Schuyler had already learned to conduct business for the English: He was dispensing petty cash for contributions to a military operation.[72]

Neither the size nor quality of the farms around Albany changed dramatically from the 1660s. Ninety-two tenantries of eighteenth-century Rensselaerswyck averaged only 153 acres, with only three over 300 acres and fifty-two between 100 and 149 acres. In fact, the tendency to subdivide continued so that the average farm was likely to have been smaller than 153 acres and showed one authority a "conspicuous difference" in the pattern of larger leaseholds in the southern manors of New York. Livingston and van Rensselaer believed that, "the smaller their

70. Ex. sess., May 19, 1679, CRA, 413; 412.
71. Ex. sess., April 30, 1679, CRA, 406; Armour, Merchants of Albany, 51.
72. Schuyler to Dongan, "An Account of Sundry Disbersements for Sundry Gifts & Presents made to ye Indians to Reliefe of Christian Prisoners," March 12, 1687/8 [Albany], BL189, Box 3, HL.

farms, the more the land will hould, and the better the Improvements will bee," so a diligent farmer could provide for a family of four or five on "80 to 120 acres," that is, forty to sixty morgen.[73] That would be near Kiliaen van Rensselaer's notion of a workable farm in the 1640s and Andros's figure for an immigrant and his wife in 1675.[74]

The proprieties of dividing land were ritualized in dramas that involved friends, associates, and family, apparently including children as well as adults. Those rituals surrounding bequests were daily occurrences. Marite Damen apparently often gathered friends around to hear her speak of her will and its provisions. She meant to divide her considerable estate equally because "all [were] equally entitled to it . . . [and] she wanted to increase not decrease her estate." As late as 1809, some families were carrying out the rituals that such a desire entailed. The five daughters of Jacob Vanderhuyden received equal portions of their father's land and directives about drawing lots after folding the papers carefully and seeing to the courtesies of the proceedings.[75] When seven burghers assembled "for a division" of "lands named Saragtoge," they did so in the presence of a surveyor and three witnesses, who were there to see that the partition was both precise and, paradoxically, a matter of luck. The children of the owners were present and they drew "seven tickets in a hat." Each was numbered and corresponded to portions of the land called lots. But the division did not end there. By intricate arrangments the lots were immediately subdivided among the owners. The man who drew lot "no. 1" was expected to "take his homestead in lot no. 2 . . . it being understood that he who draws no. 2 shall have the first choice of a homestead & that no. 1 shall take but one morgen [two acres] for his homestead. . . . The person who gets no. 3 shall have the privilege of taking his homestead within the limits of no. 4" and so on. Land partitioned at Canajoharie to four men underwent the same complex subdivision, with "home lots" carved out of "expense lots" and the whole a puzzle of private holdings.[76]

73. Sung Bok Kim, *Landlord and Tenant in Colonial New York: Manorial Society 1664–1775* (Chapel Hill, N.C., 1978), 190; 190, see table 5.1.

74. See KvR to Wouter van Twiller, April 23, 1634, *VRBM*, 286–7, for his estimate of twenty morgen of arable and "pasture land and hay fields" as a useful farm. Council minutes, August 5, 1675, *DRCH*, 8:485. The average Rockland County, N.Y., farm in 1712 was fifty acres (see Carl Nordstrom, *Frontier Elements in a Hudson River Village* [New York, 1973], 34).

75. Ord. sess., March 3, 1684/5, *CRA*, 520; Will of Jacob Vanderhuyden, April 3, 1809, Van Vechten Papers, AQ7006 Wills No. 2, Folder 19, NYSA.

76. "Articles of Agreement for Division of Arable Land of Saratoga," April 15, 1685, *ER2*, 347–9; Survey of the "Otsquaga Patent," filed August 24, 1772, accompanied by Field Book, describing partition of patent lands as issued September 2, 1729, to Rutger Bleecker, Nicholas Bleecker, James Delancey, and John Haskel. Canajoharie,

Farming around Albany was still a discouraging task, and no husbandmen stood out for conspicuously improving the quality of his land. No one moved noticeably ahead of his fellows by initiating agricultural experiments or even carefully manuring the land. Late in 1673, van Rensselaer had identified only five farms worth coveting, and by the account of one knowledgeable observer, those who lived upon the land did so while depending "wholly upon Trade."[77] No one could identify the ordered fields characteristic of the English countryside. No man, perhaps excluding Livingston, coveted the broad acres that might show the status of "the rich man lifted up by his lands." When Gerrit van Vechten received a patent to a parcel of land within Rensselaerswyck's bounds in 1678, he immediately played the entrepreneur. He parceled it to tenants who may well have expected the right of purchase.[78]

In fact, the presence of a Dutch gentry on the land was as delayed on the Hudson as it was at the Cape of Good Hope in South Africa. There, in the founding year 1652, twenty-nine acres of land was considered a useful, if not generous, landholding. A system of leased land (*erfpact*) developed alongside freehold land blurring the line between freehold and land in loan. The result was small freeholds distributed in consolidated and seemingly equal plots that fronted a run or *kil* and had "low [and] corn and mountain land." A rural gentry did not appear at the Cape until perhaps 1705.[79] Similarly, in Canada, where land tenure and farming of *rotures* also resembled Albany, a settled agricultural routine with attachment to family land did not occur until the eighteenth century. In New York, an eighteenth-century Anglo-American like William Smith, Jr. made it his business to know the entire province well. Yet at mid-century he was dismayed to find that "gentlemen of estate rarely reside in the country, and hence a few or no experiments have yet been made in agriculture."[80] In Albany, a Dutch landed gentry emerged only in the

Map (NEW 160) Closet 1, Drawer 21, Office of the County Clerk, Albany; Division of Sachtekook Land, July 10, 1708, *AA*, 5:183, 184.

77. "Governor Dongan's Report on the State of the Province" [ca. December 1686], *DRCH*, 3:397.

78. Gerard Winstanley quoted in Christopher Hill, *The World Turned Upside Down: Radical Ideas during the English Revolution* (Harmondsworth, 1975), 344; Nissenson, *Patroon's Domain*, 67.

79. Leonard Guelke and Robert Shell, "An Early Colonial Landed Gentry: Land and Wealth in the Cape Colony, 1682–1731," *Journal of Historical Geography*, (July 1983), 9:266, 268. For *erfpaght* (sic) in Schenectady, see J[unius] W. MacMurray, ed. *A History of the Schenectady Patent in the Dutch and English Times: Being Contributions toward a History of the Lower Mohawk Valley by Prof. Jonathan Pearson, A.M. and Others* (Albany, 1883), 28, 29.

80. Richard Colebrook Harris, *The Seigneurial System in Early Canada: A Geographical Study* (Madison, 1968), 161; William Smith, *The History of the Province of New-York, from the First Discovery, to which is annexed a Description of the Country, an*

Possessing Albany

mid-eighteenth century, that is, about 125 years after first settlement. If we may judge by his distribution of titles, Dongan had aided in impeding the development of such a Dutch social class by his policy of withholding titles from Dutch families. The burghers contributed as well by consistently choosing to camouflage social distinctions.

House design masked socioeconomic inequality as well. This is a matter for more careful attention but requires some consideration here. Dwellings within the town were uniformly erected at the front of house lots, thereby diminishing the display of spaciousness achieved by presenting a house set well back on a lot. Architecture also muted grandness. The notably sloping roof conveyed sobriety and snugness at the same time as it minimized the ostentation a second story might have conveyed. It moved the eye downward, producing an effect opposite to that of deliberately extended second-story eaves.[81] A large house could be designed to hide riches as well. The interior of the Lansingh house built just north of the palisades in 1710 was designed to deny an easy sense of spaciousness. Split levels masked the length of the house, while the inclusion of Dutch features on the exterior prevented the ordered symmetry and grandeur of Georgian design.

Such dwellings were typical of the Low Countries, where even furniture arrangement made a man *"zoals ieder burgerman"* (like any burgher). In 1667, Philip Pietersz Schuyler had two large and adjacent houses on Jonckheerstraat. This would certainly have suggested a display of wealth. From what we know of the houses, however, they were distinctive only in their size. But this was not spaciousness for the purpose of display or entertainment. Schuyler's enlargements of the houses "on the hill" in 1654 and 1656 had been undertaken in order to accommodate more merchandise.[82] They were, like Kiliaen van Rensselaer's Keisersgracht premises, forcefully functional, representing continued enterprise and work as much as gain. Schuyler undoubtedly rented out the second house and in doing so resembled a common burgher like van Ilpendam. The notary's estate was considerably less than Schuyler's, but his manipulations with real estate would have been essentially the same. "We have

Account of the Inhabitants, their Trade, Religious and Political State, and the Constitution of the Courts of Justice in the Colony (London, 1776), 272.

81. For an excellent discussion of vernacular architecture and the Dutch farming community, see McLaughlin, Dutch Rural New York: Flatbush, 88; see, for example, "Early Settlers of the Hudson," *AA*, 5:112; "gravity and decorum" were the qualities of Albany's houses to J. S. Buckingham in 1837, but he also noted a house, built in 1732, with a "low body and immensely disproportionate sloping roof," "J. S[ilk] Buckingham in Albany," *AA*, 9:304, 291.

82. See Roderic H. Blackburn, "Dutch Material Culture: Architecture," *de halve maen* (1982), 57:2; Ord. sess., March 31, 1654, *CRB*, 131, and Ord. sess., May 30, 1656, *CRB*, 276.

two small houses here," he wrote at the age of sixty-three. "Upon one, in which we dwell, we have spent more than the interest of two years amounts to; from the other we receive now not more rent than . . ." (leaf torn).[83]

Nothing English affected house design. The earliest dwellings were probably built of wood and expected to "wear out in a few years."[84] One early settler built a "light [wood] house," and others also consciously put up temporary structures. Whatever their structure, in time they were replaced with more permanent dwellings of brick masonry and underlying wood framing. Townsmen daily hauled sand from the land of "koopman" van Bael in the 1670s; some of it must have found its way into bricks for houses.[85] Pieter Bronck built a stone house in 1663. Its construction in stone was unusual for the time, but it did not depart notably from the homogeneous cultural profile in craft techniques and house design that marked New Netherland.

Alongside these permanent dwellings were those constructed to allow their removal to another site. In 1678, one of the young men at van Rensselaer's funeral arranged that his house beyond the north gate be "taken down and carried to Schenectady." Two years later another trader moved "a house, mostly dilapidated" away from the city and "into the country."[86] Certainly townspeople knew the distinction between a small and a large dwelling. They thought Wyant Gerritsz's house was little because he could not get a cask through the door. Livingston's house, on the other hand, involved haulage of 57,000 stones, suggesting that its construction and size must have drawn attention. We need to know more about the uses of houses, but the evidence certainly points away from the mentality of a man like Dongan whose manor house on Staten Island had a hipped roof, was set on 25,000 acres of land, and included a "hunting lodge where he killed bears."[87]

In the Byzantine procedures surrounding land division and house construction, the burghers enacted beliefs that the physical landscape should reflect an equitable social structure. Inequalities were real, but they were acted out in private dramas. The van Rensselaer ledgers are a playgoer's program to these dramas about land. There are hundreds of plays, each performed by a cast of three, four, or five characters and staged in the

83. Van Ilpendam to Dammas Guldewaghen [n.d., ca. 1681], *ER3*, 495.
84. KvR to AvC, July 18, 1641, *VRBM*, 563.
85. Contract between KvR and Planck, March 4, 1634, *VRBM*, 252, and see 259; Memorandum from KvR to Megapolensis, June 3, 1642, *VRBM*, 619; Land sold to Jan Hendricksz van Bael, July 18, 1672, SC11676–30, NYSA.
86. Ord. sess., January 29, 1677/8, *CRA*, 292; Ord. sess., December 7, 1680, *CRA*, 47.
87. Ord. sess., June 6, 1680, *CRA*, 15, Livingston's house contract, Robert Livingston: General Correspondence, 1667–1728, L-RP, n.p.; Dorothy V. Smith, *Staten Island: Gateway to New York* (New York, 1970), 31.

house of Maria van Rensselaer, her treasurer, or secretary. Some transactions (in many instances, the leasing of land) were complicated, others
seemingly straightforward. Some episodes had two scenes – for example,
when an arrangement was first arrived at and then a reconsideration
made and a marginal apostil added. Others had an altered cast of characters as, for example, when a widow came forward to ask young Kiliaen
van Rensselaer for reconfirmation of land given to her husband by his
father.[88] Each was a private performance, and it was by such cloistered
arrangements that the land was appropriated for the most part. Though
English influence around "fortres Albany" already meant a pasture set
aside for the cavalry and the presence of other military installations,
Dutch values still organized the lay of the land.[89]

The younger generation of men and women at the funeral of van
Rensselaer were, unlike their parents, socialized into living two cultures.
Yet they were experiencing situations that provided little direction as to
how the problems of merging them would be resolved. There had been,
for example, a contest between English authorities and powerful local
burghers over the status of domini Nicolaes van Rensselaer in 1675, and
it may have been taken as a metaphor for many undisguised, but unre-
solved conflicts. The townspeople would have observed the minister – a
man ordained to Anglican orders but arbitrarily appointed by Andros to
serve the Reformed congregation – defended in court according to English
custom, that is, represented by a lawyer. They would have seen his an-
tagonist, Jacob Leisler, follow Dutch custom and act on his own behalf.
It was a confrontation played for very high stakes as the extraordinarily
large sums put up as securities testify. In the end, the court's search for
conciliation was futile, and its final pronouncement was against Leisler:
He was to pay court charges and van Rensselaer was to remain as minister.[90] But the event could not have seemed a clear victory for Andros
or a resolution of the ecclesiastical issues under debate. Van Rensselaer
was deposed by the governor himself the next year. No party or policy
was a winner.

Albany's burghers were the artisans and traders with whom it annoyed
men of a feudal cast like Nicolls, Andros, and Dongan to covenant. But
they remained essentially unchanged. They continued to construct a land-

88. Agreement of Jeremias van Rensselaer and Barent Albertsz Bradt, February 24, 1671/
   2, Ledger, 1666–1708, SC10643, NYSA; entry of November 6, 1688 [preceding entry
   for January 10, 1689/90], Ledger, 1666–1708, VRMP, SC10643, NYSA.
89. Ord. sess., July 20, 1671, *CRA*, 266.
90. See "Correspondence and Memoranda," in Hugh Hastings, ed., *Ecclesiastical Records:
   State of New York* (Albany, 1901), 1:688–92.

scape that reflected *burgherlijk* virtuosity rather than the *virtu* of the aristocracy or orderliness of the squirearchy. They continued to locate real estate transactions within private investment portfolios. Merchants were still the principal men and women of the city, and their skills were the measure of its welfare. Their sharp practices drew opposition from other townspeople, and Livingston, the major wholesaler to the town, was openly detested. Moreover, their adroitness was now exercised more widely, marketing flour as well as furs. Yet vicious or virtuous, their versatility (even Livingston's) signified that the proprieties were still in place.

5

Contesting the Land, 1689–1691

Leisler's Rebellion on Manhattan Island: The Walled City and the Countryside

In the centuries-long alteration of the European medieval world order, several traditions were affected. One was the feudal system. Landed aristocracies lost their authority to gentried families who also dispersed themselves over the land but capitalized it in a different way. That was England's story. Another institution that failed to survive intact was the independent city.[1] Dominant in northern Europe, the city was the *axis mundi* of the social order. Its ruling elites were impresarios of public rituals, bankers of princes' fortunes, and keepers of the church's shrines. Yet at the time of Leisler's Rebellion, few municipalities felt secure. Certainly the giant Hanseatic cities of Hamburg, Bremen, and Lubeck did not. They were fighting for their survival against princes and kings made increasingly powerful by war and newly dependent populations.

This was particularly the case in the United Provinces. A foreboding omen was the murder of John de Witt in The Hague in 1672. De Witt was the embodiment of civic autonomy. His office as *raadpensionaris* (grand councillor) was the sign of the superordination of the municipal communes, powerful and enleagued, in the States General. He was murdered at the hands of a populace determined to contain the power of the urban bureaucracies by calling on a military leader who could harness the nation, the *stadhouder* William of Orange.[2] Even Amsterdam could see the writing on the wall. The contest for global empires brought about

---

1. I am accepting the "urban failure" position put by Fernand Braudel, *The Expansion of Europe and the "Longue Duree,"* in H. L. Wesseling, ed., *Expansion and Reaction: Essays on European Reaction and Reactions in Asia and Africa* (Leiden, 1978), 17–27, and others. It is contested by Jan de Vries, *European Urbanization, 1500–1800* (New Haven, 1974), 6.
2. Herbert Rowen, *John de Witt: Grand Pensionary of Holland, 1625–1672* (Princeton, 1978), 543.

by technology, increased population, and available capital generated needs that only the nation-state could answer. The struggle for power in northern Europe then was not primarily between court and county gentries, as it was in England. It was one between the new centralizing courts and the great cities.

They were still precarious days for Dutch monarchists. The crises of the late seventeenth century were precisely those precipitated by over-extension of the *stadhouder*'s powers. His role was meant to be a later type of the Roman consul, that of a military officer empowered to hold a province or fortified city for the republic but restrained from exercising civil jurisdiction. In the United Provinces, the rulers of the House of Orange were consuls for the States' alliance of republican cities against the invading Spaniards. Inside Orange-Nassau, the *stadhouders* were lords of a principality that lay east and west along the Rhine River and close to Frankfurt, Jacob Leisler's home.[3] Beyond the bounds of the principality, they were soldiers leading a fighting force that was in effect an army of mercenaries. As required, they effected rescue operations of the imperiled Dutch cities.[4] Paradoxically their coat of arms expressed the structure of the Dutch political order they were intended to serve but were already jeopardizing: "Except the Lord keep the *city*, the watchman waketh but in vain."[5]

The political events of New York City and Albany in the 1690s fitted into this structure. The actions taken by participants were not those of individuals shaping political scenarios in an English way. For most, it was Dutch ways of coping that the times provoked. That is, while the destabilization aroused by the overthrow of James II was English, the constitutional issues it raised and the solutions searched out were Dutch. As they traditionally had, the issues turned around the hegemony of translocal authority and, structurally at odds with it, the independence claimed by each of the cities. Over the decades and at home, the Dutch had somehow worked the magic of maintaining an equipoise among the contestants. All of Dutch politics was, in fact, pointed to sustaining that equilibrium – the murder of De Witt was ominous precisely because it

3. J. A. Houtte, *An Economic History of the Low Countries, 800–1800* (London, 1977), 132.
4. For the organization of Dutch defensive forces, see Barry Harold Nickle, The Military Reforms of Prince Maurice of Orange (Ph.D. diss., University of Delaware, 1976); G. De Bruin, "De soevereinitiet in de republiek: een machtsprobleem," *BMBGN*, (1979) 94:33 uses *stadhouder* and *opperbevelhebben van leger* (commander-in-chief) synonymously.
5. William L. Brower, *1626–1926: Tercentenary of the City of New York. A Tribute to the Settlement on Manhattan Island, now New York, by the Dutch, Early in the Seventeenth Century* (New York, 1926), 101 (my italics).

signaled that the old magic was no longer working. In New York, it was these constitutional issues and this search for equipoise that were activated in the actions of Jacob Leisler, who played a translocal role, and Stephen van Cortlandt and Pieter Schuyler, who were mayors of chartered cities.

The City under Siege

Jacob Leisler consistently acted as though his defense of political power in New York on behalf of William III was a North American version of the Low Countries' stand against the Spanish: It was a *burgeroorlog*, literally a townspeoples' war. The political power defended was essentially resident in municipalities. Throughout the years, he considered himself defender of the fort of New York City for William and Mary. He said as much on the day of execution following his trial for treason. On the scaffold, the city and its fort were the objects of his vision.[6] There and beyond, he played the *stadhouder*, holding himself responsible for plugging the holes in provincial security and making attempts to bring local communities to allegiance to William.

The political order that Dutch men and women like Leisler constructed from 1689 to 1691 began with defenses. In August of 1689, the Catholic French threatened to put New York under siege from the sea. The populace immediately used an analogy with the city of Zutphen to give shape to its terror. Those in the fort and city would suffer the fate that Protestants like themselves had met there in the early seventeenth century. They would be sold to the enemy by papists and Catholic-sympathizing officials within their own walls. On April 27, 1689 and with townsmen in "tumult" at the fear of siege, the Dutch mayor had already encouraged the English commander of the fort and his council to prepare defenses, in fact, to activate the same mechanism for defense that Stuyvesant had in 1664. Together, they arranged a *kriegsraad* to be held in two days' time. It would be a meeting of Captain Francis Nicholson, his councilors, and the city officials including the captains of the burgherguard. Nicholson had failed to maintain adequate defenses and now requested that "part of the Citty Militia keep a guard in the fort."[7] Guarding the fort, rather than the city was an unorthodox task for the *schutterij*, so the

6. "Colleccons (*sic*) made on the Dying Speeches of Captain Jacob Leisler & Jacob Milborne, his son in Law, who both Suffered in New York City on the 16th of May being Saturday in the Year of our Lord, 1691," *DHNY*, 2:378.
7. Extract of Bayard's Letter [Albany], September 23, 1689, *DRCH* 3:621; Van Cortlandt to Andros, July 9, 1689, *DRCH*, 3:591.

customary delay and debate followed before grudging agreement was given.

By the end of May, the English officer at the fort considered the local guards to be turbulent and, in fact, in rebellion. At the same time, rumors of a French fleet beyond the harbor led many of the populace to accept that papists in their midst – those like the present mayor who was "Popishly affected" – were conspiring their betrayal and massacre. Nicholson, they also heard, was considering "firing the town," and the country people, threatened by papists on Staten Island and hoping to seek refuge in the city, were already "in their boats and lay upon the [East] river."[8] Earlier rumors, quickly spread from Pennsylvania, had it that following William's landing at Torbay, "the Protestant party had captured Dublin" but only after "a massacre made by the Papists upon the Protestants." Stephen van Cortlandt described the fear in an idiom that expressed Dutch attitudes perfectly. The populace he wrote, felt it was "time to look [out] for themselves."[9] Within hours the burgherguard, which consistently argued for tighter security, had gained the support of all but twenty citizens (said one observer) and demanded and received the keys to the fort.[10]

From that point on, the *vroedschap* and commonalty met the expenses of holding the city (and province) for William and Mary against both the French and, within their midst, the representatives of a monarch sympathetic to the French and a Catholic ascendancy in England. They contributed for the two years Leisler was in authority. A reported £773 12s.3d. was made available by summer of 1689 for "repayring the ffort." Even Stephen van Cortlandt, a man who had hedged his bets – hoping to win on the performance of James or William – and someone who many burghers suspected would barter away their security, dared not fail to make a public and substantial contribution. By his own account, "the people worked hard at the City fortifications" and indeed "were very willing to worke and fortify the towne." He noted that a leading burgher, Abraham de Peyster, was fulfilling his role as a captain of the civil guard by directing the erection of one set of defenses. He demon-

8. Van Cortlandt to Andros, July 9, 1689, *DRCH*, 3:591; 595, 594; Affidavit against Bayard and certain parties on Staten Island, September 25, 1689, *DHNY*, 2:29.
9. Council meeting in the governor's lodgings, held in the house of Griff. Jones, December 24, 1688–89, *Pennsylvania Archives, selected and arranged from Original Documents in the Office of the Secretary of the Commonwealth, conformable to Acts of the General Assembly, February 15, 1851 and March 1, 1852 by Samuel Hazard. Commencing 1644* (Philadelphia, 1852), 1:247; Van Cortlandt to Andros, July 9, 1689, *DRCH*, 3:594, and, for general anticipation of a French attack by sea, see Memorial in behalf of Leisler's adherents imprisoned in New York, October 15, 1691, *DRCH*, 3:809.
10. Deposition of Johannes Wessels, February 19, 1691, *DHNY*, 2:400, and, for corroboration, see Deposition of John Pieterson, February 19, 1691, *DHNY*, 2:399.

strated his own support by providing planks for the gun platforms and carriages, making a contribution properly proportionate to his extensive income. He clearly sensed nothing self-serving or mercenary in expressing the expectation that Leisler, who was now in command, would "pay... [him] for the same." When Jochim Staats helped command the fort in Albany as Leisler's appointed lieutenant, he too kept an account of expenses incurred on the city's behalf for which he expected reimbursement.[11]

The situation of possible siege and capture stimulated a range of these sorts of civic formalities. The captains of the burgherguard assumed an authority alongside that of the civic officials. By custom, they were seldom office bearers of the city, but, like them, their authority was collegial. They rotated command at the fort. Their original protocols could not have been unlike the arrangements agreed to by about seventy Albany citizens in 1810. "We do," they pledged, "voluntarily enroll ourselves for the purpose of establishing and keeping a private night Watch... and we do hereby severally agree to do duty as it may come to our turn in the proportion of twelve of us and a Captain for each night."[12] Leisler was captain on the night when the guard and citizens demanded the fort. Whether his actions as military leader after June of 1689 were made routine by an earlier choice of signing on as a soldier for the West India Company is impossible to know. The point is that, in the dangerous times of that year, the role and the structure were there to fill, and he did so.

Leisler's previous years as a soldier with the Company and then as an active member of the civic guard gave him some competence in the role he now assumed. His early letters as commander of the fort express a soldier's expertise and concerns. They do so in much the same way that seventeenth-century Dutch painters or mapmakers pictured cities under siege, that is, they direct his correspondent's attention to the walled city in exactly the way Braun, Hogenberg, Morgan, and other illustrators of

11. Memorial, October 15, 1691, DRCH, 3:809; Van Cortlandt to Andros, July 9, 1689, DRCH, 3:597; 593; 597; [Jochim Staats], Account book, Entry of November 17, 1689, Folio 28, SC16205, NYSA; for Hendrick Jochemsz's expectation in 1654 that Stuyvesant would make "restitution" to him "through one merchant or another" for gl 100 put to defenses, see Minutes of May 9, 1655, RNA, 1:218.

12. Citizens' agreement to form a private nightwatch to protect the 2nd ward of the City [Albany, August, 16, 1810], MS238, NYSA; for the relationship of burgherguard to magistrates, see J. J. Woltjer, Dutch Privileges, Real and Imaginary, in J. S. Bromley and E. H. Kossmann, eds., Britain and the Netherlands, Volume V: Some Political Mythologies: Papers Delivered to the Fifth Anglo-Dutch Historical Conference (Hague, 1975), 29, J. A. Jochems, Amsterdams Oude Burgervendels (Schutterij) 1580–1795, met Historische Aantekeningen (Amsterdam, 1888), 1, and Robert Du Plessis, Urban Stability in the Netherlands Revolution: A Comparative Study of Lille and Douai (Ph.D. diss., Columbia University, 1974) 504.

Figure 5.1. Walter Morgan, "Moord te Naarden door de Spanjaarden, 30 November, 1572," *An Expedition into Holland, 1572*. Reprinted by permission of the Warden and Fellows of All Souls College, Oxford.

siege warfare guided the eye in bird's-eye views completed earlier in the century but still popular in the 1680s (Figure 5.1).[13] The walled city is, like Leisler's descriptions, their only focus and specification. Leisler composed his scene this way: The well of the fort is now "seven foot very good water and is 36 feet deep ... all the platforms renewed." He offered views of "all the gunes ... the powder house ... the engine [now mounted] from 13 to 36 degrees ... a battery under the fort." It was martial iconography, a series of views similar to the plans of installations and fortresses drawn in Europe by military engineers (see Figure 6.3). Leisler drew the attention of one correspondent, Robert Treat of Connecticut, to a corner of his word-picture where an installation stood below the fort. There "an halfe moon [is] in construction. It is of

13. For Leisler's early interest in the fort, see Report of Leisler on the fort at New York, January 17, 1674, *Third Annual Report of the State Historian* (1897), 2:177–8; for the vividness of illustrations of sieges, see Pieter Christiaensz Bor, *Oorsprongk begin ende vorvolgh der Nederlandschen oorlogen, beroeten ende burgerlijke oneenigheden* reprinted in H. Wansink and C. B. Wels, eds., *Zeven Pijlen, Negen Pennen: Negen Nederlandse Historici over de Vaderlandse Geschiedenis* (Zeist, 1963), 9.

100 feet over grass which defends the landing of both rivers and also the comeing in." He might also see men at a "spurre," where a company under captain Hendrick Cuyler struggled with "50 load of stone."[4] Treat was given to see New York's military posture. He was not persuaded to a civil leader's political position.

Leisler also described the city poised for siege in a letter to Governor Simon Bradstreet of Massachusetts. He offered him pictures of two cities, Saint Christopher in the Barbados and New York. In the first view, the French were seizing Saint Christopher, burning its habitations, and confining "all the people in the fort," where they were "besieged by land with 2 or 3000 men and twenty two vessels by water." In the second, he presented New York. It waited. The work of "500 men . . . and upwards of 30 bots" used to fetch sod and planking for palisades had put the city in a satisfactory "posture of defence." Leisler's further description duplicated in words the more elaborate sketches of sieges like that of Goes in 1672. Such sketches usually featured a *waterpoort*, a gate that breached the city's walls and would require defense. Leisler gave particular attention to such a point in New York City's defenses. He wanted Bradstreet to imagine it, singling it out as "one water port [which] is now made to the westward of the fort." It was the point he "hope[d] to defend" himself "with . . . [his] life and fortune."[5]

Leisler had the eye of the defender. He could not see beyond a policing operation. Still, after the summer of 1689, it became evident that the province lacked direction and that the French threat lay along an extensive frontier. The task of defense was vastly more complex than preserving New York City, and a *gemeente lantdagh* chose Leisler to organize defenses that would prevent or repel invasion. He was called "lieutenant-governor" of the province. He later called himself commander-in-chief, a term that, like *stadhouder*, had military overtones.[6] Nevertheless, Leisler seldom left Fort William in New York City during the two years of his administration. Except for occasional meetings with New England allies in Hartford, and one meeting two miles outside New York City in the home of a burgherguard captain, he remained steadfastly at Fort William. He commissioned subordinates to lead troops against the French and presented himself only once as military commander at Albany, as far as we know.

Footnotes

14. Leisler to Treat, August 7, 1689, *DHNY*, 2:20, 21.
15. Leisler to Bradstreet, August 19, 1689, *DHNY*, 2:24; see T. S. Jansma, "Een Engels kroniekje over de eerste jaren van de Opsland" (1572–1574), *BMBGN* (1978) 93:474 Leisler to Bradstreet, August 19, 1689, *DHNY*, 2:24.
16. G. De Bruin. "De soevereinitiet in de republiek: een machtsprobleem," *BMBGN*, 94 (1979), 33. For the form of the "*Gemeente Lantdagh*" gathered in 1664, see p. 148, Chapter 3.

Leisler remained within the fort. Not surprisingly, only his accounts give us such detail as the presence of statues in the church within the fort before its seizure.[17] Indeed his fixation on defensive responsibilities is one way in which the "governors' papers" of the period are notably un-English. The customary contextualization of policy within a vision of increasing land acquisition – territories for the crown, estates for oneself as loyal courtier, lands for heirs – is absent. Nor were military and civil administrative matters intermixed as a matter of course. Leisler's framework was European in another way. The containment of France was his vital concern. It was one of William's reasons for contracting with Parliament to defend England and Leisler's reason for providing military security to New York. His "totall Intent" was "to maintaine" the province by commanding "the Garrison" as its principal fortification. One loyal observer described him paying mercenaries in North America just as William had in the Low Countries. "Eighteen pence a day," he reported, "was for the use of the private men to whom it was paid, for their subsistence in defending the Government."[18] France and her crypto-Catholic allies would be defeated, and that defeat would come, just as it had traditionally done throughout sixteenth- and seventeenth-century Europe, by defending cities.

Dutch Tableaux of Municipal Sovereignty

Leisler adhered scrupulously to the formal structures of seventeenth-century Dutch politics. Above all, he respected the autonomy of the province's two chartered cities, New York and Albany, and recognized their privilege of making war or peace. This meant accepting certain geographical realities, for the *stadhouder* could not freely enter the city or its dependencies (*stad en jurisdictie*). If he was commissioned to demand the political or religious loyalty of a city to his prince, his responsibility was to make camp outside its jurisdiction and to halt the advance of men and siege equipment while the *vroedschap* staged its

17. Depositions of Andries and Jan Meyer [against Nicholson], September 26, 1689, signed by Leisler, *DHNY*, 2:17. For an excellent study of religion as a factor in Leisler's actions, see David William Voorhees, "In behalf of the true Protestants religion": the Glorious Revolution in New York (Ph.D. diss., New York University, 1988). I am indebted to Voorhees for enriching my understanding of Leisler.

18. Colleccons (*sic*) made on the dying speeches of Leisler and Milborne, n.d., *DHNY*, 2:378; "A Particular Account of the Late Revolution at Boston in the Colony and Province of Massachusetts" [1689], in Charles M. Andrews, ed., *Narratives of the Insurrections, 1675–1690* (New York, 1915), 386; for William's motives, see J. P. Jones, *The Revolution in 1688 in England* (New York, 1972), 190.

decision making and considered offering entry.[19] "The Dutch," as one
Englishman observed sixty-five years earlier, "provide well that the General shall have small means to invade their liberties."[20] If allowed entry,
the *stadhouder* would be expected to exchange loyalty to his prince for
public affirmation of the city's privileges, franchises, and freedom of
conscience. He would either retain the magistrates or allow the *vroedschap* to make new choices from among their own membership. Even in
this situation, however, the *stadhouder*'s place, or that of his field deputy,
was inside the fortress of the town. The *stadhuis* remained the magistrates' citadel, and the blockhouses and other municipal defenses remained in control of the *burgerwacht* (civic guard). The *stadhouder* was
the stranger; like his soldiers, he was a tolerated transient.

The unquestioned nature of these structures and their impact on political behavior and expectancies is best seen in tableaux of action set in
New York City and Albany. Each was a scene of men and women enacting
civic formalities; no one acted as bureaucrat of a state or agent of the
court. The formalities were, like Leisler's word-pictures, *burgerlijk* descriptions of public actions; they were those of the commune, of men
and women still enacting Dutch republicanism.

In July 1689, Stephen van Cortlandt, a merchant who had survived in
New York City by accommodating to English rule, gave Edmund Andros
an account of Leisler's first movements in New York City. In it he explicitly promised Andros exactitude, and his detail was plentiful. Its
presentation duplicated that of a burgher, Joris Craffurd, who related
"eye-witness accounts" of the disturbances during the *aansprekersoproer* (rioting about funerals) in Amsterdam seven years later.[21] Van
Cortlandt's account was in the form of a journal. He was writing in a
hurry, copying passages for Andros from his own daybook. He apologized that the account was *blotheer* (sparse) and undoubtedly hoped
to have tidied it and enlarged some descriptive passages. The daily
events were recorded like items in a ledger, that is, in a form second
nature to Netherlanders. In all but four instances, he made sense of
incidents by citing the date first, then a name, and finally, as it were,

19. For limitations on the *stadhouder*, see J. Scheurkogel, "Het Kaas en Broodspel,"
    BMBGN, (1979), 94:197.
20. *Sir Thomas Ovrbvry his observations in his travailes vpon the state of the xvii provinces,
    as they stood Anno. Dom. 1609. The treatie of peace being then on foote* (London,
    1626) in Edward F. Rimbault, ed., *The Miscellaneous Works in prose and verse of Sir
    Thomas Overbury, knt., now first collected* (London, 1856), 229.
21. Van Cortlandt to Andros, July 9, 1689, *DRCH*, 3:590; *Joris Craffurd over het Aan-
    sprekersoproer te Amsterdam in 1696*, reprinted in R. M. Dekker, *Oproeren in Holland
    gezein door tijdgenoten: Ooggetuigeverslagen van oproeren in de provincie Holland
    ten tijde van de Republiek (1690–1750)* (Assen, 1979), 38.

the business of the day. Reading for structure, it goes as follows: "The 29th of Apr. Capt Nicholson.... The 10th day of May all Magistrates and Officers.... The 11th Ebenezer Platt, Matthew Howell, John Wheeler and John Jackson.... The 12th of May Capt Nicholson and Councill.... The 18th of May Mr Wedderburn.... May the 24th The Mayor of Albany.... The 27th Major Baxter.... The 31st of May Capt Nicholson.... The 22 June came Major Gold and Capt ffitts [Fitch] from Connecticut.... The 24th Mr William Merrit...."²² Clearly the journal format served to stitch together action episodes for van Cortlandt. Some required the space of a paragraph, but most took up the few lines appropriate to an account book. There was no translation of the events into a narrative form, into allegory.

Van Cortlandt's daybook differed from accounts coming from Boston. Those efforts emphasized the deeper meanings of the happenings in "the revolution." Reverend Robert Ratcliffe, rector of King's chapel and author of a "A Particular Account of the Late Revolution, 1689," used the extended metaphor of the birth of a monster child to hold together the action of rebels in Boston. The "detestable Monster" was the offspring of disloyal preachers, and its "strugglings" were apparent months before delivery. The interpretation of events required a mystical reading, and the grammar for it, found among dissenters and Jacobites alike, was paternity.²³

In van Cortlandt's daybook, the entry of June 22 presented a tableau in which the traditional Dutch division between the role of the *stadhouder* and that of city magistrates was enacted and ritualized. Van Cortlandt reported that Leisler had just been given "printed papers" from an embassy of Connecticut officials proving that William and Mary had indeed been proclaimed king and queen in England and Ireland. He asked to retain the documents for one or two hours, obviously to have them copied into Dutch in the fort. He then had the drums rolled and proclaimed the king and queen at the fort in the forenoon. At about 3 o'clock, van Cortlandt (who was then mayor of the city) had his first meeting of the day with Leisler. Leisler had specifically designated a place that drew him away from the *stadhuis* for the meeting. As the mayor put it, "they sent for me to be at my house [and] I went home there."²⁴ Leisler arrived with two Connecticut officials as well as the officers of the civic guard seconded to the defense of the fort and now loyal to him. These *bur-*

22. Van Cortlandt to Andros, July 9, 1689, *DRCH*, 3:597; 591, 592, 593, 595.

23. "A Particular Account," in Charles M. Andrews, ed., *Narratives of the Insurrections, 1675–1690* (New York, 1960), 196.

24. Van Cortlandt to Andros, July 9, 1689, *DRCH*, 3:595; 595.

gherwacht officers, like guards in the Netherlands in similar circumstances, were now prepared to act independently of the city magistrates.[25]

The unsteady alliance that always existed in Dutch cities between magistrates and the burgherguard was now played out. As the mayor quite properly reported to Andros, the *schutterij* with Leisler were men still serving, though without loyalty, under "our [the city's] capts." Some came with *halberdiers*, the symbol of judicial chastisement.[26] At this point, Leisler showed himself prepared to recognize the right of van Cortlandt and his council to continue in office if they would declare allegiance to William and Mary. "Leyslaer," Van Cortlandt wrote, "asked me wheither I would not proclaim the King and Queen. I told him it was already done [at the fort]. He answered if I would not do it [for the city] he would do it at the Towne hall. I told him he might doe what he pleased." Both men were bluffing. Leisler's threat to breach protocol by going to the *stadhuis* was an empty bluff, for he dropped it after quarrelsome words were exchanged. Van Cortlandt also backed down. Particularly after Leisler had threatened to ask the Connecticut officials to use the town hall to make the pronouncement, he agreed to consult his aldermen and consider the offer. Continuing what delaying tactics he could in the one hour's time they gave him, van Cortlandt consulted his associates. Leisler – if we turn briefly to his account of the happenings – had made his position clear to van Cortlandt and his council: "I . . . [told] them that I had the charge from the country to defend the fort for their Ma[ties], and so I intended not to burden them [the magistrates] . . . and I doubt not if they should meet as justices, no boddy should oppose them." In fact, he recognized that he needed authorized civil officials because only they could administer oaths of allegiance to his soldiers.[27]

Meanwhile van Cortlandt and the city council determined to force Leisler into public usurpation of the city's privileged autonomy. They drew him and other military officers to the *stadhuis*, where he was kept waiting outside. He came "at the Towne hall" and again asked van Cortlandt to declare the city loyal to William: Let his clerk read the proclamation. Van Cortlandt refused, trying instead to lure Leisler into overreaching his position: "He [your clerk] that read it before the fort can read it here; I have no clarke." In a rage Leisler refused. The spectators

25. Van Cortlandt to Andros, July 9, 1689, *DRCH*, 3:591; for the structural independence of the civic guards, see N. J. J. De Voogd, *De Doelistenbeweging te Amsterdam in 1748* (Utrecht, 1914).

26. *Pieter van der Schelling over een hongeroproer te Rotterdam in 1740*, reprinted in Dekker, *Oproeren in Holland*, 125.

27. Van Cortlandt to Andros, July 9, 1689, *DRCH*, 3:595, Leisler to officials of Connecticut, July 10, 1689, *DHNY*, 2:8.

grew violent and the magistrates complied with demands that they return with Leisler to the fort. There, where he could exercise authority properly, Leisler forced the magistrates to join a large gathering drinking the king's health. Leaving the fort, van Cortlandt received humiliating abuse, and for some burghers, his presence aroused fears of the city being set afire. They alleged later that with him in the fort were some papists who set fire to three of the turrets. But he had bought time, enough to declare two days later that he possessed a codicil written by their majesties on February 14 and justifying his government as of December 1, 1689. He proclaimed the document in a carefully staged ritual, with the city's common council assembled before the *stadhuis* and him as mayor "charging and commanding... [the people] to take notice thereof."[28]

Leisler's repudiation of this action followed swiftly. Within a fortnight, he warned van Cortlandt that any attempt to convene the city court would bring him John de Witt's fate. The "people would hale the Magistrates by the legs from the Town Hall, and he would not hinder them." Meanwhile he convened a *lantdagh* on June 25 at Fort William to authorize a provincial defense force. Like Stuyvesant, he encountered delegates stubbornly resistant to nonlocal needs. Kingston "concluded to stand aloof." Others held back in traditional fashion, looking to the alliances Leisler might make with New England, rather than supporting a provincial mercenary army.[29] Nevertheless, the delegates appointed him "captain of the fort at New York, until orders shall be received from their Majesties." At the same time, he called upon powers given by the *lantdagh* to require city elections out of their normal time. It was analogous to the reelections required in Utrecht by the Prince of Orange. There, as we have seen, the States General allowed the *stadhouder* to take the quasi-constitutional step of turning out of government those in whom he did not have confidence. Leisler did this in New York City and Albany. On Manhattan Island, elections were held in October, and Leisler, acting as "commander in chief" under a Committee of Safety, confirmed the officials in office. The results were posted at the fort – which was inadvertently called Fort Amsterdam.[30] In Albany, he commissioned Captain Jochim Staats to command the fort and instructed him to ensure that "the Magistracy doe order y[t] a ffree Election bee made of a Mayor & Aldermen." Leisler was prepared to continue the courtesies

28. Van Cortlandt to Andros, July 9, 1689, *DRCH*, 3: 595; Nathan Gold and James Fitch to Leisler, June 26, 1689, *DHNY*, 2:17; 596.

29. Van Cortlandt to Andros, July 9, 1689, *DRCH*, 3:596; Marius Schoonmaker, *The History of Kingston, New York, from Its Early Settlement to the Year 1820* (New York, 1888), 85.

30. Schoonmaker, *History of Kingston*, 84; "Leisler's Proclamation Confirming the Election by the Citizens of the Mayor, Sheriff, Clerk and Common Council of New York," October 14, 1689, *DHNY*, 2:35.

essential to succession and rotation in office. "I am," he wrote, "willing to have the undermentioned p'sons chosen if ye people will Elect them ... [I am] hoping that [the obligation of] the Monthly Courts will be of Ease to them." Once loyal municipal officers were installed in the two cities, he withdrew his oversight of civil affairs.[31]

Leisler continued to direct military affairs. He called a *kriegraad* at Fort William when it seemed necessary, and he summoned his own field officers and those of the city's militia when required. He sent soldiers to take up disaffected citizens whom he called "prisoners of war." He authorized military commissions, mostly to civic guards. He took the position that he would write only to soldiers and commissioned officers, not to civil authorities. His direct contacts with Albany were solely with the burgherguard and with one of the "ould [West India Company] soldiers" who reported receiving a letter from the English commander of the fort there offering him a sergeant's place if he would help recruit burghers against Leisler "2 or 3 at a time."[32] Over the months, Leisler's government was like that of the Netherlands, where laws were often called regulations and government had restricted powers. It paralleled that of the contemporary Swedish leader, Johan Printz, who was "Governour over the District of Jennekloepingh, *Stadhouder* of the same fortress and Commander of the garrison there."[33]

Leisler's public letters during his final weeks at Fort William in 1691 were again word-sketches of fortifications. The scenarios were those of military men in the Dutch manner: Leisler again defending the fort with a terrible industry and refusing to surrender it to an English major lacking credentials (*commissiebrieven*); Leisler offering the major billeting in the city but withholding keys to the gates and access to the burgherguard's blockhouses; the major demanding "absolute possession of his Majesty's said fort" and declaring Leisler a traitor; governor Henry Sloughter arriving two months later, demanding surrender of the fort at night — contrary to the rules of war — and refusing Leisler's request "Please only to Signify" his authority by producing his commission. (It was the first

31. Leisler to Staats, December 28, 1689, *DHNY*, 2:52; Leisler to justices of the New York counties, December 19, 1689, *DHNY*, 2:50.
32. Leisler to Governor of Boston, June 19, 1689, *DHNY*, 2:6; Convention sess., September 17, 1689, *DHNY*, 2:92; Leisler to the assembly of Maryland, September 29, 1689, *DHNY*, 2:32.
33. A. Th. Van Deursen, *Het kopergeld van de Gouden Eeuw: Volk en Overheid*, 3 (Assen, 1979), chap. 1; Obligation of Joost de la Grange to Sieur Johan Prints (*sic*) and Lady Armgart Prints (*sic*), entered before Notary Walewyn van den Veen, August 21, 1663 in Berthold Fernow, ed., *Minutes of the Orphanmasters Court of New Amsterdam, 1655–1663: Minutes of the Executive Boards of the Burgomasters of New Amsterdam and the Records of Walewyn Van der Veen, Notary Public, 1662–1664* (New York, 1907), 59.

demand made by the four English officers who surrendered the same fort to Squadron Commander Evertsz in 1673.)[34]

The surrender that Sloughter finally achieved repeated, at least in part, the formalities that had engaged Stuyvesant, Nicolls, and the New Amsterdam burgomasters in 1664. Eyewitnesses (one, an English major and, another, Leisler's son) testified that Leisler and his associates had "proposed a Capitulation" and agreed "to offer him [Sloughter] the possession."[35] Leisler's secretary and the major bore this collegial decision to the English commander. Presumably they would have expected to haggle over conditions and see to the recording of proceedings. It is what had happened in 1664. Instead, the two officials were taken prisoner; one was hanged with Leisler following his surrender.

Sloughter wrote of it all to William Blathwayt in England. He did not say that he was the first European to hang and behead two burghers of New York nor that he was the first to send the mayor of a chartered city for trial after commital proceedings held in the "city hall." But he was sufficiently uneasy to redraft the letter and cast final responsibility on the Court of Oyer and Terminer. The court was in fact composed largely of Anglo-Americans, who, he implied, the Dutch prisoners would nonetheless take to be men of "their Countrey."[36]

Sloughter remembered incorrectly the day he had set for Leisler's execution, writing that it was May 17. It happened on May 16, in the rain.

Civic Worlds and Uncivilized Men

Leisler's execution took place outside the city walls. Sloughter, who was soon to die of "acute alcoholism following a drunken debauch," signed the death warrant at the fort, also outside the city's bounds.[37] Portentously, the execution was not the ritualization of a civic world, but court theater. Setting Leisler aside, the chief actor was a surrogate for the king, a man bearing absolute power from London. The judges were either the court's overseas bureaucrats – placemen of James II like van Cortlandt

---

34. Declaration of Leisler against Ingoldsby and his council, March 16, 1691, *DHNY*, 2:343; Leisler to Sloughter, March 20, 1690/1, *DHNY*, 2:360; see C. de Waard, ed., *De Zeeuwsche Expeditie naar de West onder Cornelis Evertsen den Jonge, 1672–1674: Nieuw Nederland een jaar onder Nederlandsche Bestuur* ('s-Gravenhage, 1919): De Engelschen verspechten toen den commiseebrief van Evertz te zeen," xxxix.
35. Petition of Leisler's son to King [New York], n.d., *DHNY*, 2:423, and Ingoldsby and Council to Lords of Trade, July 29, 1691, *DHNY*, 2:386.
36. Draft of a Letter [of Sloughter] to Blathwayt [New York], n.d., *DHNY*, 2:382, and 382, n.n. 1, 2, 3.
37. Clifford P. Morehouse, *Trinity, Mother of Churches: An Informal History of Trinity Parish in the City of New York* (New York, 1973), 9.

– or men like the Bostonian Robert Dudley, who may never have been within New York City before 1691. The Dutch New Yorkers were insightful when they placed the execution within that theater by muddling Sloughter's known alcoholic excesses with his signing of the death warrant and making an analogy of it with Henry II's murder of Thomas à Becket. After Leisler's hanging, the Dutch people of Kingston told the story that Sloughter had first hesitated about signing the death warrant. But his signature was procured "at the close of a feast when the governor was overpowered with wine, and the men [Leisler and his son-in-law] were executed before he recovered from his debauch sufficiently to realize what he had done."[38]

Like all allegories, this account gave substance to impressions difficult and dangerous to express. Protected by fabulation, it typed English political power as absolute in the king and then said he had the power to murder. Monarchy was located in a place of private feasting, a courtly setting away from public view and where state papers, even death warrants, could be signed in fits of anger or inadvertence. Justice was inaccessible to the gaze of the populace. By contrast, the Dutch saw that Thomas à Becket's place was in a cathedral, a municipal site available to the people and their judgments. The court's power, always moving with the king and his creatures, was not fixed, as municipal and episcopal jurisdictions were. In the end, Leisler could not discover its place, though it was there to claim his life. At one point, for example, he tried to disentangle the status of the Court of Oyer and Terminer from that of a county court; at another, he protested that he should be brought before William III, as though he had some simple proposition to present.[39] Perhaps he had in mind the Dutch practice of recalling to Holland high officials whose governance overseas had come into question. Whatever the case, the fable made Leisler a local martyr. But if the myth underwrote the city as the primary place of political action, it also called upon a strong sense of encroaching monarchical power. Unlike Thomas à Becket, Leisler was not defeated in a conflict between church and state but rather

38. See Schoonmaker, *History of Kingston*, 89. For the expansion of Dutch men and women on the theme of à Becket's murder and Englishmen having tails as a result, see Keith Thomas, *Man and the Natural World: Changing Attitudes in England, 1500–1800* (London, 1983), 134; Jozef Cornelissen, *Nederlandsche Volkshumor op Stad en Dorp, Land en Volk* (Antwerp). 4:244; see Koenraad W. Swart, "Brave New World: The Miracle of the Dutch Republic," *Delta* (1970), 13:38, and [David Pietersz De Vries], *Short Historical and Journal Notes*, CNYHS, 2nd ser. (New York, 1857), 3 (Part 1):41.

39. See Leonard Hochberg, "The English Civil War in Geographical Perspective," *Journal of Interdisciplinary History*, 14 (1984), and for the county as the military base of the king's authority, see 750; for Leisler's confusion, see Memorandum on how Leisler was to plead [New York], n.d., *DHNY*, 2:365.

in one between monarchies and republican communes, of which New York City and Albany were the most highly developed, and now the last examples in North America.

However, it was not a conflictual process that took Leisler's life. He died for appearing uncivilized. He was unsuitable or, rather, emblematic of the unsuitability of the Dutch to undertake tasks importantly English. Laughing at the Dutch was an instinctual condescension among English state bureaucrats of the seventeenth and early eighteenth centuries in North America. The laughter was inadvertent and construed for private amusement. It could also be contrived and public. In all cases it helped define person, orienting the social definition of the civilized person to the model of the English man or woman.

Consider two accounts of the death of one of Leisler's associates, a Mr. Willson, in midsummer of 1689. Van Cortlandt was eyewitness to the event and recounted it to an English correspondent. Leisler and the civic guard had sent Willson "to proclaim their Majestys in New Yersey [Jersey] and returning fell outt a Canoe at States [Staten] Island and drouned." This inaugurated the solemnities of mourning that had marked Jeremias van Rensselaer's funeral and burial: "He is buried in a great state, the whole town invited, Every man and woman [wearing] gloves, all ships and vessels their flaggs halfe staff, firing all when he was carried to the grave. The Kings flagg at the fort halfe staff, all the men upon the Fort in arms, the Drumms beating mournfully the gunns firing continually till he was in the grave. His death is much lamented by them, as being a man that stood up for the liberty of the people and protestant Religion, ettc."[40] Van Cortlandt mocked the political position of Willson and his mourners but, being Dutch, understood the appropriateness of the ceremonies.

John Tudor, an English attorney in New York City, offered a different description of the same occurrence. He confused Willson with a Mr. [William] Cox:

> Mr Cox to shew his fine cloaths undertooks to goe to Amboy to proclaime the King, who comeing whome again was fairely drowned, which accident startled our Commanders here very much, there is a good rich widdow left. – The manner of his being drowned was comeing on board in a Cannow from Captⁿ Cornelis point at Statten Islands, goeing into the boate slipt downe betwixt the Cannow and the boate the water not being above his chinn, but very muddy, stuck fast in and striving to get out, bobbing his head under receaved to

40. Van Cortlandt to Nicholson, August 5, 1689, *DRCH*, 3:609.

much water in. They brought him a shore with life in him, but all would not fetch him againe – So much for A f_____.⁴¹

Tudor expected no rebuff from his English correspondent for the derision heaped so gratuitously on "Mr. Cox" and a Dutch sense of clothing, gesture, and protocol. The figures were ludicrous. Tudor's burlesque inscribed ineradicable differences between Dutch and English men. Leisler's government, he related elsewhere, had not "two men of sense." The Dutch leader was without style. He lacked manners, proclaiming "King William and Queen Mary... in the most meanest manner as you can imagine." Leisler knew of Tudor's mockery. He also recognized that Connecticut's leaders refused him the dignity of his office. They "spit in our faces," he wrote, "within our jurisdiction." Others, he knew, despised him as a hopeless drunk.⁴²

New Netherlanders had long been derided as ignorant. The word was used in the 1630s, and it was still around in the 1720s, when it went on stage in *Androborus*, governor Robert Hunter's satirical play on New York society. In 1649, a visitor to North America noted that the Dutch were "a laughing-stock" to the English. In 1653, English Long Islanders ridiculed a letter from Stuyvesant for its obscurity and improper literary form. Governor Dongan reported them generally ignorant. Governor Richard Bellomont wrote to England that "those that are honest of the Dutch... are very ignorant." His measure was the improper use of language, a gauge universally applied by conquerors to suppressed peoples and more than anything else likely to constitute a source of laughter: They "can neither speak nor write proper English."⁴³

New England's leaders read letters carefully for their tone. They could find a shadow of irony or slab of poor prose as surely as we.⁴⁴ We have only fragmentary evidence that Leisler's letters to officials in New Eng-

41. Tudor to Nicholson, August [?], 1689, *DRCH*, 3:617.
42. Tudor to Nicholson, August [?]. 1689, *DRCH*, 3:617, 616; for Leisler's awareness of Tudor's mockery, see Fragment of a letter supposed from Leisler to Connecticut, [June?], 1690 *DHNY*, 2:262; Leisler to gentlemen [of New England ?], September 30, 1690, *DHNY*, 2:303, and see Governor and Council of Connecticut to Leisler and Council of New York, March 5, 1689–90, *DHNY*, 2:79; Leisler to Officials of Connecticut, July 10, 1689, *DHNY*, 2:9.
43. "A Few Extracts from a Description of New Netherland in 1649," in Du Simitiere Mss., CNYHS, 2nd ser. 1:274; Bernice Schultz, *Colonial Hempstead* (New York, 1937), 61; "Dongan's Report to the Committee of Trade on the Province of New York," February 22, 1687, *DHNY*, 1:148; Bellomont to Lords of Trade, May [?], 1699, in Hugh Hastings, ed., *Ecclesiastical Records: State of New York* (Albany, 1901), 2:1299.
44. For this deftness with satire and irony, see "Council of Connecticut to Andros, January 31, 1675," in J. Hammond Trumbull, ed., *The Public Records of the Colony of Connecticut from 1665 to 1678; with the Journal of the Council of War, 1675 to 1678* (Hartford, 1852), 404.

land, the Barbados, or England made him a figure of ridicule. It was common among New England officials, however, to deny their Dutch New York counterparts the courtesy of careful responses to letters. Both van Cortlandt and Leisler experienced it during these years; Colve had in 1673. And on one occasion, the Upper House of Maryland, which was not particularly hostile to Leisler at the time, found a petition of his "a Dark Ambiguous thing."[45] Moreover, letters that Leisler wrote in the two years of his command are, even to Anglo-Americans distanced from them by almost three hundred years, syntactically and lexically funny. They are the letters of the client unexpectedly come into a role of considerable responsibility and distressfully forced to use the patron's language. Not long ago, a historian of Hempstead, Long Island, deliberately treated his readers to the laughable efforts of Dutch magistrates struggling to describe themselves in English. They were composed, they wrote, of a "Constable and oversers by his magistis atariti and our honowred govenars apountment under his rial hynes the duck of York."[46]

Leisler's letters were, and are, similarly laughable. There were "piple" who "starff"; there were ships "sesed one Clerd thoder Condemned"; there were enemies "at owue bak and In ouer Bossum"; and there were events occurring on "Sabeday," folk "kilt & captivated," and "nues" of the "marsch off the marilanders." Words were misspelt in ungrammatical sentences. Pages filled up with Ks and Ts instead of Cs and Ds; there were Ws for Vs, Ys for Js. Leisler seems to have read English but did not always see to the translation of his own letters.[47] They were also vulgar. They put into public message things meant to be private. His criticism of the New Englanders for their failure of leadership in taking Canada was set in such a gaucherie: "Mistake not yourselues to imagine such figg leaves sufficient covering for your strenious evils."[48] Such words forced the reader into collusion with a bumbling, patronizing man and his dull and "foreign" associates. A heaviness sheathed his prose as it

45. See Leisler to gentlemen [of New England?], September 30, 1690, and Leisler to Treat, January 1, 1690/1, *DHNY*, 2:301, 302, 316; Van Cortlandt to Andros, July 9, 1689, *DRCH*, 3:591; see Att a Special Generall Court, called by order of the Council, and assembled together in Boston, December 10, 1673, in Nathaniel B. Shurtleff, ed., *Records of the Governor and the Company of the Massachusetts Bay in New England*, 4, Part 2 (Boston, 1854) (The court had received a letter from Colve but failed to reply, though answering letters of Connecticut and Plymouth on the same issue, 572); Petition of Jacob Lesiler (*sic*) of New York, considered in Council of Maryland meeting held October 8, 1679, in William Hand Brown, ed., *Archives of Maryland, Proceedings of the Council of Maryland, 1671–1681* (Baltimore, 1896), 15:262, 263.
46. Schultz, *Colonial Hempstead*, 108.
47. Leisler to John Tathem, May 7, 1690, and Leisler to John d'Bruyn. John Provoost, and Jacob Milbourne, April 30, 1690, *DHNY*, 2:241, 241, 238; Deposition of John Dischington, June 5, 1689, *DRCH*, 3:586.
48. Leisler to Treat, January 1, 1690–1, *DHNY*, 2:318.

did his purposes. Neither was dressed in the circumlocutions meant to cover ruthlessness.

Some of Leisler's later letters to New England were properly Anglicized before being dispatched from Fort William. But if the form of letters could at times be civilized and almost match those of an Englishman, the contents still betrayed a man ignorant of the most elementary things. He did not understand the gunpowder plot, misused "liberties and bailwycks," and did not understand royal charters. He was not anti-English: men with English names were members of the burgherguard, a charter for New York "like Boston's" seemed good to him — although he confused Boston with Massachusetts — and he tried to celebrate the anniversary of the gunpowder plot properly.⁴⁹ He used English terms such as "creatures" for political placemen. However, he did not act the gentleman. Governor John Winthrop's inexcusable failure as commander of the joint forces of New York and New England sent to defeat the French in 1690 was there for all to see. But such things were meant to be excused among gentlemen, and certainly one did not imprison such a man, as Leisler had. The incident required the governor and council of Connecticut to school Leisler properly on the courtesies of gentlemen and point out that his actions had put him outside the circle of "our best friends."⁵⁰

Leisler spoke for those of the Dutch whom the English conquest had made clients. They were men and women who allowed English culture to leak into their lives and were now trying to appear civilized, that is, English. Nicolaes Bayard was one who advertised himself as having been entertained on Dongan's private barquentine and who was, in short, assimilated. He knew English ways well enough to offer Andros a simplification that summarized what Leisler's takeover meant: He was sitting in the governor's pew. He had also absorbed English narrative style. Yet to governor Bellomont and the court in London, he was still a "beggar boy."⁵¹ Samuel Staats, whose adherence to Leisler later won him Bellomont's support, wrote the governor fulsomely in 1699. "My lord's

49. "Affadavit: Mission of Joost Stool in England as Representative of the Committee of Safety of New York, November 16, 1689," in Hugh Hastings, ed., *Ecclesiastical Record: State of New York* (Albany, 1901–16), 2:981.
50. Allyn to Leisler, September 1, 1690, *DHNY*, 2:288.
51. "Affadavit against Bayard and Certain Parties on Staten Island," September 25, 1689, *DHNY*, 2:29; "Affadavit: Mission of Stool, November, 16, 1689." Hastings, ed., *Ecclesiastical Records* 2:981; for Anglicized narrative style, see [Nicholas Bayard], *A Modest and Impartial Narrative of Several Grievances and Great Apprehensions That the Peaceable and Most Considerable Inhabitants of Their Majesties Province of New-York in America Lye Under, By the Extravagant and Arbitrary Proceedings of Jacob Leysler and his Accomplices*, printed at New York, and re-printed at London [final page dated, January 21, 1690]; Bellomont to Bridgewater, October 12, 1699, EL 9767, HL.

speech," he praised, "was so admirable that I can only say with admiration. 'Is it possible that old Seneca is alive again?' " It was a sad effort to prove himself civilized, and a meaningless one in any case, for Bellomont found Staats and his Dutch associates impenetrably stupid because they had no nous about the proper ways of manipulating factional power and did not play the game with proper ferocity. "Dr. Staats and the rest of Leisler's Party," he concluded, "are just the people that Will. Nichols points Staats to be, in his pamphlet, Impenetrable B_____ [Boors, Baboons, Bastards?]."⁵²

Leisler exposed himself to meeting English qualifications for acting as lieutenant-governor when he took on the role of captain of the civil guard and found himself propelled into a close relationship with the governors of the English-speaking colonies. He let himself become a point of comment in the House of Commons. There he was a man of "neither blood or estates." He was someone who had not even taken out English naturalization. Within a year he had to put in his own handwriting the fact that he and his Dutch associates "never were thought worthy of consulting" in the enterprises undertaken to retain the North American plantations for William and Mary. In the final days, English officers "sezed & abused" those who were the least civilized, that is, those closest to Leisler's person. A visitor to New York later testified to Leisler's pleasing decorum despite his easy irritability. Leisler "spoke," he reported, "with as much smoothness and civility as I think I have heard, which was pretty strange because new to me."⁵³ Yet within ninety years, people in his own province would consider his administration a bizarre failure. William Smith, Jr., wrote that he was "destitute of every qualification necessary for the enterprise."⁵⁴

Leisler was mocked by Sloughter in his final days. He was, for example, punctilious about records, and one of his earliest requests to Boston had been for the return of the province's records known to have been taken there. Written records legitimated government, and in the Netherlands, their abuse or loss meant dismissal from office and severe punishment.

52. Staats to Bellomont, June 12, 1699, De Peyster Papers, NYPL; Bellomont to De Peyster, September 9, 1699, De Peyster Papers, NYPL.

53. "Reasons humbly offer'd to the Honourable House of Commons, against the Passing the Bill for the Reversing the Attainder of Jacob Leisler, Jacob Milburn, Abraham Governour, and others," MS813.m.18/16, British Library; Leisler to Treat, January 1, 1690/1, *DHNY*, 2:318; Declaration of Leisler against Ingoldsby and his Council, March 16, 1691, *DHNY*, 2:343; Captain George McKenzie to Nicholson, August 15, 1689, *DRCH*, 3:614.

54. William Smith, *The History of the Province of New-York, from the First Discovery, to which is annexed A Description of the Country, an Account of the Inhabitants, their Trade, Religious and Political State, and the Constitution of the Courts of Justice in the Colony* (London, 1776), 81.

On five occasions, Leisler petitioned for their return. Bradstreet refused to respond. Yet he "forwarded...the Records of that Province" to Sloughter eight days after his arrival. Neither was Leisler accorded dignity. Only a petition of five Dutch burghers to William and Mary recorded that the dishonor shown him, his secretary, and his appointee as mayor were genuine considerations to participants. They alone noted that, when Sloughter imprisoned them in the city hall, it was "to their great shame and dishonor."[55] Leisler's speech before his execution gave the hanging some dignity, but there is no record of a guard drawn up, a procession formed, or the governor present to authorize the event. One of the non-Dutch judges of the court that condemned him called him "really a rash blundering fellow...a perfect drone his sting [now] gone and unable to do more mischief." And on the scaffold, where the condemned paradoxically say those things authorities want to hear, he also played his part and accused himself of ignorance. He acted from "misinformation and misconstruction of People's interest and meaning."[56]

Sloughter worried that Leisler had successfully disaffected the Dutch populace, who were thought to constitute three-fourths of the provincial population. Many, he feared, were prepared to accept that Whitehall had manipulated affairs and acted through ignorance. He believed that "if the Cheif Ringleaders be made an example the whole country may be quieted."[57] What he meant by making an example was unclear, probably even to himself. Across England the "glorious revolution" had produced local uprisings also; there were rebels and treasons but no universal policy of making examples. Nor was such a policy executed in Massachusetts, where the king's commissioned representative, Edmund Andros, had been seized and sent back to England a prisoner. No one dared ask Sloughter what he meant – not his soldiers, not the judges, not the bureaucrats he reinstalled in office, and not the Dutch, who, whatever their politics, were again powerless or sycophants, some of them willing to wear the caricature of ignorance. "I acted," pleaded one supporter of Leisler calling upon the proper excuse, "from want of knowledge."[58]

55. "Preface," *ER*3, 6; Leisler to Governor and Committee of Safety at Boston, June 4, 1689, Leisler to Governor of Boston, August 19, 1689, Leisler to Governor of Boston, September 25, 1689, Leisler to Governor of Boston, October 22, 1689, Leisler to Governor of Boston, April 7, 1690, *DHNY*, 2:4, 24, 31, 38, 229; Bradstreet to Lord Nottingham, May 8, 1691, *DRCH*, 3:769; Memorial on behalf of Leisler's adherents imprisoned in New York [The Hague], October 15, 1691, *DRCH*, 3:811.
56. Chidley Brooke to Robert Southwell, April 5, 1691, *DRCH*, 3:759; Colleccon (*sic*) made on the dying speeches of Leisler and Milbourne, n.d. *DRCH*, 3:377.
57. A memorial [New York] n.d., *DHNY*, 2:58; Sloughter to committee, May 7, 1691, *DRCH*, 3:763.
58. See J. P. Jones, *The Revolution in 1688 in England* (New York, 1972), 299; see Rev. Robert Ratcliffe, "A Particular Account of the Late Revolution, 1689," in Andrews,

Albany: The City and the County, 1689–1691

Leisler and his Dutch associates in New York City were like the uncertain and compromised clients of the Indian subcontinent under the nineteenth-century British raj. They were men maneuvering for position within the unfamiliar political culture of the English conqueror. Unlike those of local leaders under the raj, however, their performances of clientage always meant putting municipal autonomy at risk and unavoidably contradicting the behavior needed to constitute republicanism as it was emerging in New Netherland before 1664. Such clientage structured the relationship of Dutch residents with English superiors in Albany as well as New York City. There it also arranged men according to the contributions they made to a political culture antithetical to republicanism and municipal autonomy. It rewarded those individuals who promised to make English structures of power authentic, in this case, complicit in diminishing the city in favor of the county. The contestants in the events of 1689 to 1691 were players in that slow structural transformation.

The months of Leisler's Rebellion were violent and hazardous for the city of Albany. The rituals of contest made that clear. From the start, events turned around one matter: whether political power lay within the city or the county, that is, whether it operated in a Dutch or English way. The burghers' shorthand for power on the county level was *het convencie*, that is, the convention of city and county officials (military and civic alike) who suddenly assumed the right to direct affairs in 1689. The dispute was one surrounding the *conventie*; it, and not Leisler's Rebellion, was the framework for interpreting and later remembering the events. They were events in which buildings like the *stadhuis* lost their unambiguous meanings as municipal. But they were also events that were handled in a Dutch way. In the end, for example, conflict was covered over, and efforts to contain power emanating from outside the city maintained. All of this must be considered as we observe the scenes that follow.

Contested Forces: City Guards versus County Authorities

During the six months when they chose to make conflict most visible – August 1689 to February 1690 – as many men were participants in the *oproer* as were spectators. They acted as a threatening gathering of "one hundred," as forty "principal inhabitants," as a "mob" large enough to pack the *stadhuis*, as committees of three, four, five, eight, nine, eleven

ed., *Narratives of the Insurrections, 1675–1690* (New York, 1915); Petition of Gerardus Beakman (*sic*) to Sloughter, n.d., *DHNY*, 2:369.

and twelve. They took violent action against one another in inns, at the fort, outside the church, in the *stadhuis*, on the strand, even in the court recorder's Jonckheerstraat house. They used the geographies of trading and *handelstijd* as places for military displays and the armed violence of soldiers. On Saturday, November 9, fifty-one soldiers sent by Leisler from New York City encamped on the island Kiliaen van Rensselaer had called West Island, and on Monday, November 25, eighty-seven troopers sent from New England crossed into Greenbush and were in the city within twenty-four hours.

The contest for the right to determine the city's autonomy was played out in particularly intense rituals between November 5 and January 13. Between those dates, Mayor Pieter Schuyler had to involve the *burgerij* in decisions that he and the self-appointed *conventie* were making about offering the city's allegiance to William and Mary while denying authority to Leisler.

Leisler had ordered a typically Dutch municipal election. The burghers were to select new magistrates, once again to be called commissaries. These would have the support of local *schutterij* and a core of principal men, who would have been called the *vroedschap* twenty-five years earlier. Schuyler and his council acted to avoid a reelection that would almost certainly have seen them defeated. In doing so, they denied the validity of centuries-old Dutch municipal practices.

Tuesday, November 5, was the first of twenty-one days of public demonstrations, and immediately the privileged status of the *stadhuis* was put in jeopardy by Schuyler and the *conventie*. On that day, the ringing of the bell called the burghers and inhabitants to the *stadhuis*. There Schuyler or one of the *conventie* alerted the crowd to the impending arrival of soldiers sent by Leisler to take the fort, remove its allegedly Anglo-Catholic officers, and secure the area against the French. Proposals, which amounted to refusing entry, were presented to the populace in writing "and their answer awaited." Within the day, "forty of ye Inhabitants" had composed a nine-paragraph reply. They agreed with the propositions. It was "Dangerous to lett ye men comeing from N. Yorke come into ye Citty till Such time ye Convention have Sufficient assurance of their sincere meaning." They reiterated the rubrics of municipal independence and responsibility followed by New Amsterdam in 1664: "We are fully Resolved... not to suffer them of N. Yorke or any Person else to rule over ye Same [the fort and city] Since it will be Required att our hands when a gov^r comes & not of theres."[59]

59. Proposealls made by the convention to ye people... [and] answers. November 5, 1689, *DHNY*, 2:110, 111.

But forty supporters were too few. As a consequence, on Thursday or Friday, Schuyler took a step that even the burgomasters of New York City had not contemplated. He relinquished the *stadhuis* and prepared to command the city from the fort. The *conventie* supported his move in a fanfare of approval. Again the bells were rung and a drama staged. Some of its members "writ to ye Mayers house, and told him they were come to wait upon him and Conduct him up to ye fort." A number of "ye Principle Burghers" accompanied him from his house near the south gate, up Jonckheerstraat, beyond the palisades that then divided the city from the English fort, and into the fortress overlooking the city. "After ye usuall Ceremonies [the fort] was Delivered" to him.[60] It was a maneuver that prevented a repetition of what had occurred four months earlier in New York City, when popular suspicion about the English soldiers led the populace to seize the fort. But the mayor's clear intention to direct municipal affairs from the fort sacrificed the traditional distinction between civil and military authority.

On Saturday, "three Sloops ... [hove] in Sight." They bore a "Comp^e of Souldiers ... beating of ye Drum" and following the commands of Jacob Milbourne. His appearance promised something of a *Blijde Inkomst* (Joyous Entry) for large numbers of the burghers. He expected to receive permission to march his men into the fort that night. Instead he was conducted inside the gate and to the *stadhuis*. The building was now "very full of People." He addressed them in what the court recorder called "a high Stile and Language." Exhorting the people to recognize that the powers of Schuyler and the *conventie* derived from King James, "who was a papist," that the city charter could now be considered null and void, and that they could now "choose both new Civill and Military officers as they Pleased," he called upon the mayor to respond. Schuyler was sent for twice but would not leave the fort. After further proceedings, Dirck Wesselsz ten Broeck, the court recorder, invited Milbourne to quarter his soldiers in the city "since ye Billets were Ready." Milbourne, knowing his soldiers' place was the fort, "answered no ... & so Parted y^t night" laying with his soldiers outside the gates on Marten Gerritsz's island.[61]

In the following days, the command of the *stadhuis* by the burgher-guard and townspeople was absolute. The *conventie* lost direction entirely. On Monday their intention to meet in the *stadhuis* was frustrated by a "great multitude of People assembled together there." They "stayed att ye Record^{rs} house" instead, aware that, at the same time, a "rageing

60. Convention sess., November 7, 8, 1689, *DHNY*, 2:113.
61. Convention sess., November 9, 1689, *DHNY*, 2:113.

and mutinous" crowd in the *stadhuis* was in effect putting Milbourne's mercenaries under local command. They were also confirming Jochim Staats, an officer of the burgherguard, as captain of the soldiers and "superior officer who was ... to be Commander of yᵉ fort, Distinct from the Civil function."⁶²

As both sides realized, the election of Staats was pivotal. It promised to return power to former structures: An officer of the *schutterij* would command the city's trainbands and the mercenaries sent by the *stadhouder*. Both would function, as long as needed, under a *vroedschap* and magistrates, yet to be elected. Whether the burghers thought out these structural matters consciously is unclear; their determination to carry out the election is. Three times they rejected countermanding orders sent from the *conventie*'s recorder, Wesselsz. "Finally, some of yᵉ Convention" ventured to the *stadhuis* to disperse them but "were forced to withdraw themselfs being threatened and menaced [so] that they were in danger of their life." "Near a hundred Persons" confirmed Staats as captain and, in effect, confirmed a future that would have seen a new magistracy and undoubtedly a new charter.⁶³

Only after three days was the *conventie* able to take some control of the *stadhuis*. In the interim, it employed the usual Dutch delaying tactics such as proposing that Staats be military commander but obedient to the *conventie*. He flatly refused. Meanwhile, another "great Comp of People were met together." They demanded proceeding with the election and insisted that Schuyler take part in the debates. "If he came not into Toune" they were resolved to confirm Staats and, by implication, new magistrates.⁶⁴

On Thursday, November 14, Schuyler "came down to towne." It was a full week since he had deserted the *stadhuis*. The burghers immediately appeared and awaited "yᵉ Rasons why he had Secured there Majᶜˢ fort (since he had heard that diverse were Dissatisfyed at his so doing)." They framed his actions within the opposition represented in the fort and the *stadhuis*, forcing him to state in his own words that his removal to the fort had demonstrated a break in authority. They awaited, as he was made to put it, "yᵉ Reasons yᵉ Convention did not meet Sooner at yᵉ

---

62. For an urban riot that follows the same structure, see *Twee brieven van Lijsbet Heere over het Aansprekersoproer [Amsterdam, Feberuari 1 en Feberuarij 2, 1696]*, in Dekker, *Oproeren in Holland*, 115, and Herbert Rowen, *John de Witt*, 844; Convention sess., November 10 and 11, 1689, *DHNY*, 2:121, 122.
63. Convention sess., November 11, 1689, *DHNY*, 2:122; Notice of Milbourne to convention, November 11, 1689, *DHNY*, 2:123.
64. Convention sess., November 12, 1689, *DHNY*, 2:124; 125; 125.

Citty hall."⁶⁵ Schuyler offered lengthy explanations but, by the afternoon, had retired to his house and in the evening returned to the fort.

But Friday was the day Schuyler had awaited, and planned. The stage of the drama was a three-tiered one, more spectacle than ritual in its elaborateness. The proscenium was the town land rising within about 1,800 feet from the level of the river to an elevation of 720 feet from the summit of the hill where the fort stood. Above the fort and at the highest tier was the hill overlooking the fort. Commanding Jonckheerstraat and a large concourse of burghers was Milbourne. He marched his company up the street and demanded the fort. At the summit, however, Schuyler refused, for poised above the fort and on the hill stood about eight hundred of the men who had in fact always played a deciding role when the meaning of Albany was contested and who were now following Schuyler's directions. A "Company of Maquase" were standing on the high hill, their stillness as "spectators" caught in the court recorder's account. Soon they sent word that they were "very much Dissatisfied" to see the present magistracy endangered and "if Milbourne did not withdraw with his Compeᵉ they would fyre upon him." Given this news, he and the burghers abandoned their attempt "to goe to the fort, but marched doune yᵉ towne." Milbourne delivered his men to the authority of Staats and left Albany.⁶⁶

Ten days later the *blijde inkomst* that Schuyler and the *conventie* had so long awaited occurred. On Monday, November 25, Captain Jonathan Bull marched into Greenbush at the head of eighty-seven New England troopers. The next day the magistrates of the Albany *conventie* met him "att yᵉ gate & bid [him] welcom." Entering the city "with flying Collors" he assembled his men in the middle of Handlaarstraat, "gave three volleys & was answered by 3 gunns from yᵉ fort." Schuyler had apparently regained control of affairs. These mercenaries, whom the *conventie* had so keenly awaited, took quarters in the city and then stations in the fort.⁶⁷

But the authority Schuyler had regained was tenuous. The Mohawk – whose actions had so successfully unwound the tensions which the insiders' rituals had again and again tightened – had postponed but not eliminated the decision the burghers had to make – preferably one that looked to be unanimous. The issue peaked again between January 11 and 13, 1690. The *conventie* learned that Leisler had sent a commission to Jochim Staats to command the fort and see to free elections. It immediately commanded the sheriff to require Staats's presence. He complied but insisted upon the legitimacy of his and Leisler's commissions.[68]

The *conventie* met the next day and considered information that Staats intended to "beat ye Drum & call his Comp^e together tomorrow" to declare for William and Mary. It would not have been the first time a municipal guard had deposed the magistracy of a Dutch town. As a result, the *conventie* staged a demonstration in the course of which a placard would be read "in a most Solemn manner" before the captain could initiate his performance. They arranged the event so as to draw to their side the principal symbolic landmarks of the city – the *stadhuis*, fort, church, and main streets – and formed a procession of men displaying Dutch and English symbols of authority. The "marshall" carried a white rod, the insignia of the sheriffs of London. Others carried pointed swords. A number of respected elders of the town and some faithful men of the burgherguard joined the march. The spectacle allowed the magistrates to process "from there Maj^{es} fort" to "the Plain Before ye Church" where the bell rang thrice and matched the continual beating of drums. There Schuyler read a proclamation in Dutch and English condemning Staats and his guards as rebels. He then proceeded "through ye Principle Streets of ye City and So to ye fort," where the soldiers were ceremoniously dismissed. The marshal returned down Jonckheerstraat to the church and fixed the placard to "ye Porch of ye church."[69]

The last highly theatrical incident was over. But something must be said of the troughs of action that should have completed the meaning of the recurrent highs and peaks. Paradoxically they were not periods when men whose public actions were successful sought to enforce clear resolution of the issues on the less successful. The rituals had certainly worked to define and intensify lines of separation, but neither radical divisions in the community nor new policies were institutionalized. Rather, things subsided into daily practicalities. Fear of French attack throughout 1689 and 1690 forced the burghers into finding common measures for defense. Still, the daily exigencies of warding off attack did not in themselves postpone a confrontation on matters of legitimacy and authority.

The issues were simply never composed for discussion. The goal of continuity guided behavior. The populace, although active to the point

68. Leisler to Staats, December 28, 1689, *DHNY*, 2:52, and see Convention sess., January 11, 1689/90, *DHNY*, 2:145; 146, 147.
69. Convention sess., January 12, 1689/90, *DHNY*, 2:150; Convention sess., January 12, 1689/90, and Protest of convention, January 13, 1689/90, *DHNY*, 2:154; for the white rod used in London, see Wayne Andrews, ed., "A Glance at New York in 1697: The Travel Diary of Benjamin Bullivant," Pam. revised from *New-York Historical Social Quarterly* (1956), 12; 154.

of *oproer* over the previous months, made no demands for continued participation in government. The leading men, although now deeply hostile to one another, closed ranks and were still doing so in 1699 when the English governor, bewildered by their show of unity, defined them as "Impenetrable B____" who had no sense of party politics. Within weeks of the events just described, bitter enemies were fellow committeemen and corecipients of war contracts authorized by Leisler. Richard Prettij, who gave billeting to Milbourne and had earlier been dismissed as surveyor and sheriff by Dongan and Schuyler, worked on city defenses alongside Jan Janse Bleecker and other members of the *conventie*. Staats shared command of troops with Bull. Gabriel Thomsz, whose inn was the scene of public denunciations of Schuyler, now obeyed his directives as mayor.[70] Yet it would be misleading to suggest that individuals were simply making separate decisions to be cooperative. Rather, the familiar institutions that had afforded such men the cover of playing political roles vigorously, but collegially recovered form. After the violent events, the magistracy and the burgherguard once again offered themselves as associations for political decision making.

Blurred Political Ideologies: The Recorder's Minutes

Leisler wrote that Dirck Wesselsz was a "mistery." There were, however, some highly dramatic moments when he was caught out of hiding. "Dirck Wessels record^r," as he first identified himself in the *conventie*'s minutes, was the burgher who immediately replied to Milbourne's supporters when they demanded an explanation for the magistrates' failure to offer the traditional counterdeductions to points made in Milbourne's florid oration at the *stadhuis* on November 9. He also "assumed the discourse" for the *conventie* at the *stadhuis* the following day and convened it at his house on November 11. Four days later he played a notable part in the melodrama Schuyler arranged by stationing natives on the hill overlooking the fort and giving them lines to speak about breaking the "covenant chain" and wanting Schuyler to be "Master over ye gentlemen here." He would have been seen walking out to pacify and quiet the natives, though it was another delegate who brought Milbourne the threat that they would "fyre upon him." Throughout the week's affairs, Wesselsz "represented ye May^r in his absence," as Milbourne was quick to

---

70. For the central place of continuity, see Du Plessis, Urban Stability in the Netherlands Revolution, 484, and for its continued place in twentieth-century Dutch politics, see Arend Lijphart, *The Politics of Accommodation: Pluralism and Democracy in the Netherlands* (Berkeley, 1968, 2nd rev. ed.), 144; Bellomont to DePeyster, September 9, 1699, DePeyster Papers, 1695–1710, NYPL; David Armour, The Merchants of Albany, New York: 1686–1760 (Ph.D. diss., Northwestern University, 1965), 58.

note.[71] He probably held the keys to the city's gates. A politically powerful man, he might have been mayor in the early 1690s had Schuyler not been retained in office as long as he was.

Moreover, Wesselsz kept the record of the *conventie*'s meetings. His minutes were revisions of initial notations, written in English and inscribed on both sides of fifty-six pages.[72] The narrative in these records was ideological. Although it was largely prose with the usual patches of conventional detail and opinion, there were also highly charged statements supporting a new kind of politics. Wesselsz recorded a proposition, for example, that the *conventie* had put (unsuccessfully) to the commonalty and that would have obliged them to acknowledge it as the "only Lawfull authority in the County till such time ord^{rs} come from there Maj^{ts}." Yet the *conventie* had no place in Dutch politics. It was neither a body municipally constituted nor a *kriegraad* nor a form of the *gemeente lantdagh*. On the contrary, its members had spurned the *lantdagh* summoned by Leisler and intended to supersede the municipal authority of Albany.[73] It was a quasi-legal county government prepared to justify its own legislation and call on its English-style militia units for defense in an unspoken departure from dependence on municipal governance and the *stadhouder*. Thus when Wesselsz recorded the *conventie*'s opinion that Milbourne's arrival in Albany had violated the territory of his majesty's "liege People," the words referred to the population dispersed over the county, not simply those living in the city. At one point, his words did relate usurpation to the city: Leisler meant "to turn ye government of this Citty upside downe." Yet elsewhere he widened that meaning, – just as members of the *conventie* had done in haranguing the crowd: the usurper's design was to have "*all* authority turned Upside Doune."[74]

Four times, Wesselsz minuted the phrase, "turn ye government of this Citty upside downe." It is a discordant phrase in the accounts, a metaphor curiously overused by him and the *conventie*, and outside the canon of the town's traditional political vocabulary. The phrase is

71. Leisler to Governor of Boston, October 22, 1689, *DHNY*, 2:38; Convention sess., November 9, 1689, *DHNY*, 2:114; Convention sess., November 10, 1689, *DHNY*, 2:20, and November 14, 1689, *DHNY*, 2:129; Convention sess. November 11, 1689, *DHNY*, 2:122; Convention sess., November 15, 1689, *DHNY*, 2:131; Convention sess., November 9, 1689, 2:64.
72. City of Albany Common Council minutes, Volume 3A, Minutes 1689–1690, and Mortgages, 1752–1765 [pagination in pencil to p. 113, text in English], Albany County Hall of Records.
73. "Proposealls made by the Convention," November 5, 1689, *DHNY*, 2:111.
74. Convention sess., November [10?], 1689 *DHNY*, 2:117; Convention sess., November 4, 1689, *DHNY*, 2:106, and see "Proposealls," November 5, 1689, *DHNY*, 2:109; Convention sess., November 10, 1689, *DHNY*, 2:121 (my italics).

found in Dutch literature, but its sudden appearance here and its use in speeches to a mob is unexpected because it is a reminder of established authority's fragility and, for that reason, dangerous to a member of the bourgeoisie like Wesselsz.[75] Yet he used it because the known political tradition was not able to supply him with a readymade vocabulary in this unstable period. Its structure had become unclear over the preceding twenty-five years, and its capacity to provide familiar points of reference had become compromised.

By 1689, consecutive English governors had greatly reduced the privileges and responsibilities of the court of Albany by reorganizing New York's municipal and provincial administration. The magistrates' performances, which fashioned and displayed those privileges and duties over time, were far fewer. When they did occur, they were the acts of men trying to marry two traditions. The magistrates of the early court of Beverwijck were sometimes casual in their procedures, and on occasion they were remarkably undignified, as we have already seen. However, the small rituals of calling witnesses to "step inside," of taking oaths, of haggling with the *schout* over fines, of responding to the burlesques of convicted felons sitting with their feet in irons and slandering them, all guided townspeople both emotionally and intellectually to an understanding of authority.[76]

The municipal ceremonies of Beverwijck were less richly colored than those of Amsterdam, but the structure was the same. There, too, it was ceremonies that constructed the political life of the community. The *ceremonieboeken*, that is, the books that taught magistrates the order of proceedings, were themselves rituals. Each burgomaster or *schepen* apparently tried to have his own richly decorated copy. They fused political style and political power. They made municipal power tangible and honorable by assigning roles to such men as secretary, presiding burgomaster, young *schepenen*, and *schout*. Such rites as entering the *raadkamer* and following elaborate seating arrangements gave ordinary citizens the charisma of office. The existence of the proper political order was made real in the daily ritualized behavior of the court and the recorder, whose minutes were also symbols ordering the city.

Whatever the difference in scale, Beverwijck was a facsimile of Amsterdam. The *Ceremonieboeken van de regeeren der stad Amsteldam*, for

---

75. For European usage, see David Kunzle, "World Upside Down: The Iconography of a European Broadsheet Type," in Barbara Babcock, ed., *The Reversible World: Symbolic Inversion in Art and Society* (Ithaca, 1978), 74; for the general rule of the *vroedschap*, *"cum plebe nil negotie est,"* see A. Th. Van Deursen, *Het Kopergeld van de Gouden Eeuw, III: Volk en Overheid* (Amsterdam, 1979), 190.

76. Ord. sess., February 27, 1655, CRB, 207.

example, detailed protocols for the election of municipal officials in Amsterdam. The recorder (*secretaris*) played a leading role, directing nomination procedures and recording the votes of outgoing magistrates in a vertical series of dots. The installation rites that followed were also liturgies with the recorder directing proceedings (see Figures 5.2 and 5.3). The outgoing *schepenen* stood among the presiding officers "near the end of the table on the east [sic] side of the schout" and all engaged in proceedings, which concluded with them being thanked "for their good services." Similar ceremonies gave the magistracy of Beverwijck its political power. In 1658, the recorder minuted that the presiding officers had met and voted for new magistrates. He listed the names and number of votes received by each of six burghers in vertical order:

Pieter Hartgers	7 votes
Francoys Boon	7 votes
Sander Leendertsz	7 votes
Willem Teller	5 votes
Jan Verbeeck	6 votes
Dirck Janse Croon	4 votes

At ceremonies installing three of these men, the outgoing magistrates summoned them and witnessed their oaths of office taken while standing. "After having been congratulated," they "took their seats," while the retiring men were "thanked for their good services."[77]

Such ceremonies made and remade a wholly satisfying political tradition. Even directives issued by Beverwijck's court provided a dramatization of its central role in describing order and virtue. It announced itself as acting "in order that everything may proceed in orderly fashion." It sent cases involving capital punishment to New Amsterdam, knowing that Stuyvesant would follow tradition and hear them "under the blue heaven" and in the presence of the commonalty. It surrounded its own judgments with rituals like ringing bells three times, casting criminals in irons, calling three "irreproachable witnesses," offering formulaic prayers, and making public declarations that crime "can not be tolerated in a country where justice prevails."[78] Particularly, the *schout*'s court per-

77. See "Ceremonieboek van Amsterdam. Afgeschriften van ceremonien voor de verkiezing van raden, schepenen, burgemeesters, keurmeesters, enz. van de door hen at te leggen eden, en betreffende enige rechtspraken – Handschrift van circa 1700," H 32.001, 8, GA; Ceremonieboek, H–30, 22, GA; Ord. sess., February 3, 1653, *CRB*, 106; 108.
78. Ord. sess., November 2, 1680, *CRA*, 44; see [Cornelis Melyn], *Broad Advice to the United Netherland Provinces (1649)*, CNYHS, 2nd ser. (New York, 1848), 3 (Part 1):265, and for a detailed account of rituals in criminal cases, see Katherine Fremantle, "The Open Vierschaar of Amsterdam's Seventeenth Century Town Hall as a Setting

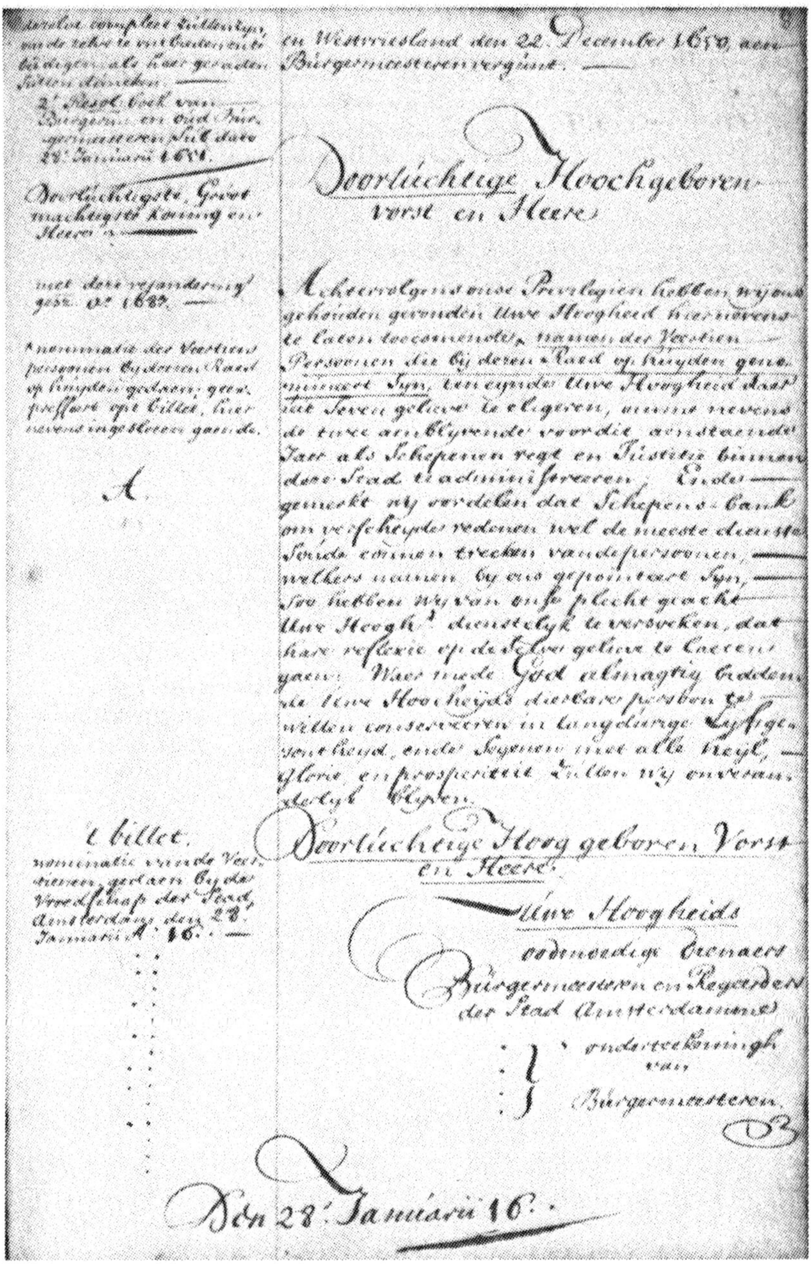
en Westvriesland den 22. December 1650 aen Burgermeesteren vergunt. —

2.e Resol. boek van Burgemeesteren en Oud Burgemeesteren sub dato 28. Januarii 1681.

Doorluchtigste, Grootmachtigste Koning en Heere

Doorluchtige Hoochgeboren Vorst en Heere

nominatie der Veertien persoonen by desen Raad op huyden gedaan; gepresenteert op billet, hier nevens ingesloten gaende.

Achtervolgende onse Privilegien hebben wij ons gehouden gevonden Uwe Hoogheid hiernevens te laten toecomen de namen der Veertien Personen die bij desen Raad op huyden genomineert zyn, ten eynde Uwe Hoogheid daar uit seven gelieve te eligeren, omme nevens de twee aenblyvende voor die aenstaende Jaar als Schepenen regt en Justitie binnen deze Stad te administreeren. Ende gemerkt wy oordelen dat Schepens-bank om verscheyde redenen wel de meeste dienst soude comen trecken van de persoonen, welkers namen by ons gepointeert zyn, soo hebben wy van onse plicht geacht Uwe Hoogh.t dienstelyk te versoeken, dat hare reflexie op deselve gelieve te laeten gaen. Waer mede God almagtig biddende de Uwe Hoocheyds dierbare persoon te willen conserveeren in langdurige Lyfsgesontheyd, ende Zegenen met alle heyl, glorie, en prosperiteit Sullen wy onveranderlyk blyven

A.

t billet. nominatie van de Veertienen, gedaen by de Vroedschap der Stadt Amsterdam den 28. Januarii A. 16..

Doorluchtige Hoog geboren Vorst en Heere

Uwe Hoogheids oodmoedige dienaers Burgermeesteren en Regeerders der Stad Amsterdamme

ondertekeningh van Burgermeesteren

Den 28. Januarii 16..

Figure 5.2. Extract from "Ceremonieboek van Amsterdam, schriften van ceremonien voor de verkiezing van raden, schepenen . . . Handschriften van ca. 1700." Courtesy of Gemeentearchief, Amsterdam.

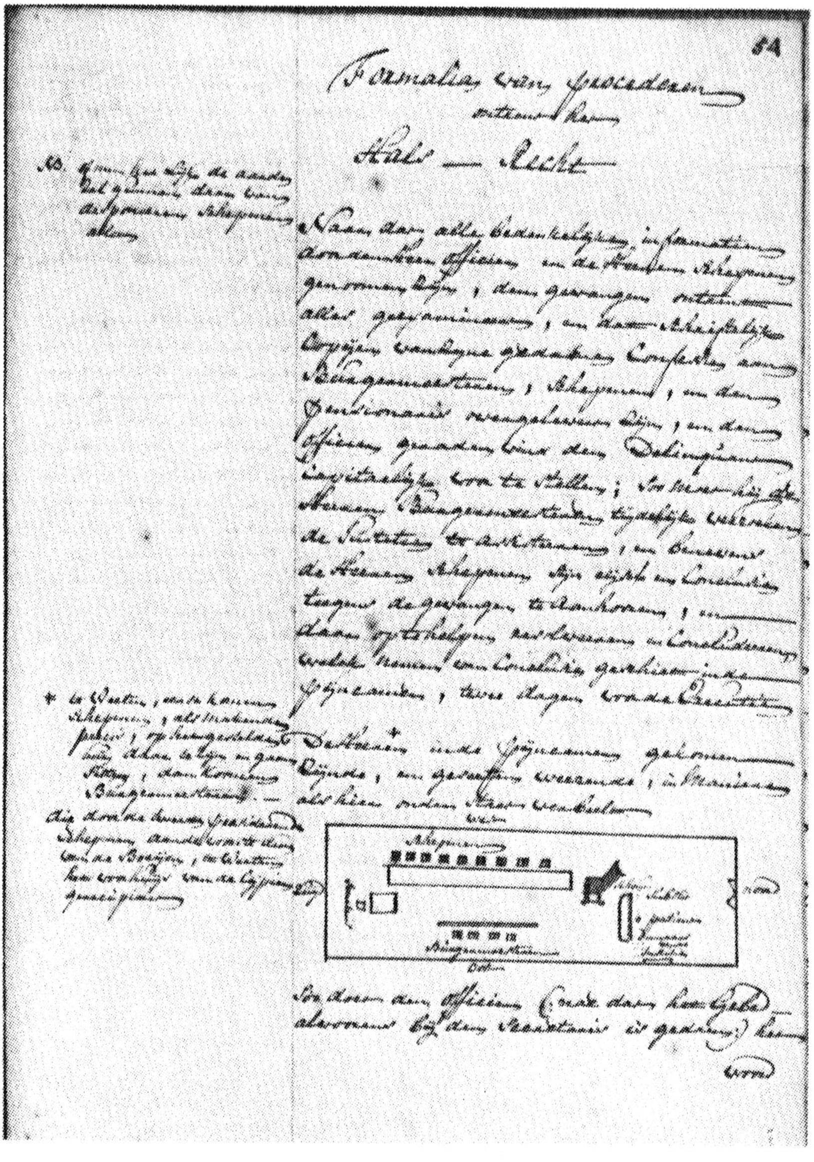

Formalia van procedeeren
ontrent het
Hals — Recht

Figure 5.3. Extract from "Ceremoniel Boek H 29." Courtesy of Gemeentearchief, Amsterdam.

formances organized the community's identification of itself as ethical. In criminal proceedings, he was superior to the magistrates, and his behavior notably shaped the outlines of law and order (Figure 5.3). His role was the immediate concern of Colve after his squadron captured New Netherland in 1673. Colve assumed that the ceremonial behavior he expected of the *schout* would be entirely understood. "Let him be present," Colve directed, "at all [judicial] meetings and preside," but should he act for himself, let him "rise from his seat and leave the Bench, and in that event he shall not have . . . a concluding vote, but the Oldest Schepen shall, then, preside in his place."[79]

These were elements of the Dutch political tradition that the English changed. Reorganization of the court of Beverwijck from 1665 to 1686 gradually cut away the ceremonial displays of municipality. An ordinance of 1665 limited court meetings and automatically left less to be seen of the town's busy affairs and the court's authority over them. Governors and military commanders felt free to sit as part of its membership. Jeremias van Rensselaer declared unequivocally that the proceedings of lawgiving were entirely altered. Meanwhile, townspeople were meant to be actors in court rituals they could not understand. Some individuals found difficulty with the English format of facing each other as accused and accuser. Others, who certainly knew what swearing an oath meant in the daily practices of Roman–Dutch law, required an explanation of "what an oath means" under English rubrics. Jurymen and local magistrates were uncertain of their roles.[80]

In 1675, Andros created a court consisting of the commander of the garrison and seven burghers. He installed Robert Livingston, a stranger, as secretary, although a burgher of longstanding residence and proven repute traditionally filled the position because his function was to advise the court in its decision making (Figure 5.3). Livingston took on the task, cooperating in some of the traditional ceremonies but acting for a court increasingly displaced as a center of the political order. Power now lay with officials of the county, that is, the justices of the peace, constables, and an increasingly intrusive provincial assembly. An Englishman acted

for the City's Justice," *Oud Holland: Driemaandelijks Tijdschrift voor Nederlandse Kunstgeschiedenis*, (Part 3/4, 1962), 77:206–34; Ord. sess., July 16, 1658, CRB, 137.

79. Fremantle, "Open Viershaar of Amsterdam," 215; "Colve's Charter to the Towns on Long Island" [Article 2], October 1, 1673, *DHNY*, 1:655–6.

80. Alterations, amendments and additions made in the laws, and confirmed at the general court of assizes held in the city of New York [1665], *Second Annual Report of the State Historian* (1897), 1:147, and see Peter Christoph, ed. *New York Historical Manuscripts: Dutch, Kingston Papers*, 2 volumes, eds., Kenneth Scott and Ken Stryker-Rodda, tr. *Dingman Versteeg* (Baltimore, 1976), 1:xiv; JvR to OvCortlandt, 12/22 September, 1665, *Corr JvR*, 382; Minutes of April 25, 1665, *RNA* 5:226; 226; Christoph, ed., *Kingston Papers*, 1:xiv.

as *schout* until his illness led to Livingston's appointment to that office as well. William Parker, a soldier, became court messenger. In 1678, the court met on twenty-five occasions. It enacted many of the customary practices, somehow managing to reinstate a Dutch man as *schout* and apparently citing Damhouder's *Practicke* when useful. Livingston kept the minutes of the court in a reasonably traditional manner. The format he adopted as well as his inclusion of detail and deployment of blocks of text and marginalia continued a form of recordation little changed from earlier times. The minutes recorded a court almost picaresque in its practice of applying the law without calling upon precedent. They displayed a court that suppressed open hostility out of its own curious quietism, asking honorable behavior because its own honor was "a tender plant" and receiving, from its own records, substantial evidence that at least some of the "formalia" proper to a Dutch town were still in force.[81]

However, the city charter continued to change the style of municipal administration. In 1686, the recorder inscribed a moment of his own confusion about the city's status. He first described Albany as existing "under ye Subjection of his most sacred majesty James." He then crossed out "Subjection" and superscribed "jurisdiction." It was an important uncertainty, for being under the jurisdiction of the crown – or within its jurisdiction – did nothing to contradict the fundamental independence of a chartered city. Being under subjection did. A subjugated or dependent city – which was in fact what the English envisaged – introduced the need for new ceremonies that would, of course, drive out earlier ones and yet would lack authenticity until the structure of authority they displayed was understood and accepted. The degree to which townspeople concerned themselves with participation in court rituals under the charter is difficult to judge. We do know that, in the first weeks of its existence, some of the officials appointed by Dongan failed to attend sessions regularly.[82] The office of "marshall" was now created and given to an English soldier – perhaps townspeople were able to make some sense of the new office because the man appointed had been court messenger. Other changes in practice have been referred to previously. They were all small marks of the existence of two traditions. When Milbourne arrived in Albany, his first pledge was to rid the burghers of the city charter. No one, as far as the records tell us, was able to respond cogently

81. Ord. sess., November 6, 1677, *CRA*, 283; Ex. sess., January 2, 1677/8, *CRA*, 287–380; for the court's use of Damhouder's *Practijcke*, see *CRA*, 147; Minutes of January 3, *RNA*, 4:1.
82. City of Albany Court Minutes, 1686–1702, Vol. 4 Entry for August 31, 1686, Albany County Hall of Records; Arthur James Weise, *History of the City of Albany, New York, from the Discovery of the Great River in 1524, by Verrazzano to the Present Time* (Albany, 1884), 204.

to that challenge or to say why the charter was in dispute. Nor was it all articulated later. Insofar as the charter was a metaphor for the whole reordering of their political world, that is not surprising.

Wesselsz was writing up political history in this context. His minutes, like the contest between the *conventie* and men like Staats, were marks of the unfamiliar country that political structures and political sentiments had moved into. Even the *conventie* had to search for its identity, variously calling itself "a Convention of yᵉ Maijor, Aldermen, Commonality and Military officers of yᵉ Citty of Albanij and Justices and Military officers of yᵉ Said Countij," a "Meeting of there Mayᵉˢ Justices of yᵉ Peace of yᵉ City and County of Albany," and "the Convention of Albny." Wesselsz had to find a phrase for a political confrontation with the scope and visibility that Dutch practice would have avoided at all costs: He discovered "the world turned upside downe." The phrase was first used by the *conventie* in conjunction with "strange rumors" that had come from New York City. In my judgment, it was a biblical phrase that had become part of New York City's vocabulary for understanding what was identified there by English and Anglicized Dutch residents as a revolutionary situation. It was probably carried to Albany by Bayard, who had fled Leisler's supporters and spent the summer and autumn in Albany, where he had doubtless attended *conventie* meetings.[83] Robert Livingston, who had numerous English and Dutch associates in New York City, offered the phrase to governor Sloughter as an easy way of understanding Albany politics. It was an image widely used in English political debate and, among royalists like himself, referred to the subversion of divinely bestowed authority by illiterate commoners. Leisler, he wrote, was interfering in Albany, seeking to "establish his Powere here and turn all upside down." The *conventie* used the words to gather support for denying entry to Milbourne. It had heard strange rumors and therefore needed assurances that "they [the New York soldiers sent by Leisler] had come with a good intent to assist us as neighbours, and to obey the Convention, and not turn yᵉ government of yᵉ Citty upside down." Five days later, Wesselsz "assumed yᵉ Discourse" for the cowering *conventie*

83. See "Att a Convention of the Mayor, Aldermen, Commonality and Military Officers of the Citty of Albanie and Justices and Military Officers of the said County," January 11, 1689–90, and "At a Meeting of their Majes Justices of ye Peace of ye Citty and County of Albany," January 12, 1689–90, *DHNY*, 2:144, 148; "Proposealls," November 5, 1689, *DHNY*, 2:109; in "A Letter from a Gentleman of the City of New York to Another. Concerning the Trouble which happened in that Province in the time of the late Happy Revolution... 1698," Nicholas Bayard reviewed the affairs of April 1689 in New York City and stated that the council members and city officials first gathered "stiled by the name of the *General Convention for the Province of New York*" (his italics) (*DHNY*, 2:427). He stayed in Albany "all summer" (429).

and answered the second of Milbourne's orations. If he had a political tradition alive enough to offer its own language, he did not call upon it. He reached for the phrase he thought would carry his argument: If Milbourne were accepted, "all authority" would be "turned upside down."[84]

Other elements in Wesselsz's records also jarred with the customary form of minutes. He often cut back on description of everyday detail. In its place were paragraphs like those in Ratcliffe's *Particular Account of the Late Revolution*. Wesselsz was no longer describing but searching out meaning behind events and creating a space for interpretation. His memorandum of November 10, for example, minuted letters received by the *conventie*, and his translations of them were uncharacteristically bracketed by three ideological paragraphs. Having inscribed one letter, he directed how it was to be read. "By which letter," he interpreted, "it is Plainly Evident ye s^d Milbourne Designs ye Subversion of ye Governm^t . . . [and should circumstances allow] would undoubtedly undertake Some Dangerous Design." This didacticism as well as his rhetoric drawing attention to men as conspirators was out of character with traditional record keeping. It hardened description into definition. Bayard's synthesis of Leisler's supporters as members of a Dutch plot had done the same.[85]

The contrast made by the newer Anglicizing style can be seen in another letter that was written to Milbourne by Adam Vrooman, the young man who once went to Springfield to learn husbandry and was now a prominent Schenectady resident. Milbourne had hoped Vrooman would take a leading role against Schuyler. In it, however, Vrooman took the traditionally recessive political stance. "Mr. Jacob Milbourne," it read. "I have just now received your letter. Firstly, I am not a person of quality; Secondly, the Indians lie in divers squads in and around the place and should we all repair to Albany [to vote against Schuyler] great disquiet would arise among the Savages to the general ruin of this Country." He then identified himself again as one who was not only dismissible as a political actor, but unconcerned about political affairs. Therefore, "please excuse me," he concluded, "as I am a person of no power nor authority." The stance was proper Dutch politics. In writing, "I am not a person of quality," perhaps Vrooman was taking measure of his social status and acting accordingly, that is, following the rule *"Het volk sijn stil"* (The ordinary people should be silent).[86] Perhaps this motivated him rather

84. Draft of a letter, Livingston to Sloughter, January 20, 1689–90 [addressed on outside, Copy: Letter of ye Convention to Col. Slater, when he comes] NYSA, "Proposealls," November 5, 1689, *DHNY*, 2:110; Convention sess, November 10, 1689, *DHNY*, 2:121.
85. Convention sess., November [9?], 1689 *DHNY*, 2:117 (see also 178); "A Memoriall of What Has Occurred in Their Maties Province of New York . . . [n.d.]," *DHNY*, 2:34.
86. Vrooman to Milbourne [n.d., ca. November 10, 1689], *DHNY*, 2:117; Van Deursen, *Het kopergeld*, 3:48.

than fear of taking an exposed role in politics. In either case, the posture was predictable.

Johannes Wendell repeated Vrooman's performance two months later, in January 1690. Asked to offer an opinion on the legality of Leisler's commission to Staats, the Albany trader insisted that "his understanding cannot Comprehend" whether Leisler was "luytenant Governeur" or "Commandeur an Chef" and he would say nothing more. It was typical of the concealment that persisted as a characteristic of Dutch political behavior well into the eighteenth century. In 1708, an observer described the useless efforts of a New York gentleman of English descent to arouse the Dutch people of Bergen County to rebel against authority. The residents professed that "they did not understand oversetting of Government and pulling Magistrates, Judges, and Justices from the Bench: It was a werke they had no liking to; and so closed their Resolutions among themselves." At almost the same time, Robert Hunter, who was governor from 1710 to 1719, grasped something of this political culture in *Androborus*, his satirical play set in New York. "*Dat week ick niet*" (That I don't know) were the words he put in the mouth of Cobus, a Dutch man asked to state his opinion on a set of resolutions.[87] It was Hunter's metaphor for Dutch political culture or, rather, its remnants.

Structurally, both Vrooman's letter and Wesselsz's didactic paragraphs were intrusions in the memorandum. Yet of the two, the Schenectady trader's was truer to the rules of earlier political behavior and was in fact true to much of what Wesselsz was doing elsewhere in the records; for the recorder's stirring emotional passages were cargo – an incongruous import from an alien culture. His willingness to intensify political confrontation by defining adversaries and suggesting conspiracies, his definition of the burghers as men of the county, his departures from transcription to interpretation – all were cargo as well. They were devices by which Englishmen managed political power. Yet they were cargo in Albany because their meanings and values were still being awkwardly incorporated into traditional understandings about the management of power. "All authority turned Upside Doune" was an unsuitable generalization not because authority was secure in 1690 and 1691, but because drawing attention to authority and inspecting its boundaries was unsuitable. Wesselesz's records generally followed that Dutch intuition. For the most part, they hid the kind of authority the *conventie* meant to exercise. The minutes gave no hint of how it was first conceived or of its specific plans. They left no account of how the *conventie* worked with

87. Convention sess., January 12, 1689/90, *DHNY*, 2:148; Ruth M. Keasey, "Rivers and Roads in Old Bergen County; I," *de halve maen* (1964), 39:9; Lawrence H. Leder, "Robert Hunter's Androborus," *Bulletin of the New York Public Library* (New York, 1964), 68:168. "Cobus" is Jacobus van Cortlandt (1658–1739).

the city court or with the commissioners set up by Leisler in 1690; they left no account of how it went out of existence. Wesselsz would have been pleased that his minutes are difficult to find today, forming as they do part of a volume labeled *Mortgage Book 4*. To the end, he evaded the chance to map out what was really happening in Albany. Yet his evasions were not made in bad faith. His moments of trying to understand Albany, as power in the city and county were being inverted, were genuine. Like the *conventie* itself, they represented the process by which English meanings of the land were being collected and taken on.

Leisler considered Wesselsz "a mistery to many" and a "recorder in Albany in noe quality for that office." Particularly, he detested him as being a sycophant who had obtained land from Dongan "40 mi [north] from Albany toward the French to build a fort upon his land." The land in question was the Saratoga grant mentioned earlier. For Dongan it marked the northernmost boundary of the county and needed to be occupied by at least a token force of men. So the *quid pro quo* for commissioning it to Wesselsz and others was the same payback that English authorities had exacted of vassals placed along the crown's northern borders with the highland Scots. The recipients were expected to guard the frontier. Leisler's information was that Wesselsz had played his part, sending "12 men to guard it" in 1689. Dutch men forced to act as soldiers on lands north of Albany in the late seventeenth century was not uncommon.[88] It was only one of the costs of clientage that men like Wesselsz would have been socialized into paying most of their adult lives. Ironically, he was one of the merchants with a keen eye for trade routes and native customers as distant as Lake Oswego. Yet he was paying men to be stationary, to secure not a trade route but borderlands. This was a militarization of the land that we must now consider.

88. Leisler to Governor of Boston, October 22, 1689, *DHNY*, 2:38; 38.

6

A Military Presence on the Land,
1690–1710

The English authorities coped with events in New York from 1690 to
1710 within an image of themselves as men of empire in an outpost
fashioned to drive the French from North America. Their configuration
of the land was as a theater of war: Correct conjunctures were those
made between fortifications and towns, natives' castles and commissaries,
military highways and hospitals, parade grounds and barracks. A steady
increase of field maps, coastal surveys, military patents, and drawings of
installations affirmed this order iconographically. There was, in other
words, a martial poetics of space. And within that structure of properly
related parts, always beyond interrogation's reach, the Dutch inhabitants
of Albany went about possessing the land.

The military establishment that ruled New York from the end of Leisler's Rebellion until the end of Queen Anne's War was made up of players
in a conflict in which military strategies were essential, but the transformation of the native populations was not a necessary goal. English commanders meant to civilize the Dutch to the ways of carrying weapons,
building redoubts, managing transport, sustaining trading alliances, and
quartering soldiers – in short, arranging themselves for service. At the
same time, however, the officers were the strangers (or enemies) that
manuals of discipline required: They followed the codes that institutionalized the physical and psychological distance between themselves and
the civilians.[1] All-male, mobile, and trained to inflict violence, they lived
out their design for a place apart in time and space. None of them felt
obliged by the articles of war to transform Dutch men and women into
English men and women; rather, civilians were implicitly described as
the objects of a surveillance operation.

Famine, disease, population dislocation, and decline were all outcomes
of war felt in Albany. It had epistemological consequences as well. In-

1. See J. A. Houlding, *Fit for Service: The Training of the British Army, 1715–1795*
(Oxford, 1981). For articles of war regulating Dutch soldiers in the Low Countries, see
Barry Harold Nickle, The Military Reforms of Prince Maurice of Orange (Ph.D. diss.,
University of Delaware, 1975), appendixes.

dividuals were unavoidably constrained to alter their knowledge of themselves as the military imposed its meanings on buildings and land, on
memory and self-identity. In the 1690s, military commanders made the
stadhuis part of a tactical headquarters for campaigns, and the land
between the south boundary of the city and Normanskil became a militia
district. These and other meanings edged into those already assigned by
the Dutch. The measure of the military's power was the quotient of them
they could enforce.

Had English families arrived in considerable numbers in Albany, they
might have effected a far-reaching transformation of Dutch culture by
contesting the full range of traditional Dutch meanings for child, house,
death, privacy, trading, self. As it happened, Albany's residents were
confronted by English culture exclusively in the form of commanders
and troopers of England's "garrison government."[2] English families did
not accompany the garrisons or follow immediately in their wake. In
addition, the martial imagery, which imposed meaning on other aspects
of English overseas imperialism in New York, was contradictory to the
Dutch. English culture was litter on the land – and a littered cultural
landscape is still what most American historians see when they look at
this period of colonial New York's history.

A Military Landscape: English Images

The military administration that governed Albany from 1690 to 1710
was a venal and violent edition of seventeenth- and early-eighteenth-
century English culture. Englishmen of this age were a violent people,
with recourse to arms considered a routine and, indeed, honorable pur-
suit.[3] British North Americans constituted themselves easily into the
armed yeoman militias that had been the kingdom's traditional military
system. Although New England men were trained to defend towns set
up as military bases ("strategic villages") with meetinghouses doubling
as "garrison houses," the eligible males were essentially an armed yeo-
manry organized as an offensive force, expected by provincial and local

2. The term is Stephen S. Webb's in *The Governors-General: The English Army and the
Definition of the Empire, 1569–1681* (Chapel Hill, N.C., 1979). For an extensive review
of Webb's interpretation and related issues, see Richard R. Johnson, "The Imperial
Webb: The Thesis of Garrison Government in Early America Considered," *William and
Mary Quarterly*, 3rd ser. (1986) 23:513.
3. Lois G. Schwoerer, *No Standing Army: The Antiarmy Ideology in Seventeenth-Century
England* (Baltimore, 1974) 17; see also John Brewer and John Styles, eds., *An Ungov-
ernable People: The English and Their Law in the Seventeenth Century and Eighteenth
Century* (London, 1980).

officers to "seeke out and molest" the enemy or "sweep the valley clear." In Virginia in 1676, Nathaniel Bacon could imagine one thousand fighting men raiding and plundering native settlements, ranging as patrols between the forts on the Virginia frontier.[4] He, like the others, could imagine the annihilation of the natives – could accept it – because in a prior way he could entertain the image of himself as warrior.

Even in times of peace in New England and Virginia, local and provincial magistrates or gentry were pleased to wear military titles, regularly mustering the "troope of foote" or parading "troops of horse." In Massachusetts, one-third of the gentlemen of the General Court had used military titles since 1634; its military force was supremely well organized by 1690, having modeled itself on Cromwell's New Model Army. The province organized its soldiers under a major general. His local militias were known as forces or regiments and could be filled up by impressment. Three majors were authorized to conduct such impressments as well as quarter soldiers if required. The image is unequivocal: Massachusetts could summon "an army," and when it was "on foote" under the major general's council of war, civilian society ceased in the face of the state.[5]

In New York, the vision of a province brought to the service of military men sent to defeat the French in Canada gave a succession of army commanders – Benjamin Fletcher, Richard Coote, Edward Hyde, and Robert Hunter – their jobs. It also gave them opportunities to fleece their soldiers, rob the king's treasury, and skim the top off taxes. The governors-general pared governance down to their own style of military rule. They surrounded themselves with "a military pomp that no other colonial governors received," commanding a drum roll on entering and leaving the fort, introducing military parades in the city, and allowing the captains stationed at Albany to behave, as one English soldier put it in 1716, as "lords of the frontier."[6]

Unlike New England and Virginia, the military government of New

4. John Shy, *A People Numerous and Armed: Reflections on the Military Struggle for American Independence* (London, 1976), 28; 26; for military activities on the provincial level, see Nathaniel B. Shurtleff, ed., *Records of the Governor and Company of the Massachusetts Bay in New England* (Boston, 1854), 5:95, and Joseph H. Smith ed., *Colonial Justice in Western Massachusetts (1639–1702): The Pynchon Court Record, An Original Judge's Diary* (Cambridge, Mass., 1961) 40; Shy, *People Numerous and Armed,* 25.

5. Timothy H. Breen, *Puritans and Adventurers: Change and Persistence in Early America* (New York, 1980), 39, 28, 38; Report to the King, May 16, 1665, *Records of Massachusetts Bay,* 4(Part 2):203, and see 28, 253.

6. Stanley McCrary Pargellis, "The Four Independent Companies of New York," in *Essays in Colonial History Presented to Charles McLean Andrews by His Students* (New York, 1966), 117; James Grant Wilson, ed., *The Memorial History of the Colony of New York from Its First Settlement to the Year, 1892* (New York, 1893) 4:209; Pargellis, *Four Independent Companies,* 119.

York operated above the heads of the populace, beyond its reach. Law was a mixture of courts-martial exercised under the articles of war, royalist codes, and feudal enactments that continually imperiled soldiers and civilians alike. In a fit of anger in 1699, Coote blustered that "those are only to be acknowledged Englishmen that live in obedience to the laws of England."[7] Yet it is doubtful that he himself knew the alleged legal system of the province. The collection of provincial laws he sent to his superiors as complete was, they found, "not so perfect as it ought to be: not only some of the Acts seeme to be misplaced, in respect to the order of time in which they were past, but there are also...leaves [that is, pages] wanting, which breake [*sic*] the sence."[8]

English law as practiced at home was nonexistent in New York. In England, systematization of the courts' jurisdiction meant sanctions that were predictable to citizens. That was not so in New York. A case requiring court-martial proceedings might be transferred to local authorities simply because the military governor found it too tedious. On the other hand, citizens might be called upon to make up a jury in the case of the murder of a soldier by natives. Local field officers could be empowered to issue warrants of arrest. Civilians acting as quartermasters could withdraw a citizen's trading rights, acting upon the power of the governor.[9] The right of Englishmen to security in their property and therefore freedom from quartering was a "cause" to be pleaded by Albany's Dutch residents. As the Albany magistrates put it with reference to one case, we "have no power...because the law gives no positive direction."[10]

Arbitrary and threatening, the military establishment had rejected the legitimacy of Dutch law (and native tribal law) but only pretended to be legitimate on its own whim. It was a system energized, in large part, by ill-concealed styles of lawbreaking. Law was not enacted to validate the ethics of a ruling class nor to integrate citizens into a society that deserved

---

7. Bellomont to Lords of Trade, April 27, 1699, *DRCH*, 4:508. For critical evaluations of the British military administration in New York, see Pargellis. *Four Independent Companies*, 96, 107, 122, and Stanley McCraery Pargellis, ed., *Military Affairs in North America, 1748–1765: Selected Documents from the Cumberland Papers in Windsor Castle* (New York, 1936), William A. Foote, The American Independent Companies of the British Army, 1664–1764 (Ph.D. diss., University of California, 1966), John Childs, *The Army of Charles II* (London, 1976), Frederick B. Wiener, *Civilians under Military Jurisdiction: The British Practice since 1689, Especially in North America* (Chicago, 1967).
8. Lords of Trade to Bellomont, January 5, 1699, *DRCH*, 4:456.
9. Ex. sess., May 16, 1678 (Council of New York, Minutes, May 23, 1678), *CRA*, 326–8; Ord. sess., August 6, 1678, *CRA*, 343 and 337.
10. "Memorial to Earl of Loudoun...1757," No. 13886, NYSA; the City Records, February 25, 1695/96, in *AA* (1852) 3:12.

the subordination of individual consciences for the common good. Dutch and English residents knew this at the time and knew their own venality and shabbiness as well. No one contradicted a contemporary Dutch minister who wrote of "our own great sins," of "public morals . . . greatly corrupted," and new modes of criminality. He was putting in shorthand a broad awareness of faction, moral lassitude, and pervasive dishonor.[11]

Whatever their other appetites for gain, Netherlanders were not hungry for land or the soldiery that would hold it.[12] Soldiers meant war, and war was a metaphor for insecurity. Jeremias van Rensselaer's brother had put it pragmatically as "one country turning against another, [so] they ruin each other." In his own home province of Gelderland, the court was keeping a record of soldiers (and sailors) wandering across the land as solitary figures or in bands, stealing, molesting children, murdering, rioting, and provoking the citizenry to violence. Even English soldiers appeared before the court – one in a band of five thieves, another stealing animals with two Dutch soldiers, another paired with a Dutch soldier and robbing farmers. War spread their names across the records for a space of forty years after 1594.[13] The presence of a large army for one week in the average farming district of northwestern Europe meant a village forced below the subsistence level; a longer stay meant "the total elimination of agricultural production for an entire year." It meant towns relying on translocal markets and higher prices for goods, accepting structural disruption to trade, and collecting crippling taxes to pay off mercenary armies, whether Spanish, French, German, or Dutch.[14]

Remaking the Land by War

The period 1690 to 1710 was a time of war in Albany. The liturgies of armed combat were most fully expressed from 1689 to 1697 and again from 1702 to 1714, when England and France were officially at war,

11. Domini Henricus Selyns to Classis of Amsterdam, September 30, 1696, in Hugh Hastings, ed., *Ecclesiastical Records; State of New York* (Albany, 1901), 2:1173, and Classis to Selyns, June 10, 1697, Hastings, ed., *Ecclesiastical Records*, 2:1184.
12. Herbert Rowen, *John de Witt: Grand Pensionary of Holland, 1625–1672* (Princeton, 1978), 827: for Amsterdam's policy regarding a peaceful border with Maryland, see "Gerrit Van Sweeringen's Account of the settling of the Dutch and Swedes at the Delaware, May 12,1684," *DRCH*, 3:345.
13. RvR to JvR, March 19, 1657, *Corr JvR*, 44; Archief van het Hof Criminele Processen, 1600–1629. M.S. Inventaris No. 7–E1, entries for May 13, 1626 and November 24, 1624. RG.
14. Myron Peter Gutmann, War and Rural Life in the Seventeenth Century: The Case of the Basse-Meuse (Ph.D. diss., Princeton University, 1976), 81; see Christopher Frederichs, *Urban Society in an Age of War: Nordlingen, 1580–1720* (Princeton, 1979), 158.

contesting one another's occupancy of North America. Then, for example, the commanders' ideal of having three full armies of regulars at Albany came closest to actuality. But even between 1697 and 1702, the land resembled war-ravaged Gelderland, with soldiers yet to be discharged and "ye People being so wearly of them."[15] Certainly the townspeople understood the devastation consequent upon war. The military commander would interdict grain leaving the city, arrest townspeople absconding from the city to support a family elsewhere, extort insupportable taxes, and quarter soldiers who would in turn burgle homes and bring disease like smallpox. Men would live with the expectation that a farm's value would be "notably diminished" by "war, fire or otherwise." People would desert the region in large numbers; the court would be supplicated to help support the illegitimate children of English soldiers; the rich would become richer and the poor poorer.[16]

All of this occurred in Albany, as it did in comparable regions of the Low Countries.[17] The burghers may even have had a pictorial image. For example, in 1710, Robert Livingston recorded the arrival of an issue of *'t Mercurius* he had ordered. It was a *courant* known by Jeremias van Rensselaer and valued by merchants like himself and Livingston because it familiarized them with movements in overseas trade. Its depictions of war were unsparingly graphic, depicting civilians as grotesques. In wartime, people were debased or debased themselves. All looked criminal. The Albany Dutch said it of themselves after ten years of war: Even the outbreak of smallpox in 1702 was "less punishment than . . . we have deserved."[18]

In Albany, the land was a text for understanding both the military purposes of the English administration of New York and the degree of

---

15. Rev. Joseph Hooper, *A History of St. Peter's Church in the City of Albany* (Albany, 1900), 48; City Records, May 9, 1697–98, *AA*, 3:33.
16. N. Anthony [Kingston] to Johannes deBruyn, Johannes Provos (*sic*), and Jacob Millborne (*sic*) [Albany], April 11, 1690, *DHNY*, 2:131, 132; for extortion in Europe, see petition to Imperial Diet (1721), quoted in Frederichs, *Urban Society in an Age of War*, 168; Deposition of Carsten Fredericksz and wife regarding burglary committed by Philip Brown, soldier, 1667, in Livingston Papers, Folder 3, W10031, Group A1–6 [A8], NYSA; City Records, August 29 and September 2, 1702, *AA*, 4:160.
17. See note 16 this chapter and also, Will of Marte Gerritse (1691), in Arthur B. Gregg, *Old Hellebergh: Historical Sketches of the West Manor of Rensselaerswyck, Including an Account of the Anti-Rent Wars, the Glass House and Henry R. Schoolcraft* (New York, 1975 reprint), 79; City Records, September 30, 1696, and December 3, 1695, *AA*, 3:15, 10.
18. Copy of account on Robert Livingston from Amsterdam, Robert Livingston: General Correspondence, 1667–1728. *L-RP*. The bill is made out to Willem Van Nuijs, Amsterdam, August, 1711; for David Schuyler's insistence to Montreal officials that the Albany Dutch were aware of European affairs, see City Records, May 5, 1701, *AA*, 4:129; City Records, Proclamation, September 2, 1702, *AA*, 4:160.

townspeople's collaboration in those goals. There were landmarks and locales where the English presence was fixed. But it is better to see it as mobile, moving through the city and its surrounds, touching all buildings and roads, the strand, the river, and the *plein*. It wound into the woods across the Hudson River, where three soldiers molested a young girl; it crept along the strand, where soldiers and a resident fought over firewood; it moved into the blockhouses, where members of the burgerguard fought repeatedly with regulars, communicating without a common language but in a gestural repertoire of both good humor and contempt; it moved to Livingston's manor where soldiers were employed to repair his stone house.[19] It moved wherever the soldiers went as carters, watchmen, gatekeepers, customs collectors, gaugers, traders, constables, sheriffs. Military ordinances carried war into all homes. In 1704, twenty-four householders had to quarter soldiers but only after citizens in about 200 houses had drawn lots. At any time, a householder might find his house on a "Forfitt Lyst." Pieter Vosburgh's house was hired for Governor Benjamin Fletcher's use from November 1695 to March 1697; James Parker's was sequestered for three years against his continual protest. Another was taken for the use of two lieutenants and their wives. There was not, in other words, the isolation of civilians from armies that military reorganization brought to Europe in the course of the eighteenth century. Commanders in New York ordered civilians into military service. Whenever the troop of horse was incomplete as a result of death or desertion, the governor-general might fill it from a list "of the principal inhabitants and gentlemen of the city." In 1693, 359 men trained for the militia.[20]

War entered public buildings as well. It became the consuming business of the court, further eroding its stature. "Red coats" entered the *stadhuis* as parties to suits involving paternity, property, debt, and assault. John Collins, appointed by Hyde as sheriff of the county, acted as lawyer in one such case and, like Livingston before him, humiliated the court as to its ignorance of English jurisprudence. Some soldiers were well known – Stuart, Barritt, MacGregory, Weems, Fyne, Hogan. By 1710, they and

19. City Records, August 15, 1701, *AA*, 4:139; Ord. sess., April 3, 1677, *CRA*, 218; Fred Ellis, June 9, 1687, and R. Shaw, March, 1688, *L-RP*, Reel 1; "Memoriael van d'Incidente Onkosten Int' Repareeren van mijn huijs begonnen den 8 Decr 1683," *L-RP*.
20. For the estimated two hundred houses, see Victor Hugo Paltsits, ed., *New York Considered and Improved, 1695 by John Miller* (Cleveland, 1903), 72; City Records, November 21, 1704, *AA*, 4:197; City Records, November 15, 1695, *AA*, 3:9; City Records, July 17, 1697, *AA*, 3:23; City Records, December 5, 1704, *AA*, 4:198; City Records, November 15, 1700, *AA*, 4:120; Synopsis of the principal acts relating to Albany ... 1691 to 1713, *AA*, 4:203; Arthur James Weise, *The History of the City of Albany, New York, from the Discovery of the Great River in 1524, by Verrazzano to the Present Time* (Albany, 1884), 254.

others were the minor public officers of the city. And a few were in-marriers. But most — and the garrison numbered between thirty and fifty except when large offensives were in train, and then the number could be 8,000 — were transients. The three troopers who molested Maria Gerritsz across the river were the strangers that the manuals of discipline wanted: She knew the men "by sight" but not "by name."[21]

For the burghers, the fort signified the English presence as no other building did. In fact, they identified as English the crest of the hill where it stood. They called it the "fort hill." Residents seem to have carefully measured out any contact with the fort. They approached it as strangers, furnishing firewood at a price and bringing visitors to the non-Dutch-speaking commandant, as to a foreigner. Their bills to commanders for necessary repairs were the notes of distanced clients. They showed themselves so disaffected about it that one army engineer concluded he would have to "explore everything [about the reconstruction of the fort] myself."[22] Governor Edmund Andros had planned the fortress to "defend and command the whole town of Albany." If he was proposing the fort as a guard post covering a resentful populace, he was exercising a view taken by his successor, Thomas Dongan. The province needed, advised Dongan, several new forts because "the people [are] growing every day more numerous and they [are] generally of a turbulent disposition."[23] By 1713, use of the vital road to Schenectady meant passing the southern angle of the structure, now named Fort Anne.

The fort was also a purposefully arranged pile of stone, pine palings, and armory that stood for England's frontier line against the French. Again and again, Fort Albany was a metaphor for England's entire war effort in northeastern North America. In the eighteenth century, there were other English forts, some that were meant to hang like "thunder-clouds" over Canada. But no "key outpost" or "frontier town" was so continuously hammered into being by official discourse as Albany.[24] How the Dutch burghers imagined the territorial nature of the frontier is difficult to know. The English governors' mental map of the frontier is

21. City Records, October 6, 1696, *AA*, 3:17, and entries for February 8, 1720/1, and October, 1722, in Minutes of Court of Sessions, 1717–1723, City and County of Albany, County Clerk's Office, Albany, non. pag.; City Records, May 25, 1703; *AA*, 4:178; City Records, August 15, 1701, *AA*, 4:139.

22. City Records, November 29, 1699, *AA*, 4:101; Jasper Danckaerts (1679–1680), as quoted in Weise, *History of the City of Albany*, 175; Ord. sess., August 24, 1675, *CRA*, 12, 17; Römer to Bellomont, June 13, 1698, *DRCH*, 4:330.

23. Weise, *History of the City of Albany*, 164; "Dongan's Report to the Committee of Trade on the Province of New-York," February 22, 1687, *DHNY*, 1:150.

24. Gov. William Shirley to Lord Halifax, August 20, 1754, as quoted in Pargellis, *Military Affairs*, 23; for the other terms, see Loudoun to Cumberland, August 20, 1756, in Pargellis, *Military Affairs*, 228; City Records, 1753, *CHA*, 1:82.

clearer. Though always changing in some particulars, it was a wilderness where the enforcement of political power rested on the presence of less than a half-dozen English and French forts and a string of tribal castles. The map was set down in scores of official and personal papers and could be pieced together from them. However, the vision was caught with direct and dramatic clarity in the maps and sketches of Colonel Wolfgang William Römer, an engineer and surveyor of the English army under Richard Coote.

The Field: Military Mapping of the Land

To recall Colonel Römer reminds us that military organizations must have maps. They must put a topography under their gaze, under a scrutiny that will exercise its power over the meaning of the land even as it records it. And so it happened with Albany in the eighty years from 1690 to 1770. The iconographical archive depicting the city during that time was entirely a military one. With one exception, it was a portfolio of maps executed by English army personnel and exclusively available to military men and their superiors.[25] The collection was their property, eventually filed among other imperial paraphernalia and now stamped "Her Majesty's State Papers Office" or "British Museum" or "Found in the Records ... of Military Patents (M.P.)."

Römer gave Coote two, and possibly three or more, maps necessary for the conquest of Canada. His "Plan de la Ville d'Albanie dans la Province de la Nouvelle Yorck en Amerique" (1698) may have been the first meticulously executed plan of the city put into the hands of an English administrator (see Figure 2.4). He gave a topographical view of the settlement. His plan of the city of Albany was scarcely comparable to bird's-eye views of European cities drawn earlier in the century. Rather, it was a skillful sketch of a fortified site on a wide terrain of high hills, rivers, cleared agricultural land, and roads. His attention to the cliffs rising behind the fort was an obvious way of conveying a worry expressed elsewhere about the fort's "very irregular and difficult... situation."[26] He made no attempt to show private houses or built up areas of the city.

25. Maps of John Miller, Wolfgang Römer, William Brazier, and Francis Pfister and maps executed for Abercrombie and the Duke of Gloucester in 1758 and 1763. The known exception was that of Robert Yates in 1770.
26. See illustrations in Chapters 3 and 6, and for a plan of Schenectady's fortifications dated about 1698, which may have been executed by Römer as well, see Map Collection (74744 [1698?] cop. 1) NYSA; for his request that Römer examine Albany's fortification, see Bellomont to Lords of Trade, May 8,1698, *DRCH*, 4:305, and Instructions of Bellomont to Römer, May 17, 1698, *DRCH*, 4:328; Römer to Bellomont, May 27, 1698 *DRCH*, 4:329.

Römer was the first of a succession of engineers to put on paper the army's classification of notable landmarks. Invariably they were itemized in a key, and invariably the "King's Fort" appeared first.

Coote admired Römer's work and commissioned him to map the frontier between the English and French. In the map that resulted, Römer Europeanized a large region of the interior north and west of Albany. He inhabited it with the fauna Europeans expected in Nearctic landscapes, the fox and beaver, even the turkey.[27] He selected as icons for large settlements – Albany and La Gallette – those used by Kiliaen van Rensselaer's draftsman in 1633 and Simon Metcalfe in a map of Albany land patented to Barent Pietersen Coeymans in 1770. Using French words for rivers and lakes he seemed to give most of the wilderness over to the French. He mapped Corlars-Lack (Lake Champlain), and Lac des Sacrament. Cadragqua (Lake Ontario) dominated his sketch perhaps because its control by the French was then dominating the anxieties of the English governor. He located Fort Frontenac on Cadragqua Lake and inspected to within ten miles of a point south of the lake where Fort Oswego would one day satisfy Coote's desire for a fort near the lakes. He delivered the remainder of the charted wilderness to the native tribes, sketching miniature castles to signify their indisputable dominion in this world without boundaries.

Engineers like Römer were the men professionally concerned for strategic installations on the terrain. Their concern for elevations and foundations, military roads and bridges imposed military meanings on the land. Their segmentations of it into frontiers – Römer advised his superiors that Albany and Schenectady had separate frontiers – redescribed the relationship between settlements like Albany and their environments.[28] Not civilian surveyors, but army draftsmen like Francis Pfister of the First Battalion Royal American Regiment (1758) composited the land. And Pfister's symbols for Oswego, Albany, New York City, and Montreal were the blackened squares and hexagonals that engineers throughout the seventeenth and eighteenth centuries had used to depict the objects they knew military men wanted to locate on a landscape: fortified cities and towns either secured to one's own forces or awaiting assault.

War made a place like Albany understandable as well. Half a century after Römer and during another war with France, the engineer William

---

27. Wilma George, *Animals and Maps* (London, 1969), 94.
28. Römer to Bellomont, May 27, 1698, *DRCH*, 4:329. For Governor Cornbury's attempt to erect a proper fort in Albany, see Weise, *History of the City of Albany*, 272; see also Map Collection (74744 [1698?] cop. 1 [of Schenectady]), and "Ratzer's Fort Schuyler, Build (*sic*) in July, 1760" (74763 [1760] Fort Schuyler [Utica]), NYSA.

Brazier reduced the city to its martial essentials in highly skilled plans and drawings. In one projection, he combined a number of already existing military structures with buildings he hoped to erect. He offered it as a proper "City of Albany." His city was the installations that a field officer needed to know: the Fort, Old Barracks, New Barracks, New Hospital, Main Guard, Well, Road to Fort Edward, Magazines, the King's Stables, New Battery under which is the Powder Magazine, and Stockades (Figure 6.1). The rest was backdrop. At the same time, another engineer mapped the city promoting his plan for better securing it against enemies. He would engineer a ditch and sites for magazines as well as batteries for guns to command the river (Figure 6.2). Either he or a later engineer offered elaborate plans for redesigning the fort's vaults, half moons, and sally points. Like him, those who had the power to determine the contours of the built-up environment directed all resources to military installations. They concentrated the mathematical and engineering reasoning, the skills of hydraulics and architectural design, in short, the esteemed learning of eighteenth-century England on fortifications (Figure 6.3). To them, it was a legitimate variation on occupying the land.

Many of the installations proposed by Römer and later engineers did not materialize. Similarly, expeditions undertaken to gather intelligence or search out and destroy villages and enemy encampments in the wilderness were often inconclusive or outright failures. Outposts were deserted by soldiers, hastily erected forts fell into weeded disuse, stockade palings became the winter fuel of thieving civilians and troopers alike. Nevertheless, places symbolic of desertion and defeat worked as well as those of stability and victory to clothe increasingly more points on the landscape in military dress.

Within the city of Albany and in addition to "fort hill," the military acquired control of the south pasture and the road leading north out of the city to Half Moon, Saratoga, and ultimately Canada. To one army engineer, the south pasture was near "the remains of an old fort," possibly all that he knew of Fort Orange (Figure 6.2). The English soldiers had confiscated properties there, meeting military logic in as much as it was the only area suitable for pasturing horses, stationing wagons, and erecting barracks. In the course of exercising its claim to the land, a sequence of English officers vacated Dutch titles, drew rents from confiscated land, brought suit against the Reformed church, and erected residences, one of them called Whitehall.[29] Like the fort hill area, it was a place where

29. For the fort and south pasture, see Paul R. Huey, *Memorandum on the Original Site of Fort Orange, Albany, New York* (Philadelphia, 1966), 254–60 and Merwick, "Dutch Townsmen and Land Use: A Spatial Perspective on Seventeenth-Century Albany, New York," *William and Mary Quarterly*, 3rd ser. (January, 1980) 37:73; Alice P. Kenney,

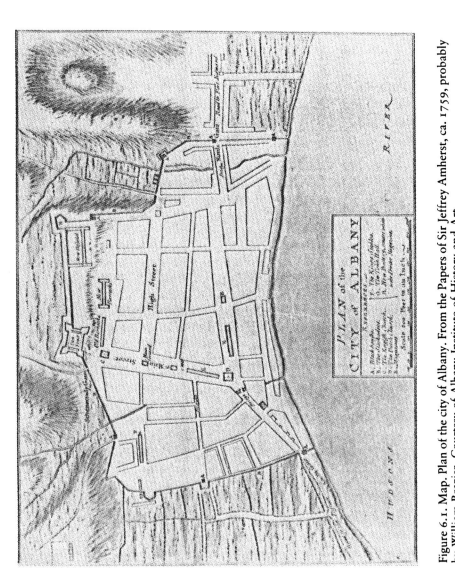

Figure 6.1. Map. Plan of the city of Albany. From the Papers of Sir Jeffrey Amherst, ca. 1759, probably by William Brazier. Courtesy of Albany Institute of History and Art.

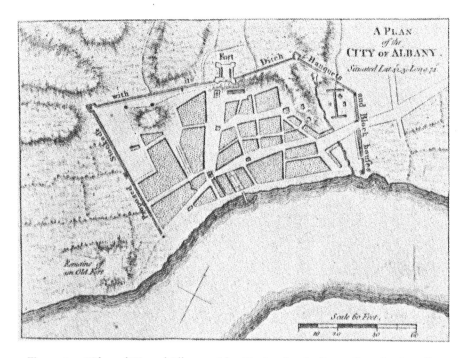

Figure 6.2. "Plan of City of Albany with a Design for the Better Securing It . . . "
Appropriation: Mary Ann Rocque, plan of ca. 1763. By permission of the British
Library.

soldiers and burghers met – possibly pasturing horses side by side along
the Beverskil – and quarreled. To our knowledge, their encounters were
a string of contained incidents involving either townspeople harassed by
field officers or those willingly engaged with soldiers in business
activities.[30]
      Land north of the city's stockades was a topographical and psycho-
logical counterpoint to the south pasture. It was poor, undesirable land.
By the 1690s, Vossen Kill, which steep hills had formed into a drainage
canal, was carrying the wastes of tanners and bisecting generally over-
grown and uneven land. Only a few families, like the Meyndertsens,
Lansinghs, and Gerritsens, were showing interest in properties bordering

The Gansvoorts of Albany: Dutch Patricians in the Upper Hudson Valley (Syracuse,
    1969), 73.
30. Ord. sess., July 20, 1671, CRA, 266; Ord. sess., April 3, 1677, CRA, 217.

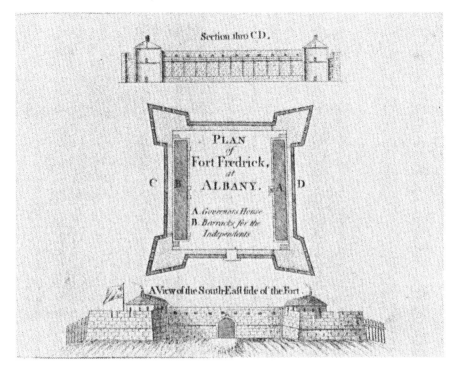

Figure 6.3. Plan of Fort Frederick at Albany [undated]. Courtesy of the British Library.

the road that bridged the kill and led north. Römer and English commanders saw the road as a vital artery carrying troops to the forts at Half Moon and Saratoga. By the 1760s, the highway was importantly the "Road to Fort Edward." Yet to the burghers, the road was a way that led "from the Citty of Albany to the water fleet" (Watervliet), that is, the mill, farms, and possibly logging lands. Well into the eighteenth century, they persisted in understanding it as "the way leading to the Patroon's Mills." The military could not control the meaning of this vital landmark. And as on paper so on the land itself. The military had made the path "the king's highway" and given its maintenance special attention. But they could not isolate it from nonmilitary landmarks. In the 1690s, for example, "a house and barn joined together" stood just north of the city, on a property bounded by the king's highway."¹ As long as such

31. See Loudoun to Cumberland, August 20, 1756, Pargellis, ed., *Military Affairs*, 228, and see Frederic Van de Water, *Lake Champlain and Lake George* (New York, 1969

buildings as this Old World Dutch barn existed in a Dutch community, the danger of their interfering with the appropriation of English meanings anywhere on the same landscape was real.

There was always the danger that things military might be ignored or misinterpreted. The Dutch could not be commanded to take a single meaning from seeing a military object on the land. They might take a fort or barracks as an optional component of a scene. Cartography too was necessarily subject to multiple meanings. Military maps inadvertently told of Dutch trading and might likewise reinforce a *burgerlijk* understanding of the land. The same French map of Lake Champlain meant to display lands "*depuis le fort Chambly jusquau [jusqu'au] fort St. Frederic*" and showing grants made to reduced officers and disbanded soldiers of the English forces, also prominently featured the *handelshuis* of a Dutch trader (Figure 6.4).[32] The cartographer's earlier map of Oswego (1727) depicted military installations – a redoubt, tents for troops, pickets for a fort – but pictured a rendezvous point for natives and English and Dutch traders as well (Figure 6.5).[33]

Dutch Commentary

The Englishman remained the stranger. When the Dutch could burlesque him openly, they mocked him for taking pleasure in armed violence. In 1676, a group of Dutch revelers and some English soldiers in Albany ridiculed a New England officer for his wanton cruelty against the natives in what we call King Philip's War. They made a comedy of a military system that honored violence and whitewashed as valiant men who delighted in aggression. In the nineteenth century, Kingston burlesqued itself for a militarism that its Dutch inhabitants had comically tried, but failed to adopt. The parades of militia companies in the nineteenth century repeatedly drew popular ridicule. Special laughter was reserved for "Jobuncker Companies" – units led out by clumsy Dutch men in displays of "ridiculous foppery" – and the "fantasticals," who mimicked the military system by parading as militiamen carrying "grotesque arms of

reprint), 79; Lease of land from Kiliaen van Rensselaer to Jacob Lansing, May 1, 1707, and Deed, Jacob J. Lansing, July 20, 1779, Lansing Papers, GZ11961, Box 1, Folder, NYSA; Indenture dated July 26, 1689: Sale of land by the city of Albany to Claes Janse van Bockhoven, Albany Papers: Folder, 1680–1689, NYHS.

32. For grants mapped here and conflicting English and French claims, see Frederic Van de Water, *Lake Champlain and Lake George*, 76, 77.

33. For the installations at Oswego, see Milton W. Hamilton, *Sir William Johnson: Colonial American, 1715–1763* (New York, 1976), 18, 19, 363.

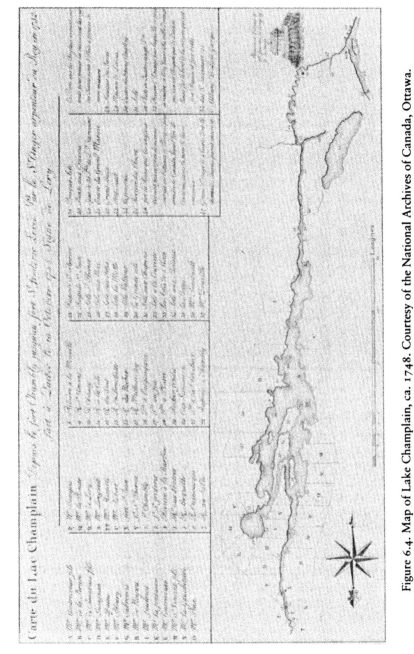

Figure 6.4. Map of Lake Champlain, ca. 1748. Courtesy of the National Archives of Canada, Ottawa.

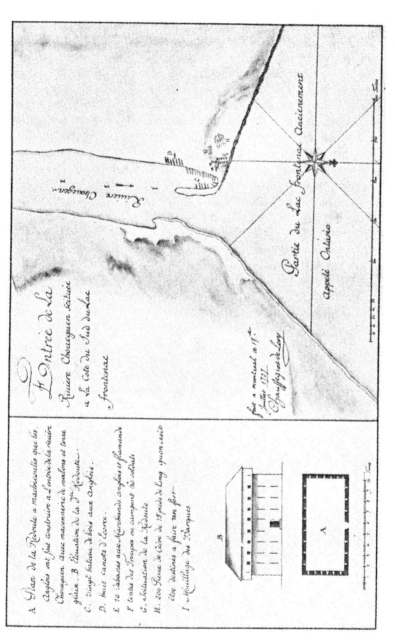

Figure 6.5. Plan of Oswego, 1727. Courtesy of the National Archives of Canada, Ottawa.

various descriptions, from the old musket to the cane and broomstick, and with fantastic [women's] dresses to match."[34]

Burlesque permitted the rejection of a way of life that would have been dangerous to express – or, in the nineteenth century, unpatriotic – in any direct way. Between 1690 and 1710, there were no burlesques recorded. But records reveal that a tendency to concealment became more pronounced. The decision of the city court to sit in the mayor's own home in order to conduct in privacy the hearing surrounding the soldiers' assault on Maria Gerritsz in 1701 was as strong a statement about boundaries that the English could not cross as the advice a man had urged upon a female relative twenty years earlier: "When the constaple comes [for information] put him off... when... mention is made of the governor, [be sure] not to say anything to the detriment of Sir Edmund [Andros], but to say that all he did was for the best interest of the province."[35]

Superficially the community accepted the imposed order: Some men acted as interpreters and filled militia posts, a few assumed commanding roles, and one at least referred to the fort as "our fort." The nineteenth-century historian George Chalmers saw such soldierly expertise in Pieter Schuyler's leadership in the expedition against the French that he mistakenly called him "the first English officer who had led an army into Canada."[36] Yet Dutch men and women continued to be overrepresented in court cases involving contempt of authority throughout the period. By 1693, Fletcher was convinced of their enduring and hidden resentment. They will not, he wrote, "fight for themselves or part with money for those who will do it for them." In 1699, Coote found the mayor disingenuous and lacking candor.[37] Unfortunately it is out of that concealment and closure that their self-identity during this period must be reconstructed.

34. Donna Merwick, "Becoming English: Anglo-Dutch Conflict in the 1670s in Albany, New York," *New York History* (October 1981), 389; Marius Schoonmaker, *The History of Kingston, New York, from Its Early Settlement to the Year 1820* (New York, 1888), 433, 434.

35. City Records, August 15, 1701, AA, 4:139; Stephen van Cortlandt to MvR, April [?], 1681, A[rnold] J. F. Van Laer, ed., *Correspondence of Maria van Rensselaer, 1669–1689* (Albany, 1935), 48.

36. [Pieter] Schuyler, Report on the fort, March 11, 1696/7, MS 10202. NYSA; *Political Annals of the Present United Colonies, from Their Settlement to the Peace of 1763, Compiled Chiefly from Records, and authorized by the Insertion of State Papers*, by G[eorge] C[halmers], Book 2, CNYHS (New York, 1868), 74.

37. Douglas Greenberg, "Persons of Evil Name and Fame": Crime and Law Enforcement in the Colony of New York, 1691–1776 (Ph.D. diss., Cornell University, 1974), 87; Fletcher to Blathwayt, January 12, 1693, *DRCH*, 4:32; Bellomont to DePeyster, August 21, 1699, DePeyster Papers, 1695–1710, NYPL.

Navigating the Land for Trade Continues

The Dutch continued to understand the city and the land lying between it and the Saint Lawrence River as an area for trade. It was a place of commercial exchange, storehouses, and trade routes with ever-receding terminal points. After 1727, Oswego was an emblem of this. In New York City, Dutch- and French-speaking merchants operated the Oswego Market near the old departure point for "Fort Orangiensche oft N. Albanische" on the north river (see Figure 3.2). Goods went from the city to Albany merchants, who transshipped them to the *handelshuis* at Oswego. Oswego, then, meant part of New York City's and Albany's livelihood, but it also signified the whole enterprise of the Dutch in the wilderness lands of the Indian nations. In nineteenth-century myth, the "hard-working Dutchman" was a fur trader who returned with riches after "his labors at Oswego" and then lived out his life contentedly "smoking a pipe in the morning air."[38] But in the late seventeenth century, the trade exchanged along the southern shores of Lake Ontario (where Oswego would be established) was an insignificant part of a wider network of *handelshuizen* of the French, Mohawk, and far Indians. It was the wilderness that the Albany traders intended to know and possess.

On March 2, 1697, an unknown trader made a draft of what he simply called "this Countrey," and his chart gives some sense of this. He organized the same territory Römer had mapped, taking in land from Albany west to Lake Ontario, north to Montreal and Quebec, and northeast around Lake Champlain (Figure 6.6). Like Römer, he was also at pains to locate the Five Nations. Yet his was a trader's map. It was an itinerary map marking two trade routes. One put Leake of Caderaquee (Lake Ontario) squarely as a center of trade west from Montreal and Albany; the other showed the well-worn trading route between Albany and Quebec using Lake Champlain and the Richelieu River. The draftsman made no identification of forts. He wrote Caderaquee for Römer's Fort Frontenac, for example, and Laek Alettae for his Fort La Gallette. It was a time when Dutch traders would have exchanged goods illegally with Ottawa brigades bringing furs to villages along the north shore of Lake Ontario. Like their French and native counterparts, they treated

38. Gorham A. Worth, *Random Recollections of Albany, from 1800 to 1808* (Albany, 1866), 26, n. 2.; for the Oswego Market in New York City, see Thomas F. De Voe; *The Market Book, Containing an Historical Account of the Public Markets in the Cities of New York, Boston, Philadelphia and Brooklyn, with a Brief Description of Every Article of Human Food Sold Therein, the Introduction of Cattle in America and Notices of Many Remarkable Specimens* (New York, 1969 reprint), 1:264.

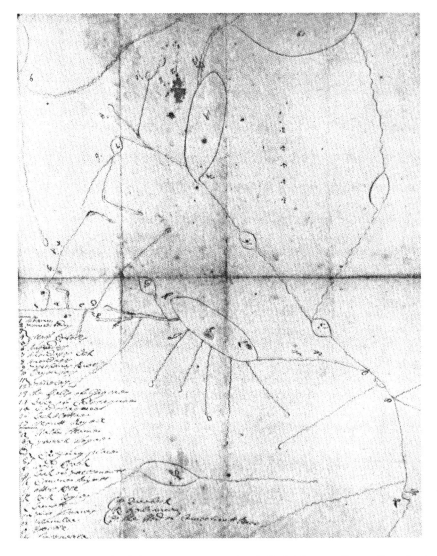

Figure 6.6. "Draft of this Country, 1696/1697." "Livingston Papers," on loan to the Franklin D. Roosevelt Library.

nearby Fort Frontenac as an anachronism, simply moving around it. If there was a farthest point at which French and Dutch–English power contested, the merchants would have found it in the north shore villages where traders exchanged furs for liquor and introduced considerable violence. In this country, actors in the power game were not located in

Römer's castles or forts. They lived in Montreal, Quebec, and all the *handelshuizen* where natives and Frenchmen, who had most of the furs by now, continued to trade with the Dutch. In a report of 1701, the *handelaar* David Schuyler effortlessly elided the meanings of "Mont Reyall" as a military headquarters and as a *handelshuis* terminating the long route from Albany via Lake Ontario. He and three other Albany traders were in Montreal for several days in April 1691. There he listened to French authorities speaking of the fresh outbreak of war in Europe. He also gained the French governor's permission to auction merchandise he had conveyed there for trade. Unlike Dongan, who considered the French authorities in Canada to be "trained soldiers and great officers, come [like himself] from Europe," Schuyler's last exchange of courtesies was with a French "gentm" about the route to Onondage and trading there.[39]

Albany, too, remained a *handelshuis*. Trading now lacked the regularity dramatized in the liturgies of *handelstijd* in the mid-seventeenth century, but redirection of the merchants' concerns into grain exports would have brought new rituals. We know relatively little about the capital accumulation of the Dutch merchant families. We do know that such diversification made some men wealthy, but they had to be merchants who could withstand extreme market fluctuations. In 1699, for example, the value of the beaver exported was £5,071; it fell to £38 in 1706.[40]

In a war year like 1695, British-made merchandise sold in New York City for as much as 400 percent markup. Such prices would have driven out smaller merchants, at least temporarily. But in the same year, Albany merchants like Johannes Rooseboom, Dirck Wesselsz ten Broeck, Margaret Schuyler, and Johannes de Wandelaer continued to trade, using Livingston as agent. They exchanged merchandise with French traders who still called the Hudson River "*Riviere d'Orange*" and, if they agreed with one French cartographer, thought of Albany as *La ville d'Orange*, and *fort belle*. The traders took furs at Albany as well as Montreal, where goods like English-made strouds were cheaper than blankets imported from France. Even during the war years of the early eighteenth century, a Canadian could more easily and profitably smuggle his beaver to Albany in spring and "have his merchandise back [to Montreal] within six weeks" than deal directly with the French. As a result, the Albany

39. City Records, May 6, 1701, *AA*, 4:129, 130; Dongan to Denonville, September 8, 1687, *DRCH*, 5:268; City Records, May 5, 1701, *AA*, 4:130.
40. Stephen Hosmer Cutcliffe, Indians, Furs and Empires: The Changing Policies of New York and Pennsylvania, 1674–1768 (Ph.D. diss., Lehigh University, 1976), 81, Table III–1 following 86. It had returned to a higher level by 1714.

merchants handled possibly one-half to two-thirds of the entire French market in furs.[41] Pelts continued to be a significant export commodity for the province.

The merchants also had many strings to their bows. Despite furs brought by French and native traders, the commerce declined, and they turned to shipping grain. But that commerce fluctuated as well. In 1690, war and natives' raids near the city caused a flight of farmers. As it would have in Europe, the market collapsed; pease and wheat had to be imported to feed the garrison. By 1694, farm laborers had returned, and there was surplus grain for export. The merchants traded this to the West Indies, and in early 1696, maintained a high price for their grain by imposing an embargo. Later that year, skirmishing near Albany again caused some farmers to flee; the resultant grain shortage persisted until 1698. Generally, reliance on grain as an export commodity continued through the period, perhaps the result of a return to population numbers slightly in excess of those counted in 1689.[42]

No merchant, wrote one authority, could have thought himself prosperous before 1698. Estimates about population and wealth would seem to bear that out for the seventeenth and early eighteenth centuries as well. War caused unnatural population fluctuations. During King William's War, 557 residents fled. That number was recovered after 1698, but the number of householders stayed at about 156 throughout the period, indicating a steady rather than growth state. Dutch men, of course, did not necessarily equate prosperity with increased population. There is considerable evidence that operations conducted efficiently with a minimum of personnel was the goal. Nonetheless, a balance needed to be maintained between production and markets, and that meant reliance on an adequate number of agriculturalists. Alice Kenney's recent studies of Albany's demographic profile during the period suggests fluctuations due to war but nothing like a demographic catastrophe.[43] Production meant subsistence, and profits for some.

Estimates of economic well-being based on wealth are equally unsat-

41. Paltsits, ed., *John Miller: New York Considered*, 45; Armour, Merchants of Albany, 53; Lunn, "Illegal Trade," 66; 69; 65.
42. See Allen W. Trelease, *Indian Affairs in Colonial New York: The Seventeenth Century* (Ithaca, 1960), 216; and see Armour, Merchants of Albany, 56; 56, 57, 49, and for trade with Amsterdam, see 53, 54; and see A List of the Ffreeholders of the City and County of Albany, 1720, DHNY, 1:370–3.
43. Armour, Merchants of Albany, 49, and see Herbert Alan Johnson, *The Law Merchant and Negotiable Instruments in Colonial New York, 1664–1720* (Chicago, 1963), 2; on unconcern for large population settlements, see Chapter 2, and for Table Bay at the Cape, see C. F. J. Muller, ed., *Five Hundred Years. A History of South Africa* (Pretoria, 1969), 24; Alice P. Kenney, "Patricians and Plebeians in Colonial Albany," *de halve maen*. 45–46 (April 1970 to April 1971).

isfactory. In 1703, the total value of "the estates" was put at £2,774. A comparison of that figure with the assessed value of wealth in Boston in the 1690s has obvious drawbacks, not least because Boston was then a city of almost seven thousand people. Real property for its regular residents in 1692 was valued at £91,500; personal wealth – livestock, trade goods, loans, commissions, and professional salaries had a total taxable value of about £150,000.⁴⁴ The disparity is remarkable and would require another book to explain. But this factor deserves consideration: In Albany and despite increased emphasis on grain exports, wealth was still generated by modes of production and exchange that had not changed technologically since the 1660s and would not do so until well into the eighteenth century. A culture which required technologically complex routines of farming was seemingly unattractive. The pattern was much the same among the upriver fur-trading settlers of the Saint Lawrence, counterparts to the men and women of Albany. Even when it was evident that the ways of the *coureurs de bois* were past, the attraction to farm routines was weak. Perhaps, as one writer put it, urban men and women simply accustom themselves slowly to farm routines. In Albany, an economy structured on the contracting fur trade, intermittent war contracts, and an indifferent agricultural base meant, as it did across Canada at the time, that poverty was natural. In 1695, a chaplain of the English garrison in New York summarized Albany's inhabitants as people who "care not for more than from hand to mouth." The suggestion cannot be taken seriously. More compelling is the proposition that they were caught in a structure producing widespread immiseration. Coote's estimate in 1700 was probably close to accurate, except that he was looking at persons rather than families. There were, he estimated, "half a dozen [persons] who have competent estates, but all the rest are miserable [*sic*] poor."⁴⁵

But if the merchants could not see prosperity in the streets and shops of Albany, they nonetheless had the same image of it as in the 1660s and 1670s. The city was still a market town open to non-Dutch traders either as permanent or seasonal residents. The terms of acceptance were those of the 1680s, when a small group of New England traders and garrison soldiers were seen to be of profit to the town and accepted. Their enter-

---

44. City Records, July 26, 1703, *AA*, 4:181 (the figure is given as £2704 on 188). G. G. B. Warden, "The Distribution of Property in Boston, 1692–1775," in Bernard Bailyn and Donald Fleming, eds., *Perspectives in American History* (Cambridge, Mass., 1976), 10:82, 83.
45. Richard Colebrook Harris, *The Seigneurial System in Early Canada: A Geographical Study* (Madison, 1968), 164; Paltsits, ed., *John Miller: New York Considered*, 45; for structural immiseration, see Robert Brenner, "Agrarian Class Structure and Economic Development in Pre-Industrial Europe," *Past and Present* (February 1976), 70:30–75; quoted in Weise, *History of the City of Albany*, 269.

prises and numbers (in the case of the traders) were continually regulated, but then, as we have seen, the business activities and numbers of Dutch residents were controlled as well. Calibrating inclusiveness was the purpose of the *burgherrecht*. English authorities were suspicious of such "mixtures of nations" and distrusted practices that allowed natives, for example, to enter towns to "pow-wow or perform worship of the devil."[46]

War added a legal dimension to suspicion and distrust. It gave the crown's commanders full power to control the economies of New York City and Albany. In a situation that would have been unthinkable in the Low Countries, they were chartered cities without whose consent war had been entered into and whose commerce was now subject to interdictions. Albany's determination to continue trade with the French and their native allies was now denounced as smuggling. The Dutch clearly recognized this. Yet they continued trafficking in contraband with the enemies of the garrison and its allies in New England and Delaware. To morally outraged outsiders, they smuggled because they were greedy. From the viewpoint of European political structures, it was something else. Ironically – or perhaps comically – smuggling was one of the last expressions of European municipal life in North America. That way of life lay behind Albany's resistance to centralizing government in the form of the English army and regulations, even if resistance came in so demeaning a practice as smuggling. The Earl of Loudoun, whose coercion of Albany's residents into providing quarters, storehouses, and provisions for his forces led to bitter altercations between himself and the mayor in the 1750s, put the dialectic between municipal authority and that of the state lodged in the form of its army succinctly: "If they [the city magistrates] would not [assist me], I must follow the Custom of Armies, and help myself."[47]

Continuities and Contrasts

Society remained *burgerlijk*. From within the city, the *handelaars* still took political decisions for the city and county. Unlike the English gentry, they did not idealize the countryside; its occupancy did not confer status. It was neither the place for building country houses nor parading the

46. Merwick, "Becoming English," 396-405; the Duke's Law quoted in Bernice Schultz, *Colonial Hempstead* (New York, 1937), 87.
47. For the Dutch as "an odd and very bad Sort of People," see remarks of Warren Johnson in the 1730s, quoted in Milton W. Hamilton, *Sir William Johnson: Colonial American, 1715–1763* (New York, 1976), 10; Earl of Loudoun to Earl of Cumberland, August 29, 1756, quoted in Pargellis, *Military Affairs*, 231.

militia. Admittedly they commanded troops and went out after the enemy alongside English troopers. General John Winthrop thought some of their men to be fine soldiers in 1696, and Pieter Schuyler directed the construction of the first military road in North America. North of the city, Kiliaen van Rensselaer's great-grandson began to see his tenant farmers properly, that is, as an armed retinue when needed. In 1744, he boasted he could "muster 600 men fit to bear arms." At Kinderhook by 1767, *"het bovenste Compeney"* now spoke for a settlement of men who had learned to relate defense of the place with the countryside, though they used a traditionally Dutch geographical designation. Near Albany, extramural militia units developed and gained some permanence.[48] But even in the early eighteenth century, a sketch of the Albany Militia District seemed to highlight the dominance of the municipal burgherguard. Within the city were 305 men (including the regulars). Only 99 men of forty-three families could be counted on as militiamen in the large area north of the city, and these were joined by males from just thirteen families south of the city to Normanskil. The burgherguard remained a stubbornly self-conscious Dutch group.[49] They seem not to have retained the *papegaaschoet*, but neither did they take to parading in the English fashion.

There were no country houses to express the innate superiority of a ruling gentry. Certainly there were none during the twenty-five years of war after 1690. In the 1690s, Coote took Livingston's manor house to be a venue of sociability in the area, but Fletcher could find none at all and resided either in a sequestered house or on his ship anchored in the Hudson. In the 1740s, a visitor who had an eye for an Englishman's estates and conversation found himself short of civilized forms of entertainment. He was properly entertained by Robert Livingston – though at a city tavern – but bored by the patroon, who did, however, show him the only garden and parks of a country house in the district.[50]

48. "Journal of Winthrop's March from Albany to Wood Creek, Rec'd September 18, 1696," *DRCH*, 4:194; Robert T. Roberts, *New York's Forts in the Revolution* (London, 1980), 85; Van de Water, *Lake Champlain*, 79; "Journal of a Trip to Albany, Cohoes and Mohawk Town" [by Alexander Hamilton], Typescript 11706 [Loose Folder], NYSA; Edward A. Collier, *A History of Old Kinderhook from Aboriginal Days to the Present Time: Including the Story of the Early Settlers, Their Homesteads, Their Traditions, and Their Descendents; with an Account of Their Civic, Social, Political, Educational, and Religious Life* (New York, 1914), 161.

49. *Third Annual Report of the State Historian of the State of New York, 1897* (New York, 1898), following 774; Major Peter Schuyler's report to Governor Fletcher, covering February 8 to 21, 1693; *DRCH*, 4:16.

50. Bellomont to DePeyster, April 5, 1700, DePeyster Papers, NYPL; Account of severall passages of the treaty of...Fletcher...with the Indians of the Five Nations in June and July, 1693, *DRCH*, 4:44; Albert Bushnell Hart, ed., *Hamilton's Itinerarium, Being a Narrative of a Journey from Annapolis, Maryland Through Delaware, Pennsylvania, New York, New Jersey, Connecticut, Rhode Island, Massachusetts and New Hamp-*

Architecturally, the few country houses that were later erected failed to follow the Georgian style so eagerly taken up elsewhere in northeastern North America. The original family home of the Schuylers south of the palisades was "highly ornamented in the Dutch style." Its replacement was a Georgian house built by the wife of General Philip Schuyler in 1760–1. It is now considered a radical departure from Dutch tradition, though, to an early-nineteenth-century visitor the absence of formal gardens made it and the country house of Stephen van Rensselaer north of Albany "powerfully [reminiscent] of some of the fine villas in Holland." The first notably imposing house was not built in Albany until 1725 and was of Dutch design. Later townhouses built by the Lansingh and Pruijn families in the mid-eighteenth century were basically Georgian but with noticeable violations of symmetry and balance. Not until 1780 was the first house designed and erected in unimpeachable Georgian style. [51]

For such violations of English fashion, the Dutch were regarded as comical. British regimental officers in Albany in the 1720s considered the behavior of leading merchants pretentious and held them in the highest ridicule. Even kindlier observers remarked that "the People [are] mostly Dutch, and have something Odd about them."[52] Doubtless they did. For English culture fell like litter on the Amerindians and then the Dutch. It came in all the miscellaneous items that made sense in England but lacked authenticity among both sets of strangers in upstate New York. One could itemize them endlessly – the damask altar cloth sent by Queen Anne to the so-called "Onondagas" and representing the bombardment and capture of Namur by the Duke of Marlborough; the complete works of Addison, Marlborough, and Godolphin supposedly brought to Albany – and read? – by Pieter Schuyler after his trip to England in 1710;[53] rules passed for the proper celebration of Guy Fawkes's Day; the hundreds of English words inscribed in wholly in-

shire from May to September, 1744 by Doctor Alexander Hamilton (New York, 1971 reprint), 75, 77.
51. The Schuyler Mansion at Albany, Residence of Major General Philip Schuyler, 1762–1804, by The Spirit of '76 (New York, 1911), 13; "Benjamin Silliman Inspects the City, 1819," CHA, 2:337; see Vanderhuyden Palace in H. P. Phelps, The Albany Handbook: A Stranger's Guide and Residents' Manual (Albany, 1884), 122, and "J. S. Buckingham in Albany [1837]," AA, 9:302, 304; see "The Lansing House," CHA 1:496–9.
52. Mrs. John King Van Rensselaer [in collaboration with Frederic Van de Water], The Social Ladder (New York, 1924), 18; James Grant Wilson, ed., Memoirs of an American Lady, with Sketches of Manners and Scenes in America as They Existed Previous to the Revolution, by Mrs. Anne Grant (New York, 1903), 284.
53. Hooper, St. Peter's Church, 489; Paul Wilstach, Hudson River Landings (New York, 1969 reprint), 100.

appropriate, if not nonsensical, ways by Dutch residents writing receipts, letters, and wills.

Robert Hunter, governor from 1710 to 1719, caught the cultural incoherence best in *Androborus*, a satirical play set in New York City. He called the city a place of fools. Laughably, Dutch men were trying to be Englishmen, English colonials were aspiring to be London gentlemen, all were acting as though power were everybody's business when it was, of course, the king's. Hunter's irony uncovered a society without points of reference. He found what John Miller, a chaplain to the regiments, had discovered in the 1690s: that New York, steeped in its Dutchness, could never be more than a stepmother to Englishmen. Forty years later, William Smith, Jr., also looked at the ship of fools Hunter had discovered in early-eighteenth-century New York. His interest was in the historical factors that had prevented understanding of the basic statutory law of England before 1776 and thereby retarded the development of jurisprudence in New York. Had the colony been "first settled by the English," he concluded, then "the cultivation of science," including the law, would have paralleled the admirable progress seen in other colonies.[54]

The lack of advancement in knowledge that he bemoaned, however, was not due to New York's settlement by the Dutch, but to the demands of biculturalism placed on Dutch residents after 1664. More than scientific knowledge, self-knowledge was made problematic. Dispossessed of familiar meanings and of a system of stability caught in the metaphor, navigating the land, they had, from the time of England's conquest, been given the task of possessing the land and their lives in unknown ways.

54. *Androborus, A Biographical Farce in Three Acts, Viz. The senate, The consistory and The apotheosis*, by Governour Hunter. Printed at Monoropolis since 1 August, 1714 [corrected by Hunter to Moropolis, i.e. the City of Fools] (New York, by William Bradford, 1714); Paltsits, ed., *New York Considered*, 46; Smith, *History*, 2:41.

7

Reflections on Looking at the Land

The Dutch looked at the New World with their own eyes. They put the new continent under their gaze, and by that, began the process of exerting their power over it. The English, too, looked at this already possessed world with their eyes. By that, they also began to exert power as they bent the gaze of the Dutch to this other world. They came to possess the land because they controlled its interpretation. That has been the thesis of this book.

The archives of the State University of New York at Albany hold an artifact of 1665. An archivist of the 1950s cataloged it as "Contract of Sale from the Indians to Juriaen Teunissen, Jan Cloet and Jan Hendricksen Bruyn for land on the *Moordenaers* (Murderer's) *Kil*, near Athens, New York, March 21/31, 1665." The archivist assumed that land was the object of the men's dealings with the natives and that land ownership lay behind the careful recording of the transaction. That was his way of seeing. It was not that of the three Albany burghers. They saw a paper that gave them access to water. They saw creeks and a river bounding the property on three sides (*Moordenaers Kil, Cleyne Kil,* and the North River [Hudson river]). They saw a trade route, *"Kats Kil* Path," forming the fourth boundary. The men had very nearly acquired an island. It was ideal for the small rivercraft that they and the natives would use to traffic in furs (Figures 7.1 and 7.2).[1]

The conveyance included a primitive chart. It was a view relating the men's property to the region lying to the north, as far as Albany. It edited the region into a transport system, illustrating trade routes and destinations. The *Kats kil* Path and the North River led to Albany. A second and third path also went north. The first found its way to Schenectady, and the second went north and then west around the Helderberg ranges and into the far valleys of the Mohawk River. There the men may have hoped to pick up the northern reaches of the streams that would carry

---

1. Contract of sale from the Indians to Juriaen Teunissen, Jan Cloet and Jan Hendricksen Bruyn for the land on the Moordenaers (Murderer's) Kill, near Athens, New York, March 21/31, 1665, SC12303 NYSA [Acquisitioned in 1950].

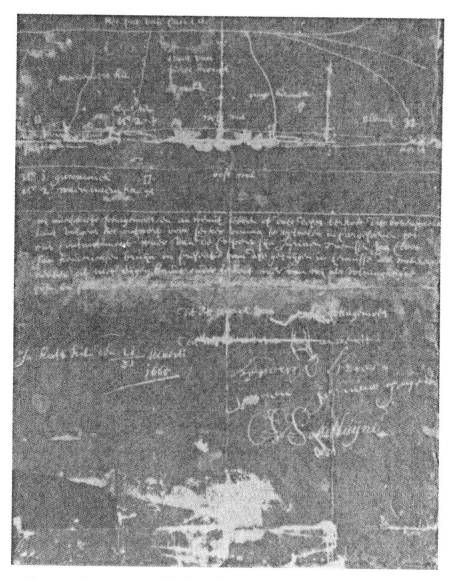

Figure 7.1. Contract of sale, dated April 20, 1665. Courtesy of the State University of New York Library, Albany.

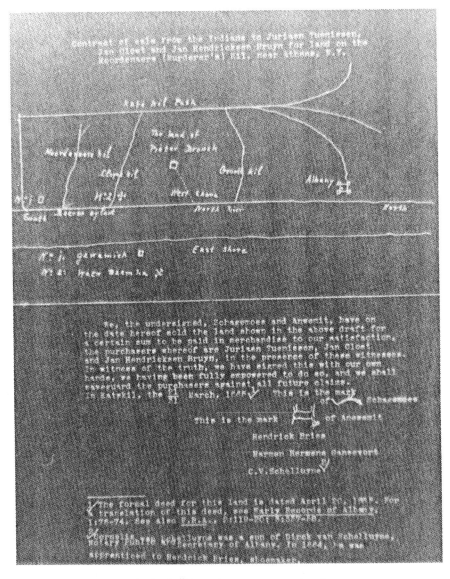

Figure 7.2. Contract of sale, dated April 20, 1665 (translated transcript). Courtesy of the State University of New York Library, Albany.

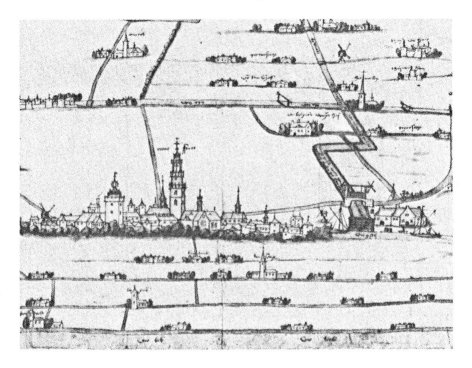

Figure 7.3. Montfoort, detail of a map, 1554. Courtesy of Gemeentearchief, Amsterdam.

them and their furs south to the Delaware River. The chart pictured a region that accommodated itself to commercial ventures. In Dutch fashion, the vast distances were already being made familiar: It was all good to the eye.

The chart was an attempt to make the New World congruent with the Low Countries. It was a faithful rendition of fundamental preferences about land and water and, for that reason, would have been as readable to Dutch men and women at home as the cartographic work of Netherlands mapmakers like Ortellius and Mercator. Maps printed at home were also illustrations enabling travelers to journey from one point of trade to another. The itinerary maps as well as the district and urban bird's-eye views foregrounded the important elements of a commercial system – cities and towns, roads and canals, and rivers – and treated the countryside with relative disregard (Figures 7.3 and 7.4). They pictured a landscape in which nature and man had elided land and water. They showed this amphibious world because Dutch people had gained a sense of the equal value of land and water; they no longer made the same

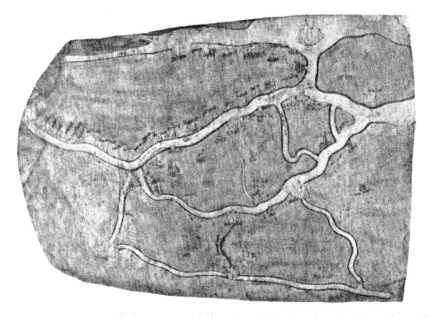

Figure 7.4. Map of the courses of the rivers Rijn, Waal, Lek, Merwede, and Maas, 15th century. Collection Hingman, VTH, 236. Courtesy of Algemeen Rijksarchief, 's-gravenhage.

distinctions as people who had not experienced water in the same way. Netherlanders had given themselves a geography in which they could see masts in the streets of towns and sails moving in the fields. The elemental juxtaposition was not just charming but showed that they were controlling both land and water for all the purposes of well-being. New Netherlanders had tried to construct a similar geography. Sails drifted into the streets of New Amsterdam, and the masts of Hudson River scows would move through the land belonging to Teunissen, Cloet, and Hendricksen.[2] They were crude equivalents, but they offered the assurance that the New Netherlanders were harnessing both land and water and, by that, laying the foundation of an economic system that would give them control of the New World.

Thirty years before the contract of sale, Harmen Meyndertsen van den

2. Teunissen, Cloet, and Hendricksen did not take up permanent residence on Murderer's Creek, but they retained the property until at least 1684. See Deed to Cornelis Van Dyck and Marte Gerritsz, June 13, 1684, Van Vechten Papers, LZ 15213, No. 3, NYSA. They may have kept it as a commodity or one of them may have lived on it seasonally, that is, when there was profit in forestalling natives carrying furs to their neighbor to the north, Pieter Bronck, or to Albany.

Bogaert inscribed a journal with the details he knew would give him and the West India Company greater control of the Mohawk and Oneida lands northwest of Fort Orange. In the winter of 1634, he and two companions traveled overland from Fort Orange to the Oriskany River, interrogating natives about the volume of furs being traded with the French and hoping to lure the trade back to the fort. He went into the natives' land expecting to establish a system of barter that would convert it from wilderness into a civilized trading environment. To accomplish this he made careful entries in his journal and, in effect, gave himself a verbal map that dissected an extended trade route into manageable segments. This strip map included the location of native villages, already fortuitously established as transit stops along the way and open to Europeans peddling wares for furs. Like the Roman's portolan chart, or the medieval traveler's strip map, or the cheap roadmaps (*wegwizers*) popular among seventeenth-century Dutch men and women, it was a reusable guide to the riches that a sound trading system might make available.[3]

Meyndertsen had no eye for the day when the Mohawk Valley would come under the control of Dutch agriculturalists. He called it "the land of the Maquaesen" and was satisfied to leave it at that.[4] Nor was he concerned to control the natives by converting them to Christianity cr to alter a settlement pattern that served his needs and those of the Company. His eye was that of the transient ethnographer. He looked at natives engaged in rituals whose exotic performances would seem to us to demand close attention. Yet he had no interest in bringing the aborigines' ways within his own cultural system by giving them considered reflection or interpretation. Back at Fort Orange, he reported on his journey, and like any captain sailing for the Dutch provinces overseas, he logged the details of the sea-lanes that had made possible his navigation of the vast ocean wastes of upstate New York.

Meyndertsen and the three Albany burghers were bringing the New World into a Dutch order of things. Inadvertently, however, it was becoming a variation on Dutch culture at home. The contract of 1665 and the journal of 1635 show the resistance of the physical and human environment to the strenuous imaginative exertions of the settlers. The contract documented that burghers like Teunissen, Cloet, and Hendricksen had come to accept as accurate, geographical measurements of the most rough-and-ready sort. They had also learned to cope with nearby

3. Charles T. Gehring and William A. Starna, trs., and eds., *A Journey into Mohawk and Oneida County, 1634–1635: The Journal of Harmen Meyndertsen van den Bogaert* (Syracuse, 1988).
4. Gehring and Starna, eds., *Journal into Mohawk and Oneida Country*, 12.

landowners, who signed legal papers with strange hieroglyphics and with the names of landmarks that were unintelligible as well as uncertain – was it Gawamick that lay behind Beeren Eylant, as indicated on the conveyance, or was it Machawemeck, as given on the deed of sale?[5] In Europe, Dutch merchants extended the economic power of the United Provinces and of their own companies by using secure and well-traveled roads to reach far distant cities – such a stable transportation system, for example, made it possible for Kiliaen van Rensselaer to be apprenticed to a merchant in Prague in 1608. For Albany merchants, the principal component in the trading system on land south of the city was – with the significant exception of the river – a footpath.

The same improprieties lurked in Meyndertsen's journal. It was a travel account of a seventeenth-century man of commerce, but it told of entering lands where customers allowed their dogs to eat desperately needed provisions, where there were settlements with only graves to be seen, where communication was possible only in sign language and possibly primitive pidgin, and where the lands were cut by dangerous rivers and endless stretches of wilderness.[6] Meyndertsen was already preparing to mix some Mohawk words into his vocabulary, and one of his companions had tried to see the Mohawk River valley through native eyes by asking several of them to help him draw a map.[7] In the late 1670s, Jasper Danckaerts visited Albany from Holland and found that some of the Dutch had forgotten their language and were unconsciously using English terms like "valleyen" (valleys).[8] The New Netherlanders were so much the strangers that his entire account is a sustained ethnography.

Before 1664, New Netherland was a version of European Dutch culture. By that, it was not a weaker or flawed culture and therefore somehow readily susceptible to or in need of redeeming English ways. Yet this is how the records have been read. Not really Dutch and not yet English, New Netherland has been read by later historians as having been a loose collection of greedy entrepreneurs, careless of their lives and those of others and living under only the flimsiest hint of legal and political order. It awaited a unifying, and civilizing, political structure.

This would not have been a valid interpretation in the eyes of the New Netherlanders themselves. In reading their own records – or other texts,

---

5. See Indian deed for Caniskek (Athens, Greene County), April 20, 1665, *DRCH*, 13:397, 398.
6. Gehring and Starna, eds., *Journal into Mohawk and Oneida Country*, 3; 5; see notes 63–5; 7.
7. "Wordlist," in Gehring and Starna, eds., *Journey into Mohawk and Oneida Country*, 51–63; 14.
8. Bartlett Burleigh James and J[ohn] Franklin Jameson, eds., *Journal of Jasper Danckaerts, 1679–1680* (New York, 1913), 117, 213.

like the landscape, where they were recording their culture – they would not have appropriated an account of irrecoverable disorder. However, the conquest of 1664 meant not only surrendering the land but also losing the power of interpreting their culture to others. They lost control of the archive of themselves, and because of the same conquest, their descendants were in no position to recover it. As a result, the texts that would tell how this New World Dutch culture diverged from that of the home provinces and in what ways it was an elaboration on it have awaited the gaze of outsiders willing to see with an insider's eye.

After 1664, men with an English way of seeing also tried to tame the wilderness. In 1666, individuals of both cultures had occasion to take stock of the landscape around Albany when a French force was halted in its campaign against the Mohawk by an ambush just outside Schenectady. The incident, and the events that followed it, generated hundreds of artifacts, including the correspondence of civil and military officers as well as accounts written by men like a Dutch surgeon and the wounded French soldiers cared for in the city during the spring and summer months.[9]

The literature shows that the invasion caused the English to visualize the Albany area in a new way. Before that time, they had already begun to reorganize New York province around the unifying principle of the Crown. They had never shared the Dutch view that the wilderness would be civilized by creating conditions for a way of life based on mercantile exchange. Nor had they expected it to be civilized by individuals who believed that free people are bound together by contractual alliances. Rather, they were civilizing the lands in New York because they were bringing them under the king's possession. Those in authority had made that clear. Land was already being distributed by privilege and by rela-

---

9. For the account of the raid by two Dutch men twenty-two years later, see Depositions of Symon Groot, July 2, 1688, and Jan Labatie, August 2, 1688, in Lawrence Leder, ed., *The Livingston Indian Records, 1666–1723* (Gettysburg, 1956), 144, 145, and for Dutch reactions, see *Corr JvR*, 388, and, among English accounts, see [Captain John Baker], "Relation of the Governor of Canada his march, with 600 volunteers into the Terretorys of His Highness, the Duke of Yorke in America." *DRCH*, 3:118, 119; Winthrop to Secretary of State Arlington, October 25, 1666, *DRCH*, 3:137; see Nicolls to de Tracy, August [?], 1666, *DRCH*, 3:133 and for French references, see de Tracy to Nicolls, April 30, 1667, *DRCH*, 3:152, and ratification of the treaty by the Oneidas and Mohawks, July 12, 1666 [Quebec], *DRCH*, 3:126, 127, and for the natives' recollections of the raid, see Proposals, July 9/19, 1666 in Leder, ed., *Livingston Indian Records*, 30; Dongan to M. de la Barre, July [?], 1684, *DHNY*, 1:102, and Ratification of the treaty, July 12, 1666, *DRCH*, 3:126, 127.

tionship to the king. One's ownership of acres was already a public measure of one's proximity to the throne.

Now the invasion of the French presented the English with a reason for refining their image of a northern border separating Nova Francia from the "plantations" of his majesty of Great Britain. From accepting loose descriptions of the northern territory as the "Mahauke" lands or as the trading posts of the Dutch, they now began the process of naming and describing the region as properly related to England. They refined an image of the king's "dominions."[10] It gave contiguity to Albany, New England, and New York, places that were not contiguous at all – not geographically, not conceptually, not temperamentally. On the contrary, the relationship of New England to Albany and of each to England and empire was vague. "Frontier" was an ill-defined term, and its correspondence to a definite topography not yet clear enough to map.[11] Yet the reconnoitering of soldiers and the opportunities of commanders to read the communiques of field officers stationed at "bounds and limits" and in frontier forts were moments when the English way of seeing New York was acquiring form.[12]

The king's "dominions" was an image that filled up land.[13] In New York, the king's sovereignty occupied land without the need of settlers, traders, or even an occupying army. Unlike the Dutch, the English did not abide enclaves of strangers, or wastes that were not worth claiming, or points along borders where crossing was not an invasion of royal ownership. To the Dutch, distance was familiar, not foreign. To the English, distance was other and dangerous, because it was filled in by a foreign power or by wilderness without civilized power.

During all this clarification about dominions, much of it achieved as a result of rhetorical skirmishes with French adversaries in Canada, the Dutch continued to act upon a republican landscape. They played leading roles in many affairs of 1666 but situated themselves "below the battle," protecting the privileges and independence of the city while carrying on the fur trade and arranging meetings among the combatants. In all of it, they activated the familiar trajectories out of Albany – to Schenectady via the Schenectady–Albany road, to Montreal via the Albany–Lake Champlain–Montreal trade route, to hidden rendezvous points with natives along the trails that men like Arent van Curler and Jan Cloet would have known. At the same time, the magistrates took directions from the

---

10. [Baker], "Relation," *DRCH*, 3:118.
11. Samuel Willis to Nicolls, July 16, 1666, *DRCH*, 3:121.
12. Nicolls to de Tracy, August [?], 1666, *DRCH*, 3:133.
13. See [Baker] "Relation," *DRCH*, 3:119, and John Winthrop to Arlington, October 25, 1666, *DRCH*, 3:141.

English, forced to recognize that their construction of Nova Francia as an implacable enemy was creating a new political geography. It was already a topography marked by redistributed native settlements, flash points of violence, and insecure trade routes.

The French raid had led the English governor and his subordinate officers on the northern "frontier" to see Albany in a new way. Captain John Baker was the commanding officer at Albany and someone who struggled to see where his garrison outpost fitted into a frontier comprising Canada, Montreal, Quebec, "the frozen Lake of Canada" (Lake Champlain), New England, Massachusetts, Hartford, Schenectady, the Mohawk River, and native castles.[14] In addition to being a fur-trading town, Albany had a new meaning cast up by the contests of the kings of England and France. Out of their enterprises, he saw Albany within a dialectic: It was part of a massive geography where, above all, French troops from the Saint Lawrence River could march south across "the vast wilderness" and capture "territories" now made subject to "his Ma[ties] obedience."[15]

Baker's moments of recognizance and his moments of finding words to describe the frontier in communiques were experiences that came and went quickly. They may seem trifling. They were, however, full of the immediacies and small distinctions that lay behind our models of the great wars for empire between England and France in seventeenth- and eighteenth-century North America. And as they were the evanescent experiences that lay behind English control of New York. They were part of the process by which an English way of seeing New York was gathering strength and would be the proper way of doing so until the American Revolution.

14. See [Baker] "Relation," *DRCH*, 3:118, 119, Nicolls to Baker, November 20, 1666, *DRCH*, 3:148, and Winthrop to Arlington, October 25, 1666, *DRCH*, 3:137.
15. [Baker], "Relation," *DRCH*, 3:118.

Index

Printed in the United States
24894LVS00003B/262-279

9 780521 533249